The Dawn
of
Islamic Literalism

RISE OF THE CRESCENT MOON

Joseph A. Butta

authorHOUSE®

AuthorHouse™
1663 Liberty Drive
Bloomington, IN 47403
www.authorhouse.com
Phone: 1-800-839-8640

Published by AuthorHouse 3/5/2013

ISBN: 978-1-4772-9530-4 (sc)
ISBN: 978-1-4772-9529-8 (hc)
ISBN: 978-1-4772-9531-1 (e)

Library of Congress Control Number: 2012922987

TABLE OF CONTENTS

PREFACE

Greetings to you: People of the West! Thank you very much for deciding to spend your time with this book. My motivation for writing it is to provide a one-stop introduction for people who want to know more about Islamic Literalism. Many people unfamiliar with this subject matter can be easily confused by the meaning of Qur'anic verses or seek context for these verses in order to understand the motivation of Islamic Literalists. The Qur'an was not constructed chronologically. It was constructed according to the length of each *surah* ("chapter"). The longest surahs are found in the front of the Qur'an and the shortest surahs are found in the back of the Qur'an. In brief, the Qur'an goes from the longest to shortest surah. The Sirah, Hadith, and History of Al-Tabari are needed to help place the Qur'an in a chronological sequence. These sources provide a great aid to Westerners who tend to be linear in their thought process. It is quite difficult to read a text that does not have a sense of chronology. Without chronology, it is extremely difficult to understand how these events are connected. These books, excluding the Qur'an, include the words and deeds of Muhammad and his early followers. Only the Qur'an surpasses these works in importance to Muslims, although all are considered either holy writ and/or authoritative by most Muslims.

INTRODUCTION

Arguably the most important authoritative book in Islam, the *Sirah*, is the biography of Muhammad. It was written by Ibn Ishaq, who died in 773 AD. Unfortunately, we do not have Ishaq's original work. It appears that his original manuscript was lost. However, according to Alfred Guillaume, Ibn Hisham, who died in 834 AD, was an understudy of Ibn Ishaq. Ibn Hisham left evidence that he edited Ishaq's original work when he stated:

> "I have omitted things which are disgraceful, matters which would cause distress, and are not trustworthy."
>
> —Ishaq:691

This strongly suggests that Ibn Hisham edited Ibn Ishaq's original. Hisham's work was translated into English by Alfred Guillaume in 1955. Today, it is known as *The Life of Muhammad*. Ishaq's work is considered excellent by many.[1] At the same time, it must be said that some scholars see these sources as unreliable.[2] A number of Muslim scholars and scribes contributed hadith, which is a saying or action attributed to the Prophet. The most widely used hadith among the Muslim community are the *Al-Kutub Al-Sittah* ("The Six Books" or "The Authentic Six") which includes: (1) Sahih Bukhari, (2) Sahih Muslim, (3) Sunan an-Nasa'i, (4) Sunan Abu Dawud, (5) Jami' at-Tirmidhi, and (6) Sunan Ibn Majah. Muhammad Ibn Ismail al-Bukhari, the author of Sahih Bukhari, and his student, Muslim Ibn al-Hajjaj, the author of Sahih Muslim, are the two most famous providers of hadith.[3] Between these two collections, the hadiths of Bukhari have the highest standing in the Islamic community.[4] Muhammad ibn Ismail al-Bukhari, who lived from 810–870 AD, claimed that in the year 850 AD, there were 600,000 hadith. He examined 300,000 records and accepted about 3,000 as being reliable.[5] Muslim ibn al-Hajjaj lived from 821–875 AD. He examined the other 300,000 Hadith and accepted 4,000. Abu Dawud, the author of Sunan Abu Dawud, who died in 888 AD, accepted 4,800 traditions from the 500,000 that he collected.[6] Other hadiths were compiled by Ibn Majah, who died in 896 AD, Al-Tirmidhi, who lived from 824–893 AD, Al-Nasa'i, who died in 915 AD, and also Malik ibn Anas, the author of the Muwatta', who lived from 715–801 AD.[7] These hadith are usually arranged by topic rather than chronology and they describe what is *halal* ("acceptable") and *haram* ("forbidden"). [8] Muhammad's words and deeds are his *Sunnah* ("traditions").[9] Sunnis accept all of it, Shi'ites accept most of it. Abu Muhammad bin al-Tabari, who died in 923 AD, wrote an epic account from the creation of man to the life of Muhammad, including the history of the Caliphs. His work was constructed from 870–920 AD. One will notice that these sources sometimes provide diverse accounts of the same events and at other times, al-Tabari in particular, quotes directly from earlier sources. Some Islamic scholars claim when comparing these traditions with one another there seems to be a lack of continuity.[10]

Muhammad and his early followers are made known through the words in these books. The intent of the Qur'an was to disclose the will of Allah as it escaped from the mouth of Muhammad. For these reasons, only the Qur'an surpasses the Sunnah in importance to Muslims, but all are considered authoritative and binding by most Muslims.[11] Allah speaks through Muhammad in the Qur'an and Allah acts through Muhammad in the Sunnah.[12] The verses from the authoritative texts of Islam, the Qur'an and the Sunnah (i.e., the Sirah, the Hadith, and the History of Al-Tabari), when read and applied literally, advocate radical Islamic "peace". However, this is not peace as Westerners understand it. Peace, as defined by Islamic Literalists, means the end of opposition to Allah's Will, Allah's Prophet, and Allah's Law.

The goal of this book is to accurately reflect the generally accepted Islamic texts in order to portray the original intent. This will be done by placing the Qur'anic text in the most likely chronological order, according to the most authoritative sources, along with corresponding passages from the Sirah, Hadith, and History of Al-Tabari. Since this book is written for Western readers, it is written in a style that should be easy to follow, while conveying Islamic ideology as derived by Islamic Literalists. The Qur'anic style has a circular structure that places its emphasis on the points being conveyed not the historical sequence of events. The Sirah and History of Al-Tabari are essential aids in determining the proper chronology of the Qur'an.

Each chapter in this book will represent a period of time. Within each chapter, numerous sections of the Qur'an will be presented which correspond to a specific grouping of years. Every one of these sections will consist of five segments: (1) Scripture; (2) Preface; (3) Surah; (4) Sunnah; and (5) Summation. The "Scripture" segment will list all of the scripture that is quoted in each section. The "Preface" segment will be a compilation of statements made by Maulana Muhammad Ali in his work *The Holy Qur'an with English Translation and Commentary* and by Mohammad Marmaduke Pickthall in his work *The Meaning of the Glorious Koran*. The "Surah" segment will consist of verses from the Qur'an that correspond to the Preface. It must also be mentioned that not all sources are convinced that the Qur'an came from Muhammad. Some feel that it was compiled by others in the first two centuries of Islam.[13] The "Sunnah" segment contains quotes from the Sirah, Hadith, and History of Tabari that correspond to the Surah. Finally, in each section, there will be a summation. The "Summation" segment will be divided into two parts. (1) The first part will be an explanation of the Islamic Literalist point of view, which will be labeled with the designator IL, or *Islamic Literalist*; and (2) The second part will be a critical analysis of the Islamic material presented which will be labeled with the designator WA, or *Western Analysis*. The summation in each section will strive to discern the bottom line or meaning of each surah and its corresponding hadith.

In sharing the Qur'anic textual interpretations of Ali and Pickthall, I've made one adjustment for western readers. In Islam, the Arabic word *Rasul* ("Messenger") is one who comes with his own revelation. Moses had the Torah, Jesus the Gospel, and Muhammad the Qur'an. So they all earn the title *Rasul*. Islam only claims a few people as having that title. In the Bible, the word *angel* ("Messenger of God"), in the sense that it is used, is usually a spirit being who can appear in human form. In modern day English, a messenger is "one who is sent". There is nothing in the English interpretation of this word that implies religion or one sent by a force outside of this world. The Arabic word *Nabi* signifies a Prophet. All of those who are Rasul are also Nabi; however, not all Nabi are a Rasul. Islam claims that all peoples have been sent a prophet. In total, over 100,000 prophets have been sent. If they did not come with their own book, then they cannot be a Rasul. Although the Arabic word for messenger has a more important meaning for Arabs, it does not for non-Muslim English readers. Those who read English understand the word "Prophet" has having a religious meaning or standing for one with tremendous insight. Therefore, in this book, I will often substitute the word "Prophet" for the word "Messenger" in the summation segment.

INTRODUCTION NOTES

1. Akram, *The Sword of Allah*, Introduction
2. Peters, *Muhammad and the Origins of Islam*, p. 265
3. Shahrazuri, *Introduction to the Science of the Hadith*, p. 1245
4. Siddiqui, *Sahih Muslim*, Introduction
5. Sabini, John, *Islam: A Primer*, p. 14
6. Swarup, *Understanding the Hadith*, p. 7
7. Spencer, *The Truth About Muhammad*, p. 26
8. Ankerberg/Caner, *Islam & Jihad*, p. 52
9. Dien, *Islamic Law*, p. 38
10. Crone, *The Evolution of Islamic Polity*, p. 11
11. Hallaq, *A History of Islamic Legal Theories*, p. 60
12. Swarup, *Understanding the Hadith*, p. 4
13. Rawandi, *Origins of Islam*, p. 111

PART I

Muhammad:
Allah's Prophet

CHAPTER 1

Jahiliyyah

(570-609 AD)

SCRIPTURE:

Ishaq:70-73, 79, 82-85, 90; Muslim:B1C75N311; Tabari VI:44, 46, 48, 56, 58-59, 64, 66

PREFACE:

Muhammad was born in the year 570 AD. He was the son of Abdullah, son of Abdul Muttalib, son of Hashim, son of Abd Manaf, who was the son of Qusayy. Abdullah's brothers were Harith, Talib, Lahab, Jahal, Abbas, and Hamza. His mother Amina was a descendent of Qusayy's brother Zuhar, all of the Quraysh tribe. Muhammad never knew his father Abdullah, who died before he was born. Muhammad's mother died when he was six. He was then protected by his grandfather Abdul Muttalib until his grandfather's death. From that time until he reached adulthood, Muhammad was raised by his uncle Abu Talib. Muhammad as a youth travelled with his uncle to Syria in caravans. Eventually he joined a caravan owned by a wealthy widow named Khadijah. Muhammad managed to impress her in his business dealings and she married him. When they married in 595 AD, Muhammad was 25 years old and Khadijah was 40 years old.

Muhammad was *not* born into a Jewish or Christian family. He was born to polytheists who worshipped many gods.[1] The most popular gods were: Hubal, the Moabite man image; Al-lah, the oval dark rock moon deity; and Al-lah's daughters, the three goddesses, Al-lat, Uzza, and Manat. There was a group of Arabs who were not polytheists. They were known as Hanifs, who drew their beliefs from Hellenistic philosophy and Christianity. It is believed by some that Muhammad joined their ranks. One of their practices was to visit the cave Hira for one month per year in order to meditate. It was during one of these visits in 610 AD that the Qur'anic revelations began.

SURAH:

This section does not contain any Qur'anic revelations. The time period being described preceded the Qur'anic revelations by many years

ISLAM'S NATIVITY

Ishaq:70: "I heard a Jew calling out at the top of his voice from Yathrib [Medina], O Jews, tonight has risen a star under which Ahmad is to be born.' [...] After his birth his mother sent to tell his grandfather Abd Al-Muttalib...It is alleged that Abd al-Muttalib took him before Hubal in the middle of the Ka'aba where he stood and prayed to Al-lah thanking him for this gift."

Ishaq:71: "When Halima [a Bedouin woman] reached Mecca, she set out to look for foster children [...] And when we [Halima and those with her] decided to depart, I said, 'I do not like the idea of returning with my friends without a suckling. I will take that orphan [Muhammad].' I took him for the sole reason that I could not find anyone else."

ADOLESCENT CRISIS

Ishaq:72: "But she sent him [Muhammad] back [to Mecca]. Some months after his return to the desert two men in white seized the boy [Muhammad], threw him down and opened up his belly, stirring it up. Halima said, 'I am afraid that this child has had a stroke, so I want to take him back before the result appears.' She carried him back to Aminah and said, 'I am afraid that ill will befall him, so I have brought him back to you.' She asked what had happened. I said, 'I fear that a demon has possessed him.'"

Muslim:B1C75N311: "Gabriel came to Muhammad while he was playing with his playmates. He took hold of him and lay him prostrate on the ground and tore open his breast and took out his heart. Then he extracted a blood clot out of it and said: That was the part of Satan in you.' Then he washed it with the water of Zamzam in a golden basin and then it was joined together and restored to its place. The boys came running to their mother and said: 'Muhammad had been murdered.' They all rushed toward him. I myself saw the marks of needle on his breast."

THE ORPHAN

Ishaq:73: "When he was 6 years old his mother Amina died. [...] Thus the Apostle [to be] was left to his grandfather."

Ishaq:79: "There was a seer [an occultist prophet] who came to Mecca to look at Muhammad. She said, 'Bring me that boy, for I saw just now that by Al-lah he has a great future."

Tabari VI:44: Abdul Muttalib died eight years after the Year of the Elephant. He entrusted the future Messenger's care to his uncle Abu Talib because Abu and Abdullah had the same mother....Talib took pity on him [Muhammad]...The caravan halted at Busra in Syria where there was a learned Christian monk named Bahira in his cell...When he saw the Messenger, he observed him very intently, noting features of his person whose description he had found in his Christian book...Finally he looked at his back, and saw the seal of prophethood between his shoulders in the very place described in his book....'By Al-Lat and Al-Uzza', Bahira said, 'Take him back to your country, and be on your guard against the Jews, for, by Allah, if they see him and recognize what I have, they will seek to do him harm.' [...] The monk walked among them, coming up and taking the hand of the Messenger. He said, 'This is the Chief of the Worlds, the Messenger. This person has been sent by Al-lah as a mercy to the Worlds.'"

Tabari VI:46: "I also recognized him by the seal of prophethood which is below the cartilage of his shoulders and which is like an apple. While Bahira was standing by them beseeching them not to take the Messenger to the land of the Byzantines, since if these saw him, they would recognize him by his description and would kill him [...]"

A BUSINESS WOMAN, WIFE, AND MOTHER

Ishaq:82: "Khadijah was a wealthy and respected merchant. She was determined and intelligent, possessing many properties. She was the best born woman of the Quraysh, and the richest, too."

Tabari VI:48: "She used to employ men to engage in trade with her property and gave them a share of the profit, for the Quraysh were merchants. When she heard of Muhammad's truthfulness and nobility of character she sent for him and proposed that he should go to Syria and engage in the trade with her property. [...] When he arrived in Mecca.... She sent for the Messenger and, it is reported, said to him, 'Cousin, your kinship to me, your standing among your people...makes you a desirable match.' She offered herself to him in marriage."

Ishaq:83: "Khadijah was the mother of all of the Apostle's children, except Ibrahim [who was born of a future concubine, Maryrum the Copt], namely al-Qasim, al-Tayyib, and al-Tahir. They all died in paganism [They are all damned]."

THE KA'ABA AND THE BLACK STONE

Ishaq:84: "[...] There was a snake which used to come out of the well in the Ka'aba into which votive objects were thrown. It would lie on top of the Ka'aba everyday to sun itself. It was a terror. People were terrified of the snake because whenever anyone went near, it would draw itself up, make a rustling noise, and opened its mouth. One day, as it was laying on top of the Ka'aba as usual, Allah sent a bird which seized it and carried it off."

Ishaq:85: "[...] The Quraysh found in the corner [of the Ka'aba] a writing in Syriac. They could not understand it until a Jew read it for them. It read: 'I am Allah Lord of Mecca. I created it on the day that I created heaven and earth and formed the sun and moon.'"

Tabari VI:56: "[...] Muhammad was thirty-five. When they made the decision to demolish and rebuild the Ka'aba, Abu [Omaiyah bin Mugheerah Al-Makhzumi] took a stone from it which leapt from his hand and returned to its place."

Tabari VI:58: "[...] When they reached the place where the black stone was to be put they began to dispute about it, since every clan wished to lift the Stone to its place."

Tabari VI:59: "[...] when they saw him they said, 'This is the trustworthy one with whom we are satisfied. This is Muhammad.' He came up to them and they told him about the matter, and he said, 'Bring me a cloak.' They brought him one, and he [Muhammad] took the Black Stone and placed it [the cloak] on it [the Black Stone] with his own hands. Then he said, 'Let each clan take one side of the cloak, and then lift it up altogether.' They did so, and when they had brought it to its place he [Muhammad] put it [the Black Stone] in position with his own hands."

Tabari VI:64: "Zayd bin Amir said, 'I expect a prophet from the descendents of Ishmael, in particular from the descendents of Abd al-Muttalib.' I shall inform you of his description so that he will not be hidden from you. He is neither short nor tall, whose hair is neither abundant nor sparse, whose eyes are always red, and who has the seal of the prophethood between his shoulders. His name is Ahmad, and this town is his birthplace and the place in which he will commence his mission. Then his people will drive him out and hate the message which he brings, and he will emigrate to Yathrib and triumph."

Ishaq:90: "Jewish rabbis, Christian monks, and Arab soothsayers had spoken about the Apostle of Al-lah before his mission when his time drew near. The rabbis and monks found his description in their scriptures. The Arab occultists had been visited by satans [devils] from the jinn with reports that they had secretly overheard [concerning Muhammad] before they were prevented from hearing by being pelted with stars."

Tabari VI:66: "Then Umar said, 'By Allah I was [standing] by one of the idols of the Jahiliyyah. An Arab sacrificed a calf to it, and we were waiting for it to be divided up in order to receive a share. I heard coming from the belly of the calf a voice, which was more penetrating than any I've ever heard—this was one year before Islam [609 AD]. The dead calf's belly said, 'There is no god but Allah.'…"

SUMMATION:

IL: Islamic Literalists learn that the Jews knew from their own books that Muhammad was the Prophet. Muhammad never knew his father and before his mother's death Muhammad was being nursed by a Bedouin woman who did not understand the Angel Gabriel had to miraculously remove the imperfections in Muhammad's being before the onset of his prophetic mission. After being purified by Gabriel, a pagan seer, and a Christian, came to recognize Muhammad as a prophet. The Christian monk stated that he found evidence of Muhammad's call in his Christian book and warns Muhammad's protector to keep Muhammad from the Jews and Christians because they know who he is and will try to harm or kill him. It was reported by Ibn Sa'd that a Jewish man saw the mole on Muhammad's back and said, "Prophethood has gone from the Israelites and the Scriptures out of their hands. It is written that he will fight with them and kill their scholars."[2] Allah then permitted Muhammad to meet his older female cousin who was wealthy. They were married but it was not Allah's will that Muhammad's sons would survive. Ten years into his marriage Muhammad became involved in the rebuilding of the Ka'aba which was the central focus of Arab paganism. Muhammad's wisdom brought about cooperation between the clans who lifted the Black Stone into its place. The Black Stone was the object of Arab circumambulation and touching.[3] Another claim, attributed to Muhammad, of prophethood is that he placed the Black Stone in its resting place. Before this period ended Muslims were reminded that rabbis and monks knew Muhammad was the Prophet from evidence in their scriptures. Soothsayers even learned of his status from more occult methods. Further evidence to Muhammad's prophethood was the uttering from a cow's stomach that "There is no god but Allah."

WA: Western Analysis can only make determinations on what is known from the text, not on what is believed by Muslims. Muhammad appears to have been raised in less than ideal surroundings. He never knew his dad. After his birth Muhammad's mother gave him to his grandfather who brought him before Hubal while he prayed to Al-lah. Al-lah was the high god of the Meccan pantheon.[4] Hubal was brought from Mesopotamia to the Ka'aba by Amr ibn Luhayy.[5] He was a member of the ruling Khuza'I before they were overcome by the Quraysh. Hubal was in the form of a man and was the largest idol in the Ka'aba.[6] Muhammad's pagan grandfather dedicated him to these pagan deities. Afterward his mother allowed him to be raised by another woman. The experience with the two men or angel figuratively opening Muhammad's chest seems to have been traumatic since the terms "stroke", "devils", and "Satan" are used in the Islamic text. One may ask how could a very young boy, who was to become the Prophet of Allah, have a demon that needed to be removed by two mysterious men or the Angel Gabriel. Regardless, after this event, a polytheistic pagan seer associated Muhammad with pre-Islamic Al-lah, the moon god, father of the three goddesses Al-lat, Uzza, and Manat.

According to various encyclopedias, Al-lah was one of the Meccan deities before the time of Islam.

> "The Arabs, before the time of Muhammad, accepted and worshipped, after a fashion, a supreme god called Allah."[7]

> —*Encyclopedia of Islam*, I:302

> "Al-lah was known to the pre-Islamic…Arabs; he was one of the Meccan deities."[7]

> —*Encyclopedia of Islam*, I:406

> "Allah' is a pre-Islamic name…corresponding to the Babylonian Bel."[8]

> —*Encyclopedia of Religion*, I:117

> An Islamic scholar, Caesar Farah, asserted, "In Arabia, the sun god was viewed as a female goddess and the moon as the male god. As has been pointed out by many scholars such as Alfred Guilluame, the moon god was called by various names, one of which was Allah…There is no reason, therefore, to accept the idea that Allah passed to the Muslims from the Christians and Jews"(9)

> —Farah, *Islam*, pp. 7, 28

> "Allah, the moon god, was married to the sun goddess. Together they produced three goddesses [the daughters of Allah], Al-Lat, Al-Uzza, and Manat. All of these 'gods' were viewed as being the top of the pantheon of Arab deities. Along with Allah, however, they worshipped a host of lesser gods and the 'daughters of Al-lah.'"[10]

> —*Encyclopedia of World Mythology and Legend*, I:61

Al-lat was venerated among the Thaqif and Meccans although Uzza was more favored by the Meccans. Manat was more favored among the Aws and Khazraj of Yathrib.[11] After Muhammad's Uncle Abu-Talib assumed the role of guardian, a Christian monk claimed to have found evidence of Muhammad in his Christian book. From a Christian perspective, the only Christian book that could matter in this regard is the New Covenant.

> "Of [concerning] the New Testament, however, we have two splendid manuscripts of the fourth century, at least ten of the fifth [century], twenty-five of the sixth [century] and in all a total of more than four thousand copies in whole or in part of the Greek New Testament."[12]

> —Cook, *Muhammad*, p. 10

Therefore, we have at least 37 New Covenant manuscripts that pre-date Muhammad. None of those manuscripts contain what Tabari VI:44 claimed. The book that the monk had in his possession could not have been the New Covenant. He may have been an Arian or Gnostic. These sects were not recognized by the western or eastern churches. Arianism believed that Jesus was created. Gnostics believed that Jesus was human but attained divinity by acquiring intuitive knowledge. The sects that were present in Arabia were the Monophysites and the Nestorians. The Monophysites believed Jesus only had a divine nature. He did not have a divine and human nature. The Nestorians believed there was disunion between the divine and human nature of Christ. All of these were considered heretical sects.[13] The "Christian" monk then spoke in the name of the Arab goddesses while warning of Jewish treachery. He also proclaimed that Allah, one of the gods of the Arab pantheon since the revelations had not occurred, and Muhammad will have global authority. Why would the monk say this when these words contradict the words found in the New Covenant? Simply put, there are no historical records stating that Christians or Jews were awaiting an Arab prophet.[14] Before Muhammad met his first wife, the Christian monk warned the Arab polytheists that the Byzantines may want to kill Muhammad. So a Christian monk warned Arab polytheists that Christian Byzantines wanted to murder an innocent Muhammad.

Muhammad's marriage to Khadijah was not at all surprising. She was an affluent woman, who, because of the age difference—she was fifteen years older than Muhammad—, may have been able to assume the role of a mother figure for him since his mother did not appear to be all that involved in his life. Curiously, Khadijah pursued Muhammad in regard to their nuptials. The issue of succession, which has plagued Islam since the 7ᵗʰ century, could have been avoided if any of his sons had survived. Sunni Muslims do not believe being a blood relative to Muhammad is a requirement to become Caliph. Having so many sons die in infancy must have had a psychological impact on Muhammad, as it would on most people.

Zayd bin Amir, a Hanif poet, not a Christian or Jew, seems to predict perfectly Muhammad's mission, but there is a problem. The problem is this *prophecy* was recalled by al-Tabari 300 years after the recorded event. We know from history that most of the hadiths collected by Sahih Bukhari were rejected for not being true. If this had been recorded in the Tenakh or in the New Covenant, it would have been more convincing to the Jews and Christians.

As for the Ka'aba, Muslims believe Allah created the prototype to it 2000 years before the world was created. After Adam was created, he was in the environs of Mecca when the Jewel of Paradise was sent down so that Adam could circumambulate it. Then Allah sent down Gabriel to help Adam build the cubed building (Ka'aba) so that Adam would continue to circumambulate it. So the Ka'aba houses the Jewel. The Jewel of Paradise eventually turned black after menstruating women touched it. The Ka'aba was then removed before the great flood. Allah told Abraham to follow a spirit that coiled like a snake at the place where the new Ka'aba was to be built by Abraham and Ishmael. As for the snake, Mecca's premier local historian stated the serpent protected the Ka'aba's sanctuary and treasure for more than 500 years.[15] According to Islam, a snake-like spirit designated where the Ka'aba was to be built and a snake protected the Ka'aba for more than 500 years. This does not bode well since the snake/serpent of the Bible is always associated with the devil. After the Ka'aba was finished, Gabriel handed the Black Stone to Abraham and he set it in place. Knowing this, the text ties Muhammad to Abraham when Muhammad raised the stone into the place in the rebuilt Ka'aba in 605 AD.[16]

As this section comes to a close, Christians, Jews, and polytheists recognized that a Prophet of Allah was to be revealed, when in reality they could have only recognized Al-lah as the moon-god companion of Hubal and the father of the three goddesses. The saying, "There is no god but Allah," heard in 609 AD, could only mean that Al-lah, the moon-god, was the only god at that time. It could not be understood any other way since it was still the time of Jahiliyyah.

CHAPTER 1 NOTES

1. Haeri, *Elements of Islam*, p.12
2. Sa'd, *Kitab al-Tabaqat*, Vol. 1, p.186
3. Haeri, *Elements of Islam*, p.11
4. Henninger, *Pre-Islamic Bedouin Religion*, p.12
5. Al-Azraqi, *Ahkbar Makka*, pp.73-74
6. Kalbi, *Book of Idols*, p. 28-29
7. Encyclopedia of Islam, I:302, 406
8. Encyclopedia of Religion, I:117
9. Farah, *Islam*, pp. 7, 28
10. Encyclopedia of World Religion and Mythology, I:61
11. Kalbi, *Book of Idols*, pp. 12-14, 27
12. Cook, *Muhammad*, p.10
13. Spencer, *The Truth About Muhammad*, p. 38
14. International Standard Bible Encyclopedia, pp. 2950-2957.
15. Al-Azraqi, *Ahkbar Makka*, pp. 108-109
16. Tabari I:216, 293-294,303; Tabari II:69-71

CHAPTER 2

Early Meccan Revelations

(610-614 AD)

"The Clot"

610 AD

SCRIPTURE:

Qur'an 96:1-5, 15-19

Bukhari:V1B1N3, V6B60N478; Ishaq:100-102; Tabari VI:67

PREFACE:

This was the first surah revealed in the Qur'an. The beginning of mankind's creation started with a clot of blood; likewise, Muhammad, starting with Mecca, would raise humanity both morally and spiritually.[1]

SURAH:

Qur'an 96:1-5: "[After receiving this revelation from Allah, Gabriel tells Muhammad] Read in the name of thy Lord who creates — creates man out of a clot, read and thy Lord is most Generous, who taught by the pen, taught man what he knew not."

Qur'an 96:15-19: "Nay, if he [Abu Jahl, a Meccan leader] desist not, we will seize him by the forelock — a lying, sinful forelock! Then let him summon his council, we will summon the braves of the army. Nay! Obey him not, but prostate thyself, and draw nigh to Allah."

THE MENTOR

Ishaq:100-102: "[Zayd ibn Amr, a Meccan Hanif who may have schooled Muhammad before his initial revelation, cited the following poem:] O Ilah, if I only knew how you wished to be worshipped I would do so; but I do not know. Then Zayd prostrated himself on the palms of his hands while facing the Ka'aba. I worship one Lord. I renounce Al-Lat and Al-Uzza. I will not worship Hubal [Bel, Baal], though he was our lord. Ilah has annihilated many men whose deeds were evil. I serve my Lord Ar-Rahman so that the forgiving Lord may pardon my sin. So keep fearing Ilah, your Lord, and you will see the Gardens. While for the infidels [or Kuffar], hell fire is burning. Shamed in life, when they die their breasts contract in anguish […]. Beware of associating another with Ilah, for the straight path has become clear. […] Zayd was determined to leave Mecca to travel about in search of the Hanif religion, the religion of Abraham. […] Zayd faced the Ka'aba inside the mosque and said, 'I am a sincere worshipper in truth. Here I am at your service. I take refuge in what Abraham took refuge when he stood and faced the Qiblah. I am a humble slave. I put my face in the dust. Whatever I am commanded, I must do. […] I submit myself.'"

THE REVELATION BEGINS

Bukhari:V1B1N3, V6B60N478: "[According to Aisha years later], the commencement of divine inspiration to Muhammad was in the form of dreams [while sleeping] that came true like a bright light. The Prophet loved the seclusion of a cave in Hira [in the month of Ramadan where he practiced *Tahannuth* ("self-justification"), a Hanif/pagan rite during Jahiliyyah]. The angel came to him and asked him to read. The Prophet replied, 'I do not know how to read.' The Prophet added, 'Then the angel caught me forcefully and pressed me so hard that I could not bear it anymore. He released me and asked me to read. I replied, "I do not know how to read." Thereupon he caught me again and pressed me till I could not bear it anymore. He asked me to read but I replied, "I do not know how to read or what shall I read?" Thereupon he caught me for the third time and pressed me, "Read in the name of your Lord who has created man from a clot. Read! Your Lord is the most generous." Then the apostle returned from that experience; the muscles between his neck and shoulders trembling, and his heart beating severely. He went to Khadijah and cried, 'Cover me! Cover me!' She did until his fear subsided. He said, 'What's wrong with me? I am afraid that something bad has happened to me.' Khadijah replied, 'Never! By Allah, Allah will never disgrace you […].'"

Tabari VI:67: "[Another version according to Aisha who was not alive when these events occurred] Aisha reported: 'Solitude became dear to Muhammad and he used to seclude himself in the cave of Hira where he would engage in the Tahannuth worship for a number of nights before returning to Khadijah and getting provisions for a like period, till truth came upon him while he was in a cave. The first form of revelation was a true vision in sleep. He did not see any vision but it came like the break of dawn […] Muhammad, you are the Messenger.' The Prophet said, 'I had been standing, but fell to my knees; and crawled away, my shoulders trembling, I went to Khadijah and said, "Wrap me up!" When the terror had left me, he came to me and said, "Muhammad, you are the Messenger of Allah."' Muhammad said, 'I had been thinking of hurling myself down from a mountain […], but he appeared to me as I was thinking about this and said, "I am Gabriel and you are the Messenger," Then he said, "Recite!" I said, "What shall I recite?" He took me and pressed me three times. I told Khadijah, "I fear for my life." She said, "Rejoice, for Allah will never put you to shame."'"

SUMMATION:

IL: For Islamic literalists, the initial revelation signaled the beginning of the end of Jahiliyyah for the Arabs. In retrospect Muhammad married Khadijah, in 595 AD, because he needed her to withstand Gabriel's visitation. Gabriel's mention of prophethood was endorsed by Khadijah and this helped convince Muhammad. Allah's wrath from inception was kindled against anyone who opposed the Prophet's mission. In this case, Abu Jahl, Muhammad's foe, was directly mentioned by Allah.

WA: From the analytical Western perspective the entire event occurred while Muhammad was participating in a pagan rite at Hira.[2] When one considers Ishaq's words, it appears that Muhammad was also influenced by Zayd ibn Amr and the Hanif faith. Participation in the Tahannuth was a Hanif rite which included prayer while facing the Ka'aba. Since Muhammad was practicing this pagan rite at the time of his spiritual encounter it was likely that he also prayed facing the Ka'aba at Mecca. The problem at that time was that it was still a pagan shrine, not an Islamic shrine. Later, as we will see, the direction of prayer will change to Jerusalem before once again changing to the Ka'aba. Also, according to the text, he appeared to have dreamt the spirit visitation. Clearly he was illiterate, terrified, and troubled, for he seriously contemplated suicide, thinking that a devil had seized him. He was fortunate that his 'mother/ wife' Khadijah was there to comfort him as he succumbed to her embrace and assurance.

"The One Wrapping Himself Up"

610 AD

SCRIPTURE:

Qur'an 74:1-56

Ishaq:105-106

PREFACE:

The Angel Gabriel once again appeared to Muhammad. Afterward, Muhammad entered a trance and wrapped himself in a cloak. Like the first appearing, this visit by Gabriel also occurred on Mt. Hira. Muhammad was admonished by Gabriel to take his mission to the public. Up to this point he was in seclusion. Muhammad was told to warn others of the evil consequences that would result from their deeds.[3]

SURAH:

Qur'an 74:1-7: "O thou who wrappest [wrap] thyself up, arise and warn, and thy Lord do magnify, and thy garments do purify, and uncleanness do shun, and do no favour seeking [worldly] gain, and for the sake of thy Lord, be patient."

Qur'an 74:8-14: "For when the trumpet is sounded, that will be — that day — a difficult day, for the disbelievers anything but easy. Leave Me alone with him, who I created, and gave him vast riches, and sons dwelling in his presence, and made matters easy for him."

Qur'an 74:15-20: "And yet he desires that I should give more! By no means! Surely he is inimical to Our messages. I will make a distressing punishment overtake him. Surely he reflected and determined, but may he be destroyed by how he determined! Again, may he be destroyed by how he determined!"

Qur'an 74:21-25: "Then he looked, then frowned and scowled, then turned back and was big with pride, then said: this is naught but magic from old! This is naught, but the word of a mortal [man]."

Qur'an 74:26-30: "I will cast him into hell. And what will make thee realize what hell is? It leaves nothing and spares nothing. It scorches the mortal. Over it are nineteen."

Qur'an 74:31: "And We have made none but angels wardens of the Fire, and We have not made their number but as a trial for those who disbelieve, that those who have been given the Book may be certain and those who believe may increase in faith, and those who have been given the Book and the believers may not doubt; and that those in whose hearts is a disease and the disbelievers may say: What does Allah mean by this parable? Thus Allah leaves in error whom He pleases, and guides whom He pleases. [...] This is naught but a Reminder to mortals."

Qur'an 74:32-39: "Nay, by the moon! And the night when it departs! And the dawn when it shines! — surely it [hell] is one of the gravest misfortunes. A warning to men, to him among you who will go forward or will remain behind. Every soul is held in pledge for what it earns, except the people of the right hand."

Qur'an 74:40-47: "In [the] Gardens, they [will] ask one another, about the guilty: What has brought you into hell? They will say: We are not of those who prayed, nor did we feed the poor; and we indulged in vain talk with vain talkers; and we called the Day of Judgment a lie; till the inevitable overtook us."

Qur'an 74:48-51: "So the intercession of intercessors will not avail them. What is then the matter with them, [...] they turn away from the Reminder. As if they were frightened asses, fleeing from a lion?"

Qur'an 74:52-56: "Nay, everyone of them desires that he be given pages spread out! By no means! But they do not fear the Hereafter. Nay, it is surely a Reminder. So whoever pleases may find it. And they will not mind unless Allah please. He is Worthy that duty should be kept to Him and Worthy to forgive."

SUNNAH:

SUICIDE IS CONTEMPLATED

Ishaq:105-106: "The Apostle would pray in seclusion on [Mt.] Hira every year for a month [Ramadan] to practice Tahannuth as was the custom of the Quraysh in the heathen days [In the period of *Jahiliyyah*, or Barbarism]. [...] I awoke from my sleep. These words were written on my heart. None of Allah's creatures was more hateful to me than an ecstatic poet or a man possessed. I thought, 'Woe is me, I'm a possessed poet.' I will go to the top of the mountain and throw myself down that I may kill myself and be at rest. So I climbed to the mountain to kill myself when I heard a voice saying, 'Muhammad, you are Allah's Apostle.' I raised my head to see who was speaking and lo, I saw Gabriel in the form of a man with feet astride the horizon. I stood gazing at him and that distracted me from committing suicide. I couldn't move. Khadijah sent her messengers in search of me, and they gained the high ground above Mecca so I came to her and sat by her thigh. She said, 'O Abu'l-Qasim [My uncle's son], where have you been?' I said, 'Woe is me. I am possessed.' She said, 'I take refuge in Allah from that Abu'l-Qasim. Allah would not treat you that way. This cannot be, my dear. Perhaps you did see something, 'Yes, I did,' I said, I told her of what I had seen. She said, 'Rejoice, son of my uncle, and be of good cheer. Verily, by Him in whose hand is Khadijah's soul, I have hope that you will be the prophet to this people.' He read from the scriptures and learned from those who followed the Torah and the Gospels."

SUMMATION:

IL: Although not immediately understanding the complete will of Allah, Muhammad still allowed Allah to use his host to transmit this surah. The revelation makes clear that those polytheists who resist Islam will be thrown into hell.

WA: During this period while Muhammad was experiencing psychological distress, he still revealed a surah that recalled his sunken state. This occurred while Muhammad was practicing *tahannuth*, an ascetic practice observed during Ramadan on Mt. Hira, which included fasting and sexual abstention.[4] Muhammad, fearing he was possessed by an evil spirit, uttered revelation that damned his oppressors to hell. Predestination is hinted at in 74:31. It appeared that 19 angels, who folks usually associate with heavenly places, are the wardens of fire for the diseased infidels. Al-Qaida used this surah as inspiration, noting that the "magnificent 19" destroyed the World Trade Center Towers. Curiously, as this surah concluded, Allah swore by the moon, darkness of the night, and called hell a great sign.

QUR'AN 1

"The Opening"

610 AD

SCRIPTURE:

Qu'ran 1:5-7

Tabari VI:68, 70; Ishaq:107; Bukhari:V1B1N3

PREFACE:

This surah established the basis for all Muslim prayer. The verses contained are mandatory for all Muslims. The *Bismillah* is the first phrase that Muslims utter. In doing so, the Muslim *ummah* ("community") becomes the Kingdom of Allah. The Bismillah announces the glory of Allah and the kingdom of his believers. These words separate Islam from the religions of the People of the Book. Jews and Christians are included as those who went astray.[5]

SURAH:

Qur'an 1:5-7: "Guide us the right path, the path of those whom Thou hast bestowed favours, Not those upon whom wrath is brought down [Jews], nor those who go astray [Christians]."

SUNNAH:

DOUBT AND VALIDATION

Tabari VI:68: "Then she took me to Waraqa and said, 'Listen to your brother's son.' He questioned me and I told him what had happened. He said, 'This is namus [virtue] which was sent down to Moses, son of Abraham.' [...] The first parts of the Qur'an to be revealed to me after Iqra were: 'By the pen and that which they write. You are not a madman. Yours will be a reward unfailing, and you are of a great nature. You shall see and they shall see.'"

Tabari VI:70: "He went to Khadijah and said, 'I think I have gone mad.' Khadijah said, 'No, by Allah,' she said. 'Your Lord would never do that to you. You have never committed a wicked act.' Khadijah went to Waraqa and told him what had happened. He said, 'If what you have said is true, your husband is a prophet...' After this Gabriel did not come to him for a while and Khadijah said, 'I think that your Lord must hate you.' In the beginning of the Messenger's prophetic mission he used to spend a month every year in religious retreat on Hira. This was part of the practice of Tahannuth [...]."

Ishaq:107: "When she related to him what Muhammad had told her [what] he had seen and heard, Waraqa cried, 'Holy! Holy! If you have spoken the truth, Khadijah, there has come unto him the Namus [law], the spirit who appeared long ago to Moses. Tell Muhammad to be of good cheer, for he is to be the Prophet of his people.' So Khadijah returned to her husband and told him what Waraqa had said. As a result, his fears were somewhat calmed."

Bukhari:V1B1N3: "Khadijah then took Muhammad to Waraqa bin Naufal [her cousin]. He was the only man in town [Mecca] who had to embrace Christianity in the pre-Islamic Days of Ignorance [the period of Jahiliyyah]. He used to write the writing in Hebrew letters. He would write from the Gospel in Hebrew as much as Allah wished him to write. He was very old and lost his eyesight. Khadijah told Waraqa, 'Listen to the story of your nephew, my cousin!' Waraqa asked, 'Nephew, what have you seen?' Muhammad described whatever he had seen [concerning the event at Mt. Hira]. Waraqa said, 'This is the same one who keeps the secrets whom Allah had sent to Moses. I wish I were young and could live up to the time when your people would expel you!' Muhammad asked, 'Will they drive me out?' Waraqa said, 'Yes! Anyone who came with something similar to what you have brought was treated with hostility.' A few days later Waraqa died, and the divine inspiration was paused for a long while."

SUMMATION:

IL: Shortly after the initial verses of the Qur'an were recited by Muhammad, he received the Bismillah—In the name of Allah, the Beneficent, the Merciful. The Bismillah established Islam as the only true religion of Allah. It separated Allah from the other gods of the Ka'aba as it does from those who anger Allah, the Jews, and those who go astray, the Christians. Thus, Islam was instituted as the straight path.[6] It was the proclamation of the Bismillah that lowered the status of Arab polytheism, which, in turn, led to verbal attacks against Muhammad. In the Sunnah, Waraqa the Christian prophet affirmed that Muhammad was being persecuted like the prophets before him, thus, endorsing his prophethood.

WA: Those who were accusing Muhammad of being mad were his relatives who knew him from the time of his youth. They witnessed a change in behavior and the Muhammad they knew believed that he spoke for one of the gods of the Meccan pantheon. Their verbal attacks on him took such a toll that Khadijah, his wife, intervened. There was no indication that the revelation of the Bismillah eased Muhammad's mental state. Rather, the words of Khadijah's blind Christian cousin, who also answered to Allah's inspiration, temporarily eased Muhammad's fears.

QUR'AN 68

"The Pen"

610 AD

SCRIPTURE:

Qur'an 68:1-16, 35, 42-44, 48, 51

Tabari VI:73-74

PREFACE:

This surah was revealed after the Meccans accused Muhammad of being a madman. In response Allah promised their doom. When events go bad, remember, the Qur'an helps humanity triumph over the trials of life. Therefore, the Qur'an ("the recitation") is for all nations.[7]

SURAH:

Qur'an 68:1-2: "By the inkstand and the pen and that which they write! By the grace of thy Lord thou [Muhammad] art not mad."

Qur'an 68:3-14: "And surely thine is a reward never to be cut off. And surely thou hast sublime morals. So thou will see and they too will see, which of you is mad. Surely thy Lord knows best who is erring from His way, and He knows best those go aright. So obey not the rejectors. They wish that thou shouldst be pliant, so they too would be pliant. And obey not any mean swearer, defamer, going about with slander, hinderer of good, outstepping [exceeding] the limits, sinful, ignoble, besides all that, notoriously mischievous — because he possesses wealth and sons."

Qur'an 68:15-16: "When Our messages are recited to him, he says: Stories of those of yore! We shall brand him on the snout."

Qur'an 68:35: "Shall We then make [treat] those who submit [Muslims] as the guilty [like disbelievers]?"

Qur'an 68:42-44: "On the day when there is a severe affliction, and they are called upon to prostrate themselves, but they are not able — their looks [eyes] will be cast down, abasement will cover them. And they were indeed called upon to prostrate themselves, while yet they were safe. So leave Me alone with him who rejects this announcement. We shall overtake them by degrees, from whence they know not.

Qur'an 68:48: "So wait with patience for the judgment of thy Lord, and be not like the Companion of the fish, when he cried while he was in distress."

Qur'an 68:51: "Those who disbelieve would almost smite thee with their eyes, when they hear the Reminder, and they say, surely he is mad."

SUNNAH:

SPIRIT OF INFLUENCE

Tabari VI:73: "'Cousin, can you tell me when this visitor comes to you?' Muhammad said, 'Yes.' She said, 'Tell me then, when he comes.' Gabriel came to him as before and Muhammad said, 'Here is Gabriel who has just come to me.' She said, "Yes, Come, cousin, and sit by my left thigh.' He came, and she said, 'Can you see him?' [Muhammad said,] 'Yes.' 'Move around and sit by my right thigh.' He did so and she said, 'Can you see him?' [Muhammad said,] 'Yes.' She said, 'Sit on my lap?' He did so and she said, 'Can you see him?' He replied, 'Yes.' She was grieved, and she flung off her veil and disclosed her body while the Apostle was sitting in her lap. [According to one version the text of the next sentence says:] Khadijah put the Messenger inside her shift next to her body. [According to another version, the text of this sentence says:] I heard that she made the Apostle come inside her shift. Then she said, 'Can you see him?' [Muhammad said,] 'No.' At that she said, 'Rejoice cousin. By Allah, this spirit is an angel and not Satan.'"

Tabari VI:74: "[...] Jabir said: 'I am telling to you what the Messenger told me. He said: "I stayed in the cave for one month and when my stay was completed, I came down and went into the valley. Somebody called me. I looked but I did not see anybody. I was again called but saw nothing. I raised my head, and there on the Throne in the atmosphere he was sitting. I began to tremble because I was afraid of him.""""

SUMMATION:

IL: In these opening surahs of the Qur'an, Allah declared that his chosen, Muhammad, was not mad, in fact, he will be rewarded and his persecutors will be punished for declaring that Allah's Prophet was possessed by Satan.

WA: After the revealing of this surah, the revelations stopped for a few years. Muhammad's mental state was still troubled. It was Khadijah who stated Muhammad had not committed a wicked act. The same Khadijah stated, "I think your Lord must hate you." Then frustrated by not being able to see the invisible Gabriel, proving she was not a prophetess, she revealed her body to Muhammad. Since his attention was now on her body and not on his invisible visitor, she was pleased and believed that the spirit that afflicted Muhammad's mental state was an angel and not Satan. We also see that Muhammad's experiences with Gabriel were associated with the Quraysh pagan practice of Tahannuth Therefore, we now know that Muhammad experienced a spiritual being, even seeing that creature sitting on a throne up in the atmosphere while or after he was participating in a non-Jewish, non-Christian pagan rite. Those who accused Muhammad of being mad were his relatives who have known him for his entire life.

QUR'AN 94

"The Expansion"

613 AD

SCRIPTURE:

Qur'an 94:1-8

Tabari VI:75-76

PREFACE:

Muhammad was reminded through revelation that his difficulties with the Meccans would come to an end. Allah promised to remove his anxiety. Although Muhammad was being derided and shunned, Allah claimed that his name would be exalted.[8]

SURAH:

Qur'an 94:1-8: "Have We not expanded for thee thy breast [chest], and removed from thee thy burden, which weighed down thy back, and exalted for thee thy mention? Surely with [every] difficulty is ease [relief], with [every] difficulty is surely ease. So when thou art free from anxiety, work hard, and make thy Lord thy exclusive object."

SUNNAH:

A TRAUMATIC EXPERIENCE

Tabari VI:75: "'Messenger, how did you first know with absolute certainty that you were a prophet?' He replied, 'Two angels came to me while I was somewhere in Mecca [...]. One angel said, "Open his breast and take out his heart." He opened my chest and heart, removing the pollution of Satan and a clot of blood, and threw it away. [...] Then one said, "Wash his breast as you would a receptacle." He summoned the Sakinah ["God's presence"], which looked like the face of a white cat, and it was placed in my heart [...].Then one said, "Sew up his breast." So they sewed up my chest and placed the seal between my shoulders.'"

Tabari VI:76: "'The inspiration ceased to come to the Messenger for a while, and he was deeply grieved. He began to go to the tops of mountain crags, in order to fling himself from them [commit suicide]; but every time He reached the summit of a mountain, Gabriel appeared to him and said to him, 'You are Allah's Prophet.' Thereupon his anxiety would subside and he would come back to himself [peace of mind].' Muhammad explains: 'I was walking one day when I saw the angel who used to come to me at [Mt.] Hira. I was terror-stricken by him.'"

SUMMATION:

IL: Muhammad became the Prophet of Allah after two angels came to Muhammad and supernaturally opened his chest to remove the pollution of Satan and a clot of blood. The spirit of Allah, resembling a white cat, was placed inside of him. After the spirit of Allah was placed within him, he knew and began to carry out the will of Allah.

WA: The Qur'anic verse relates to an event that occurred during the time of Jahiliyyah. The Sunna details an Arab woman who described two men taking a younger Muhammad against his will and purportedly opening his belly. She feared demonic possession (Ishaq:72). For her to say this, the event in her judgment changed Muhammad for the worse. Why would she tell his mother that she feared possession? Muslim's account, which is a later version of the event, changed the two men to the angel Gabriel. This account contends that Satan was removed from him. The text states that Muhammad had no choice in this matter. The Qur'anic verse and the later account by Tabari seem to agree. The "We" in the Qur'an must be Allah working His will through Gabriel to Muhammad. What was the "Satan" that had to be removed Muhammad? Could have been Muhammad's polytheistic upbringing? Muhammad was raised to worship Uzza.[9] At the time of this occurrence, all appeared normal since Muhammad was playing with his friends. It appears to be the will of these spirit beings to fill Muhammad with the white cat-like spirit of Allah.[10]

During the nearly three year drought of revelation, Muhammad's state of mind was clearly in decline. The passage indicated more than a few times that Muhammad wanted to commit suicide. Gabriel appeared in every instance to convince him otherwise. Obviously, given the accounts of Khadijah and her "Christian" cousin Waraqa in the hadith, Allah's revelation did not work. Gabriel made numerous appearances to save Allah's Prophet. Muhammad was pleased to think of himself as a prophet, but his direct encounters with this Spirit Being(s) did not bring him peace, instead it left him terror-stricken.

QUR'AN 93

"The Brightness Of The Day"

613 AD

SCRIPTURE:

Qur'an 93:3-8

Bukhari:V4B52N267; Ishaq:113; Tabari VI:82

PREFACE:

Three years had gone by since the early revelations were announced. The Meccans then declared, "Allah of whom we used to hear so much has forsaken poor Muhammad and now hates him." After that statement this revelation was revealed. The Meccans continued to think of him as mad. What came later would be better than what had already occurred. This meant the truth of Islam would gradually be on the rise.[11]

SURAH:

Qur'an 93:3-8: "Thy Lord [Ar-Rahman] has not forsaken thee, nor is He displeased. And surely the latter state is better for thee than the former. And soon will thy Lord give thee [much] so that thou wil[l] be well pleased. Did not He find thee [as] an orphan and give thee shelter? And find thee groping [perplexed] and so He showed you the way? And find thee in want so, He enriched thee?"

THE OBJECTIVE IS DEFINED

Ishaq:113: "When I was a merchant I came to Mecca during the Hajj pilgrimage. While I was there a man came out to pray and stood facing the Ka'aba. Then a woman and boy came out and stood praying with him. I asked him, 'What is their religion? It is something new to me.' Abbas said, 'This is Muhammad who alleges that Allah has sent him with it so that the treasures of Chusroes [Persia] and Caesar [Rome] will be open to him. The woman is his wife Khadijah who believes in him.'"

Tabari VI:82: "During Jahiliyyah I came to Mecca and stayed with Abbas bin Muttalib. The sun rose while I was looking at the Ka'aba. A young man [Muhammad] came up and gazed at the sky. He turned to face the Ka'aba. Soon after, a woman [Khadijah] and a youth [Ali] came and stood behind him. The young man bowed and the woman and youth bowed; then the man stood erect, followed by the woman and youth. The young man prostrated himself, and they did the same. Abbas asked, 'Do you know what this is?' 'No,' I answered, 'this is Khadijah, my nephew's wife. He has told me that his Lord has commanded them to do what you see them doing. Allah's oath, I do not know anyone on the face of the earth but these three who follow this religion.' I asked Abbas, 'What is this religion?' He answered, 'This is Muhammad bin Abdallah, who claims that Allah has sent him as His Messenger with this religion and that the treasures of Chusroes and Caesar will be given to him by conquest.'"

Bukhari:V4B52N267: "The Prophet said, 'Khosrau will be ruined, and there will be no Khosrau after him, and Caesar will surely be ruined and there will be Caesar after him, and you will spend their treasures in Allah's Cause [Jihad].'"

SUMMATION:

IL: Following a period of testing, the revelations once again began. Ar-Rahman promised Muhammad that what was coming would be much better than what Muhammad endured from his relatives. Ar-Rahman promised to protect and enrich the Prophet. Early in his prophetic mission,

Muhammad confessed that the treasures of Persia and Rome lay before him.

WA: As Muhammad's psychological state improved, the revelations continued. Immediately, he was again accused of being crazy, but seemed to be better prepared to defend his position. We are now in the third year of Muhammad's mission since the initial revelation. At this point only Muhammad's wife and Ali, his cousin, believed that he was a prophet. Insights into Muhammad's inner motivations were also coming to the surface. A non-believer, Abbas, claimed Muhammad said that his god Allah wanted him to acquire the wealth of the two biggest empires of his day. He was speaking of Persia and Byzantium (Rome). From early on, this vision of acquiring the wealth of the Zoroastrians and Christians was conveyed to believers and non-believers. This also helped explain why Muhammad's pagan relatives thought he was mad. Before the revelations started, Muhammad knew about Ar-Rahman from the Hanifs. Since Muhammad only knew Allah as part of the Meccan pantheon, it is not surprising that he was seen praying at the polytheist's shrine.

You may have noticed that I used the name "Ar-Rahman" in both sections. This is because the term Ar-Rahman is designated as Lord instead of Allah in surahs: 56, 68, 78, 89, and 93. In fact, Ar-Rahman was worshipped in Yemen.[12] Verses 13:30; 21:36; 25:60 all mention Ar-Rahman, not Allah.

QUR'AN 73

"The One Covering Himself Up"

613 AD

SCRIPTURE:

Qur'an 73:1-6, 10-13

Ishaq:115-116

PREFACE:

This surah encouraged Muhammad to bear patiently the opposition that he received from the Meccans. After being opposed by the Meccans, Muhammad went to his wife Khadijah and she wrapped him in a cloak. Muhammad was admonished to pray at night and Allah promised to protect him just like Moses was protected. As Pharaoh, the enemy of Moses was destroyed, so the enemies of Muhammad will also be destroyed.[13]

SURAH:

Qur'an 73:1-6: "O thou covering thyself up! Rise to pray by night except a little, half of it, or lessen it a little, or add to it, and recite the Qur'an [as you have been told], in a leisurely manner [slow measured rhythmic tones]. Surely We shall charge [entrust] thee with a weighty word. The rising by night is surely the firmest [devout] way to tread and most effective in speech."

Qur'an 73:10-11: "And bear patiently what they say and forsake [depart from] them with a becoming withdraw [graciously]. And leave Me and the deniers, possessors of plenty, and respite them a little.

Qur'an 73:12-13: "Surely with Us are heavy fetters and a flaming Fire, and food that chokes and a painful chastisement [doom]."

SUNNAH:

Ishaq:115: "Now Muhammad did not want his secret to be divulged before he applied himself to the publication of his message."

Ishaq:116: "I heard the Apostle say, 'I have never invited anyone to accept Islam who hasn't shown signs of reluctance, suspicion and hesitation.'"

SUMMATION:

IL: Allah began to prepare Muhammad for the constant criticism of the Quraysh. Muhammad was comforted by his wife. He was told to pray at night in rhythmic tones. Muhammad was promised that all those who opposed him will perish in great pain and sorrow.

WA: The promise of destruction for Muhammad's non-believing relatives comforts Muhammad. However, Muhammad was reluctant because he knew those who opposed him would reject him and his message. Muhammad was looking for people who were showing signs of reluctance, suspicion and hesitation. In this fashion, he could prove how Islam changed lives.

QUR'AN 67

"The Kingdom"

613 AD

SCRIPTURE:

Qur'an 67:1-2, 5-8

Bukhari:V4B54N461; Muslim:B1C74N304; Ishaq:117

PREFACE:

Allah decreed the Kingdom of Allah was about to be established. Allah's law was made to work in the spiritual realm to delineate good from evil. In the end, doom awaited the disbelievers.[14]

SURAH:

Qur'an 67:1-2: "Blessed is He in Whose hand is the Kingdom, and He is Possessor of power over all things, [He] who created death and life that He might try you — which of you is the best in deeds. And he is mighty, the Forgiving."

Qur'an 67:5-8: "And certainly We have adorned [beautified] this lower heaven with lamps and We make them means for conjecture for the devils, and We have prepared for them the chastisement of burning [Hell]. And for those who disbelieve in their Lord is the chastisement of hell, and evil is the resort. When they are cast therein, they will hear a loud moaning of it as it heaves, almost bursting for fury. Whenever a group is cast into it, its keepers ask them: Did not a warner come to you?"

THE REINITIATION

Ishaq:117: "Three years elapsed from the time Muhammad concealed his state until Allah commanded him to publish his religion according to information that has reached me. [Allah says:] 'Proclaim what you have been ordered and turn away from the polytheists. Warn your family and your nearest relations [relatives].' When these words came down to the Apostle he said, 'Allah has ordered me to warn my family and the task is beyond my strength. When I make my message known to them I will meet with great unpleasantness so I have kept silent. But Gabriel has told me that if I do not do as ordered my Lord will punish me.'"

Muslim:B1C74N304; Bukhari:V4B54N461: "While talking about the period of pause in revelation, the Prophet said, 'While I was walking, all of the sudden I heard a voice. I looked and saw the angel who had visited me at the cave sitting on a chair in the sky. I got scared of him and ran back home and said, "Wrap me in blankets, Khadijah." And then Allah revealed the Verses of the Qur'an to me. [Allah says:] "O Muhammad, the shrouded one, wrapped up in garments, arise and warn the people against the Lord's Punishment, and abandon the idols." After this the revelation started coming strongly, frequently, and regularly.'"

SUMMATION:

IL: The Prophet, with Allah's assurances, was commanded to boldly promote Islam to the unbelievers. Allah's messages to the non-believing Quraysh were harsh and to the point. Muhammad came to his people and they continued to reject him. They are all bound for hell.

WA: Allah revealed through Muhammad that unbelievers will be cast into hell; however, believers will be forced to choose between giving their lives up for Allah and accumulating good deeds in this life. Muhammad was still not comforted by Gabriel who promised that Muhammad would be punished by Allah if he did not promote the message. Muhammad did not like being rejected and scolded by his family, yet he was so terrified by the sight of the angel who threatened him that he willingly complied. Afterward, Muhammad saw the angel Gabriel sitting on a throne. At this point, the Quraysh rejection and the appearance of the angel both greatly troubled Muhammad enough that he ran to his wife for protection. Her comfort succeeded as the revelations began to gain momentum.

QUR'AN 109

"The Disbelievers"

613 AD

SCRIPTURE:

Qur'an 109:1-6

Tabari VI:83, 89; Ishaq:118, 120, 123, 126;

PREFACE:

This revelation was in response to the Meccans who tried to persuade Muhammad to compromise his religion. The Meccans were told they would pay for their misdeeds while Muhammad and the Muslims would reap the rewards. [15]

SURAH:

Qur'an 109:1-6: "Say: O disbelievers [Infidels], I serve not what you serve, nor do you serve Him Whom I serve, nor shall I serve that which ye serve, nor do you serve Him Whom I serve. For you is your recompense and for me my recompense."

SUNNAH:

THE FIRST REVERT

Tabari VI:83: "Ali was the first to accept Islam. He submitted at the age of nine. One of the favors Allah bestowed on Ali bin Talib was that the Messenger was his guardian before Islam. The Quraysh were afflicted by severe drought, Muhammad said to his uncle Al-Abbas, one of the richest of the Banu Hashim, 'Abbas, your brother Abu Talib has many dependents, and you see how people are suffering. I will take one of his sons and you take one.' Abu Talib said to them, 'As long as you leave me Aqil, do as you wish.' Muhammad took Ali [bin Talib] […] Ali accepted Islam [one] year after the Prophet began his mission and […] he remained in Mecca for twelve years. […] The first man to believe and follow the Prophet was Zayd bin Harithah [Khadijah's slave, adopted by Muhammad]. […] Zayd was the first male to accept Islam and to pray after Ali. Then Abu Bakr accepted Islam.

FAMILY CONFLICT

Tabari VI:89: "Three years after the beginning of his mission, Allah commanded His Prophet to proclaim the divine message […] publically to the people. In the previous three years […] he kept his preaching secret and hidden […] because the Muslims were few in number and practiced their faith in secret. […] Many responded to his summons and accepted Islam […]. They came to blows and Sa'd struck one of the polytheists with a camel's jawbone and split his head open […]. He [Muhammad] said, 'I am a Warner in the face of terrible doom.' Abu Lahab responded, '[…] may this religion perish in which I and all other people should be equal!' The Prophet said, 'Then I warn you that you are heading for torment.' […] Abu Lahab said to his sons, 'I forbid myself seeing and meeting you until you divorce the daughters of Muhammad.' […] Utalbah [one of Abu Lahab's sons] became so nasty that he came before the Prophet and said, 'I repudiate Islam.' Then he spat on him. […] The Prophet prayed, 'Allah, subject him to the power of a dog from among your dogs.'"

Ishaq:118: "Abu Lahab [Muhammad's uncle] said, 'Muhammad is trying to bewitch you. With that the Quraysh got up and left before the Messenger could speak. The following day they gathered again. This time the Apostle said, 'Kinsmen, I know of no Arab who has come to his people with a nobler message than mine. I have brought you the best of this world and the next. So which of you will cooperate with me in this matter, my brother, my executor, and my successor being among you?' The men remained silent. [Ali said,] 'I...will be your helper' Muhammad laid his hand on my back and said, 'He is my successor. Listen to him and obey him.' The Meccans got up laughing. They told Abu-Talib [Ali's father], 'He has ordered you to listen to and to obey your ten-year-old son.' [One day] When the Apostle's companions prayed they went to the glens [a narrow valley] so that their people could not see them. But one day they were rudely interrupted. The Muslims protested and then turned to blows. They smote [hit] a polytheist with the jawbone of a camel and wounded him. This was the first bloodshed in Islam. When the Prophet openly displayed Islam as God [Allah] ordered him, his people did not withdraw or turn against him […] until he spoke disparagingly of their gods. When he did that [talked trashed about their gods] they took great offense and resolved unanimously to treat him as an enemy […]"

Ishaq:120: "Every tribe [of the Quraysh] fell upon the Muslims [companions of Muhammad] seducing them from their religion."

Ishaq:123: "[Abu Talib recites,] 'By the Black Stone […] By Abraham's standing place […] By the running between Marwa and Safa […] By the station of Mina […] By the great stone heap […] For if we are men we will take revenge. And you will suffer the full effects of war.'"

Ishaq:126: "[Abu Talib said,] 'Tell Qusayy that our cause will be blazed abroad. Give Qusayy the good news that after us there will be a falling apart among our enemies.'"

SUMMATION:

IL: Islamic tolerance is displayed through Allah's revelation to the Prophet by stating to an unbelieving uncle and mob, "To you your religion and to me my religion." Although Muhammad's own uncle, Abu Lahab, opposed him by forcing his sons to divorce Muhammad's daughters, Muhammad's ten-year-old cousin Ali believed that he was the Prophet. Soon thereafter, others started to follow the straight path as determined by the Prophet.

WA: Muhammad's relatives were trying to persuade Muhammad to compromise since he appeared to be unyielding in his new belief. The Qur'anic revelation at first glance appeared to be moderate until one realized that Muhammad's kin were being addressed as "K-F-R" ["Kuffar," i.e., infidels]. It may have been the language in this surah that really upset them. Ishaq's account also appeared to bolster the position of the Shi'a community when Muhammad stated that the ten-year-old Ali would be his successor. This is the position that the Shi'a community believe in to this day. Abu-Talib, who was still an unbeliever, was reminded by the Quraysh that Muhammad placed Ali, Abu-Talib's son, in authority over Abu-Talib. A little while afterward, Muhammad's small band of followers were interrupted at prayer. These Muslims attacked a polytheist, wounding him with a camel's jawbone. The Meccans responded by treating the Muslims terribly, persecuting most all of them, except the Prophet who was protected by the Banu Hashim and the Bani Abd al-Muttalib. Abu-Talib then recited a poem swearing by things, places, and attitudes that are embraced by contemporary Islamic literalists. He invoked the name of Qusayy, who was responsible for moving the Quraysh into Mecca, when he stated that revenge, division, and war would now be the outcome.

We also gain more insight into Muhammad's character. After his uncle rejected Muhammad's religion and spat on him, Muhammad responded by praying that his uncle be subjected to dogs. In other words, his uncle was unclean.

QUR'AN 69

"The Sure Truth"

613 AD

SCRIPTURE:

Qur'an 69:5-6, 10, 30-32, 35-37, 40-46

Bukhari:V6B61N535

PREFACE:

This revelation answered the Meccans' accusations that Muhammad was a poet, a diviner, an imposter, and also mad. Allah then assured Muhammad that the evildoers will experience doom when the Muslims triumph at the end of time. This is the promise of Allah.[16]

SURAH:

Qur'an 69:5-6: "Then as for the Thamud, they were destroyed by the severe punishment. And as for [the] Ad, they were destroyed by a roaring, violent wind."

Qur'an 69:10: "And they disobeyed the messenger of their Lord, so He punished them with a vehement punishment.

Qur'an 69:30-32: "[It will be said at the judgment] Seize him, then fetter him, then cast him into the burning Fire, then insert him in a chain the length of which is seventy cubits."

Qur'an 69:35-37: "Therefore he has not here on this day [of Judgment] a true friend, nor any food except refuse [filth, pus, what is washed off of dirty bodies], which none but the wrongdoers eat."

Qur'an 69:40-46: "Surely, it is the word of an honored Messenger, and it is not the word of a poet. Little is it that you believe! Nor the word of a soothsayer. Little is that you mind! It is the revelation from the Lord of the worlds. And if he had fabricated against Us certain sayings, we would certainly have seized him by the right hand, then cut off his heart's vein."

SUNNAH:

Bukhari:V6B61N535: "Whenever the Prophet became ill he used to blow his breath over his body hoping for its blessing."

SUMMATION:

IL: In the face of being insulted by being called a liar, a poet, a sorcerer, a soothsayer, and possessed, Muhammad, through revelation, reminded the Quraysh of the destruction that occurred to the Thamud and Ad.

WA: Muhammad was being insulted by people who were related to him and knew him. Allah decreed through Muhammad that his unbelieving relatives will be lowered into hell after being impaled on a chain that is seventy cubits, or 150 feet long. They will be made to eat the pus off of their dirty bodies because they did not believe that the Muhammad they knew was a Prophet. Allah spoke through Muhammad, and said, if Muhammad made any of this up, Allah would personally sever the artery in his heart. If this was true, then Muhammad either had no choice but to follow the god that chose him or Muhammad was in perfect accord with his god.

QUR'AN 103

"The Time"

613 AD

SCRIPTURE:

Qur'an 103:1-3

Bukhari:V4B54N513

PREFACE:

Those who accept the truth of Islam will prosper if they exhort others to the Islamic truth. Those who love wealth and not Islam will surely lose their wealth.[17]

SURAH:

Qur'an 103:1-3: "By the time! — surely man is in loss, except those who believe and do good, and exhort one to [the] Truth [that is Islam], and exhort one another to patience [when faced with trials]."

SUNNAH:

Bukhari:V4B54N513: "Allah's Apostle said, 'A good dream is from Allah, and a bad dream is from Satan; so if anyone of you has a bad dream and is afraid, he should spit on his left side, for then it will not harm him.'"

SUMMATION:

IL: All those who have great wealth in this life will lose it if they do not accept the religion of truth. These same people will lose much more than their wealth on the Day of Judgment. As for the true believers, they must help support the Muslim Brothers when they are a minority living in a land of mostly non-believers.

WA: This surah is not precise concerning when unbelievers with wealth will lose their wealth. This implies that their loss of wealth is meant to be experienced in this life. If this is so, some Muslims could interpret this as approval from Allah to relieve non-Muslims of their possessions. Until that happens, Muslim's are obligated to support other Muslims in their struggle.

QUR'AN 104

"The Slanderer"

613 AD

SCRIPTURE:

Qur'an 104:1-3

Bukhari:V8B81N780

PREFACE:

At this point, the Meccans were trying to convince other Meccans not to follow Muhammad. The Meccans were viewed as those who amass wealth, reject truth, and slander others.[18]

SURAH:

Qur'an 104:1-3: "Woe to every slanderer, defamer! Who amasses wealth and counts it — he thinks that his wealth will make him abide [immortal]."

SUNNAH:

Bukhari:V8B81N780: "The Prophet said, 'The hand should be cut off for stealing something that is worth a quarter of a Dinar or more.'"

SUMMATION:

IL: Those that conspire against the truth of Muhammad's words do so because they are perceived by others as having great influence because of their wealth. The accusers of the Prophet did this, but not to the Prophet's face. They clearly said things that were not true. The Quraysh will be relieved of their wealth like a thief who will have his hand severed.

WA: The point was made early on in the Qur'an that those who opposed Muhammad had money. It also suggested that Muhammad had very little, if any, wealth. If his accusers were not wealthy, then something other than wealth would be blamed for making the Quraysh feel untouchable. Since these Meccans who opposed Muhammad were wealthy, they would surely lose what they valued most.

QUR'AN 79

"Those Who Yearn"

614 AD

SCRIPTURE:

Qur'an 79:1, 6-9, 17, 25-26, 29, 34-39

Bukhari:V6B60N378

PREFACE:

Those who brave all opposition in Mecca were instrumental in bringing about the transformation of the world. This will occur through a great revolution and they initiated this revolution.[19]

SURAH:

Qur'an 79:1, 6-9: "I swear by them [believers] who drag them [unbelievers] forth to destruction…the day when the quaking one shall quake — the consequences will follow it. Hearts that day will palpitate, their eyes downcast."

Qur'an 79:17, 25-26: "Go to Pharaoh, surely he has rebelled [...]. So Allah seized him with the punishment of the Hereafter [Hell] and of this life. Surely there is in this a lesson for him who fears."

Qur'an 79:29, 34-39: "And He made dark its night and brought out its light [...]. So when the great Calamity comes; the day when man remembers all that he strove for and hell is made manifest [for] him [to see]. Then as for him who is inordinate, and prefers the life of this world, hell is surely the abode."

SUNNAH:

Bukhari:V6B60N378: "Whoever tells you that Muhammad saw his Lord is a liar...After his appointment to Prophethood, and before he started preaching Islam, Muhammad began performing the prostration prayer facing Allah's House [the Ka'aba] the way Allah taught him. Watching the technique, the Quraysh assumed that he adopted a new religion...but Abu Jahl in his arrogance and pride threatened the Prophet and forbade him to worship in that way [towards] the Ka'aba."

SUMMATION:

IL: These Muslims, like the prophets of Allah who came before, must be tested. Those who survived were responsible for changing the world. The Muslims were then comforted by Allah who assured them that the Meccans would be defeated and eventually cast into hell. The Islamic revolution was born by Muhammad and his companions who resisted the Meccan persecution.

WA: In these revelations, Allah revealed, through Muhammad, that part of their mission was to initiate revolution. In this revolution, those who oppose Islam in this life and those who die in unbelief will be punished. Therefore, Muslims are assured that they rightly believe and this belief must bring fear into the hearts of the non-believers.

QUR'AN 80

"He Frowned"

614 AD

SCRIPTURE:

Qur'an 80:17-22, 34-37, 40-42

Bukhari:V4B54N430, V4B54N506

PREFACE:

This revelation occurred after Muhammad became annoyed when a blind man interrupted him while he was trying to convince other Meccans to believe in Islam. The revelation reminded Muhammad that the Qur'anic revelation will give rise to new Islamic followers and make possible future conquests. Muhammad was reminded that a man's importance should not be judged by his appearance.[20]

SURAH:

Qur'an 80:17-22: "Woe to man! How ungrateful is he! Of what thing did He create him? Of a small life germ. He creates him, then proportions him, then [He] makes the way easy for him, then He causes him to die, then assigns him a grave. Then, when He will, He raises him to life again."

Qur'an 80:34-37: "The day when a man flees from his brother, and his mother and his father, and his spouse and his sons [children]. Every one of them, that day, will have concern enough to make him indifferent to others.

Qur'an 80:40-42: "And faces on that day will have dust on them, darkness covering them. Those are the disbelievers, the wicked."

SUNNAH:

Bukhari:V4B54N430: "Allah's Apostle, the true and truly inspired said, 'Regarding the matter of the creation of a human being: humans are put together in the womb of the mother in forty days. Then he becomes a clot of thick blood for a similar period. He becomes a piece of flesh for forty days. Then Allah sends an angel who is ordered to write four things: the new creature's deeds, livelihood, date of death, and whether he will be blessed or wretched. He will do whatever is written for him'"

Bukhari:V4B54N506: "When a human being is born, Satan touches him at both sides of the body with his two fingers. That is why it cries."

SUMMATION:

IL: The importance of a person is determined by Allah's decree at conception. The righteous in Islam have been selected by Allah. Therefore, Muslims are chosen of Allah and must do what Allah commands.

WA: In the Muhammad gestation story, perhaps he was thinking that after 120 days in the womb an angel visits and starts to log vital statistics. Surely it was observable, in his day, that babies needed 270 days in the womb until they were born. Since most Westerners have not been chosen by Allah, then one can conclude that people in the west are wretched as determined by Allah. Therefore, Muslims who are familiar with this surah and the hadith will view us as their deity views us.

QUR'AN 81

"The Folding Up"

614 AD

SCRIPTURE:

Qur'an 81:10-14, 19-22, 25, 28-29

Bukhari:V1B3N68

PREFACE:

Allah stated that a time will come when the light will no longer shine. Ultimately, the truth of Islam will experience the eventual triumph.[21]

SURAH:

Qur'an 81:10-14: "And when the books are spread [pages are laid open], and when the heaven has its covering removed [is stripped off], and when hell is kindled [to intense heat], and when the Garden [of bliss] is brought nigh [near] — Every soul [person] will know what it has prepared [what is waiting for him]."

Qur'an 81:19-22: "Surely it is the word of a bountiful Messenger, the possessor of strength [power], established in the presence of the Lord of the Throne, One to be obeyed, and faithful. And your companion [Messenger] is not mad."

Qur'an 81:25: "[The Qur'an] is not the word of an accursed devil."

Qur'an 81:28-29: "For him among you who will [want to] go straight [...]

you will not [embrace Islam], except [if] Allah please [wills it], the Lord of the worlds."

SUNNAH:

Bukhari:V1B3N68: "The Prophet preached at a suitable time so that we might not get bored. He abstained from pestering us with sermons and knowledge."

SUMMATION:

IL: On the Day of Judgment heaven and hell will be brought near. The tally of one's good and bad deeds will determine their eternal destination. As for the unbelievers, they will know the Prophet should be followed because he is honorable. Calling Muhammad mad is fruitless. Allah and Muhammad must be obeyed. This is Allah's will.

WA: It was necessary to understand that Muhammad's relatives, the Meccan Quraysh, thought Muhammad was nuts and they, the polytheists, associated Muhammad's early revelation with Satan. To counter this, Allah stated that Muhammad was given power. From this point on, Allah and Muhammad in the Qur'an become "We" and "Us". Some even claim this plurality is Allah and Jibril. Nevertheless, they both must be obeyed. Allah then disclosed that those who succeed at the judgment will only succeed if Allah permits it. As for the Meccans, they were condemned for not listening to Muhammad and putting aside the revelation from the Qur'an. The Sunnah clearly displayed that the early Muslims were not crazy about Muhammad's preaching style. It bored them. Muhammad then realized that continuing his sermons could be considered "pestering". It also showed that the early Muslims were not seekers of knowledge.

QUR'AN 87

"The Most High"

614 AD

SCRIPTURE:

Qur'an 87:6-7, 12-13, 16-19

Bukhari:V6B61N550

PREFACE:

This surah promised that Muhammad would rise to the highest position. The previous scriptures mentioned Abraham and Moses rising to prophetical heights. In a similar way, the Qur'an also states that the previous scriptures predicted the advent of Muhammad. Allah promised abrogating verses that would ensure Muhammad's rise just as the Qur'an abrogates erroneous biblical scriptures.[22]

SURAH:

Qur'an 87:6-7: "We shall make thee recite so thou shalt not forget — except what Allah please [permits]. Surely he knows the manifest, and what is hidden."

Qur'an 87:12-13: "And the most unfortunate one will avoid it [the Reminder], [it is he] who will burn in the great Fire [...]. Therein he will neither live nor die."

Qur'an 87:16-19: "But, you prefer the life of this world, while the hereafter is better and more lasting. Surely this is in the earlier scriptures, the scriptures of Abraham and Moses."

SUNNAH:

Bukhari:V6B61N550: "The Prophet said, 'It is a bad thing that some of you say, "I have forgotten such-and-such a verse of the Qur'an." For truly, I have been caused by Allah to forget it. So you must keep on reciting the Qur'an because it escapes [from the hearts of men] faster than a runaway camel.'"

SUMMATION:

IL: Because the flood gates of new scripture have been opened, Muhammad was told, by way of revelation, to continue to recite and remember. Furthermore, anything he forgot was in accordance with Allah's will. Just as Muhammad was foretold in the scriptures, which are abrogated by the Qur'an, so abrogating verses will be introduced in the Qur'an to ensure the Prophet's success.

WA: The Islamic doctrine of abrogation was first introduced in this surah. Muhammad's detractors realized that he could not remember everything that he claimed was divinely inspired from Allah. After being scorned, Allah reassured Muhammad that his coming was foretold in the scriptures of Abraham and Moses. For clarification, scriptures attributable to Abraham do not exist, in other words, scriptures penned by Abraham—unless there was an assumption that Abraham's story was found in the books of Moses in the Genesis account. Also, the earthly Quraysh were promised plagues during their lifetime, and a great fire in the hereafter.

QUR'AN 88

"The Overwhelming Event"

614 AD

SCRIPTURE:

Qur'an 88:2-6, 23-26,

Bukhari:V4B55N544

PREFACE:

Doom is assured for those who oppose the Prophet. This doom is promised for evildoers in this life and the next.[23]

SURAH:

Qur'an 88:2-6: "Faces on that day [of Judgment] will be downcast, laboring, toiling, entering burning Fire, [and] made to drink from a boiling spring. They will have no food but [only] of thorns [to eat].

Qur'an 88:23-26: "Whoever turns back and disbelieves, Allah will chastise [punish] him with a greatest chastisement [punishment]. Surely to Us is their return. Then it is for Us to call them to account."

SUNNAH:

Bukhari:V4B55N544: "Allah's Apostle said, 'The first group who will enter paradise will be glittering like the moon and those who will follow will glitter like the most brilliant star. They will not urinate, relieve nature, spit, or have any nasal secretions. Their combs will be gold and their sweat will smell like musk. Their companions will be houris [maiden virgins]. All of them will look alike and will be sixty cubits [180 feet] tall."

SUMMATION:

IL: The true believer is given every reason to believe. Denying Islam will result in torment. Those who are accounted worthy will be relieved of life's unpleasantness and embrace amazons [cooperative women 180 feet tall].

WA: For denying Allah and Muhammad, the unbeliever will face a burning fire, will drink boiling water, and will eat thorns for eternity. One must assume that Muhammad did not care much for going to the bathroom, spitting, and blowing his nose. The text does indicate that he did like gold, the smell of musk, and must have dreamt of being with some very huge women.

QUR'AN 89

"The Daybreak"

614 AD

SCRIPTURE:

Qur'an 89:5-13, 17-26

Bukhari:V8B77N616

PREFACE:

This surah was revealed as the *Hajj* ("pilgrimage") brought trade and many Arabs into Mecca. However, this revelation also warned that Mecca would be overthrown just as Ad and Thamud were overthrown.[24]

SURAH:

Qur'an 89:5-13: "Truly in this is an oath for men of understanding. Hast thou not considered how thy Lord dealt with Ad, of Iram, having lofty buildings, the like of which were not created in the land, and with Thamud, who hewed out rocks in the valley; and Pharaoh, the Lord of hosts, who exceeded the limits in the cities, and made great mischief [transgression] therein? So the Lord poured on them a portion of chastisement punishment]."

Qur'an 89:17-26: "Nay, but you honor not the orphan [Muhammad], nor do you urge one another to feed the poor, and you devour heritage, devouring all, and you love wealth with exceeding love, Nay, when the earth is made to crumble to pieces and thy Lord comes with the angels, ranks on ranks; and is made to appear that day. On that day men will be mindful [of his deeds], and of what use will being mindful [of your deeds] be then? He will say: O would that I had sent before for this my life! But none can punish as He will punish on that day. And none can bind as He will bind on that day."

SUNNAH:

Bukhari:V8B77N616: "Allah's Apostle said, 'Plague is a means of torture which Allah sends upon whom-so-ever He wishes.'"

SUMMATION:

IL: Lessons from the past stand as a warning to those who have the upper hand over Muslim. Those who have the upper hand over Muslims transgress. Therefore, Muslims are assured by Allah that He will punish these transgressors. None of those who oppose Islam will escape Allah's punishment.

WA: No matter how dire the plight of Muslims in various parts of the world, the Qur'an assures them that the non-Muslims will be punished. This of course begs the question: What do Muslims do that is worthy of punishment? When this surah was revealed, Muhammad identified himself as the orphan who was not protected by his Quraysh relatives. Allah, speaking through Muhammad, was bitter towards the Quraysh. The surah implied the Quraysh were beyond redemption, so Muhammad continually reminded them of how Allah would make them suffer.

QUR'AN 90

"The City"

614 AD

SCRIPTURE:

Qur'an 90:1-2, 4, 13-16, 19

Muslim:B28C2N5612

PREFACE:

The city spoken of in this is Mecca. A city that persecuted the first Muslims would become the spiritual center for all Muslims.[25]

SURAH:

Qur'an 90:1-2: "Nay, I call to witness this City! And thou wil[l] be made free from obligation in this city."

Qur'an 90:4: "We have certainly created man to face difficulties."

Qur'an 90:13-16: "It is to free a slave, or to feed in a day of hunger an orphan nearly related [to you], or the poor man lying in the dust."

Qur'an 90:19: "And those who disbelieve in Our messages, they are the people of the left hand."

SUNNAH:

Muslim:B28C2N5612: "Allah's Apostle said, 'He who played chess is like one who dyed his hand with the flesh and blood of swine.'"

SUMMATION:

IL: The city that first persecuted the Prophet would become the center of the Islamic world. Muslims are told they will have difficulty, but when Islam triumphs it will be liberating. The Prophet then condemned games that did not originate in the Islamic world.

WA: The great sin that Allah alluded to was that Muhammad's relatives should have cared for and fed Muhammad as a child. Rather, the Prophet was left to languish without a father. Finally, Muhammad condemned chess players. This meant those individuals who play chess are defiled. Since the game was not created in Islam it has no value. One can only imagine what the Prophet's opinion would have been in regard to other family-oriented games that originated in the West.

QUR'AN 91

"The Sun"

614 AD

SCRIPTURE:

Qur'an 91:11-15

Bukhari:V6B61N536

PREFACE:

In this surah, the Prophet was called "The Sun of Righteousness," meaning that, through him, the way to perfection is displayed to mankind.[26]

SURAH:

Qur'an 91:11-15: "[The tribe of] Thamud rejected the truth in their inordinacy, when the basest of them broke forth with mischief — so Allah's Messenger said to them: leave alone Allah's she-camel, and give her [something] to drink. But they called him a liar and slaughtered her. So their Lord destroyed them for their sin and [leveled] them with the ground. And He [Allah] fears not its consequence."

SUNNAH:

Bukhari:V6B61N536: "When the Prophet went to bed he would cup his hands together and blow over them reciting surahs. He would then rub his hands over whatever parts of his body he could reach, starting with his head, face and frontal areas."

SUMMATION:

IL: Allah revealed this surah as a warning to the Quraysh who would not heed the warnings given by the Prophet. The Prophet's private practices are to be repeated by devout Muslims. Acting like the Prophet, while reciting surahs, will bring blessings to Muslims.

WA: In this surah another Arab non-biblical Prophet came to the Thamud to warn them of their wrong doing. We are told that Allah destroyed them because they killed a she-camel. In the 21st century this makes little sense. We can only surmise that she-camels had great worth in 7th century Arabia. If one killed a she-camel it had consequences for the community. The point was made. The Quraysh would be destroyed for the same reasons the Thamud were destroyed.

QUR'AN 92

"The Night"

614 AD

SCRIPTURE:

Qur'an 92:8-11, 14-21

Bukhari:V8B76N542

PREFACE:

The night of disbelief will give way to the light of day. Those who strive after good will find the light and those who go after evil will find the night.[27]

SURAH:

Qur'an 92:8-11: "And as for him who is niggardly [greedy], and considers himself self-sufficient, and rejects what is good. We will facilitate for him the way to distress [misery]. And his wealth will not avail him when he perishes."

Qur'an 92:14-21: "So I warn you of the Fire that flames. None will enter it but the most unfortunate, who rejects the truth and turns his back. And away from it shall be kept the most faithful to duty, who gives his wealth, purifying himself, and none has with him any boon for a reward, except the seeking of the pleasure of his Lord, the Most High. And he will soon be well-pleased."

SUNNAH:

Bukhari:V8B76N542: "Allah's Apostle said, 'The believers, after being saved from the Fire, will be stopped at a bridge between Paradise and Hell and mutual retaliation will be established among them regarding wrongs they have committed in the world against one another. After they are cleansed and purified through the retaliation, they will be admitted into paradise.'"

SUMMATION:

IL: Those who strive after good give what they have. Those who submit to the truth and give from their wealth purify themselves before Allah. Disbelief can be determined by observing those who do not give. These disbelievers will burn in hell.

WA: In 614 AD, Muhammad and his god were still taking aim at his well-to-do Quraysh relatives. Allah insinuated that they could be made pure if they gave to the Islamic cause in Allah's name. If they did not, hellfire would result. The hadith goes on to speak of Muslim believers. After death, these believers still must be stopped at a bridge between Paradise and Hell to engage in mutual retaliation against one another. According to Islam, they must retaliate against one another before they reach paradise because they can only be purified through retaliation. Therefore, believing Muslims must know if they escape Hell they must still endure abuse from other Muslim believers before they can be accounted acceptable to Allah and be admitted into Paradise.

QUR'AN 95

"The Fig"

614 AD

SCRIPTURE:

Qur'an 95:4-7

Bukhari:V7B62N52

PREFACE:

In this surah a comparison is drawn between the Mosaic dispensation and the Islamic dispensation. If a person is not guided and does not act upon right principles, he will be degraded to the lowest position of creation.[28]

SURAH:

Qur'an 95:4-7: "Certainly We created man in the best make. Then We render him [down, reducing him to] the lowest of the low, except those who believe and do good; so theirs is a reward never to be cut off. So who can give the lie [deny] to thee after this about the Judgment [of Allah]? Is not Allah the Best of the Judges."

SUNNAH:

Bukhari:V7B62N52: "[...] Allah's Apostle said, 'If a man and a woman agree to marry temporarily, their marriage should last for three nights, and if they like to continue, they can do so; and if they want to separate, they can do so.'"

SUMMATION:

IL: Islamic law is an improvement over Mosaic Law because it takes into account the errors of the previous dispensation. Both sets of guidelines will be considered at the Judgment. An example of the improvement brought by Islam is the marriage amendment. This amendment prevents one from fornicating and committing adultery.

WA: The premise introduced in this surah implies that Allah contributes towards inequality. Allah promises unending reward but that reward must be in the next life since many Muslims suffer terribly at the hands of other Muslims in this life. The marriage amendment that is practiced, especially by the Shi'a, cannot be regarded as a type of improvement over Mosaic Law and in the contents of the New Covenant. This law does not appeal to just single men, but also married men. It gives no consideration to wives when their Muslim husbands choose to practice temporary marriage. Their feelings are not considered in this law. This law gives no consideration for the bond of love between a husband and wife. However, it has everything to do with legalizing, and making acceptable the lustful instincts of human beings.

QUR'AN 97

"The Majesty"

614 AD

SCRIPTURE:

Qur'an 97:2-5

Bukhari:V6B60N475

PREFACE:

This relates to the last ten nights of Ramadan when the original revelation occurred at Mt. Hira during the night of majesty. The word majesty referred to the revelation and the Prophet who received it.[29]

SURAH:

Qur'an 97:2-5: "And what will make thee comprehend what the Night of Majesty is? The Night of Majesty is better than a thousand months. The angels and the Spirit descend in it by the permission of their Lord — for every affair — peace! It is till the rising of the morning."

SUNNAH:

Bukhari:V6B60N475: "Allah's Apostle became sick and could not offer his prayer. A lady came and said, 'Muhammad! I think that your Satan has forsaken you, for I have not seen him with you for two or three nights!'"

SUMMATION:

IL: Allah revealed the Night of Majesty, the initial revelation that came to Muhammad, commemorated the last ten nights of Ramadan. This is true because Allah permitted the spirit (Jibril/Gabriel) to be accompanied by angels and transmit the heavenly Qur'an to Muhammad. Thus, there is nothing that can occur over 1000 months, or over 80 years that can compare to the Night of Majesty.

WA: The Night of Majesty referred to permission given by the Islamic deity who conveyed the Qur'anic revelation through *Jibril* ("Gabriel") all the while aided by other angels. One must ask this question: Did Muhammad believe the night of revelation was majestic? According to Tabari VI:67, Muhammad was troubled by the encounter and contemplated suicide. At the time, it was suggested that a devil was doing this to him. This notion gained traction when a woman, mentioned in the hadith, commented on Muhammad's illness and stated she did not see his devil for three days. In consideration of this, why was this night better than 1000 months? Also, this surah stated, 'when the "spirit and angels come" there will be peace until the dawn of the next day.' This did not occur in Muhammad's experience on the Night of Majesty.

"The Quraish"

614 AD

SCRIPTURE:

Qur'an 106:1-4

Muslim:B4C23N863

PREFACE:

This revelation asserted the importance of guarding the Ka'aba. Thus, the importance of the Ka'aba in Islam was established.[30]

SURAH:

Qur'an 106:1-4: "For the protection of the [Quraysh] — their protection of their journey [caravans] in the winter and the summer. So let them serve the Lord of this House [Ka'aba], who feeds them against hunger and gives them security against fear."

SUNNAH:

Muslim:B4C23N863: "People should avoid lifting their eyes towards the sky while supplicating in prayer, otherwise their eyes would be snatched away."

SUMMATION:

IL: For the past 1400 years, Muslims have been praying in the direction of the Ka'aba at Mecca. This was commanded by Allah and revealed in his Qur'an. It is important because Allah promised the Quraysh that they would be safe, along with their possessions, as long as they honored the god of the Ka'aba...Allah. This can only be done by putting ones head to the ground in total submission to Allah. One risks losing their eyes if they would look towards the heavens.

WA: In 614 AD, the Ka'aba was a center of polytheistic worship. Allah was still part of the Meccan Pantheon, but in this revelation, Allah, Jibril, and Muhammad claimed the Ka'aba was a monotheistic shrine. The revelation conveyed the lives of the Quraysh and their possessions would not be safe until the Quraysh recognized the Ka'aba as belonging to Allah. So this revelation made the point that polytheists wrongly took possession of the Ka'aba from Allah. Therefore, Muhammad was sent to retake the Ka'aba. We have no proof the Ka'aba was ever a monotheistic shrine before Muhammad's time. Furthermore, the hadith, as stated, is not true. I'm not aware of anyone losing their eyesight by not supplicating in prayer. It is clear that Allah wants one's head in the ground in total submission when he is being addressed.

"The Assaulters"

614 AD

SCRIPTURE:

Qur'an 100:1-4

Bukhari:V4B52N104, V4B52N112

PREFACE:

The great disasters spoken of in the last revelation will occur through warfare. When Islamic warfare is decreed a spiritual awakening will follow. (31)

SURAH:

Qur'an 100:1-4: "By those running and uttering cries [panting horses]! And those producing fire, striking! And those suddenly attacking [raiding] at morn[ing]! Then thereby they raise [clouds of] dust, then penetrate thereby gatherings [deep into the midst of a foe] — surely man is ungrateful to his Lord."

SUNNAH:

Bukhari:V4B52N104: "The Prophet said, 'Good will remain in the foreheads of horses for Jihad for they bring about reward in Paradise or booty.'"

Bukhari:V4B52N112: "Allah's Apostle said, 'Horses are kept for one of three purposes. For some they are a source of reward, for others a means of shelter, and for some a source of sins. The one of whom they are a source of reward, is he who keeps a horse for Allah's cause [Jihad]."

SUMMATION:

IL: Because of the great resistance to the Prophet's message, Allah predicted the disagreement between the Muslims and the Quraysh would be settled on the battlefield.

WA: Not only are those who would not accept Muhammad promised hell in the next life, they were also threatened with repeated cavalry charges. The idea of lesser Jihad, paradise for jihadists, and confiscated booty were already being considered.[32]

QUR'AN 83

"Default in Duty"

614 AD

SCRIPTURE:

Qur'an 83:10-16, 29-36

Bukhari:V9B86N98

PREFACE:

This revelation condemns those who cheat others. Those who do so are guilty. They will suffer and perish, but the righteous will prosper.[33]

SURAH:

Qur'an 83:10-16: "Woe on that day to the rejectors! Who give the lie to the day of Judgment. And none gives the lie to it but every exceeder of limits, every evil one; when Our messages are recited to him, he says: Stories of those of yore! Nay, rather, what they earned is rust upon their hearts. Nay, surely on they are that day debarred from [thrust from the presence of] their Lord. Then they will surely enter the burning Fire."

Qur'an 83:29-36: "Surely they who are guilty used to laugh at those who believe. And when they passed by them, they winked at one another, and when they returned to their people, they returned exulting. And when they saw them they said, 'Surely these [people] are in error — and they were not sent as keepers over them. So this day those who believe laugh at the disbelievers — on raised couches, gazing [downward]. Surely the disbelievers are rewarded as they did.

SUNNAH:

Bukhari:V9B86N98: "The Prophet said, 'A virgin should not be married until she is asked for her consent.' It was asked, 'O Apostle! How will the virgin express her consent?' He said, 'By remaining silent.'"

SUMMATION:

IL: Originally, these verses were meant for the non-believing Quraysh. Using the term "their Lord" also related to the Quraysh who already had Allah but refused to recognize Allah as the only god. Those who deny, reject, and repudiate Allah's message will also enter the burning fire. Those who scoff at Islam will not laugh in the Day of Judgment.

WA: This surah was a response to constant ridicule that was confronting Muhammad's message. Since the Quraysh were unlikely to hear or read these words, the revelation that escaped from Muhammad's lips was solely for Muhammad to assure him that his tormentors would be damned. Although the Hadith cited here was probably from a later period and involved the young Aisha, it espoused the importance of non-verbal cues. In one set, like-mindedness and ridicule were affirmed by the Quraysh. In the other example Muhammad interpreted female silence as permission. In the West, one would think that the woman would say 'Yes.' In Islam, this was not true, in Muhammad's eyes, because it was expected that women remain silent. This silence was interpreted as an affirmation. If a woman would open her mouth in disagreement then she could experience the distain of her father, brothers, clan, and tribe.

QUR'AN 84

"The Bursting Asunder"

614 AD

SCRIPTURE:

Qur'an 84:20-24

Bukhari:V8B76N545

PREFACE:

Once Islam is established, it will burst asunder upon the world just like a cloud gives way to a heavy downpour.[34]

SURAH:

Qur'an 84:20-24: "But what is the matter with them that believe not? And, when the Qur'an is recited to them, they adore Him not [they do not bow in adoration]? Nay, those who disbelieve give the lie [reject the message and the Prophet] — And Allah knows best what they hide. So announce to them a painful chastisement [a tormenting punishment]."

SUNNAH:

Bukhari:V8B76N545: "Allah's Apostle said, 'All who are called to account on the Day of Doom will be ruined.' Aisha said, 'O Allah's Apostle! Hasn't Allah said, "For him who will be given his record in his right hand, he surely will receive an easy reckoning"?' [Qur'an 84:7]. The Apostle said, 'That verse means only the presentation of accounts, but anybody whose account is questioned will be punished.'"

SUMMATION:

IL: Allah knows that those who deny Islam lie because they know that Islam is the truth. Since they already are aware they are liars, Islam will burst upon the earth to bring the disbelievers tidings of doom.

WA: There is an important lesson to be learned here. Muslims are taught not to question and not to doubt the word of Allah and his Messenger. By keeping silent they affirm their belief. When Allah calls people to account, they are already doomed. In the same way, Muslims do not like having their beliefs challenged or brought to account. This was true in 614 A.D and remained true a few years later when Aisha, daughter of Abu Bakr, entered Muhammad's life.

"The Stars"

614 AD

SCRIPTURE:

Qur'an 85:10-11, 19-22

Bukhari:V7B67N427

PREFACE:

The zodiac plays a part in foretelling the defeat of the Christians in Arabia at the hands of the Jewish King Dhu Nawas. This led to Abyssinian intervention in Yemen until they were defeated during the War of the Elephant in 570 AD, which was the year of Muhammad's birth. This means that the Arabs will prosper as long as they accept Muhammad's message, but they will suffer the same fate as the Arab Christians experienced at the hands of the Jews, if they reject his message. In order to assure Arab victory, Allah promised to introduce abrogating verses to give the Arabs divine favor and assure their victory.[35]

SURAH:

Qur'an 85:10-11: "Those who persecute believing men and believing women, then repent not, theirs is the chastisement of hell, and theirs is the chastisement of burning. Those who believe and do good, theirs [is the] Gardens, wherein flow rivers [the fulfillment of all of their desires]. That is the great achievement."

Qur'an 85:19-22: "Nay, those who disbelieve give the lie — and Allah encompasses [surrounds] them on all sides. Nay, it is a glorious Qur'an, in a preserved tablet."

SUNNAH:

Bukhari:V7B67N427: "The Prophet said, 'If I take an oath and later find something else better than that, then I do what is better and expiate my oath.'"

SUMMATION:

IL: The unbelieving polytheistic Arabs were presented with an example from their recent history. They were assured of defeat unless they accepted Muhammad's message. Those who refused were considered liars. These deniers were to be surrounded by Muslims who acted according to Allah's guidance. Victory was assured for the Muslims since Allah preserved the Qur'an…a Muslim's inspiration.

WA: The 'believe or else' scenario is repeated over and over. This surah, however, raised some questions when compared to a hadith by Sahih Bukhari. Like the previous surah, those who do not believe in the Qur'anic revelation are liars, yet Muhammad said that he could enter an agreement via a sworn oath and not honor the agreement if circumstances changed while the agreement was in effect. In the West, when one expiates an oath, treaty, or any agreement, they are considered untrustworthy. This surah also states the Qur'an is a preserved tablet. Since Muslims already believe the Torah and Gospel came from Allah in their uncorrupted form, but became corrupted, how can it be explained that Allah could not prevent the Torah and Gospel from becoming corrupted, yet promises the Qur'an is a preserved tablet?

QUR'AN 86

"The Comer By Night"

614 AD

SCRIPTURE:

Qur'an 86:5-7, 13-14, 15-16

Dawud:B14N2631

PREFACE:

In this story, the morning star became Muhammad. Allah, through Muhammad, will fertilize the world as a sperm fertilizes an egg. Muhammad is the light that came into a dark world and knocked on the door. For 600 years the earth was in darkness and Muhammad was responsible for its spiritual resurrection. In doing so, the enemies of Islam wanted to destroy it. As the enemies of Islam plotted against the Prophet, so Allah schemed against them to defeat them.[36]

SURAH:

Qur'an 86:5-7: "So let man consider from what he was created. He is created of water pouring forth [gushing], coming from between the back[bone] and the ribs."

Qur'an 86:13-14: "Surely it [Qur'an] is a decisive [conclusive] word; and it is not a joke [it is not for amusement or for pleasantry]."

Qur'an 86:15-16: "Surely they plan a plan [they are scheming], and I [Allah] plan a plan [scheme]. So grant the disbelievers a respite — let them [leave them] alone for while."

SUNNAH:

Dawud:B14N2631: "When the Prophet intended to go on an expedition, he always pretended to be going somewhere else, and he would say: 'War is deception.'"

SUMMATION:

IL: Allah continued to reveal verses to aid Muhammad as the Quraysh continued to oppose his message. The seriousness of the consequences for not following the Prophet would soon become apparent. Victory was assured. Allah will scheme and plot against those who reject Islam. Doubters have declared war on Islam by not giving heed to the Prophet's teaching; therefore, the use of deception is permissible.

WA: The creation account is perplexing unless the gushing water represents the seed that comes out of a man. However, if that is true, wouldn't Allah know that it does not come from between the backbone and the ribs? Furthermore, why would Allah need to plot and scheme against a few Arab polytheists at Mecca? Nevertheless, Muslims believe their god plots and schemes against the unbelievers. Also, the hadith verified that Muhammad permitted the use of deception against the perceived enemies of Islam.

QUR'AN 75

"The Resurrection"

614 AD

SCRIPTURE:

Qur'an 75:1-17

Bukhari:V4B52N233

PREFACE:

Islam has become a spiritual resurrection brought by Muhammad which will be confirmed by the physical resurrection at the end of time. The animal nature that can appear in man must be accused by the human nature of man—this allows the spiritual awakening to occur.[37]

SURAH:

Qur'an 75:1-17: "Nay, I swear by the day of Resurrection! Nay, I swear by the self-accusing spirit! Does man think that We shall not gather his bones? Yea, We are Powerful to make complete his whole make [resurrect him]. Nay, man desires to go on doing evil in front of him. He asks: when is the day of Resurrection? So when the sight is confused, and the moon becomes dark, and the sun and the moon are brought together — man will say on that day: Whither to flee? No! There is no refuge! With thy Lord on that day is the place of rest. Man will that day be informed of what he sent before and what he put off. Nay, man is evidence against himself, though he put[s] up excuses. Move not thy tongue therewith to make haste with it [do not speak hastily concerning the Qur'an]. Surely on Us rests the collecting of it and the reciting of it."

SUNNAH:

Bukhari:V4B52N233: "Allah's Apostle forbade the people to travel to a hostile country carrying copies of the Qur'an. [He said:] 'Unbelievers will never understand our signs and revelations.'"

SUMMATION:

IL: Muhammad, the most favored of Allah, will be permitted to signal the final resurrection at the end of time. Allah gave unto Muhammad the ability to recite and rightly interpret the Qur'an. It is for this reason the Qur'an should not be given to infidels without the proper Islamic interpretation that came from Allah through Muhammad.

WA: In Islam, the animal nature (bad) must be accused by the human nature (good). This assumed that human nature is made subordinate to Islamic teaching. Once this happens, according to Islam, the spiritual awakening can occur. This theory insinuates that Muslims who submit in Islam will not act according to the animal nature. One must then question if Muslims really believe this and if they have ever acted in a barbaric or animalistic way towards other Muslims and non-Muslims. This surah states those who do not submit will be judged as guilty. Although they will know their guilt, they will make excuses. According to this logic, non-Muslims must not read the Qur'an without Muslims telling them what to think and what to believe. This flies in the face of what Westerners think. Western thought would suggest that all books should be made available to all people and those who read should be able to make their own judgments concerning what they choose to believe and what they choose to reject. From the Christian perspective, all people are encouraged to read the Bible. Interestingly, the Muslim clergy discourages or forbids Muslims from reading the Bible. In Saudi Arabia, it is a capital offense. The prohibition, as stated in the hadith, infers that Muhammad knew there were passages in the Qur'an that are distasteful to unbelievers. When read without Islamic instruction, this could prevent a non-believer from coming to Islam.

QUR'AN 70

"The Ways Of Ascent"

614 AD

SCRIPTURE:

Qur'an 70:1-2, 6, 11-17, 19-21, 29-31, 36, 40-44

Bukhari:V4B54N459

PREFACE:

Although punishment is a certainty, the faithful are promised nearness to Allah. Simultaneously, the opponents of Islam shall not only be disgraced but shall also be replaced by the Muslims.[38]

SURAH:

Qur'an 70:1-2, 6, 11-17: "A questioner asks about the chastisement to befall the disbelievers [infidels] — there is none to avert it [...]. Surely they see it far off [...]. The guilty one would fain redeem himself [will want to be able to ransom himself] from the chastisement [punishment] of that day by [offering] his children, and his wife and his brother, and his kin that gave him shelter, and all that are in the earth [to be sacrificed in his stead] — then deliver him — by no means! Surely it is the flaming Fire [for him], plucking out his extremities [dismembering the body] — it [Hell] shall claim [drag] him who retreats and falls back [him who tries to flee]."

Qur'an 70:19-21: "Surely man is created impatient — fretful [irritable and perturbed] when evil afflicts him, and niggardly when good befalls him."

Qur'an 70:29-30: "And those who restrain their sexual passions, *except* [emphasis added] in the presence of their mates or those whom your right hands possess [slave girls] — for such surely are not to be blamed."

Qur'an 70:36, 40-44: "But what is the matter with those who disbelieve, that they hasten on to thee [who rush to listen to you] [...]. I swear by the Lord of the Eastern lands and the Western lands! [...] We are certainly powerful to bring in their place others better than them, and We shall not be overcome. So leave them alone to plunge in vain talk and to sport, until they come face to face with that day of theirs [Day of Judgment] which they are promised — the day when they come forth [rise] from the graves in [great] haste, as hastening onto a goal, their eyes downcast [lowered in dejection], disgrace covering them. Such is the day which they are promised."

SUNNAH:

Bukhari:V4B54N459: "Allah's Apostle said, 'If a husband calls his wife to his bed [to have sex] and she refuses and causes him to sleep in anger, the angels will curse her till morning.'"

SUMMATION:

IL: Those who reject the Islamic revelation will gladly offer their children, wife, and other family members in order to escape the doom of the flaming fire. This is true because the damned will know their body will be dismembered and their skin roasted. People were created in a fallen state and the only medicine for this sickness is Islam. Muslims are exhorted to restrain their passions. This does not apply to their relationship with their wives, women who were sold to Muslims as slaves, or women captured by Muslims in any future conflict. These women become the possession of a Muslim male just like his wife. As for the infidels, their doom is assured.

WA: Allah and Muhammad really had a low opinion of the Quraysh who were Muhammad's relatives. This surah stated—and to Muslims it cannot be in error—that these cowards would rather damn their own family members and wives to redeem themselves from the wrath to come. This would mean that all were devoid of love. An Islamic literalist would read this to apply to all non-Muslims. Not only will they roast in hell, but they will be conquered and their religion will be replaced with Islam.[39] The creation account does not speak of a fall from grace, but rather how people were created by Allah with an impatient and greedy nature. They easily become irritable, perturbed, and niggardly in their actions. So for Muslims, the best they can hope for is to be a slave of Allah; otherwise, they will be reduced to becoming fuel for Allah's hell. The lack of love in the Islamic marriage bond is, again, on display. Men who are married can have sex with non-Muslim slave girls. The wife does not have an opinion or feelings in this regard. Furthermore, if a Muslim wife refuses her husband's advances, Muhammad assured these believing women that the angels of heaven, who are supposed to be holy, will curse Muslim women for the simple reason that they were not in the mood. Passages like these shout at Muslim women that they really do not matter and they have no say when it comes to their own bodies.[40]

QUR'AN 77

"Those Sent Forth"

614 AD

SCRIPTURE:

Qur'an 77:25-33

Muslim:C31B20N4645

PREFACE:

Those who accept Islam, meaning those who strive to attain Allah's perfection, learn that those who reject the Islamic message will bring evil consequences on themselves.[41]

SURAH:

Qur'an 77:25-33: "Have We not made the earth draw to itself the living and the dead and made therein lofty mountains, and given you drink of sweet water? Walk on to that which you call a lie. Walk on to the shadow, having three branches, neither cool, nor availing against the flame. It sends up sparks like palaces, as if they were tawny camels."

SUNNAH:

Muslim:B20C31N4645: "[...] the Messenger of Allah said: 'Abu Sa'd, whoever cheerfully accepts Allah as his Lord, Islam as his religion, and Muhammad as his Apostle is necessarily entitled to enter Paradise.' He [Abu Sa'd] wondered at it and said: 'Messenger of Allah, repeat that for me.' He [Muhammad] did that [repeated it] and [also] said: 'There is another act which elevates the position of man in Paradise to a grade one hundred (higher), and the elevation between one grade and the other is equal to the height of the heaven from the earth.' He [Abu Sa'd] said: 'What is that act?' He [Muhammad] replied: 'Jihad in the way of Allah! Jihad in the way of Allah!'"

SUMMATION:

IL: The Quraysh and then all non-believers will feel the torment of hell-fire. A hadith by Sahih Muslim states how a person can gain paradise. One must accept Allah as the only true God, Islam as the only true religion, and Muhammad as the Prophet. If anyone is to be exalted in Islam, they must participate in Jihad. The ultimate goal of Jihad is the *Dawah* ("the call"), to spread the faith. This can be done through persuasion or by ending the resistance of Islam's enemies.[42]

WA: According to Allah, if one cannot be persuaded by Muhammad, then one should be threatened into conformity by Allah's endless promises of a holocaust. The minimum requirements for Islamic salvation are belief in Allah, acceptance of Islam, and Muhammad. The additional caveat is that Muslims are encouraged to participate in Jihad, which elevates the participant to a higher position in paradise. In 614 AD, there was no call for violent Jihad, but that would change. The steps required to attain paradise depart at this point from what Jesus said in the Gospel. During the crucifixion (Muslims reject the notion that Jesus was crucified) one of the thieves crucified with Jesus said, 'We are receiving what we deserve for our deeds but this man (Jesus) has done nothing wrong.' He then said to Jesus, 'Lord, remember me when you come into your kingdom.' Jesus said to him, 'Truly I say to you, today you will be with me in paradise.' In this instance, an evil doer acknowledged that Jesus did nothing wrong and was the Lord. The result was the promise of paradise. Muslims will not agree that believing in Jesus as Lord will merit paradise. Both Allah and Muhammad are right, or the Jesus found in the Christian Gospel is right. If Allah and Muhammad are wrong, then Allah cannot be God and Muhammad cannot be the Prophet. If Jesus acknowledged that he was the Lord, then he cannot be an Islamic Prophet. If Jesus was wrong, then he cannot be the Son of God.

QUR'AN 78

"The Announcement"

614 AD

SCRIPTURE:

Qur'an 78:21-33

Bukhari:V8B74N290

PREFACE:

Allah will give life to the earth through Muhammad. The truth of Islam will bring about the doom of the infidels. Islam's truth must bring about martyrs who are willing to shed their blood to fulfill the Qur'anic promise. Those who oppose Islam will meet their doom.[43]

SURAH:

Qur'an 78:21-30: "Surely hell lies in wait, a resort for the inordinate, living therein for long years. They taste not therein coolness or drink, but boiling and intensely cold water, requital corresponding. Surely they feared not the [day of] reckoning, and rejected Our messages [as lies]. And We have recorded everything in a book. So taste, for we shall add to you naught [nothing] but chastisement [punishment]."

Qur'an 78:31-33: "Surely for those who keep their duty [the righteous] is achievement [triumph], Gardens and vineyards, and youthful companions [with big bosoms], equal in age, and a pure cup."

SUNNAH:

Bukhari:V8B74N290: "Allah's Apostle said: 'Shall I inform you of the biggest of the great sins?' They said, 'Yes, O Allah's Apostle!' He said, 'To join partners in worship with Allah, and to be undutiful to one's parents.'"

SUMMATION:

IL: Rejecting Muhammad and his message will result in hell for the deniers. Allah assures those who are doomed of their pending peril. For true believing Muslims, their reward will be a beautiful garden, vineyards, and big-busted virgins. As for the Quraysh polytheists or any Christian who does not repent of the belief that Jesus is the Son of God, they will definitely go to hell.[44]

WA: For the most part the West is made up of atheists, cultural Christians, practicing Christians, and Jews. All of these groups are excluded from Paradise and are included in the Islamic description of hell. Therefore, it is correct to say that Islam damns the West to hell for rejecting their belief system. In terms of the Islamic Paradise, why would a Muslim, who becomes a spirit-being after death, want or need a garden, a vineyard which produces grapes for wine, and big-busted virgins? This could only apply to a period after the resurrection and judgment. If this is true then one can only conclude that drinking wine in paradise and having sex with big-busted women in paradise is permitted—one could say encouraged. The hadith warns Christians and polytheists that their eternity will be spent in torment. Knowing this, literalist Muslims can only view non-Muslims with contempt since westerners are already viewed by them as lost in their infidelity.

QUR'AN 112

"The Unity"

614 AD

SCRIPTURE:

Qur'an 112: 1-4

Bukhari:V9B88N174

PREFACE:

The summation of Qur'anic teaching is given here. It was revealed to answer the queries of some Jewish doctors. The Unity of Allah was declared as was the doom of Polytheism.[(45)]

SURAH:

Qur'an 112:1-4: "Say: He, Allah, is One. Allah is He on Whom all depend. He begets not, nor is He begotten; and none is like Him."

SUNNAH:

Bukhari:V9B88N174: "I heard the Prophet saying, 'Islam cannot change.'"

SUMMATION:

IL: Although in the minority, Muhammad was assured of Islamic truth through his channeling of Allah. Allah once again confirmed that he does not have a son.

WA: Prior to 610 AD, there was no evidence that anyone viewed the Allah of the Ka'aba as the one and only God. The declarations of the Islamic deity place the New Testament authors as corruptors of the Gospel. Allah detests the thought that Jesus is the Son of God.[46] The hadith is a warning from Islamic Literalists to the Western World that Islam cannot change or be changed. When it comes to Islamic Literalism, polarization is assured.

"The Dawn"

614 AD

SCRIPTURE:

Qur'an 113:1-5

Bukhari:V7B71N643

PREFACE:

This revelation told Muhammad and the Muslims to seek Allah and his protection from all fear. The promise was made that the truth of Allah will eliminate darkness.[47]

SURAH:

Qur'an 113:1-5: "Say: I seek refuge in the Lord of the Dawn, from the evil of that which He has created, and from the evil of intense darkness, when it comes, and from the evil of those who cast evil suggestions in firm resolutions [malignant witchcraft], and from the evil of the envier when he envies."

SUNNAH:

Bukhari:V7B71N643: "I heard the Prophet saying, 'If anyone of you dreams something he dislikes, when you get up, blow thrice [three times] on your left [side]. If you spit on the left side of your bed the bad dream will not harm you.'"

SUMMATION:

IL: Obviously, Allah must have conveyed to the Prophet that blowing in a certain way and rubbing one's body was important in warding off evil.

WA: In this surah Muhammad sought refuge from the Lord of the Dawn who created the evil darkness, malignant witchcraft, who was the envier. The acts of blowing and rubbing are not seen in the doctrine of the People of the Book. It seems more likely that Muhammad inherited these traits from the Hanifs or the polytheistic Quraysh.

QUR'AN 56

"The Event"

614 AD

SCRIPTURE:

Qur'an 56:17, 22, 36-38, 41-43, 52-56, 75, 78-80, 92-95

Bukhari:V7B69N494

PREFACE:

This surah declares there are three classes of humans: the faithful, the believers, and the guilty opponents. In the judgment to come, all will get what they deserve. The implication here is that the martyr is elevated above and beyond the believer and is the most highly esteemed by Allah.[48]

SURAH:

Qur'an 56:17, 22: "Round about them will go youths never altering in age…and pure, [and] beautiful ones."

Qur'an 56:36-38: "So We have made them virgins, loving, equals in age, for those of the right hand."

Qur'an 56:41-43: "And those of the left hand; how wretched are those on the left hand! [They shall be] In hot wind and boiling water, and shadow of black smoke, neither cool nor refreshing.

Qur'an 56:52-56: "Eat of the tree of Zaqqum, and fill your bellies with it; then drink after it of boiling water; and drink as drinks a thirsty camel [like a thirsty camel]. This is their entertainment on the day of Requital."

Qur'an 56:75, 78-80: "But nay, I swear by revelation of portions of the Qur'an! — And it is a great oath indeed, if you knew — Surely it is a bounteous Qur'an, in a book that is protected, which none touches save [except] the purified ones. A revelation from the Lord of the worlds."

Qur'an 56:92-95: "And if he is one of the rejectors, the erring ones, he has an entertainment of boiling water, and burning in hell. Surely this is a certain truth."

SUNNAH:

Bukhari:V7B69N494: "I heard the Prophet saying, 'From among my followers there will be some who will consider illegal sexual intercourse, the wearing of silk, the drinking of alcoholic drinks and the use of musical instruments, to be lawful. Allah will destroy them during the night and will let mountains fall on them. He will transform the rest into monkeys and pigs and they will remain so until the Day of Doom.'"

SUMMATION:

IL: Allah began to reveal the classes of people who were pleasing to Him and those who will earn eternal scorn. To those who are righteous in the sight of Allah—*delight,* and to those who claim to be believers but disregard Qur'anic injunction and all infidels—*torment.* According to Al-Misri:

> "Allah Almighty and Majestic, sent me (Muhammad) as a guide and a mercy to believers and commanded me to do away with musical instruments, flutes, strings, crucifixes, and Jahiliyyah (Pre-Islamic ignorance). On the day of resurrection, Allah will pour molten lead into the ears of whoever sits listening to a female singer. Song makes hypocrisy grow in the heart as water does herbage. This community will experience the swallowing up of some people by the earth, some will be changed into animals and be rained upon with stones [...] This will occur when female singers and musical instruments appear and the drinking of wine becomes lawful. There will be people of

my community who will hold fornication, silk, wine, and musical instruments lawful."[49]

WA: The promise to the faithful is a very sensual paradise. Why is there a need for sensuality in Allah's paradise? There is no evidence that procreation after the resurrection occurs. Why the need to convey that houris will remain ever-virginal despite continual sex? Why is heaven described as a bordello?[50] The Allah-rejecting and Allah-disobedient folks are placed in a hot desert setting. They are drinking boiling water. Allah, through Muhammad, then swears by his own Qur'anic revelation that the Qur'an is being protected, unlike the Torah and the Gospel that Allah inspired, but were corrupted by the Jews. How so? Only the rightful believing Muslims can touch and record this revelation for posterity. In the hadith, Muhammad began to break down behavior that he and Allah did not welcome. This included having illegal sex—which is still to be defined, wearing silk, drinking alcohol, and playing music. Muhammad said these sins were so grave that those doing such will be crushed and transformed into unclean animals. Having sex outside of marriage can certainly get folks into trouble. Wearing silk can only refer to a class distinction that Muhammad wanted to avoid. Imbibing alcohol can be a problem if it leads to drunkenness. Neither the Torah of Moses nor the words of the New Testament forbid alcohol consumption; however, the Bible does condemn drunkenness. As for condemning music, are we all to think that the great composers, musicians, and some Bible characters are condemned because they played musical instruments? If Muhammad was speaking for Allah, then the music and talents that Allah created are to be avoided. No big band leaders and musical geniuses? If the world would have listened to Muhammad 1400 years ago, there never would have been Caruso, Pavarotti, Bucelli, Sinatra, or any of the other music that we in the West have come to enjoy.

According to Muhammad, Allah sent him to get rid of all musical instruments. Furthermore, Muhammad was not fond of Catholic symbols or the religious ignorance that existed before his initial revelation. According to Muhammad, Allah so hates music and singing that everyone who listens to a woman sing will have molten lead poured into their ears. Muhammad then predicted a time when people would permit what Allah forbade (female singers, musical instruments, and wine drinking). He stated those people will be consumed by the earth and changed into beasts. Among the Muslim Ummah, some claiming to be Muslim will have sex with unmarried Muslim virgins, wear silk, drink wine, and permit music. These proclamations Muhammad and his god amount to a total condemnation of Western Civilization.

QUR'AN 52

"The Mountain"

614 AD

SCRIPTURE:

Qur'an 52:11-13, 29-34, 45-47

Bukhari:V4B54N524

PREFACE:

This surah draws a comparison between Moses at Sinai and Muhammad at Hira. The Torah was revealed to Moses and the Qur'an to Muhammad. Jews worship in their synagogues and Muslims worship in their mosques. Just as those who opposed Moses and the Israelites were defeated and removed from the land, so will the opponents of Islam be defeated and removed from the land. Just as those who obeyed the Torah were blessed, so those who follow the Qur'an will also be blessed. The opponents to Muhammad will be judged, just as the theme in this surah is judgment. Muhammad is not only compared with Moses, but is greater. So, if those who opposed Moses were punished, those who opposed Muhammad, will be punished in this life and the next.[(51)]

SURAH:

Qur'an 52:11-13: "Woe on that day to the deniers, who amuse themselves by vain talk [falsehood]. The day will come when they are driven [by force] to the hell-fire with violence."

Qur'an 52:29-34: "So remind [yourselves], by the grace of thy Lord, thou art no soothsayer, nor madman. Or say they: A poet — we wait for him the evil accidents of time. Say: Wait, I too wait along with you. Or do their understandings bid them this? Or are they an inordinate people? Or say they: He has forged it. Nay, they have no faith. Then let them bring a saying like it, if they are truthful."

Qur'an 52:45-47: "Leave them then [alone] till they meet that day of theirs wherein they are smitten with punishment: The day when their struggle will avail them naught, nor will they be helped. And surely for those who do wrong there is a chastisement besides that [an additional punishment], but most of them know not [are ignorant of it]."

SUNNAH:

Bukhari:V4B54N524: "The Prophet said, 'A group of Israelites were lost. Nobody knows what they did. But I do not see them except that they were cursed and changed into rats [...]'"

SUMMATION:

IL: The parallels between Moses and Muhammad are undeniable. Those who refuse to see the similarities and refuse to conclude that Muhammad is the greatest of the prophets will share a fate of torment and doom.

WA: The introduction speaks of what Jews and Muslims have in common. The Jews were blessed for obeying the Torah and the Muslims are blessed for obeying the Qur'an. This comparison was being made because Muhammad continued to be under assault from his Quraysh relatives. We know this because Allah was telling Muhammad what to say in his revelation. The Quraysh believe Muhammad was a soothsayer, madman, and forger. Allah once again comforted Muhammad by assuring him that his relatives, who did not have a good opinion of him, will burn in hell. Interestingly, while the introduction strives to bring commonality between Jews and Muslims, the hadith recalled Muhammad saying that a group of Jews were cursed and turned into rats.

QUR'AN 38

"Sād"

614 AD

SCRIPTURE:

Qur'an 38:3-8, 17-19, 26-27

Tabari VI:93, 95-96

PREFACE:

This revelation came after the Quraysh (Meccans) tried to persuade Muhammad's uncle, Abu-Talib, to withdraw his protection from Muhammad. When persecution of the prophets became intense, triumph was assured. This vehement opposition was attributed to the devil, for the devil attacked all the Prophets.[52]

SURAH:

Qur'an 38:3-8: "How many a generation [have] We destroyed before them, then they cried [out for mercy] when there was no longer time for escape! And they wonder that a warner from among themselves has come to them, and the disbelievers say: This is a sorcerer, a charlatan, a wizard telling lies.' He has made all the gods into one God. This is an enchanter, a liar. [He makes] the gods a single God? Surely this is a strange thing. And the chief among them say: Go and steadily adhere to your gods: surely this is a thing intended. We have never heard of this in the former faith: this is nothing but a forgery. Has the Reminder been revealed to him from among us? Nay, they are in doubt as to My Reminder. Nay, they have not yet tasted My chastisement [punishment]."

Qur'an 38:17-19: "[...] and remember Our servant David, [was] the possessor of power [by Allah] [...]. Truly We made the mountains subject to him, [by] glorifying Allah at nightfall and sunrise, and the birds gathered together. All were obedient to him."

Qur'an 38:26-27: "O David, surely We made you a ruler in the land; so judge between men justly and follow not desire lest it lead thee from the path of Allah. Those who go astray from the path of Allah, for them is surely a severe chastisement [punishment] because they forgot the day of Reckoning [Judgment]. And [those who disbelieve say] We created not the heaven and earth and what is between them in vain...So woe to those who disbelieve on account [because of] the Fire [Hell]."

SUNNAH:

A TRIBAL DIVIDE

Tabari VI:93: "The Quraysh [Hajjaj's eight sons] went to Abu Talib and said, 'Your nephew has reviled our gods, denounced our religion, derided our traditional values, and told us that our forefathers were misguided. Either curb his attacks [stop him from attacking us] or give us free hand to deal with him, for you are as opposed to him as we are.' They said, 'We asked you to forbid your nephew from attacking us, but you did nothing. By Allah, we can no longer endure this vilification of our forefathers, this derision of our traditional values, and this abuse of our gods.' This breach and enmity with his tribe weighed heavily on Abu Talib. [They said,] 'Abu Talib, you are our elder and our chief, so give us justice against your nephew and order him to desist from reviling our gods, and we will leave him to his god.'"

Tabari VI:95: "Abu Talib sent for Muhammad. [Abu Talib said,] 'Nephew here are the shaykhs and nobles of your tribe. They have asked justice against you. You should desist from reviling their gods and they will leave you to your god.

Tabari VI:96: "Abu Talib said to Muhammad. 'Nephew how is it that your tribe is complaining of you and claiming that you are reviling their gods and saying this, that, and the other?' The Messenger said, 'I want them to utter one saying. If they say it, the Arabs will submit to them and the non-Arabs will pay the jizyah [penalty tax] to them.'"

SUMMATION:

IL: Allah, the Lord of the Worlds, did not like when the Prophet he picked, from the Arab people, was called a sorcerer, a charlatan, a wizard telling lies, and a forger. The Quraysh did not believe the Allah, they knew from the Ka'aba, was the only god. Since the Prophet told them the truth, and they rejected it, they must be reminded that previous prophets also faced similar rejection. If the Quraysh would change their mind, punishment in the fires of hell was assured.

WA: The harmony of the Quraysh at Mecca was now totally disrupted. The issue for the Quraysh was not about Allah. The issue was with Muhammad verbally reviling their gods, denouncing their religion, bashing the traditional values at Mecca, and telling them their forefathers were misguided. They wanted Abu-Talib, Muhammad's uncle, who did not believe Muhammad was a prophet, to convince Muhammad not to verbally attack them. Muhammad did not heed his Uncle's words because he already had a vision of where he wanted this to go. He was trying to convince the Quraysh about his new faith, because they were the keepers of the Ka'aba. Muhammad understood that unity was not possible unless the Arabs unified under Islam and rejected their polytheism. If the Arabs, who were splintered, would submit, eventually the non-Arabs would have to pay them tribute. This tribute known as the jizyah or penalty tax was already conceived by Islam's founder as early as 614 AD.

QUR'AN 101

"The Calamity"

614 AD

SCRIPTURE:

Qur'an 101:6-11

Bukhari:V8B76N537

PREFACE:

This revelation not only hints towards a physical destruction, but also a spiritual destruction for those who oppose the Prophet.[53]

SURAH:

Qur'an 101:6-11: "Then as for him whose measure of good deeds is heavy, he will live a pleasant life. And as for him whose measure of good deeds is light, the abyss is [will be] a mother to him. And what will make thee know what that is? A burning Fire."

SUNNAH:

Bukhari:V8B76N537: "The Prophet said, 'Allah will say, "Adam!" Adam will reply, "I am obedient to your orders." Allah will say, "Bring out the people of the Fire." Adam will say, "How many are the people of the Fire?" Allah will say, "Out of every thousand take out nine-hundred and ninety-nine persons." At that time children will become hoary-headed and every pregnant female will drop her load. You will see the people as if they were drunk. Allah's punishment will be very severe.'"

SUMMATION:

IL: Good deeds, as defined by the Qur'an, will determine who goes to paradise and who will burn in the flames of hell. The damned will be spiritually and physically destroyed.

WA: One can see from this surah that Islam is a works-based ideology based on what the Qur'an says is acceptable and unacceptable behavior. As for those who have deeds that are light, according to Muhammad, Allah will take 999 of them at a time and show them what is about to happen to them. Children will instantaneously become aged and women, who somehow become pregnant in the next life, will suffer miscarriages before they are thrown into hell.

QUR'AN 102

"The Abundance Of Wealth"

614 AD

SCRIPTURE:

Qur'an 102:1-6

Bukhari:V4B56N793, V4B56N795

PREFACE:

The pursuit of wealth keeps people from the real objective in life. Therefore, it is necessary for them to flee from these comforts. For this reason, Allah permits disasters upon people.[(54)]

SURAH:

Qur'an 102:1-6: "Abundance [wealth] diverts you [leads you astray], until you come to the graves. Nay, you will soon know, nay, again, you will soon know. Nay, would that you knew with a certain knowledge! You will certainly see hell."

SUNNAH:

Bukhari:V4B56N793: "The Prophet said, 'If you live long enough the treasure of Khosrau will be opened and taken as spoil. You will carry out handfuls of gold and silver.'"

Bukhari:V4B56N795: "I [Muhammad] have been given the keys of the treasures of the world by Allah."

SUMMATION:

IL: Those who attain great wealth but do not use this wealth for Islamic causes will experience hell-fire. Muslims are to sacrifice their wealth in order to attain the wealth of the infidels.[(55)]

WA: Muslims are to use their wealth in order to finance the Jihad, or the Dawah, against those who resist the message of the Prophet. Hell is threatened against any Muslim who withholds his wealth. In a later hadith, Muhammad predicted that obtaining the treasure of Khosrau (the Persian King) was an Islamic objective. He told his believers that they would get their hands on the gold and silver of the Persians because he was given the keys of the treasures of the world by Allah. So according to Muhammad, his god Allah wanted him and the Muslims to possess the wealth of their enemies. This can only happen through voluntary reversion [Muslims believe that all people are born Muslim] to Islam, subjugation through infiltration, or military conquest.

QUR'AN 105

"The Elephant"

614 AD

SCRIPTURE:

Qur'an 105:1-5

Bukhari:V4B54N530

PREFACE:

This revelation recalls the siege against Mecca by the King of Abyssinia, Abraha. The attackers from east Africa used elephants but were not able to destroy the Ka'aba. The invading army was destroyed. The attack occurred in 570 AD, the year of Muhammad's birth.[56]

SURAH:

Qur'an 105:1-5: "Hast thou not seen how thy Lord dealt with the possessors of the elephant? Did He not cause their war to end in confusion And send against them birds in flocks? Casting at them decreed [great] stones — so He rendered them like straw eaten up."

SUNNAH:

Bukhari:V4B54N530: "Ibn Umar used to kill snakes, but when Abu Lubaba informed him that the Prophet had forbidden the killing of snakes living in houses, he gave up killing them."

SUMMATION:

IL: Allah encouraged the Muslims, though they were outnumbered, to recall the lessons of the past. Just as Allah prevented the Abyssinians from destroying the Ka'aba, Allah will also ensure an Islamic victory in the end of time.

WA: The Muslims, during Muhammad's time were told that Allah intervened to protect them. In this one instance, Allah intervened to protect the Quraysh polytheists. Allah did not protect them because they were polytheists. He protected them because Allah wanted the Ka'aba preserved. Why would Allah want the Ka'aba preserved? According to Tabari II:69, Allah sent Sakinah, a gale force wind with two heads which coiled like a snake, to the place where the Ka'aba was to be built. When one considered that a spirit-like entity coiled like a snake at the location of the Ka'aba, Muhammad's prohibition against the killing of snakes in houses began to make sense.

QUR'AN 107

"Acts Of Kindness"

614 AD

SCRIPTURE:

Qur'an 107:1-7

Bukhari:V2B24N498

PREFACE:

This revelation states that needy and poor believers must be uplifted by the Muslims.[57]

SURAH:

Qur'an 107:1-7: "Hast thou seen him who belies [slanders] religion? That [he] is the one who is rough to [repels] the orphan [Muhammad], and urges not the feeding of the needy. So woe to the praying ones [worshippers], who are unmindful [pay no attention] of their prayer! Who do good to be seen, and refrain from acts of kindness!"

SUNNAH:

Bukhari:V2B24N498: "[Adi bin Hatim] heard the Prophet saying: 'Save yourself from the Fire [Hell] even with half a date to be given in charity.'"

SUMMATION:

IL: Since the needy and poor were not cared for by the indifferent Quraysh, Allah established that Muslims should care for Muslims who were poor and needy. By giving charity, a Muslim can save himself from hell and its consequences.

WA: Allah continued to heap blame on the Quraysh. They were the ones who ridicule Muhammad. The orphan and needy spoken of in this surah was none other than Muhammad. The Quraysh were wealthy, whereas Muhammad, also belonging to the Quraysh, was not wealthy. This surah reflected his early days when his father died and his mother passed away. Allah agreed with Muhammad that he was neglected by his own people. By 614 AD, neglect had turned into conflict. This event was so important in Muhammad's life that he declared the giving of charity could merit paradise and cause the believer to escape from hell.

QUR'AN 82

"The Cleaving"

614 AD

SCRIPTURE:

Qur'an 82:9-16, 19

Muslim:B19C11N4327

PREFACE:

Celestial signs will occur before the final triumph of Islam in the world. The opponents of Islam will, in time, find themselves in a helpless situation. (58)

SURAH:

Qur'an 82:9-12: "Nay, but you give the lie to the Judgment [deny the Judgment], and surely there are keepers over you, honourable recorders, they know what you do.

Qur'an 82:13-16: "Surely the righteous are in bliss, and the wicked are truly in burning Fire — they will enter it on the Day of Judgment and will not be absent from it."

Qur'an 82:19: "The day when no soul controls aught [anything] for another soul. And the command on that day is Allah's."

SUNNAH:

Muslim:B19C11N4327: "[...] the Messenger of Allah said: 'One of the prophets made a holy war.' ...So he marched on and approached a village at or about the time of the Asr [afternoon] prayers. He said to the sun: 'Thou art subservient to Allah and so am I [I am also subservient]. O Allah, stop it [the sun] for me a little. It was stopped for him until Allah granted him victory.' The people gathered the spoils of war at one place. A fire approached the spoils to devour them, but it did not devour them. He [the Holy Prophet] said: 'Some of you have been guilty of misappropriation [...]'"

SUMMATION:

IL: Judgment is coming as surely as Islam's victory is coming to the earth. This will occur when the enemies of Islam find themselves at the mercy of Muslims. In the hadith, everything experienced by previous prophets was fulfilled by Muhammad. Islam's victory will bring the spoils of war. At that time, Muslims were warned to guard against misappropriation.

WA: According to Muhammad, signs in the heavens will herald the final triumph of Islam. This differs from the biblical account where signs in the heavens will herald the end of this age. In the Bible no human entity will triumph. This surah tells Muslims that non-Muslims are wicked. This is unfortunate since literalists continue to believe that Muslims and non-Muslims who do not share their point of view are enemies that must be defeated. Concerning Muhammad's prophet story from the past, the only prophet this could apply to was Joshua. The account is found in Joshua 10:13-14. It is curious that Muhammad could not recall the name of Yehoshua ("Joshua"), which means Yahveh's Salvation. Instead, Muhammad attributed these events to Allah. He also included the account of the spoils of war and the fire approaching the spoils of war, which cannot be found in the biblical account. In doing so, Muhammad held sway over a biblically ignorant audience and told them the prophets of the past behaved exactly like he intended to act. This explained why the accounts differ. From an Islamic perspective, when the accounts differ, culpability falls on a corrupted biblical text.

QUR'AN 108

"The Abundance Of Good"

614 AD

SCRIPTURE:

Qur'an 108:1-3

Muslim:B35C17N6565

PREFACE:

The abundance of wealth leads men away from life's true objective. It conflicts with the obligation to pray and sacrifice for other Muslims.[(59)]

SURAH:

Qur'an 108:1-3: "Surely We have given thee [an] abundance of good. So pray to thy Lord and sacrifice. Surely thy enemy is cut off from good."

SUNNAH:

Muslim:B35C17N6565: "Abu Huraira reported that Allah's Messenger (May peace be upon him) used to supplicate in these words: 'O Allah, set right for me my religion which is the safeguard of my affairs. And set right for me the affairs of my world wherein is my living. And set right for me my Hereafter on which depends my after-life. And make the life for me a source of abundance for every good and make my death a source of comfort for me protecting me against every evil.'"

SUMMATION:

IL: Every Prophet suffered. Muhammad endured sacrifice when he lost all of his sons born to Khadijah. As a result of this sacrifice, Muhammad became the inspiration for millions of Allah's slaves. As for the woman who taunted the Prophet, her destiny was assured in the hell-fire.

WA: The woman who ridiculed Muhammad seemed to understand, very early on, there would be a problem with succession after Muhammad died. Although she could not know the future, the woman was right. To this day, the Shi'a refuse to recognize the first three Caliphs; Abu Bakr, Umar Al-Khattab, and Uthman Al-Ummayyad. This can all be traced to Muhammad not having a surviving son by Khadijah and by not naming an heir to his Islamic kingdom. It had to bother Muhammad that none of his sons survived. Muhammad may have enjoyed an "abundance of good", but this good would eventually come at the expense of the material possessions and lives of other people.

"Qāf"

614 AD

SCRIPTURE:

Qur'an 50:24-26, 29-30, 36, 45

Tirmidhi:B4C21N2687

PREFACE:

Spiritual and physical resurrection is mentioned in this surah. Every action has consequences and these consequences will come to light on the Day of Judgment. Judgment and resurrection if this life will be tied to judgment and resurrection in the next life.[(60)]

SURAH:

Qur'an 50:24-26: "Cast into hell every ungrateful, rebellious one, forbidder of good, exceeder of limits, doubter, who sets up another god with Allah, so cast him into severe chastisement [punishment]."

Qur'an 50:29-30: "My sentence cannot be changed, nor am I in the least unjust to the servants. On the day We say to hell: Art thou filled up? And it will say: Are there any more?"

Qur'an 50:36: "And how many a generation We destroyed before them who were mightier in prowess than they! [...]"

Qur'an 50:45: "We know best what they say, and thou art not one to compel them. So remind by means of the Qur'an him who fears my threat."

SUNNAH:

Tirmidhi:B4C21N2687: "Muhammad said, 'The smallest reward for the people of Paradise is an abode where there are 80,000 servants and 72 wives [...]'"

SUMMATION:

IL: Allah had nothing but distain for the Quraysh and, by extension, anyone who rejects or opposes the implementation of Islamic principles. As much as the unbelievers will be punished, so the faithful will be rewarded.

WA: Reading between the lines, one can imagine there was no love lost between Muhammad and his relatives. They thought he was a fraud and he responded with surahs that condemn their unbelief to hell. The hadith spoken of by Muhammad was aimed at young Muslim men. When the time came for Muslims to sacrifice their wealth and possibly themselves, Muhammad wanted to make sure the reward of 80,000 servants and 72 wives would nullify any doubt.

QUR'AN 51

"The Scatterers"

614 AD

SCRIPTURE:

Qur'an 51:10-14, 38-39, 56, 59-60,

Bukhari:V6B60N332

PREFACE:

In the same way a son was born to Abraham, Islam will be born to the world. Muhammad's message slowly gained ground. Eventually, all those who opposed Muhammad would be judged and their good fortune would come to an end.[61]

SURAH:

Qur'an 51:10-14: "Cursed be the liars! Who are in an abyss, neglectful; they ask: When is the day of Judgment? It is the day when they are tried [thrown] into the Fire. Taste your persecution! This is what you would hasten on [what you would make come quickly]."

Qur'an 51:38-39: "And in Moses, when We sent him to Pharaoh with clear authority. But he turned away on account of his might and he [Pharaoh] said: An enchanter or a madman!"

Qur'an 51:56: "And I have not created the Jinn and the men except that they should serve me."

Qur'an 51:59-60: "Surely the lot of the wrongdoers is as [the same as] was the lot of their companions, so let them not ask Me to hasten on. Woe, then, to those who disbelieve because of the day of theirs which they are promised!"

SUNNAH:

Bukhari:V6B60N332: "The Prophet said, 'Last night a demon from the Jinn came to me to disturb my prayer, but Allah gave me power to overcome him. I intended to tie him to one of the pillars of the mosque till the morning so that all of you could see him.'"

SUMMATION:

IL: The infidels claim the Prophet's time was without a miracle. The Jinn and mankind were created to serve Allah, so Allah gave the Prophet power over the demons, the Jinn, and power over men.

WA: Allah cursed, pronounced judgment, and damned Muhammad's relatives at Mecca. The point being, the Quraysh will pay for their evil deeds just as those in the past did. According to Allah, He created Jinn who are evil, and men who are sinful, to serve Him. Why would Allah want what is spiritually evil to serve him? As for men, there was no mention of people coming to Allah's religion through their own will. Muhammad went on to state that it was his intention to tie a demon to a pillar of the mosque so that all could see him. This either meant Muhammad was capable of doing this, but decided against it, or if he had the power to do this, he would have performed this feat. In reality, that which is physical cannot tie the invisible to anything physical and expect others who are physical to see that which is invisible. None of this was plausible.

QUR'AN 54

"The Moon"

614 AD

SCRIPTURE:

Qur'an 54:9, 16-18, 23, 33, 38, 41, 48

Bukhari:V2B23N446

PREFACE:

The Moon was the symbol of power among the Arabs; therefore, the moon will be torn asunder so that only the crescent would remain. Persecution would increase but success was assured, but not before conflict on the battlefield.[(62)]

SURAH:

Qur'an 54:9: "Before them the people of Noah rejected — they rejected Our servant and called him mad, and he was driven away."

Qur'an 54:16-18: "How terrible was then My chastisement and My warning! And certainly We have made the Qur'an easy to remember, but is there anyone who will mind [does anyone care]? Ad denied, so how terrible was My chastisement and My warning."

Qur'an 54:23: "Thamud rejected the warning."

Qur'an 54:33: "The people of Lot treated the warning as a lie."

Qur'an 54:38: "And certainly a lasting chastisement overtook them in the morning."

Qur'an 54:41: "And certainly the warning came to Pharaoh's people."

Qur'an 54:48: "On the day when they [the aforementioned disbelievers] are dragged into the Fire upon their faces: Taste the touch of hell."

SUNNAH:

Bukhari:V2B23N446: "The Prophet said, 'He who commits suicide by throttling shall keep on throttling himself in the Hell Fire [forever] and he who commits suicide by stabbing himself shall keep on stabbing himself in the Hell-Fire [forever].'"

SUMMATION:

IL: Allah reminds the Muslims that all the previous prophets went through persecution and in every instance their adversaries were destroyed. Therefore, Muslims should always take heart, no matter the circumstances, that they will eventually be victorious. The Prophet then reminded those who sought an escape from suffering through suicide that they will not escape a horrible judgment.

WA: As we approach the conclusion of the year 614 AD, Muhammad, channeling Allah's will through the Angel Gabriel, strived to cement that his actions were just like the biblical Prophets. This also applied to Ad and Thamud when he warned of their impending doom. Seeing that he could not be successful without the self-sacrifice of his companions, Muhammad warned Muslims not to give into suicidal thoughts because they would meet a horrible fate on the day of Judgment. This form of suicide has nothing to do with destroying the enemy. Therefore, in Islam it is not permitted.

QUR'AN 71

"Noah"

614 AD

SCRIPTURE:

Qur'an 71:1-3, 13-14, 21-22, 24-28

Bukhari:V4B52N73

PREFACE:

The example of Noah is given here. He prays that transgressors will be destroyed so their evil deeds may not prosper.[63]

SURAH:

Qur'an 71:1-3: "Surely We sent Noah to his people, saying: Warn thy people before there [comes upon] them a painful chastisement. He [Noah] said: O my people, surely I am a plain warner to you: that you should serve Allah and keep your duty to Him and obey me."

Qur'an 71:13-14: "What is the matter with you hope not for greatness from Allah? And indeed He has created you by [through] various stages."

Qur'an 71:21-22: "Noah said: My Lord, surely they disobey me and follow him whose wealth and children have increased him in naught [nothing] but loss. And they have planned a mighty [very great] plan.

Qur'an 71:24-28: "And indeed they have led many astray. And increase Thou the wrongdoers in naught but perdition. Because of their wrongs they were drowned, then made to enter [the] Fire, so they found no helpers besides Allah. And Noah said: My Lord, leave not of the disbelievers on the land [earth]. For if thou leave them, they will lead astray Thy servants, and will not beget any but immoral, ungrateful ones [children] My Lord, forgive me and my parents and him who enters the house believing, and the believing men and the believing women. And increase not the wrongdoers in aught [anything] but destruction."

SUNNAH:

Bukhari:V4B52N73: "Allah's Apostle said, 'Know that Paradise is under the shades of swords.'"

SUMMATION:

IL: In this instance, Allah recalled the words of Prophet Noah as an example for Muhammad to follow. Muhammad was to provide a warning just as Noah warned the people of his day that Allah was to be feared. Muhammad opposed the rich just as Noah opposed the disobedient during his time. The rich who opposed the Prophet lost what they had. Just as Noah insisted that Allah not show mercy to those who would not listen to him, so Muhammad would not show mercy to those who refused to listen. We must insist on the destruction of Allah's enemies. We must show them the sword.

WA: Up to this point, this should be the most troubling surah for westerners. In this Qur'anic account, we are told the Noah of history was a slave of Allah who wanted Allah to kill everyone on earth and bring them nothing but destruction. As you already know, this revelation came out of Muhammad's mouth. Therefore, we must conclude that these were also the desires of Muhammad towards his enemies. If we are also considered the enemies of Muslim Literalists, then they will adopt the same intentions towards us that Muhammad had towards the people he was unable to persuade. For those familiar with the biblical account, Noah never insisted upon the death of others. Yahveh told Noah the people were not redeemable because their corruption was too great. The Creator decided the course of action for Noah—to build an ark. The Islamic account is troubling because it implies that Noah demanded their death. In doing so, Muhammad then had the divine right to demand the death of his enemies.

CHAPTER 2 NOTES

1. Maulana Muhammad Ali, p. 1227; Mohammad Marmaduke Pickthall, p. 445
2. Peters, *Muhammad and the Origins of Islam*, p. 131
3. Ali, p. 1149; Pickthall, p. 419-420
4. Peters, *Muhammad and the Origins of Islam*, 129
5. Ali, p. 1-2; Pickthall, p. 31
6. Esposito, *The Straight Path*, p. 14
7. Ali, p. 1117; Pickthall, p. 409
8. Ali, p. 1223; Pickthall, pp. 443-444
9. Kalbi, *Book of Idols*, p. 19
10. Ibn Ishaq/Ibn Hisham, Ishaq:72; Sahih Muslim, B1C75N311
11. Ali, p. 1220; Pickthall, p. 442-443
12. Ryckmans, G., *Pre-Islamic Arab Religions*, 47-48
13. Ali, p. 1145; Pickthall, p. 418
14. Ali, p. 1111; Pickthall, p. 407
15. Ali, p. 1253; Pickthall, p. 452
16. Ali, p. 1124; Pickthall, p. 411
17. Ali, p. 1242; Pickthall, p. 449
18. Ali, p. 1243; Pickthall, p. 449
19. Ali. p. 1173; Pickthall, p. 427
20. Ali. p. 1178; Pickthall, p. 429
21. Ali. p. 1182; Pickthall, p. 431
22. Ali. p. 1203; Pickthall, p. 437
23. Ali. p. 1206; Pickthall, p. 438
24. Ali, p. 1208; Pickthall, p. 439
25. Ali, p. 1212; Pickthall, p. 440
26. Ali, p. 1215; Pickthall, p. 441
27. Ali, p. 1218; Pickthall, p. 442
28. Ali, p. 1225; Pickthall, p. 444
29. Ali, p. 1230; Pickthall, p. 445
30. Ali, p. 1247; Pickthall, p. 451
31. Ali, p. 1236; Pickthall, p. 447
32. Geisler, *Answering Islam*, p.179

33. Ali, p. 1190; Pickthall, p. 432

34. Ali, p. 1194; Pickthall, p. 434

35. Ali, p. 1197; Pickthall, p. 435

36. Ali, p. 1200; Pickthall, p. 436

37. Ali, p. 1154; Pickthall, p. 421

38. Ali, p. 1130; Pickthall, p. 413

39. Bulandshahri, *Illuminating Discourses on the Noble Qur'an*, Vol.1, p. 235

40. Al-Misri, *Reliance of the Traveler*, pp. 525, 542

41. Ali, p. 1164; Pickthall, p. 424

42. Al-Misri, *Reliance of the Traveler*, pp. 602-603

43. Ali, p. 1169; Pickthall, p. 426

44. Bulandshahri, *Illuminating Discourses on the Noble Qur'an*, Vol., p. 386

45. Ali, p. 1257; Pickthall, p. 454

46. Ali, *The Meaning of the Holy Qur'an*, p. 291

47. Ali, p. 1258; Pickthall, p. 454

48. Ali, p. 1051; Pickthall, p. 384

49. Al-Misri, *Reliance of the Traveler*, r40.1

50. Richardson, *Secrets of the Koran*, p. 39

51. Ali, p. 1021; Pickthall, p. 374

52. Ali, p. 893; Pickthall, p. 324

53. Ali, p. 1238; Pickthall, p. 448

54. Ali, p. 1240; Pickthall, p. 448

55. Al-Misri, *Reliance of the Traveler*, p. 272

56. Ali, p. 1245; Pickthall, p. 450

57. Ali, p. 1249; Pickthall, p. 451

58. Ali, p. 1187; Pickthall, p. 432

59. Ali, p. 1251; Pickthall, p. 452

60. Ali, p. 1009; Pickthall, p. 369

61. Ali, p. 1015; Pickthall, p. 372

62. Ali, p. 1036; Pickthall, p. 379

63. Ali, p. 1135; Pickthall, p. 414

CHAPTER 3

Middle Meccan Revelations

(615-618 AD)

QUR'AN 15

"The Rock"

615 AD

SCRIPTURE:

Qur'an 15:9, 27-48

Muslim:B39C14N6757

PREFACE:

This surah established warnings against anyone who would seek to destroy the Prophet of Islam or his message. The Qur'an, in particular, must be guarded against the evil intentions of others just as the Qur'an was protected by Allah from being corrupted. Furthermore, a fatal blow cannot be struck against the Arabs who are bringing this truth to the world. During the period of this revelation, the Thamud rejected and ridiculed the Qur'anic revelation and Allah promised their mockery would not go unpunished. The Islamic message came peacefully, but opposition to it continued to grow from the Meccans and the Thamud. Therefore, this surah established that abrogating verses would be necessary to authorize a change in tactics, especially against those who mocked the Qur'anic revelation.[1]

SURAH:

Qur'an 15:9: "Surely We have revealed [set down] the Reminder [Qur'an], and surely We are its Guardian [against corruption]."

Qur'an 15:27-44: "And the Jinn, We created before [man] of intensely hot fire. And when thy Lord said to the angels: I am going to create a mortal of sounding clay, of black mud fashioned into shape. So when I have made him complete and breathed into breathed into him of My spirit, fall down making obeisance [prostrate] to him. So the angels made obeisance, all of them together — but Iblis [Lucifer] did it not. He refused to be with those who made obeisance [...]. He [Iblis] said: I will not make obeisance [prostrate myself] to a mortal, whom thou hast created of sounding clay, of black mud fashioned into shape. He [Allah] said: Then go forth, for surely thou art driven away, and surely on thee is a curse till the day of Judgment [...]. He [Iblis] said: My Lord, as thou hast judged me erring [in error], I shall certainly make evil fair-seeming [seem logical] to them on earth, and I shall cause them all to deviate, except Thy servants from among them, the purified ones. He [Allah] said: This is the right way [fine] with Me. As regard[ing] My servants, thou hast no authority over them except such of [for] the deviators as [that] follow thee. And surely hell is promised place for them all — it has seven gates. For each gate is an appointed portion of them."

Qur'an 15:45-48: "Surely those who keep their duty are in [the] Gardens and fountains. Enter them in peace, secure. And We shall root out whatever of rancor [spite/malice] is in their breasts — as brethren, on raised couches, face to face. Toil afflicts them not therein, nor will they be ejected therefrom."

SUNNAH:

Muslim:B39C14N6757: "Allah's Messenger said, 'There is none amongst you with whom is not an attaché [attached] from amongst the Jinn [with a devil]. They [the Companions] said, 'Allah's Messenger, [is there a devil] with you too?' He said, 'Yes, but Allah helps me against him and so I am safe from his hand and he does not command me but for good.'"

SUMMATION:

IL: Allah promised that we can trust the Qur'an as being 100% true because Allah declared that He has kept it uncorrupted. In this surah we learn that Allah intended for the angels to be subjected to man, but Satan refused to pay homage to man and was cursed by Allah. Although Satan promised to pollute the earth, Allah acknowledged that his prophets could not sin. The seven gates of hell await all those who allow themselves to be influenced by Satan. The slaves of Allah will inherit paradise. As for the Prophet, Satan attacked him hoping that he would fail, but the Prophet had power over the demons of hell.

WA: Again, how can Allah who is all powerful, according to Muslims, guard the Qur'an from corruption but be unable to prevent the Torah and Gospel from being corrupted? Allah can guard the Qur'an from corruption if He is not the god of the Torah and Gospel. If that is true, then Allah's testimony concerning the Torah and Gospels in the Qur'an cannot be true. If Allah accepts no partners, i.e., does not want anyone else to be worshipped with him, why would Allah require the Jinn to worship or bow down to the first man? Allah cursed Satan for not worshipping Allah's creation, mankind. Therefore, Allah, who cursed Satan for not worshipping man, permitted Satan to pervert man, except for those whom Allah favored. As for Allah's preferred, they were promised the delights of paradise.

In this instance, the hadith is very troubling. All demons, devils, and Satan come from the Jinn. According to Muhammad, demons are assigned to everyone including Muhammad. If Allah helped Muhammad with the Jinn, why was the demon assigned to him in the first place?

QUR'AN 19

"Mary"

615 AD

SCRIPTURE:

Quran 19:30, 33-35, 54, 88-92

Tabari VI:98

PREFACE:

Some Muslims immigrated to Christian Abyssinia because the Muslims knew the Christians would protect them from the Meccans who were trying to turn them back to polytheism. The Muslims were told to resist the false doctrine of the Christians which has nothing to do with the teachings of the prophets.[2] The final point made is that faith cannot benefit anyone unless it is translated into practice. The Christian religion must be denounced as false doctrine. The point of this surah, named after Mary, is that the People of the Book have either openly disobeyed or they deliberately created false doctrine.[3]

SURAH:

Qur'an 19:30: "He [Jesus] said: I am indeed a servant [slave] of Allah. He has given me the Book and made me a prophet."

Qur'an 19:33-34: "And peace on me the day I was born, and the day I die, and the day I am raised to life. Such is Jesus son of Mary — a statement of truth about which they dispute."

Qur'an 19:35: "It beseems not [is not befitting of] Allah that He should take to Himself a son. Glory be to Him! [W]hen he decrees a matter, He only says to it, Be, and it is."

Qur'an 19:54: "And mention Ishmael in the Book [Qur'an]. Surely he was truthful in promise, and he was a messenger, a prophet."

Qur'an 19:88-92: "And they say: The Beneficent [most Gracious] has taken to Himself [begotten] a son. Certainly you make [utter] an abominable [gross] assertion [blasphemy]! The heavens may almost [are about] be rent thereat [to shatter], and the earth [is about to] cleave [tear] asunder, and the mountains fall down in pieces [are about to crumble], that [because] they ascribe [claim] a son [has been born] to the Beneficent [most Gracious]. And it is not worthy [befitting] of the beneficent [most Gracious] that He should take to Himself [beget] a son."

SUNNAH:

IRRECONCILABLE DIFFERENCES

Tabari VI:98: "The situation deteriorated, hostility became bitter, and people withdrew from one another, displaying open hatred…the Meccan chiefs conspired to seduce their sons, brothers, and clansman away from the new religion. It was a trial which severely shook the Muslims who had followed the prophet. Some were seduced […]. The main body went to Abyssinia because of the coercion they were being subjected to at Mecca. His fear was that they would be seduced from their religion. There is a difference of opinion as to the number of those who emigrates in stealth and secret. Some say there were eleven men and four women […] Ibn Ishaq claims there were ten."

SUMMATION:

IL: As a result of the unreasonableness and hatred of the Quraysh towards the Prophet and the Muslims, the Prophet believed it was prudent that some of the believers escape to Abyssinia. In Abyssinia, the Muslims came under the protection of the Christians. However, Allah sent new revelations to the Prophet which warned the Muslims not to be tempted by the Christians. Otherwise, it would have been a loss for the Muslims to have escaped the polytheists and then had these same Muslims converted to the false doctrine of the Christians. Another proof the Christian belief is false, comes from verse 54 where the promise was made to Ishmael. Since the promise was made to Ishmael, it could not have been made to Isaac. Allah once again provided proof of biblical corruption.

WA: This surah, while giving the appearance of honoring the mother of Jesus, called the eyewitness authors of the Gospels liars. The Qur'an claims that Jesus never made the statements that are found in the first century New Covenant. In this surah, it was first revealed that Jesus is not the Son of God. He is a slave of Allah. In verses 33-34, Muhammad was channeling Jesus, who is saying through Muhammad that he (Jesus) was born and did not die in the past. He went on to say that he will die in the future, and after his death, Allah will raise him to life at the Judgment. This means that Jesus had no father at all. He did not die on the cross though he will die in the future and be raised at the resurrection subordinate to Muhammad's god. The Jesus channeling by Muhammad was supposed to represent proof that Jesus never claimed to be the Son of God. This occurred in Islam because Muhammad never read the New Covenant or the Jewish Tenakh i.e. the Bible. He was familiar with heretical Christian belief. Muhammad knew that he and his god must repudiate Christian belief for Islam to be elevated above the "false" Christian belief. In essence, Muhammad and Allah realized there can be no Islam, or claim that Islam is the truth, if Jesus Christ is the Son of God. So while the Christian Abyssinians were supposed to be hospitable to the Muslims, these same Christians were guilty of such a blasphemy that the heavens were about to tear apart and the mountains crumble. If these words truly came from the Creator of the Universe, Allah, one is forced to question why this has not happened in past 1400 years. People continue to confess Jesus as Messiah and Lord, yet the world we live in has not crumbled because of it.

QUR'AN 20

"Tā Hā"

615 AD

SCRIPTURE:

Qur'an 20:48, 60-61, 70-71, 85, 87, 95-97, 100, 113-114, 133

Bukhari:V7B63N191

PREFACE:

Moses suffered persecution but succeeded, and so would Muhammad overcome oppression. The Qur'an would soon be revealed in triumph to the world. Jesus was also opposed by his enemies, but rose above the persecution. Umar al-Khattab came with a blade to murder Muhammad. He accused Muhammad of being a Sabaean but was told that vengeance would follow him if he killed Muhammad. Umar then learned that members of his family became Muslims. He attacked his brother-in-law and cut his sister. Umar was sorry that he harmed them. He then read a parchment of the Qur'anic revelation that was given to him by his wounded sister. Following this, he was convinced to revert to Islam.[4]

SURAH:

Qur'an 20:48: "It has indeed been revealed to us [Moses and Aaron] that punishment will overtake him [Pharaoh] who rejects and turns away [from the truth]."

Qur'an 20:60-61: "So Pharaoh went back and settled [devised] his plan [plot], then came. Moses said to them: Woe to you! Forge not a lie against

Allah, lest He destroy you by punishment [torment], and he fails indeed [he] who forges a lie."

Qur'an 20:70-71: "So the enchanters [magicians] fell down prostrate [on the ground]: We believe in the Lord of Aaron and Moses. Pharaoh said: You believe in Him before I give you leave [permission]? Surely he is your chief who taught you enchantment. So I shall cut off your hands and your feet on opposite sides and I shall crucify you on the trunks of palm-trees, and you shall certainly know which of us can give the more severe and the more abiding [lasting] chastisement [punishment]."

Qur'an 20:85, 87: "He said: Surely We have tried thy people in thy absence, and the Samiri has led them astray. [...] They said: We broke not the promise to thee [to you] of our own accord, but we were made to bear the burdens of the ornaments of the people, then we cast them away, and thus did the Samiri suggest [as the Samiri suggested]."

Qur'an 20:95-97, 100: "Moses said: What was thy objective, O Samiri [descendents of Simeon]? He [Samiri] said: I perceived what they perceived not, so I took a handful from the footprints of the messenger [Moses] then I cast it away. Thus did my soul I embellished it to me. He [Moses] said: Begone then! It is for thee in this life to say, Touch me not. And for thee is a promise which shall not fail. And look at thy god to whose worship thou hast kept. We will certainly burn it, then we will scatter it in the sea. [...] Whoever turns away from it, he will surely bear a burden on the day of Resurrection."

Qur'an 20:113-114: "And thus have We sent it down an Arabic Qur'an, and have distinctly set forth therein threats that they may guard against evil, or that it may be a reminder for them. Supremely exalted then is Allah, the King, the Truth. And make not hast with [do not try to anticipate] the Qur'an before its revelation is made complete to thee [comes to you], and say: My Lord, increase me in knowledge."

Qur'an 20:133: "And they say: Why does he [Muhammad] not bring us a sign from his Lord? Has not there come to them a clear evidence of what is in the previous Books?"

SUNNAH:

Bukhari:V7B63N191: "Indeed in the Apostle of Allah, you have a good example to follow."

SUMMATION:

IL: The accounts of Moses and Jesus foretold what the Prophet of Islam would experience. This was explained at length in the Qur'an. The truth of the Qur'an was so compelling that a younger Umar, who planned to harm the Prophet, heard the words of the Qur'an and was compelled to revert to Islam. The Qur'an revealed that a group of Israelites were the guilty party who led the rest of the Israelites astray. The Samiri then embellished the words of Moses. Since this happened, Allah sent an Arabic Qur'an that guarded against this ancient evil. Even so, there is still evidence of Islamic truth in the Bible. If people want to know the beauty and truth of the Qur'an, it was displayed by the Prophet Muhammad.

WA: In some verses of this surah, Muhammad was channeling Moses. Channeling Allah, whom Muhammad believed to be God, was one thing, but Moses died 1,865 years before this surah was even revealed. If this was so, it suggested that Muhammad was a medium or soothsayer, which was what he was accused of by the Quraysh. Verses 60-71 are problematic. In the Biblical account, the God of Moses revealed himself as YHVH, not Allah. The account given concerning the Egyptian magicians is also an eye opener. The biblical record is not in agreement with this account. Furthermore, the threat of crucifixion could not have happened. There was no evidence of crucifixion prior to the 7th century BC or about 500 years after these events would have occurred. This also poses another question. If Pharaoh threatened crucifixion and cutting feet and hands on opposite sides, why did Allah prescribe the same torture and death in 5:33? If Pharaoh was evil, why would Allah prescribe the same horror to others? As for the Samiri, some Islamic sources believed the Samiri were Samaritans. This gives rise to another problem. Samaritans, as a people, did not show up in Palestine until after the Assyrian invasion in the 8th century BC. Josephus and other historians did not recall Samaritans until 400 years after the Assyrian invasion. The Allah of the Qur'an did not want to blame Aaron, who was also considered an Islamic Prophet, so the Samiri became the scapegoat. Allah again declared in 615 AD that *clear* evidence of Muhammad and his god can be found in the previous scriptures. Muslim literalists are still looking for that *clear* evidence.

QUR'AN 21

"The Prophets"

615 AD

SCRIPTURE:

Qur'an 21:3, 5-6, 9, 11, 15, 18, 22-24, 29, 36, 39, 96, 98, 100, 103, 105

Bukhari:V4B54N509, V4B54N516

PREFACE:

In the same way Abraham and Moses were delivered from their enemies, Muhammad will be delivered from his enemies. Those that opposed the Prophet were assured of judgment and reckoning. Because the Prophet brought the truth with him, he was assured of deliverance. More than any other messenger or prophet, Muhammad had the most in common with Abraham. The truth of Islam is that Muslims will attain and inherit the land of those who oppose the message of Muhammad.[(5)]

SURAH:

Qur'an 21:3: "Their hearts are trifling [preoccupied]. And they — the wrongdoers — counsel in secret: He is nothing but a mortal like yourselves; will you then yield [succumb] to enchantment [magic] while you see."

Qur'an 21:5-6: "Nay, they say: Medleys [muddled] of dreams! [N]ay, he has forged [invented] it! [N]ay, he is a poet! [S]o let him bring to us a sign like the former prophets were sent with [provided]. Not a town believed before them which We destroyed: [W]ill they then believe?"

Qur'an 21:9: "[...] so We delivered [saved] them and whom We pleased, and We destroyed the extravagant."

Qur'an 21:11, 15, 18: "And how many a town [towns] which was iniquitous did We demolish, and We raised up after it another! [...] And this cry of theirs ceased not [did not stop] till We made them cut off, [and made them] extinct. [...] Nay, We hurl the Truth against falsehood, so it knocks out its brains, and lo! [I]t vanishes. And woe to you for what you describe!"

Qur'an 21:22-24: "If there were in them gods besides Allah, they would both have been in disorder. So glory be to Allah, the Lord of the Throne, being above what they describe! He cannot be questioned as to what He does, and they will be questioned. Or, have they taken gods besides Him? Say: Bring your proof. This is the reminder [book] of those with me and the reminder for those before me. Nay, most of them know not the Truth, so they turn away."

Qur'an 21:29: "And whoever of them should say: I am a god besides Him, such a one [that person] We recompense [will repay] with hell. Thus We reward the unjust."

Qur'an 21:36: "And when those who disbelieve see thee, they treat thee not but [only] with mockery."

Qur'an 21:39: "If those who disbelieve but knew the time when they will not be able to ward off [prevent] the fire from their faces, nor from their backs, and they will not be helped!"

Qur'an 21:96: "Even when Gog and Magog are let loose and they sally [come] forth from every elevated place."

Qur'an 21:98: "Surely you and what you worship besides Allah are fuel of hell; to it you will come."

Qur'an 21:100: "From them therein is groaning [mourning] and from therein they hear not [hear nothing]."

Qur'an 21:103: "The great Terror will not grieve them [the believers], and the angels will meet them [and say]: This is your day which you were promised."

Qur'an 21:105: "And certainly We wrote in the Book [scriptures] after the reminder that My righteous servants [slaves] will inherit the land."

SUNNAH:

Bukhari:V4B54N509: "The Prophet said, 'Yawning is from Satan and if anyone of you yawns, he should check his yawning as much as possible, for if anyone of you during that act of yawning should say: "Ha," Satan will laugh at him.'"

Bukhari:V4B54N516: "The Prophet said, 'If anyone rouses from sleep and performs the ablution, he should wash his nose by putting water in it and then blow it out thrice [three times] because Satan has stayed in the upper part of his nose all the night.'"

SUMMATION:

IL: The unbelieving Quraysh continued to belittle the Prophet by accusing him of doing magic and being a dreamer. Allah destroyed those who opposed the Prophets of old, so the enemies of Muhammad would suffer the same fate. Worse yet are those who claim to be God, those who mock the Prophet, and those who deny the majesty of Allah. At the end of time, the forces of Islam, comprised of Gog and Magog (Turkic peoples), will hurl their vengeance against those who dismiss the Prophet and his religion. As a result of this end time Gog-Magog war, the Muslims will inherit the land of the unbelievers.

WA: In this passage, Muhammad was speaking about what he heard Gabriel telling him. Gabriel revealed what Allah heard the unbelievers say. The accusations were responded to by Allah and by Muhammad. In the Sunnah, Muhammad answered their accusations by contrasting Satan's words from Allah's Qur'an. Muhammad believed he was experiencing a good dream. The proof was the Prophet abstained from yawning and spat on the left side to ward off Satan. Whenever he performed an ablution, he washed his nose with water and blew it three times to expel Satan. This was done because Satan slept in the noses of people during the night. Therefore, believers were reassured that non-believers will pay in this life and ultimately through the Gog-Magog Islamic invasion and conquest. Unlike the Bible, where the Gog and Magog of Ezekiel 38-39 invade the land of Israel, in the Qur'an, Gog and Magog exercise Islamic justice against the unbelievers. These slaves of Allah will inherit the land of the unbelievers—in this case, Israel.

QUR'AN 26

"The Poets"

615 AD

SCRIPTURE:

Qur'an 26:49, 91-95, 141-144, 192-197

Bukhari:V1B7N1331

PREFACE:

Allah warned disbelievers that rejecting Allah's message was like rejecting food and drink. This revelation dealt with continuing allegations that Muhammad was a poet. Muhammad was told not to despair because this was what occurred to Prophets. Those who opposed the Prophets were destroyed. Those who oppose Muhammad and his message will also be destroyed.[6]

SURAH:

Qur'an 26:49: "Pharaoh said: You believe in him before I give you leave [permission]; surely he is the chief of you who taught you enchantment [magic], so shall you know. Certainly I will cut off your hands and your feet on opposite sides, and I will crucify you all."

Qur'an 26:91-95: "And hell is made manifest to the deviators, and it is said to them: Where are those that you worshipped besides Allah? Can they help you or help themselves? So they are hurled into it [hell], they and the deviators, and the hosts of the devil, all."

Qur'an 26:141-144: "Thamud [Second Ad located north of Mecca] gave the lie to the messengers. When their brother Salih said to them: Will you not guard against evil? Surely I am a faithful messenger to you: so keep your duty to Allah and obey me." [See Qur'an 32:2-3]

Qur'an 26:192-197: "And surely this is a revelation from the Lord of the worlds. The Faithful Spirit has brought it, on thy heart that thou mayest be a warner, in plain Arabic language. And surely the same is in the Scriptures of the ancients. Is it not a sign to them that the learned men of the Children of Israel know it?"

SUNNAH:

Bukhari:V1B7N1331: "The Prophet said, 'I have been given five things which were not given to anyone else [the Prophets who came before me]. Allah made me victorious with terror [against my enemies]. The earth was made for me...Booty was made lawful for me yet it was not lawful for anyone else. I was given the right of intercession on the Day of Doom. Every Prophet used to be sent to his nation only, but I have been sent to all of mankind.'"

SUMMATION:

IL: The people of old were thrown into hell for ignoring the Prophets. Likewise, those in the future will suffer the same fate for ignoring Muhammad. As it applied to Muhammad, Allah terrorized enemies in order to give their land to the Prophet and his followers. In doing so, the Prophet could claim the possessions of his enemies because Allah communed with the Prophet and assured him, unlike previous prophets, Muhammad was sent to everyone in the world.

WA: This surah is, for the most part, a carbon copy of Qur'an 20 with some notable exceptions. A prophet named Salih was introduced. This surah started with Pharaoh but it transitioned to Thamud. The point was reiterated that Thamud did not listen so they were destroyed. Next, verses 192-197 state what was revealed in the Qur'an was revealed to those who wrote the Bible. This surah also claims the Children of Israel knew it. However, this is not true. They did not know it nor could they find it. It would have been so easy for Allah, through Muhammad, to have quoted chapter and verse to prove this point, but this never happened even once in the Qur'an.

QUR'AN 27

"The Naml"

615 AD

SCRIPTURE:

Qur'an 27:16-17, 38-39, 43-44, 76, 82

Bukhari:V9B87N127

PREFACE:

This surah addresses the mysterious and the miraculous. Comparisons were drawn from Moses and Solomon. Muhammad was declared to be the combination of the two. Muhammad was selected to resurrect the spiritually dead; however, those who will not heed his message are opponents of Islam and will be destroyed. At the time of the end, Islam will bring forth the beast, the end time Caliphate, Imamate, or Sultanate, Empire. The wrath of this beast will be directed against the materialistic nations of the West. This judgment against the West will bring doom because they refuse to believe in Islam.[7]

SURAH:

Qur'an 27:16-17: "And Solomon was David's heir, and he said: O men, we have been taught the speech of birds, and we have been granted of all things. Surely this is manifest grace. And his hosts [armies] of the Jinn and the men and the birds were gathered to Solomon, and they were formed into groups [battle order]."

Qur'an 27:38-39: "He [Solomon] said: O Chiefs, which of you can bring me her throne before they come to me in submission? One audacious among the Jinn said: I will bring it to thee before thou rise up from thy place; and surely I am strong, trusty for it."

Qur'an 27:43-44: "And that which she worshipped besides Allah prevented her; for she was of a disbelieving people [...] She said: My Lord, surely I have wronged myself, and I submit with Solomon to Allah, the Lord of the worlds."

Qur'an 27:76: "Surely this Qur'an declares to the Children of Israel most of that wherein [which] they differ [disregard]."

Qur'an 27:82: "And when the word comes to pass [is fulfilled] against them, We shall bring forth for them a creature [beast] from the earth that will speak to them, because people [mankind] did not believe in Our messages [revelations]."

SUNNAH:

Bukhari:V9B87N127: "The Prophet said, 'I have been given the keys of eloquent speech and given victory with awe [terror] cast into the hearts of the enemy, and while I was sleeping last night, the keys of the treasures of the earth were brought to me till they were put into my hand.' [...]"

SUMMATION:

IL: Just as the Jinn were subjected to the previous prophets and so they were also subordinate to Muhammad. These beings and birds as well, aided the previous prophets. Therefore, they were also at the service of Muhammad. The example illustrated how Solomon predicted what would happen concerning the unbelieving Queen. The Jinn offered to bring her to Solomon, but Solomon knew and rightly predicted she would submit to Allah. Despite the revelation of this truth, the Children of Israel still chose not to believe it. When these words are fulfilled at the end, Allah, Muhammad, and the Jinn, will bring forth the Great Beast. The end time Beast, the consuming empire, will come forth because the whole world refuses to accept Islam.

WA: The accounts given here concerning Solomon, Jinn, birds, Islam, and Allah, do not appear in the Jewish Tenakh. What does appear is the Queen of Sheba who was most impressed with Solomon's wisdom. What was not quoted in the Qur'anic account was her adoration for Yahveh...not Allah. The Queen of Sheba said, 'Blessed is Yahveh your God which delighted in you, to set you on the throne of Israel: because Yahveh loved Israel forever, therefore he made you king to do judgment and justice' (1 Kings 10:9).

Most people in the West will not accept what Muhammad preached, so according to Allah, the Islamic Beast must come upon the world. For the Mahdi/Caliphate empire to emerge, they must sway the masses and be given the authority to use terror, which will insure their victory.

"The Spider"

616 AD

SCRIPTURE:

Qur'an 29:28-29, 46

Dawud:B32N4092

PREFACE:

False beliefs, woven like a spider's web, will not stand the test of time. Afflictions and trials must be suffered before the onset of triumph. Thus, suffering and persecution are necessary. Children are told to yield to their parents except if the parents are teaching them false religion. The previous prophets were all displayed as suffering before their final victory. The words of the Qur'an are promised to purify and transform all those who follow it. The Muslim persecutors will be judged. Those who strive hard in Islam through jihad, are guided in Allah's way and succeed.[8]

SURAH:

Qur'an 29:28-29: "And We sent Lot, when he said to his people: Surely you are guilty of an abomination [you commit lewdness] like none of the nations has done before you. Do you come to males [commit sodomy], and commit robbery on the highway [rob travelers], and commit evil deeds in your assemblies? But the answer of his people was only that they said: Bring on us Allah's chastisement [doom], if thou art truthful."

Qur'an 29:46: "And argue not with the People of the Book except by what is best, save such of them as act unjustly. But say [Muhammad]: We believe in that which has been revealed to us and revealed to you, and our God (Allah) and your God (Allah) is One, and to Him we submit [ourselves]."

SUNNAH:

Dawud:B32N4092: "Asma, daughter of Abu Bakr, entered upon the Apostle of Allah wearing thin clothes. The Apostle of Allah turned his attention from her. He [Muhammad] said, 'O Asma, when a woman reaches the age of menstruation, it does not suit her that she displays parts of her body except [...] her face and hands.'"

SUMMATION:

IL: Muhammad had to deal with the vile Quraysh like the prophet Lot dealt with the evil of his day. All the prophets suffered. Since Muhammad brought the fullness of Allah's religion, Allah instructed the Prophet on how to respond when the People of the Book refused to accept the Islamic truth.[(9)] The truth is they should submit because the destiny of the world is an Islamic destiny. Part of this truth is the requirement for women to cover all but their face and hands.

WA: Allah and Muhammad did not want their modest amount of early followers to lose heart. The message to children suggested that children do not have to listen to parents if their parents are not Muslims. Muslims are told to trust in the words of the Qur'an. The Qur'an tells Muslims in the present that ancient prophets prayed in the name of Allah. This is to make the case that they understood the concept of God in an Islamic context. Another reason why Muslims are told not to argue with Christians and Jews is because if Muslims argue religion, there would be a chance they could be persuaded to change their mind about Islam. Lastly, Muhammad's clothing requirement concerning women is about as un-Western as one can imagine. What is really being said is women have no say in such matters. The Bible told women to dress modestly. There is no stipulation that women must be totally hidden.

QUR'AN 30

"The Romans"

616 AD

SCRIPTURE:

Qur'an 30:28-30

Bukhari:V2B23N441

PREFACE:

From 613-616 AD, the Persians were making gains against the Byzantines in the Levant and North Africa. Arabian polytheists saw this as a victory over monotheism. Muhammad asserted that his theocracy would triumph. In 624 AD, the Byzantines beat back the Persians and the Muslims were victorious at Badr. Allah's law of consequences was then revealed which is the key to the establishment of Allah's earthly reign. Therefore, the rise of Islam is foretold in this surah because it appeals to the nature of man. Muslims are promised by Allah that, no matter the odds against Muslims, Islam will triumph. The eventual conquest of Islam will result in the submission of all religions including the religion of the Romans. The spreading faith of Islam will be aided by dissimulating Muslims.[(10)]

SURAH:

Qur'an 30:28-30: "He sets forth to you a parable relating to yourselves. Have you among those whom your right hands possess [slave girls] partners in that which We have provided you with, so that with respect to it you are alike — you fear them as you fear each other? Thus do We make the messages clear for a people who understand. Nay, those who are unjust follow their low desires [lusts] without any knowledge; so who can guide him guide him whom Allah leaves in error [has sent astray]? And for they shall have no helpers. So set thy [Muhammad] your face for [towards] religion [of pure Islamic Monotheism; *Hanifa*, worship none but Allah Alone; and Allah's *Fitrah*, Allah's Islamic Monotheism], being upright, the nature made by Allah in [with] which He has created men. There is no altering Allah's creation [*Khalqillâh*, i.e., the Religion of Allah, Islamic Monotheism]. That is the right [straight] religion — but most of people know not."

SUNNAH:

Bukhari V2B23N441: "Every child is born [into the] true faith of Islam (i.e., to worship none but Allah alone) but [it is] his parents who convert him to Judaism or Christianity [...]"

SUMMATION:

IL: Allah provides additional partners for Muslims, but only as they command new territory for Allah's Kingdom. They are promised the reward of slave girls from among the subjugated. Those who do not understand or object to this divine command are led astray by Allah. As for the Prophet, Allah wanted him to focus on pure Islam, through which the world was created. Islam is the one straight religion which cannot change or be changed. The unbeliever cannot understand Islam.

WA: Allah's law of consequences is the key to Allah's reign on earth because it appeals to human nature. This is different from the Christian concept which teaches that the nature of mankind is inherently sinful. Muslims are told that the acceptance of Allah's law which appeals to human nature will lead Muslims to the ultimate victory. The ultimate victory is the victory over Christianity. This surah proved that the pure religion of Islam included being rewarded with slave girls who are bought or acquired after an Islamic conquest. Finally, in the hadith, the concept of reversion is introduced. Muslims believe that all people were born as Muslims, but the blame for why all people are not Muslims rests primarily with non-Muslim parents.

QUR'AN 31

"Luqmān"

616 AD

SCRIPTURE:

Qur'an 31:13, 23-24, 30

Bukhari:V5B59N727

PREFACE:

Luqman is described in this surah as an Ethiopian slave who possessed the insight and wisdom of Aesop. Therefore, he illuminated Islam. He was revered by Arabs but unknown in the Jewish scriptures.[11]

SURAH:

Qur'an 31:13: "[…] Luqman said to his son, while he admonished him: O my son, ascribe no partner to Allah. Surely ascribing partners to Him is a grievous iniquity."

Qur'an 31:23-24: "And whoever disbelieves, let not his [their] disbelief grieve thee […]. We give them to enjoy a little, then We will drive them to a severe chastisement."

Qur'an 31:30: "[…] Allah is the truth, and that which they call upon besides Him is falsehood, and that Allah is the High, the Great."

SUNNAH:

Bukhari:V5B59N727: "[Muhammad said], 'Allah's curse be on Jews and Christians.'"

SUMMATION:

IL: Islam's truth was revealed by Allah to an Ethiopian slave who knew it was a grievous sin to make any man or a prophet equal with Allah. Allah told the Muslims not to lose heart when the polytheists, Christians, and Jews   oppose the Islamic perspective. It may seem like others are winning but they will be punished in hell. Everything except Islam is false.

WA: Allah refers to the Torah and Gospel. Often the Qur'an tells Muslims these books have significance. It is clear those who believe that Jesus is the Son of God are headed for an Islamic hell. Muslims are told how Christians will be punished. Westerners must understand, from an Islamic Literalist point of view, all false doctrine that contradicts Islam must be punished. Muhammad then exclaimed that those who follow the Torah and Gospel are cursed.

QUR'AN 32

"The Adoration"

616 AD

SCRIPTURE:

Qur'an 32:2-3, 20

Bukhari:V4B52N220

PREFACE:

The Muslims are told to prostate themselves in adoration when the Qur'an is recited. Not only will Islam triumph and be established, but Allah assures that those opposing Islam will be punished in this life.[12]

SURAH:

Qur'an 32:2-3: "The revelation of the Book [Qur'an], there is no doubt in it, [for] it is from the Lord of the worlds. Or do they say: He has forged it? Nay, it is the Truth from thy Lord that thou mayest warn a people to whom no warner has come before thee that they may walk aright [upright]."

Qur'an 32:20: "And as for those who transgress, their refuge is the Fire. Whenever they desire to go forth from it [leave it], they are brought back into it, and it is said to them: Taste the punishment of the Fire, which you called a lie."

SUNNAH:

Bukhari:V4B52N220: "Allah's Apostle said, 'I have been sent with the shortest expressions bearing the widest meanings, and I have been made victorious with *terror* [emphasis added], and while I was sleeping, the keys of the treasures of the world were brought to me and put in my hand.'"

SUMMATION:

IL: Muslims prostrate at the reading of the Qur'an because it is from the Lord of the Worlds. This surah was another response to the Quraysh who continued to call the Qur'an a forgery. Hell-fire is promised to anyone who calls the Qur'an a lie. The keys of Islam are the laws of consequence found in the Qur'an. The victory of the Prophet over the Quraysh was assured.

WA: It should be understood at this point that Islamic Literalists have no intention of accommodation or compromise when the Islamic texts are cited. In verse 20, who or what kind of entity would taunt those burning in hell? This does not sound like the Creator of the universe. It sounds more like Muhammad who wanted to gloat over his persecutors getting what they deserved. Why? This was the same Muhammad who boasted that he was made victorious with terror. This means that terror will always be part of conflict when Muslim literalists are at odds with another civilization.

QUR'AN 34

"The Saba"

617 AD

SCRIPTURE:

Qur'an 34:12, 28, 50,

Bukhari:V9B92N384

PREFACE:

A flood in Yemen was contrasted with those who live in luxury. This displayed how non-believers with wealth may lose it. It is a warning to nations that an easy life fosters evil, which brings decay and ruin. Judgment will overtake evil people and nations. The deniers of Islam will be punished and their deities will not be able to aid them.[13]

SURAH:

Qur'an 34:12: "And We made the wind subservient to Solomon; it made a month's journey in the morning and a month's journey in the evening; and We made a fountain of molten brass to flow for him. And of the Jinn there were those who worked before him by the command of his Lord. And whoever turned aside from Our command from among them, We made to taste of the chastisement [punishment] of burning [hell]."

Qur'an 34:28: "And We have not sent thee as a bearer of good news and as a warner to all mankind, but most men know not [are ignorant]."

Qur'an 34:50: "[Muhammad says]: If I err [am in error], I err [am in error] only to my own loss; and if I go aright [am right], it is because of what my Lord reveals to me. Surely He is Hearing, [and] Nigh [near]."

SUNNAH:

Bukhari:V9B92N384: "Allah's Apostle said, 'All my followers will enter paradise except those who refuse' They said, 'O Allah's Apostle! Who will refuse?' He said, 'Whoever obeys me will enter Paradise, and whoever disobeys me is the one who refuses.'"

SUMMATION:

IL: Allah warns that living in luxury brings decay and ruin. Those who deny Islam are evil. The Quraysh were still not heeding Muhammad's message. Since Muhammad only revealed what Allah told him, Muhammad was right when he said whoever obeyed him would enter paradise and whoever disobeyed him would not enter it.

WA: Allah's revelation was, again, meant to bolster the Muslims so they would not lose heart in the face of Quraysh opposition. The Quraysh were perceived as living in luxury while they persecuted Muhammad so they were condemned. The Qur'an then speaks of those who are subservient to the Lord. In this case they are the Jinn. When the phrase, "Lord of the Worlds", is used for Allah, it means the Lord of above and below. This is how the Jinn, who are not holy, work by the command of Allah. This Qur'anic revelation was for the Quraysh and for the world. Therefore, in the long term if Muhammad's words, as inspired in the Qur'an, are not true it is to his loss as found in the Qur'an. If he is correct, it is because Allah is God. Muhammad said that he must be obeyed for one to enter Paradise. In contrast Jesus said, 'I am the way, the truth, and the life. No one can come to the Father but by me.'[14] Jesus and Muhammad cannot both be right. If Muhammad is not correct, then he is as the Qur'an states, 'I am in error to my own loss.'

QUR'AN 35

"The Originator"

617 AD

SCRIPTURE:

Qur'an 35:24, 36

Bukhari:V9B83N17

PREFACE:

The heavens and the earth sweep away the old ways. Therefore, a new generation of Muslims must be raised up to promote the truth of Islam. For those who promote Islam, Allah promises peace, safety, success, and abundance either in this life or the next. Those who choose evil will be punished.[15]

SURAH:

Qur'an 35:24: "Surely We have sent thee with the Truth as a bearer of good news and a warner. And there is not a people but a warner has gone among them [there is not a people that does not have a warner]."

Qur'an 35:36: "And those who disbelieve, for them is [the] Fire of hell; it is not finished with them so that they should die, nor is chastisement thereof lightened to them [will not ease up on them]. Thus We deal retribution on every ungrateful one."

SUNNAH:

Bukhari:V9B83N17: "Allah's Apostle said, 'The blood of a Muslim who confesses that none has the right to be worshipped but Allah and that I am His apostle, cannot be shed *except* [emphasis added] in three cases: In Qisas [retaliation] for murder [of another Muslim], a married person who commits illegal sexual intercourse, and the one who reverts from Islam [apostatizes] and leaves the Muslims."

SUMMATION:

IL: Muhammad was chosen for the Arabs first and for the world second. Those who do not choose to follow the words of Muhammad will be punished because they are evil. That punishment will occur in this life and the life to come. There will be no mercy for them. Since the infidels are damned, a Muslim can never be killed by a Muslim for killing one of these disbelievers. If a Muslim kills a Muslim, then he can be killed. A Muslim can also be killed for sleeping with the spouse of another Muslim and a Muslim should be killed if that Muslim leaves Islam.

WA: For those who promote Islam, peace, safety, success, and abundance are promised. This is an inducement to promote Islam but it is not always true. It may be true for some but not true for others. Certainly, the Islamic world is not a place of peace, safety, and success. It is only a place of abundance for some who Muslim literalists call corrupt. In addition to being condemned to hell in every surah in the Qur'an, non-Muslim westerners should understand the following: (1) In the Islamic world, non-Muslims are not viewed as equal to Muslims. This is why a Muslim cannot be killed for killing non-Muslims; (2) If a Muslim has sex with the wife of a non-Muslim, there is no reason for them to be killed; and (3) Being born a Muslim is the will of Allah, so a Muslim can be killed if they decide that Islam is not the truth.[16]

QUR'AN 36

"Yā Sin"

617 AD

SCRIPTURE:

Qur'an 36:9, 37-41

Musnad:N25636

PREFACE:

This revelation was given for Muslims to recite in times of adversity, illness, fasting, and death. People can attain perfection through contact with the perfect man Muhammad. This can give life to a dead humanity. The promise of the resurrection should prove sufficient to bring real transformation as Muslims seek to attain Muhammad's perfection.[17]

SURAH:

Qur'an 36:9: "And We have set a barrier before them and a barrier behind them thus, We have covered them, so that they see not."

Qur'an 36:37-41: "And a sign to them is the night: We draw forth from the day, then lo! [T]hey are in darkness; and the sun moves on to its destination. That is the ordinance of the Mighty, the Knower. And the moon, We have ordained for it stages till it becomes again as an old dry palm-branch. Neither is it for the sun to overtake the moon, nor can the night outstrip the day. And all float on in an orbit. And a sign to them is that We bear their offspring in the laden ship.

SUNNAH:

Musnad:N25636: "Muhammad looked at a baby named Um Habiba while she was nursing and said, 'If she grows up while I am still alive, I will marry her.'"

SUMMATION:

IL: The rejection of Muhammad by the Quraysh sealed their eternal fate. These were the people of the night, who in their eternal darkness will encounter the symbol of Islam...the moon in its stages. For in the night, the sun cannot overtake the moon.

WA: Muslims are told through their trials to strive for the perfection of the perfect man, Muhammad. Following Muhammad gives life to humanity. Since Muhammad was aware that Allah considered him the perfect man, what he thought and wanted to do must also be perfect. This leads to some instances that are not acceptable in the western world. In a future hadith, Muhammad looked at a baby while the female baby was nursing and declared his desire to marry her when she grew up. First, this desire in a western society would not be acceptable. Second, no consideration was given to the female. Why would a young girl want to marry a very old man? In the end, to the most perfect man that ever lived, the young girl's feelings, in this regard, were not considered.[18]

QUR'AN 37

"Those Ranging In Ranks"

617 AD

SCRIPTURE:

Qur'an 37:6-9, 19-23, 33-38, 42-49, 62-68, 102-113

Muslim:B8C19N3364

PREFACE:

Muhammad's coming coincided with a comet and many meteors. This was according to the revealing angel Gabriel.[19]

SURAH:

Qur'an 37:6-9: "Surely We have adorned the lower heaven with an adornment, the stars, and there is a safeguard against every rebellious devil. They cannot listen to the exalted assembly and they are reproached from every side, driven off; and for them is a perpetual chastisement."

Qur'an 37:19-23: "So it will be but one cry, when lo! [T]hey will see. And they will say: O woe to us! This is the day of Requital [day of doom] which you called a lie. Gather together those who did wrong [assemble the wrongdoers] and their associates [wives] and what they worshipped besides Allah, then lead them to the way to hell."

Qur'an 37:33-38: "So, that day they will sharers in the chastisement [penalty of doom]. Thus do We deal with the guilty [non-Muslims]. They indeed were arrogant, when it was said to them: There is no god but Allah; and [they] said: Shall we should give up our gods for a mad insane and possessed] poet. Nay, he has brought the Truth and [he] verifies the messengers [the Prophets]. Surely you will taste the painful chastisement."

Qur'an 37:42-49: "For them is a known sustenance: Fruits. And they are [will be] honored, in Gardens of delight, on thrones, facing each other. A bowl of running water will be made to go around them, white, delicious to those who drink. It deprives not of reason, nor are they exhausted therewith. And with them are those modest in gaze, having beautiful eyes, as if they were eyes carefully protected."

Qur'an 37:62-68: "Is this the entertainment or the tree of Zaqqum [a foul smelling tree with bitter leaves]. Surely We have made it a trial for the wrongdoers. It is a tree that grows in the bottom of hell — its produce is as it were heads of serpents. Then truly they [the damned] will eat of it and fill their bellies with it. Then surely they shall have after it [to wash it down] a drink of boiling water. Then their return is surely to the flaming Fire."

Qur'an 37:102-113: "But when he [Ishmael] became of age to work with him [Abraham] he said: O my son, I have seen in a dream that I should sacrifice thee: so consider what thou seest. He [Ishmael] said: O my father, do as thou art commanded: if Allah please [permits], thou wilt find me patient. So when they both submitted [to Islam] and he had thrown them down upon his forehead, and We called out to him, saying: O Abraham, thou hast indeed fulfilled the vision. Thus do We reward the doers of good. Surely this is a manifest trial. And We ransomed him [Ishmael] with a great sacrifice. [...] Peace be to Abraham! [...] Surely he was one of Our believing servants. And We gave him the good news [afterwards] of Isaac, a prophet, a righteous one. And We blessed him and Isaac. And of their offspring [the Jews] some are doers of good, but some are clearly unjust to themselves." [They fraudulently altered Genesis 22:1-18]

SUNNAH:

Muslim:B8C19N3364: "[...] the Jews used to say that when one comes to one's wife through the vagina, but being on her back, and she becomes pregnant, the child [will have] a squint [be cross-eyed]."

SUMMATION:

IL: Those who ridicule Allah and believe that Muhammad was an insane possessed poet shall be thrown into the flaming fire. At the bottom of hell, they will eat from a foul smelling tree that produces demons with heads like snakes. What they consume will be washed down with boiling water.

Also, the Qur'an corrects the errors of the promise made in Genesis 22:1-18 by naming Ishmael, not Isaac, as the object of Abrahams sacrifice. Isaac's seed, the Jews, can be doers of good, but most are unjust. The unjust Jews never accepted Islam.[20] To prove this; they spoke falsehood in the hadith concerning how a child gets to be a certain way.

WA: In the Qur'an, Allah revealed that stars in outer space can protect the world from rebellious devils. Allah again spoke of devils and hell. Why does it seem that Allah is incapable of speaking kind things, even occasionally? To describe hell and its torments in such detail on a constant basis, in the very least, alludes to a deep hatred of these people.

In the story concerning Ishmael, Allah/Muhammad realized that Muhammad must be able to prove that he came from the proper blood line. Since Muhammad was a descendent of Ishmael, the point had to be made for People of the Book who disagree that the Jews altered Genesis 22 to steal the divine birthright from the Arabs.[21] The hadith claimed that Jews said certain things about procreation. This was quoted for two reasons: (1) to ridicule them; or (2) to discredit them.

QUR'AN 39

"The Companies"

617 AD

SCRIPTURE:

Qur'an 39:4, 15-16, 28, 71

Bukhari:V1B12N749

PREFACE:

Two classes of people are revealed in this surah: the believers and the disbelievers. This is the precursor to the future concept of the *Dar al-Islam/Salam* (House of Islam/Peace) and the *Dar al-Harb* (House of War).[22] Those that reject Islam are evil. Allah is merciful and can show mercy to the disbeliever if he chooses. Ultimately, everyone will get what they deserve.[23]

SURAH:

Qur'an 39:4: "If Allah decided to take a son to Himself, He could have chosen those He pleased out of those whom He created — Glory be to Him! He is Allah, the One, the Subduer of all."

Qur'an 39:15-16: "Serve then what you will besides Him. Say: The losers surely are those who lose themselves and their people in the day of Resurrection. Now surely that is the manifest loss. They shall have coverings of fire above them and coverings beneath them. With that Allah makes His servants to fear; so keep your duty to Me, O My servants."

Qur'an 39:28: "An Arabic Qur'an without any crookedness, [so] that they may guard against evil."

Qur'an 39:71: "And those who disbelieve [infidels] are driven to hell in companies [groups]; until, when they come to it, its doors are opened, and its keepers of it [will] say to them: Did not there come to you messengers from among you reciting to you the messages of your Lord and warning you of the meeting of this day to you? They [will] say: Yea. [Therefore,] the word of punishment [will be] proved true against the disbelievers [infidels]."

SUNNAH:

Bukhari:V1B12N749: "Allah's Apostle said, 'Say "Amen" when the Imam says "not the path of those who earn Your anger (such as Jews) nor of those who go astray (such as Christians); all the past sins of the person whose saying (of Amen) coincides with that of the angels, will be forgiven."'"

SUMMATION:

IL: Muslims reside in the *Dar al-Salam* ("House of Peace") or *Dar al-Islam* ("House of Islam"). The infidel nations reside in *Dar al-Harb* ("House of War").[24] Allah shows mercy to the infidels to the extent that they will come to Islam. However, those who insist otherwise—those that believe Jesus is the Son of God—will be covered in fire. Allah states this for the benefit of Muslims so they will continue to fear Allah and continue to be his servants/slaves. Allah's slaves are assured by Allah's promise that the Qur'an is without flaw. The infidels have no excuse because the Prophet came to all mankind, and those who reject his warning are condemned. Muslims must avoid the Jews and Christians because the People of the Book have many flaws. Lastly, the past sins of Muslims will be forgiven whenever their "amen" coincides with the "amen" of the angels.

WA: The Qur'anic concept of separating the world into the House of War and the House of Islam ensures that war and strife will always be present. [25] Since the Qur'an states those who reject Islam are evil, any chance of goodwill and peace with these Muslim literalists is not possible. The attack on western religion is unrelenting. Allah is intent on dethroning the one referred to in the New Covenant as the King of Kings. In all of this, Muslims must believe that the Qur'an is perfect. One can never know that for sure unless the Qur'an is put under scrutiny. The Qur'anic theme is consistent that people are judged according to the group in which they belong. Jews, Christians and Polytheists are not part of Allah's religious group. Finally, Muslims learn in the hadith that Jews earn Allah's anger and Christians guide people astray.

QUR'AN 41

"Hā Mim"

617 AD

SCRIPTURE:

Qur'an 41:3, 19, 44

Bukhari:V3B49N857

PREFACE:

This revelation gives moral and spiritual aid which revives the spiritually dead. If the Prophet's warnings are not heeded then doom is assured. As Islam continued to spread throughout the region, the truth of the straight path became evident.[26]

SURAH:

Qur'an 41:3: "A Book of which the verses are made plain, an Arabic Qur'an for a people who know."

Qur'an 41:19: "And the day when the enemies of Allah are gathered to the fire, they will be formed into groups."

Qur'an 41:44: "And if We had made [...] a Qur'an in a foreign tongue, they would have said: Why have not its messages been made clear? What! [A] foreign tongue and an Arab! Say: It is to those who believe [it is] a guidance and a healing, and those who believe not, there is deafness in their ears and it is obscure to them. [...]"

SUNNAH:

Bukhari:V3B49N857: "[Allah's Apostle said,] 'He who makes peace between the people by inventing good information or saying good things, is not a liar.'"

SUMMATION:

IL: Muslims can always act in confidence because they are assured the Qur'an gives guidance.[27] It is no accident the Qur'an was revealed in Arabic. Muslims are selected by Allah and will always know their enemies will be thrown into hell with groups of people who are just like them.

WA: For a westerner, it is not evident how Islam provides moral and spiritual aid. The message being conveyed is: Listen to me or else! It is not hard for a westerner to understand that Muhammad, an Arab, received revelation from his god who speaks and prefers Arabic. The hadith that is cited has nothing to do with peace between Muslims and non-Muslims. The hadith was given to Muslims who are told to make peace with other Muslims by inventing information or by being very complementary. The intent of the revelation is to make peace between Muslims; and thus avoid that which is considered *haram* ("a sin").

"The Counsel"

617 AD

SCRIPTURE:

Qur'an 42:7, 13, 44, 46

Bukhari:V7B63N190

PREFACE:

Allah's mercy was shown by sending Muhammad as a Warner to those who disbelieved. Allah's angels solicit forgiveness for men. Allah decrees that no nation will be destroyed unjustly. The unjust will be given respite, so Muslims must be patient. Those who do not follow the Qur'an will find themselves in evil plight.[28]

SURAH:

Qur'an 42:7: "And thus We have revealed to thee an Arabic Qur'an, that thou mayest warn the mother-town [Mecca] and those around it, and give them warning of the day of gathering [the Resurrection] wherein is no doubt [it *will* happen]. A party [some] will be in the Garden and another party [others] in the burning Fire."

Qur'an 42:13: "He has made plain to you the religion which He enjoined upon [gave to] Noah and which We have revealed to thee, and which We enjoined on [gave to] Abraham and Moses and Jesus — to establish religion and not be divided therein [...]. Allah chooses for Himself whom He pleases, and guides to Himself him [anyone] who turns to Him."

Qur'an 42:44: "And he whom Allah leaves in error, has no friend after Him. And thou wil[l] see the iniquitous [see those who commit iniquity], when they see the chastisement [on the day of doom], saying: Is there any way to return?"

Qur'an 42:46: "And they will have no friends to help them besides Allah. And He who Allah leaves in error cannot find a way [out]."

SUNNAH:

Bukhari:V7B63N190: "A man divorced his wife and she married another man who proved to be impotent and divorced her. She could not get her satisfaction from him, and after a while he divorced her. Then she came to the Prophet and said, 'O Allah's Apostle! My first husband divorced me and then I married another man who entered upon me to consummate his marriage but he proved to be impotent and did not approach me except once during which he benefited nothing from me. Can I remarry my first husband in this case?' Allah's Apostle said, 'It is unlawful to marry your first husband till the other husband consummates his marriage with you.'"

SUMMATION:

IL: The mercy that Islam shows to non-believers is the Prophet Muhammad. Those nations who refuse to submit will be destroyed through Allah's justice. The primary objective of the Prophet was to bring Islam to the Quraysh at Mecca. This is the reason why the Qur'an was revealed in Arabic. Once Islam is introduced to society and rejected, those people who have no interest in the truth will most assuredly be doomed. This is accurate because Islam was revealed to Noah, Abraham, Moses, and Jesus. Allah guides the Muslims and leaves the infidels in error. They will find their doom with no recourse.

WA: Mecca became the mother-town in the Qur'an. It is the mother-town of Muhammad's Islam, but as for all the righteous prophets who lived before him in history, Mecca was not mentioned or was a non-issue. The Islamic argument has always been that the prophets of old, including Jesus, were all Muslims because Allah introduced Islam to them. Only to the extent that Noah, Abraham, Moses, and Jesus warned the people of their day can this be said. The five pillars of Islam: (1) *Shahada* ("Witness"); (2) *Salat* ("Islamic prayer"); (3) *Zakat* ("Alms tax"); (4) *Sawm* ("Fasting during Ramadan"); and (5) *Hajj* ("Pilgrimage to Mecca"), are not taught in the biblical text.[29] Also, other terms such as; Allah, Jihad, Ijtihad, Isnad, and other Arabic words more familiar to Muslims, were not spoken or taught in the Judeo-Christian scriptures by any of the biblical prophets. Allah's Qur'an makes the point that infidels will be full of regret before they are thrown into hell. Perhaps, one of the statements these damned souls will mention to Allah and Muhammad will be something like this: 'If we perceived love, holiness, and righteousness in your Qur'an and in the actions of your Prophet, we might have followed you.' An Atheist, Agnostic, Christian, Jew, Hindu, and Buddhist could all ask this question. According to the Islamic texts they would all receive the same sentence.

QUR'AN 43

"Gold"

617 AD

SCRIPTURE:

Quran 43:3-4, 30-31, 59, 74, 81

Bukhari:V5B58N266

PREFACE:

Allah states that worldly things keep people from the truth. Allah wants righteous deeds from men. This revelation is a favor from Allah. Allah described why he did not use people with wealth as prophets. The truth of the Qur'an will cause the Muslim nation to rise. Those who reject the message will regret their deeds. Arab idolaters justify their idolatry based on the Christian doctrine of the divinity of Jesus. Allah rejects Polytheism along with the Christian doctrine.[30]

SURAH:

Qur'an 43:3-4: "Surely We have made it an Arabic Qur'an that you may understand. And it is in the Original of the Book [*Umm al-Kitab* ("Mother of the Book")] with Us, truly elevated, full of wisdom."

Qur'an 43:30-31: "And when the Truth came to them they said: This is enchantment [sorcery], and we are disbelievers in it [we don't believe this]. And they say: Why was not this Qur'an revealed to a man of importance in the two towns [Mecca and Ta'if]?"

Qur'an 43:59: "He [Jesus] was naught [nothing] but a servant [slave] on

174   *The Dawn of Islamic Literalism*

whom We bestowed favor and We made him an example for the Children of Israel."

Qur'an 43:74: "Surely the guilty will abide in the chastisement of hell."

Qur'an 43:81: "[…] The Beneficent has no son […]"

SUNNAH:

Bukhari:V5B58N266: "[…] Uthman [bin Maz'un] fell ill and I nursed him till he died, and we covered him with his clothes. Then the Prophet came to us and I (addressing the dead body) said, 'O Abu As-Sa'ib, may Allah's Mercy be on you! I bear witness that Allah has honored you.' On that the Prophet said, 'How do you know that Allah has honored him?' I replied, 'I do not know. May my father and my mother be sacrificed for you, O Allah's Apostle! But who else is worthy of it (if not Uthman)?' He said, 'As to him, by Allah, death has overtaken him, and I hope the best for him. By Allah, though I am the Apostle of Allah, *yet I do not know what Allah will do to me* [Emphasis added].' By Allah, I will never assert the piety of anyone after him. That made me sad, and when I slept I saw in a dream a flowing stream for Uthman bin Maz'un. I went to Allah's Apostle and told him of it. He remarked, 'That symbolizes his (good) deeds.'"

SUMMATION:

IL: The responsibility of unbelief among the Arabs falls on the Christians who stubbornly worship the Prophet Jesus. This gave justification to the Quraysh to practice idolatry. Here it is revealed that the pure Qur'an has always existed with Allah. Allah made an Arabic Qur'an and revealed it on earth. However, this revelation was not to the liking of the Quraysh, because they did not approve of their brother Muhammad. They did not believe, because the Christian error permitted them to persist in their wrong belief. Jesus was Allah's slave and those who refuse to see this will surely be punished. Allah promises his slaves that He has no son.

WA: Up through this chronology the unbelief of the Quraysh has been the main theme in the Meccan surahs. For the first time outright condemnation of Christianity has come front and center. This is true because Muslims believe the Qur'an has always existed in heaven with Allah. This becomes problematic from a western perspective. Why would the Mother of the Book exist in the far distant past, and include sayings to Muhammad, commentary on events in the 7th century AD to include condemnation of polytheists, Christians, and Jews, when none of them would exist until the far distant future?

Given the Qur'an has anointed Muhammad as Allah's Prophet, how are we to interpret the following hadith by Bukhari? Muhammad is the Prophet of Islam, yet was unsure if Uthman was going to paradise. Also, in a bit of a shocker, Muhammad was not sure what Allah would do with him. He had faithfully done as Allah commanded yet Muhammad did not speak with certainty in terms of his eternal salvation. In this hadith, the person Muhammad was speaking to was behaving more prophet-like than the Prophet of Islam.

QUR'AN 44

"The Drought"

617 AD

SCRIPTURE:

Qur'an 44:13-14, 16, 47-48, 54

Muslim:B20C29N4635

PREFACE:

Punishment awaits those who do not repent. As for the opponents of Islam they all shall meet their doom. Before the promised demise of Islam's opponents, it may become necessary for some Muslims to give their lives for the assurance of paradise.[31]

SURAH:

Qur'an 44:13-14: "When will they be reminded? And a Messenger has indeed come [to them] making clear; yet they turned away from him and said: One taught by others a madman!

Qur'an 44:16: "On the day when We seize them with the most violent seizing; surely We will exact retribution."

Qur'an 44:47-48: "Seize him, then drag him into the midst of hell; then pour on his head the torment of boiling water."

Qur'an 44:54: "Thus shall it be. And We shall join [wed] them to pure, beautiful ones [Houris]."

SUNNAH:

Muslim:B20C29N4635: "The Prophet said: 'Nobody who enters Paradise wants [to] return even if he were offered everything on earth except the martyr who will desire to return and ten times be killed for the sake of the great honor that has been bestowed on him.'"

SUMMATION:

IL: Allah knew the struggle against the unbelief of the polytheists, Christians, and Jews would be difficult. At this juncture he began to prepare the Muslims for sacrifice, to include the possible loss of their lives. Those who ridiculed Allah's Prophet will be seized and dragged into hell drenched in boiling water. However, the Shahid will forever be married to the houris of paradise.

WA: Not only is the issue of martyrdom sanctioned in the Qur'an, but the hadith is telling Muslims to lose their lives not once, but over and over again. It is not hard to see that Muslims who really believe this are willing to forfeit all of their tomorrows for Allah's promise and Muhammad's assertion. We must encourage Muslims to think. If none of this is true then untold numbers of Muslims have thrown their lives away.

QUR'AN 45

"The Kneeling"

617 AD

SCRIPTURE:

Qur'an 7-11, 14

Bukhari:V6B60N8, V6B60N662

PREFACE:

Despite signs, the kuffar reject Islam and those who reject it will be conquered. Judgment comes to all who reject Islam. The doom of the disbelievers is certain. In order for Islam to conquer, abrogating verses were reinforced to grant Muslims the permission for physical conquest of the unbelievers.[32]

SURAH:

Qur'an 45:7-11: "Woe to every sinful liar! Who hears the messages of Allah recited to him then persists in haughtiness, as though he had not heard them. So announce to him a painful chastisement. And when he comes to know of any of Our messages, he takes them [Our messages] for a jest [joke]. For such [people] there is an abasing chastisement. In front of them is hell, and that which they have earned [all of their wealth] will avail them naught [cannot save them], nor those whom they take for protectors besides Allah, and for them is a grievous chastisement. This is guidance; and those who disbelieve in the messages of their Lord, for them is a painful punishment of an evil kind."

Qur'an 45:14: "Tell those who believe to forgive those who fear not the days of Allah that He may reward a people for what they earn."

SUNNAH:

Bukhari:V6B60N8: "Umar said, 'Our best Qur'an reciter is Ubai. And in spite of this, we leave out some of his statements because Allah's Apostle himself said, "Whatever verse or revelation We abrogate or cause to be forgotten We bring a better one.""

Bukhari:V6B60N662: "Allah's Apostle said, 'Some eloquent speech is as effective as magic.'"

SUMMATION:

IL: Through the Prophet, Allah made the truth of Islam obvious to the unbelievers. Because they treat Allah's words as a joke, nothing will save them from the harsh hell to come. Evil will visit them in this life and in the next. Verse 14 applies to Muslims who should forgive other Muslims who are, at times, not grateful for what Allah has done for them. When Muslims forgive other Muslims it is to their credit and they will be rewarded.

WA: The doctrine of Abrogation was explained to Muhammad's companions. Some Qur'anic verses were meant to be forgotten. This is what the literalists do. They disregard earlier verses that are not as toxic to non-Muslims. Unfortunately, the better verses are not actually better verses for non-Muslims. As far as pitching or selling these verses to other Muslims, Muhammad knew that he was a master of speech and a motivator who could convince Islamic converts to do what no one would normally do. With this capability of eloquent speech, death and killing became sanctified in Islam.

QUR'AN 40

"The Believer"

618 AD

SCRIPTURE:

Qur'an 40:2-6, 10-12, 18, 21, 33-35, 49-50, 53, 67, 70-72

Bukhari:V5B57N27; Ishaq:130-131; Tabari VI:101-103

PREFACE:

Muhammad was reminded that a man pleaded for Moses when Pharaoh wanted to kill him. The persecution was harsh which may have led some to flee to Abyssinia. However, comfort was offered to those who were persecuted.[33]

SURAH:

Qur'an 40:2-6: "The revelation of the Book is from Allah, the mighty, the knowing, Forgiver of sin and Accepter of repentance, Severe to punish, Lord of bounty. There is no God but He; to Him is the eventual coming. None dispute concerning the messages of Allah but those who disbelieve, so let not their control in the land deceive thee. Before them the people of Noah and the parties after them [those who came afterwards] rejected [the prophets], and every nation purposed against its messenger to destroy him by means of falsehoods to render null [and void] thereby the truth, so I seized them; how terrible was My retribution [and My retribution was terrible]! And thus did the word of thy Lord prove true against those who disbelieve that they are the companions [inmates] of the Fire."

Qur'an 40:10-12: "Those who disbelieve are told: Certainly Allah's hatred of you, when you were called upon to the faith and you rejected [it], was much greater than your hatred now of yourselves. They say: Our Lord, twice hast thou made us die, and twice hast thou given us life; so we confess our sins. Is there then a way of escape? That is because when Allah alone was called upon, you disbelieved, and when associates were given to Him, you believed. So judgment belongs to Allah, the High, the Great."

Qur'an 40:18, 21: "And warn them of the day that draws near, when hearts, grieving inwardly, [will] rise up to [their] throats [filling them with anguish]. The iniquitous will have no friend, nor any intercessor who should be obeyed [listened to for the disbelievers]...Mightier than these [Quraysh] were they [who opposed the prophets] in strength and in fortifications in the land, but Allah destroyed them for their sins. And they have none to protect them from Allah."

Qur'an 40:33-35: "The day on which you will turn back retreating, having none to save you from Allah; and whomsoever Allah leaves in error there is no guide for him. And Joseph indeed came to you before with clear arguments, but you ever remained in doubt as to what he brought you; until, when he died, you said: Allah will never raise a messenger after him. Thus does Allah leave him in error who is prodigal, a doubter — those who dispute concerning the messages [signs and verses] of Allah without any authority that has came to them. Greatly hated is it by Allah and by those who believe [...]"

Qur'an 40:49-50: "And those in the Fire will say to the guards of Hell: Pray to your Lord to lighten our chastisement for a day. They will say: Did not your messengers come to you with clear arguments? They [the damned] will say: Yea. They [the guards] will say: Then pray. And the prayer of the disbelievers goes only astray."

Qur'an 40:53: "And We indeed gave Moses the guidance, and We made the Children of Israel inherit the Book."

Qur'an 40:67, 70-72: "He it is Who created you from dust, then from a small life-germ, then from a clot, then He brings you forth as a child, then that you may attain your maturity, then that you may be old; and of you are some who die before and that you may reach an appointed term, and that you may understand. Those who reject the Book and that with which We have sent Our messengers. But they shall soon know. When the fetters are on their necks and the chains. They are [will be] dragged. Into hot [the boiling] water; then in the Fire they will be burned."

SUNNAH:

ASSAULT AND BATTERY

Bukhari:V5B57N27: "Then I saw Uqba coming to the Prophet while he was praying. He seized his robe. Abu Bakr came crying and pulled Uqba away. He [Abu Bakr] said, 'Would you kill a man just because he says: "Allah is my Lord"?' Then they left him. That is the worst that I ever saw the Quraysh do to him."

Ishaq:130 "When the Quraysh became distressed by the trouble caused by the Apostle they called him a liar, insulted him, and accused him of being a poet, a sorcerer, a diviner [soothsayer], and of being possessed. However, the Apostle continued to proclaim what Allah had ordered him to proclaim. He excited their dislike by condemning their religion, forsaking their idols, and leaving them to their unbelief."

Tabari VI:101: "The nastiest thing I saw the Quraysh do to the Messenger occurred when their nobles assembled in the Hijr [in the mosque of the Ka'aba]. They discussed Muhammad, saying, 'We have never seen the kind of trouble we have endured from this fellow. He has derided our traditional values, declared our way of life foolish, abused and insulted our forefathers, reviled our religion, caused division among us, divided the community, and cursed our Gods. We have endured a great deal from him.' While they were saying this, the Apostle walked up and kissed the Black Stone. Then he performed the circumambulation of the Ka'aba. As he did they said some injurious things about him. I could see from the Messenger's face that he had heard them. When he passed a second time they made similar remarks. When he passed them the third time, the Prophet stopped and said, 'Hear me, O Quraysh. By Him who holds Muhammad's life in his hand, I will bring you slaughter.'

Tabari VI:102: "They were gripped by what he had said...They said,

'Depart Abu Al-Qasim [Muhammad]; for by Allah, you were never violent."

Ishaq:131: "Hamza bin Abdul Muttalib […] was the strongest man of the Quraysh. A woman rose up and said, 'If only you had seen what your nephew Muhammad had to endure just now before you came. Abu Jahl spoke to him offensively.'" "Hamza was carried away with fury, as it was Allah's will to honor him this way […] instead of circumambulating the Ka'aba, he was ready to attack Abu Jahl […] Hamza raised his bow and gave Abu a blow which split his head open in an ugly way. He said, 'Do you insult him when I am a member of his religion? Hit me back if you can.'"

Tabari VI:103: "Hamza bin Abdul Muttalib […] was the strongest man of the Quraysh. A woman rose up and said, 'If only you had seen what your nephew Muhammad had to endure just now before you came. Abu Jahl spoke to him offensively.' Hamza was carried away by a fury, as it was Allah's will to honor him this way. He went off quickly, not stopping to talk to anyone. Instead of circumambulating the Ka'aba, he was ready to attack Abu Jahl when he saw him. When he entered the [Ka'aba] mosque […] Hamza raised his bow and gave Abu-Jahl a blow which split his head open in an ugly way. He said, 'Do you insult him when I am a member of his religion? Hit me back if you can.' […] Hamza's Islam was complete. He followed the Prophet's every command […] Hamza would protect him […] Umar bin al-Khattab was a staunch and mighty warrior. He accepted Islam, as had Hamza before him. The Messenger's companions began to feel stronger."

SUMMATION:

IL: This unjust and unwarranted persecution continued. The Prophet had sympathy for his Companions and approved a second flight to Abyssinia. The revelation once again convinced Muhammad that the prophets before him suffered in a similar fashion. The Prophet was assured those who deny Islam and persecute Muslims will be denizens of hell. Allah promises the good fortune of infidels is only temporary.

WA: Here we learn that Allah is severe to punish those who refuse the Islamic message. If that is not enough, Muslims learn their god has hatred for the People of the West who reject the Islamic message. Those who assigned partners were the pre-Islamic Quraysh and the Christians. Those who exercise their free will in this manner are assured of damnation—where there will be no aid. Muhammad's revelation went on to say that Allah was purposely leading people into error. These same people who question, or will not accept Islam, are hated by Allah and His literalist followers. Therefore, Muslims learn by reading this passage that we in the West are to be hated and our prayers are not heard. As for those who received the revelation in the past, the Israelites, they could not accept it and thus altered it. Those who reject Allah's true revelation through Muhammad will be fastened with iron collars attached to chains and dragged through boiling water into a burning hell.

As for proper behavior, we learn that the Black Stone of the Ka'aba is central to Islamic affection. Unbelievers, those who insult Islam and its Prophet, will be slaughtered. While practicing as a Hanif or Quraysh polytheist, Muhammad was not violent; however, his Quraysh relatives noticed a behavioral change. Uqba did not seize Muhammad's robe because he declared Allah as lord. He seized Muhammad's robe because Muhammad just threatened to kill his relatives. Finally, after becoming familiar with this dialogue, it is no wonder that Hamza reacted as he did. The fact that Allah honored Hamza when he became furious is most troubling to non-Muslims. As we continue, Hamza was angered when Muhammad was offended by Abu Jahl. By becoming furious, Hamza came into the favor of Allah. By splitting open the head of the one who insulted Muhammad, Hamza was made complete in Islam. Why? Islam is about power. It is about ultimate control and justification against those who are subjugated or injured by Muslims. Those who receive this punishment deserve it because it is inshallah [Allah's will].

CHAPTER 3 NOTES

1. Ali, p. 523; Pickthall, p. 190
2. Kathir, *Tafsir Ibn Kathir*, Vol. 8, p. 171
3. Ali, p. 613; Pickthall, p. 220
4. Ali, p. 629; Pickthall, p. 226
5. Ali, p. 647; Pickthall, p. 235
6. Ali, p. 730; Pickthall, p. 264
7. Ali, p. 750; Pickthall, p. 272
8. Ali, p. 784; Pickthall, p. 284
9. Kathir, *Tafsir Ibn Kathir*, Vol. 3, p. 326
10. Ali, p. 798; Pickthall, p. 289
11. Ali, p. 810; Pickthall, p. 294
12. Ali, p. 817; Pickthall, p. 287
13. Ali, p. 846; Pickthall, p. 307
14. Cook, *Muhammad*, p. 58
15. Ali, p. 857; Pickthall, p. 311
16. Lewis, *The Crisis of Islam*, p. 48
17. Ali, p. 866; Pickthall, p. 314
18. Esposito, *Woman in Muslim Family Law*, pp. 16-17
19. Ali, p. 877; Pickthall, p. 318
20. Bostum, *Legacy of Islamic Anti-Semitism*, p. 33
21. Kathir, *Tafsir Ibn Kathir*, Vol. 8, pp. 271-272
22. Lewis, *The Crisis of Islam*, p. 31
23. Ali, p. 905; Pickthall, p. 328
24. Al-Misri, *Reliance of the Traveller*, pp. 944-947
25. Demy, *In the Name of God*, p. 80
26. Ali, p. 932; Pickthall, p. 340
27. Khadduri, *War and Peace*, pp. 14-18
28. Ali, p. 942; Pickthall, p. 344
29. Sabini, *Islam: A Primer*, pp.15-24
30. Ali, p. 954; Pickthall, p. 348
31. Ali, p. 967; Pickthall, p. 352
32. Ali, p. 973; Pickthall, p. 355
33. Ali, p. 918; Pickthall, p. 334

CHAPTER 4

Late Meccan Revelations

(619-622 AD)

QUR'AN 18

"The Cave"

619 AD

SCRIPTURE:

Qur'an 18:1-5, 25, 27, 29, 50, 86, 94, 102-106, 110

Ishaq:132-135

PREFACE:

This surah revealed how Allah was trying to help Muhammad answer the questions posed by the rabbis. The Meccans travelled to Yathrib ("Medina") where the rabbis gave them questions that would cause Muhammad great stress and torment. After this episode, the surah then dealt with the Christians. The Son-ship of Jesus is directly renounced. It states that the Christians have gone from monks to embellishments which hinder Christians from accepting the truth. A prophetical reference is given concerning the stages of Christianity. The Christians reject Islam because of their great power and wealth. The warnings rejected by the Christians will bring judgment and then helplessness. This surah blames Christianity for the plight of Christian nations. Abrogation of the scriptures becomes a principle focus of this surah since the questions posed by rabbis and the claims that Jesus is divine are rejected.[1]

SURAH:

Qur'an 18:1-5: "Praise be to Allah! Who revealed the Book [Qur'an] to His servant [Muhammad], and allowed not therein any crookedness [to enter him], rightly directing, to give warning of severe punishment from Him [...] and to warn those who say: Allah has taken to Himself a son.

They have no knowledge of it nor had their fathers. Grievous is the word that comes out of their mouths. They speak nothing but a lie."

Qur'an 18:25, 27: "And they [Christians] remained in their cave 300 years and they add 9 [years]. And recite that which has been revealed to thee of the Book of thy Lord. There is none who can alter his words. [...]"

Qur'an 18:29: "[...] Surely We have prepared for the iniquitous a Fire, an enclosure which will encompass them. And if they cry for water, they are given water like molten brass, scalding their faces. Evil the drink! And [bad] ill [is] the resting-place!"

Qur'an 18:50: "And when We said to the angels: Make submission to Adam, they submitted except Iblis [Satan]. He was of the Jinn, so he transgressed the commandment of his Lord...."

Qur'an 18:86: "Until, when he reached the setting-place of the sun, he found it going down into the Black Sea and found by it a people. We said: O Dhu-l-qarnain [Two-horned one], either punish them or do them a benefit."

Qur'an 18:94: "They said: O Dhu-l-qarnain [Two-horned one], Gog and Magog do mischief in the land. May we then pay thee tribute on condition that thou raise a barrier between us and them?

Qur'an 18:102-106: "[...] Surely We have prepared hell as an entertainment for the disbelievers [...]. Those are they who disbelieve in the messages of their Lord and meeting with Him, so their works are in vain. Nor shall We set up a balance for them on the Day of Resurrection. That is their reward — hell, because they disbelieved and held My messages and My messengers in mockery."

Qur'an 18:110: "Say: [Muhammad] I am only a mortal [man] like you — it is revealed to me that your God [Allah] is one God. So whoever hopes to meet his Lord, he should do good deeds, and join no one in the service of his Lord."

THE QURAYSH PEACE PROPOSAL

Ishaq:132-133: "Utba who was chief, said while sitting in a Quraysh assembly, 'Why don't I go to Muhammad and make some proposals to him? If he accepts, we will give him whatever he wants, and he will leave us in peace' [...] So Utba went to the Prophet who was sitting in the mosque by himself, and said, 'O my nephew, you are one of us yet you have come to our people with a matter that is dividing the community. You are ridiculing our customs. You have insulted ours gods and our religion. You have even declared that our forefathers were infidels. So listen to me and I will make some suggestions, and perhaps you will be able to accept one of them.' The Apostle agreed. Utba said, 'If what you want is money, we will gather for you some of our property so that you may be the richest man in town. If you want honor, we will make you a chief so that no one can decide anything apart from you. If you want sovereignty, we will make you king. And if this demonic spirit which has possession of you is such that you cannot get rid of him, we will find a physician for you, and exhaust our means trying to cure you. For often a demonic spirit gets possession of a man, but he can be rid of it.' The Apostle listened patiently."

Ishaq:134-135: "'Muhammad if you do not accept our offer then ask your Lord to give us the land and water we lack, for we are shut in by these mountains, we have no river, and none live a harder life than we do. If you speak the truth, resurrect Qusayy for us for he was a true shaykh, so that we may ask him whether what you say is accurate. If you do this we will believe you and know that God has sent you as an apostle as you claim.' [...] Well then at least ask your god to send an angel to confirm your depictions of paradise and give you the mansions and gold you obviously crave. If not that, then send us the Day of Doom you threatened us with, for we will not believe you until you perform a miracle. [...] Why doesn't your god help you? Didn't he know that we were going to present you with these opportunities to prove yourself? Listen, Muhammad; we know the truth. Information has reached us that you are taught by this fellow in Yemen called Al-Rahman. By Allah, we will never believe in Ar-Rahman. [...] 'Alright then, our conscience is clear.' When they said this, the Prophet got up and left [...]. The Prophet went to Khadijah, sad and grieving."

SUMMATION:

IL: Muslims in this surah experience Allah's promise that he protected the Qur'an from error and corruption. Therefore, Muslims are assured that Christian claims about Jesus being the Son of God are lies. These lies became apparent 300 years after the time of Jesus when Emperor Constantine converted and then changed Christian dogma. Those who polluted Christian dogma will be severely punished. Those who do not submit commit sin. This is what Satan did when he refused to submit to Adam. Towards the end of time, Gog and Magog will exercise judgment to the guilty and be a benefit to those who submit (Muslims). Believers will do well by not making any god equal to Allah. The reward for those who do not listen to this Islamic command will be hell. Christians who curse the Prophet will be destroyed.

WA: The question again arises why Allah could prevent the Qur'an from being corrupted but could not prevent the Torah and Gospel from being corrupted. Verse 29 appears to be directed towards Christians. Christians in the next life will drink molten brass. Verse 50 confirms that Jinn are demons. Allah repeats the same point that those who do not accept Muhammad will be damned.

As for Muhammad, his Quraysh relatives offered him money, property, honor, Kingship. He was even offered medical attention because they concluded that he was afflicted with a demon. They offered anything to make peace. The Quraysh asked Muhammad for one miracle so they would have a reason to believe. When this did not occur, the Quraysh accused Muhammad of being a Hanif who was really devoted to their god Ar-Rahman. As Muhammad departed it was evident to them that Muhammad was a sorcerer, insane, and demon possessed. They knew him and he was somehow changed for the worse. Despite this, Christians are told they should drop the miracle performing Jesus for Muhammad who was incapable of performing a miracle. How are Christians supposed to know if Muhammad was a prophet? The Christians could not observe any visible proofs, or miracles, of Muhammad's prophethood. Regardless, Islam declared that Christians will be exterminated. The Christians are in the same boat as the Quraysh—submit to Islam.

"The Discrimination"

619 AD

SCRIPTURE:

Qur'an 25:2, 14, 17, 22, 27-29, 32, 45, 70

Ishaq:145, 155-156

PREFACE:

This surah takes aim at the superstition of the polytheists and the absence of miracles mentioned by the Christians. This surah responds by declaring Islam changes the lives of those who submit, and that Islam will change and conquer the world. This will occur through a gradual process. This surah announces the coming judgment against those who practice superstition and those who require miracles to prove the truth. Since Islam was changing some lives what followed was Allah's response to the lack of miracles. The People of the Book will also be forced to believe that Islam will change and conquer the world. Judgment is promised against those opposing Islam because Islam must be triumphant. This judgment will also be experienced by the wicked when it is too late for them to repent. Otherwise, those who oppose Islam in this life must be subdued into Dhimmitude.[2]

SURAH:

Qur'an 25:2: "He, Whose is the kingdom of the heavens and the earth, and Who did not take to Himself a son, and Who has no associate in the kingdom, and Who created everything, then ordained it for a measure."

Qur'an 25:14, 17: "Pray not this day for destruction once but pray for destruction again and again. And on the day when He will gather them, and that which they serve [worship] besides Allah, He will say: Was it you who led astray these My servants, or did they themselves stray from the path?"

Qur'an 25:22, 27-29: "On the day when they will see the angels, there will be no good news for the guilty, and they will say: Let there be a strong barrier. And on the day when the wrongdoer will bite his hands, saying: Would that I had taken a way [path] with the Messenger! O Woe is me! [W]ould that I had not taken such a one as a friend! Certainly he led me astray from the Reminder after it had come to me […]."

Qur'an 25:32: "And those who disbelieve say: Why has not the Qur'an been revealed to him all at once? Thus, that We may strengthen thy heart thereby and We have arranged it well in arranging."

Qur'an 25:45: "Seest thou seen [Haven't you seen] how thy Lord extends the shade? And if He pleased, He would have made it stationary. Then We have made the sun an indication of it."

Qur'an 25:70: "Except him who repents and believes [in Islamic Monotheism], and does good [righteous] deeds; for such [people] Allah changes their evil deeds [sins] to good ones [good deeds]. And Allah is ever Forgiving, [and most] Merciful."

SUNNAH:

Ishaq:145: "[…] It was that evil man Abu Jahl who stirred up the Meccans against them. When he heard that a man had become a Muslim […] he reprimanded him and poured scorn on him, saying, '[…] We will declare you a blockhead and brand you as a fool, and destroy your reputation.' If he was a merchant he said, 'We will boycott your goods and we will reduce you to beggary.' If he was a person of no social importance, he beat him and incited the people against him. […]"

UMAR ENTERS THE FIELD

Ishaq:155: "Umar became a Muslim, he being a strong, stubborn man whose protégés none dare attack. The prophet's companions were so fortified [strengthened] by him and Hamza that they got the upper hand on the Quraysh. 'We could not pray at the Ka'aba until Umar became a Muslim, and then he fought the Quraysh until we could pray there."

Ishaq:156: "Umar said, 'I am making my way to Muhammad, the apostate who has split up the Quraysh and made a mockery of our traditions, to kill him' [...] Umar heard her [his sister Fatima] reciting Khabbab as he came near the house. He said, 'What is this balderdash?' [She lied by saying,] 'You have heard nothing.' [Umar said,] 'By Allah, I have,' striking his sister in the face and wounding her. When he saw the blood, he felt sorry and asked to hear what Fatima was reciting. [Fatima said,] 'You are unclean in your polytheism and only the clean may listen to it' [Umar said,] 'How fine and noble is this speech. Lead me to Muhammad so that I may accept Islam.'"

SUMMATION:

IL: Islam's miracle started with one man, the Prophet Muhammad. Fourteen hundred years later 1.5 billion people follow his teaching. Eventually, the entire world will know his truth. This revealed truth looked towards the future. Destruction will come to civilizations that accept Jesus as one with Allah. Muslims are told to stay away from Christians who would lead them from the Straight Path. Allah revealed the Qur'an according to His will. This does not please the Christians. Good deeds lead Muslims to Paradise. Strength, as displayed through Hamza and Umar, permitted prayer at the Holy Mosque. The repentance spoken of in verse 70 happened to Umar. When he came to kill the Prophet, he instead found Islam.

WA: This surah gives the indication that Islamic literalism longs for destruction to reoccur against people who do not hold their belief. Muslims are conditioned in the surah not to trust Christians and are assured that Christians will ultimately lose out in this life and in the Afterlife. In the Sirah, Abu Jahl continued his persistent persecution of the Muslims. It is in this vein that we gain insight into Umar al-Khattab. He came seeking Muhammad with murder in his heart. His Muslim sister lied, so Umar belted her in the face. He regretted what he did and was reminded by his sister that he was an unclean polytheist. Apparently, this was all it took for Umar to revert to Islam. Clearly, Umar was a man capable of violence, evidenced by his desire to murder and by hitting his sister. He did not come to Islam because Muhammad changed his mind; rather, he was impressed by his sister's courage when she stood up to him even after she became a victim of battery.

QUR'AN 111

"The Flame"

619 AD

SCRIPTURE:

Qur'an 111:1-5

Ishaq:161-162

PREFACE:

This chapter was revealed after Muhammad was opposed by his uncle Abu Lahab/Abdul Uzza. The opposition was so fierce that Muhammad's aunt used to throw thorns in the ground where she knew Muhammad walked. This burning opposition to Muhammad will lead to flames of fire for his persecutors in the next life.[(3)]

SURAH:

Qur'an 111:1-5: "Abu Lahab's hands will perish and he will perish. His wealth and that which he earns will not avail [help] him. He will burn in fire giving rise to flames — and his wife — the bearer of slanderer. Upon her neck a halter of twisted rope!"

SUNNAH:

BELLIGERENCE

Ishaq:161: "Lahab and his wife Umm mocked and laughed at him so the

Qur'an came down on their wickedness. Umm carried thorns and cast them in the Apostle's way."

Ishaq:162: "Abu Jahl met the Apostle and said, By Allah, Muhammad, you will either stop cursing our gods or we will curse the god you serve.' So the Qur'anic verse was revealed, 'Do not insult those to whom they pray lest they curse God wrongfully through lack of knowledge.' I have been told that the Apostle then refrained from cursing their gods, and *began* [emphasis added] to call them to Allah [instead of Ar-Rahman]."

SUMMATION:

IL: Muhammad's uncle and aunt were so wicked towards him that they mocked and tried to injure him. Allah revealed to the Prophet and all Muslims that Abu Lahab will burn and Umm, his wife, will hang."

WA: Why would the Creator of the Universe reveal a surah meant for one person at one point in time only to describe how he and his wife will be tortured? Yes, their behavior was not desirable, but the reason for their behavior was revealed in the Sirah. Muhammad kept cursing all the gods of the Ka'aba except for Allah. His aunt and uncle were highly offended by Muhammad. This explained their behavior.

Interestingly, the Sirah displayed it was Muhammad's behavior that changed. If we were to take this literally, then Allah must have agreed with or listened to the polytheist Abu Jahl. He told Muhammad to stop cursing or they would start cursing. Therefore, the polytheists were not bad mouthing Allah. The insults were all coming from Muhammad. As this occurred, either Allah agreed with Abu Jahl, or Muhammad decided to change course based on Abu Jahl's words. Muhammad then attributed his change of mind to a new revelation from Allah.

QUR'AN 53

"The Star"

619 AD

SCRIPTURE:

Qur'an 53:2-5, 10-14, 19-23, 29, 49-53

Ishaq:165-167; Tabari VI:106-107, 110

PREFACE:

This surah states that as Muslims would rise to destroy their enemies, the position of the Prophet would rise as well. As for Muhammad, he did not commit error. Since there were no errors in him, he rose to the highest heights of any man. The proof that Islam is the truth can be seen in the destruction of its enemies, i.e., falsehood. During the "Meccan period," Allah acknowledged that better verses would have to be revealed in order to protect the Prophet, and advance Islam at the expense of its enemies. [4]

SURAH:

Qur'an 53:2-5: "Your companion errs not, nor does he deviate. Nor does he speak out of desire. It is naught but revelation that is revealed — One Mighty in Power has taught him."

Qur'an 53:10-14: "So He revealed to His servant what He revealed. The heart was not untrue in seeing what he saw. Do you then dispute with Him as to what he saw? And certainly he saw Him in another descent, at the farthest lote-tree [shade tree]."

Qur'an 53:19-23: "Have you then considered Lat, Uzza, and another, the third, Manat? Are the males for you and Him the females? Thus is indeed an unjust division! They are naught but names which you have named, you and your fathers — Allah has sent no authority to them....They follow [nothing] but conjecture and what their souls desire. And certainly the guidance has come to them from their Lord [Ar-Rahman]."

Qur'an 53:29: "So shun him [people] who turns his back [turns away] upon Our Reminder, and desires nothing but this world's life."

Qur'an 53:49-53: "And that He is the Lord of Sirius: And that He destroyed first Ad: And Thamud, so He spared not. And the people of Noah before. Surely they were most iniquitous and inordinate. And the overthrown cities, He hurled down."

SUNNAH:

THE ANGEL OF LIGHT

Tabari VI:106-107: "The revelation from Allah was coming to the Prophet continuously, commanding and threatening those who showed open hostility to him, and vindicating him against those who oppose him. The Quraysh promised Muhammad that they would give him so much wealth that he would become the richest man in Mecca, they would give him as many wives as he wanted, and they would submit to his commands. The Quraysh said, 'This is what we will give you, Muhammad, so desist from reviling our gods and do not speak evilly [sic] of them. If you will do so, we offer you something which will be to your advantage and to ours.' 'What is it,' he asked. They said, 'If you will worship our gods, Al-Lat and Al-Uzza, for a year, we will worship your god for a year.' Satan cast a false Qur'anic revelation on the Messenger of Allah's tongue."

Ishaq:165: "Walid, As, Aswad and Umayyah said, 'Muhammad, come and let us worship that which you worship and you worship what we worship. We shall combine in the matter and make you a partner in all our undertakings [...] and you shall have your share of it.' 'Let me see what revelation comes to me from my Lord.' He [Muhammad] replied. So Muhammad debated with himself and fervently desired such an outcome. Then Allah revealed, 'By the star when it sets, your comrade does not err, nor is he deceived; nor does he speak out of his own desire. And when he came to the words, 'Have you thought about Al-Lat, Al-Uzza, and Manat,' Satan, when he was meditating upon it, and desiring to bring reconciliation, cast on his tongue, because of his inner longings and what he desired, the words: 'These are exalted high flying cranes (goddesses). Verily, their intercession is accepted with approval.'

Ishaq:166-167: "When the Quraysh heard this, they rejoiced and were delighted at the way in which he spoke of their gods, and they listened to him. While the Muslims, trusting their Prophet in respect to the messages which he brought, did not suspect him of a vain desire or slip. When he came to the prostration, having completed the surah, he prostrated himself and the Muslims did likewise, obeying his command and following his example. Those polytheists of the Quraysh and others who were in the mosque likewise prostrated themselves because of the reference to their gods which they had heard, so that there was no one in the Mosque, believer or unbeliever, who did not prostrate himself. Then they all dispersed from the Mosque. Then angel Gabriel came to the Messenger and said, 'Muhammad, what have you done?' You have recited to the people that which I did not bring to you from Allah, and you have said that which he did not say to you.' The Messenger was grieved and feared Allah greatly. So Allah sent a revelation to him, consoling him and making light of the affair. He informed him that there had never been a prophet or messenger before who desired as he desired and wished as he wished but that Satan had cast words into his recitation as he had interjected them on Muhammad's tongue and into his desires."

Tabari VI:110: "Thus Allah removed the sorrow from his Messenger, reassured him about that which he had feared, and cancelled the words which Satan had cast [placed] on his tongue. [...] The Prophet said, 'I have fabricated things against Allah and have imputed to Him words which He has not spoken.'"

SUMMATION:

IL: There is no fault or error in the Prophet Muhammad. Satan tried to distort the Prophets message, but the Prophet's heart was pure. Allah's revelation erased the effort of Satan to mislead. Satan is damned by Allah.

The proof of Muhammad's prophethood and inerrancy rests with the eventual destruction of Islam's enemies.[(5)]

WA: How does Muhammad recite: "These are exalted high flying cranes (goddesses)? Truly, their intercession is accepted with approval." Wasn't he raised with the belief that Allat, Uzza, and Manat were the daughters of Al-Lah? The previous surah described how paradise and hell could be confused with one another. Now we see Muhammad's apparent inability to tell what came from Allah through Gabriel and what came from Satan. Muhammad acknowledged the goddesses after he was promised wealth, wives, and power by the Quraysh. However, Muhammad did not realize this until Gabriel told him. Both this surah and the Sunnah declare this was not Muhammad's fault. The devil made him do it. Regardless of the initial statement and recanting of the statement through another Qur'anic revelation, the Quraysh knew what they heard Muhammad say.[(6)]

"The Israelites"

619 AD

SCRIPTURE:

Qur'an 17:1, 4, 7, 13, 16, 22-26, 31-39, 59-60, 82, 86, 88, 90-93, 97, 105, 111

Ishaq:182-186

PREFACE:

This surah relates to a vision of Muhammad being carried by a steed from Mecca to Jerusalem and then into the seven heavens of Allah. The Israelites rose to power but were severely punished because of their transgressions. The world rejects Islam, but eventually the world will find itself at the brink of destruction. All those who oppose the teachings of Muhammad will eventually disappear. The miracle of the Qur'an attributes the Spirit of truth in St. John's Gospel with Muhammad. It then decries the doctrine of son-ship. This Qur'anic revelation abrogates previous revelations. The judgment that came against the Israelites will also occur against all that disobey Allah. Jihad will be waged by Muslims against unbelief.[7]

SURAH:

Qur'an 17:1: "Glory to Him Who carried His servant by night from the sacred Mosque [Mecca] to the remote Mosque [Jerusalem], whose precincts We blessed, that We might show him Our signs! Surely He is the Hearing, the Seeing."

Qur'an 17:4, 7: "And We made known to the Children of Israel in the Book: Certainly you will make mischief in the land twice, and behave insolently with mighty arrogance. So when the second warning came, We raised another people that they might enter the Mosque [Temple] as they entered it the first time, and that they might destroy, whatever they conquered with utter destruction."

Qur'an 17:13: "And We have made every man's actions to cling to his neck, and We shall bring forth to him on the day of Resurrection a book which he will find wide open."

Qur'an 17:16: "And when We wish to destroy a town, We send commandments to its people who lead easy lives, but they transgress therein; thus the word proves true against it, so We destroy it with utter destruction."

Qur'an 17:22-26, 31-39: "Associate not any other god with Allah, lest thou sit down despised, forsaken. And they Lord has decreed that you serve none but Him, and do good to parents. If either or both of them reach old age with thee, say not "Fie" to them, nor chide them, and speak to them a generous word. And lower to them the wing of humility out of mercy, and say: My Lord, have mercy on them, as they brought me up when I was little. Your Lord knows best what is in your minds. If you are righteous, He is surely Forgiving to those who turn to Him. And give to the near of his kin [provide for relatives], and to the needy [the poor] and the wayfarers [sojourners], and squander not wastefully [do not be wasteful]. And kill not your children for fear of poverty — We provide for them and for you. Surely the killing of them is a great wrong. And go not nigh [near] to fornication, surely it is an obscenity. And evil is the way. And kill not the soul which Allah has forbidden except for a just cause. And whoever is slain [killed] unjustly, We have indeed given to his heir authority — but let him not exceed the limit in slaying. Surely he will be helped. And draw not nigh [don't go near] the orphan's property except in a goodly way, till he attains maturity. And fulfill the promise; surely the promise will be enquired into. And give full measure when you measure out, and weigh with a true balance. This is fair and better in the end. And follow not that of which thou hast no knowledge. Surely the hearing and the sight and the heart, all of these it will be asked. And go not about in the land exultantly, for thou canst rend the earth, nor reach the mountains in height. All this, the evil thereof, is hateful in the sight of the Lord. This is of the wisdom of thy Lord has revealed to thee. And associate not any other god with Allah lest thou be thrown into hell, blamed, and cast away."

Qur'an 17:59-60: "And nothing hindered Us from sending signs, but the ancients rejected them. And We gave to Thamud the she-camel, a manifest sign, but they did her [the she-camel] wrong, and [now] We send not signs but to warn. And when We said to thee: Surely thy Lord encompasses men. And We made not the vision which We showed thee but a trial [as an ordeal] for men [mankind], as also the tree cursed [the Zaqqum tree] in the Qur'an. And We warn[ed] them, but it only adds to their inordinacy [impiety]."

Qur'an 17:82: "And We reveal of the Qur'an that which is a healing and a mercy to the believers, and it adds only to the perdition of the wrongdoers [infidels]."

Qur'an 17:86: "And if We please, We could certainly take away that which We have revealed to thee, then thou wouldst find none to plead thy cause against Us."

Qur'an 17:88: "Say: If men and Jinn [demons] should combine together to bring the like of this Qur'an, they could not bring the like of it, though some of them were aiders of others [even though the devils would help men and men would help devils]."

Qur'an 17:90-94: "And they say: We will by no means believe in thee [Muhammad], till thou cause a spring to gush forth from the earth for us, or thou have a garden of palms and grapes in the midst of which thou cause rivers to flow forth abundantly, or thou cause heaven to come down upon us in pieces, as thou thinkest, or bring Allah and the angels face to face with us or thou have a house of gold, or thou ascend into heaven. And we will not believe in thy ascending till thou bring down to us a book we can read. Say: Glory to my Lord! [A]m I naught [nothing] but a mortal messenger?"

Qur'an 17:97: "And He whom Allah guides, he is on the right way; and he whom He [Allah] leaves in error, for thou wilt find no guardians but Him. And We shall gather them together on the day of Resurrection on their faces, blind and dumb and deaf. Their abode [home] is [will be] hell. Whenever it [the flame] abates, We will make them burn [all] the more."

Qur'an 17:105: "And with truth have We revealed it [the Qur'an], and with truth did it come. And We have not sent thee but as a giver of good news and as a warner."

Qur'an 17:111: "And say: Praise be to Allah! Who has not taken to Himself a son, and Who has not a partner in the kingdom, and Who has not a helper because of weakness; and proclaim His greatness, magnifying Him."

SUNNAH:

THE FLIGHT TO HEAVEN AND HELL

Ishaq:182-183: "While I was in the Hijr, Gabriel came and stirred me with his foot. He took me to the door of the Mosque and there was a white animal, half mule, half donkey, with wings on its sides yet it was propelled by its feet. He mounted me on it. When I mounted, he shied. Gabriel places his hand on its mane, and said, 'You should be ashamed to behave this way. By God, you have never had a more honorable rider than Muhammad.' The animal was so embarrassed, it broke into a cold sweat. When we arrived at the Temple in Jerusalem, we found Abraham, Moses, Jesus, and along with a company of [other] prophets. I acted as their Imam in prayer. [...] Moses was a ruddy faced man, thin fleshed, curly haired with a hooked nose. Jesus was a reddish man with lank wet hair and many freckles [...] [Aisha said,] 'The Prophet's body remained where it was. Allah removed his spirit at night.' Upon hearing this many became renegades who had prayed and joined Islam. Many Muslims gave up their faith. Some went to Abu Bakr and said, 'What do you think of your friend now? He alleges that he went to Jerusalem last night and prayed there and came back to Mecca.' Bakr said that they were lying about the Apostle. But they told him that he was in the Mosque at this very moment telling the Quraysh about it. Bakr said, 'If he says so then it must be true. I believe him [...].'"

Ishaq:184-186: "Umm, Abu Talib's daughter, said: 'The Apostle went on no journey except while he was in my house. He slept in my home that night after he prayed the final night prayer.' A little before dawn he woke us, saying, 'O Umm, I went to Jerusalem.' He got up to go out and I grabbed hold of his robe and laid bare his belly. I pleaded, 'O Muhammad, don't tell the people about this for they will know you are lying and will mock you.' He said, 'By Allah, I will tell them.' I [then] told a negress [black female slave] of mine [to], Follow him and listen.' After the completion of my business in Jerusalem, a ladder was brought to me finer than any I have ever seen. An Angel was in charge of it and under his command were 12,000 angels each of them having 12,000 angels under his command. And none knows the armies of Allah better than he. Muhammad said, 'Order Malik to show me hell.' Certainly, O Malik, show Muhammad hell.' Thereupon he removed its covering and the flames blazed high into the air until I thought that they would consume everything. Adam reviewed the spirits of his offspring. The infidels excited his disgust. Then I saw men with lips like camels. In their hands were pieces of fire like stones which they thrust in their mouths. They [the stones] came out their posteriors [rear ends]. I was told that they sinfully devoured the wealth of orphans. [...] Then I saw some women hanging by their breasts. They had fathered bastards. He took me into Paradise and there I saw a damsel [woman] with dark red lips. I asked her to whom she belonged, for she pleased me much when I saw her. She said, 'Zayd [Muhammad's adopted son].' The Apostle gave Zayd the good news about her."

SUMMATION:

IL: Another proof that Muhammad is the Prophet is found in his heavenly ascent. Furthermore, he led Abraham, Moses, and Jesus in prayer. Afterward, Allah revealed the surah. Allah stated that he took Muhammad to Jerusalem. This is symbolic of the first Muslim conquest of Jerusalem during the early Caliphate and the ultimate conquest of the Jews during the last Caliphate. Muslims were commanded by Allah to bring annihilation when the Jihad began. Those adversaries who practice *shirk* ("Attributing a partner to Allah"), accepting Jesus as Son of God, will be conquered. At the Judgment that will be thrown into hell-fire. No signs will accompany the movement of Islam. When Allah permitted Moses and Jesus to perform signs, it did nothing for their followers. The Qur'an will bring mercy to Muslims and condemnation to non-Muslims. The Qur'an is divinely inspired and is demonstrated by this thought: 'Even if man and Jinn worked together they could not create something better.'

Allah guides Muslims but non-Muslims will be left in error. Allah will burn these people in hell. Allah is to be praised for sending Muhammad and for not taking a son or partner in Paradise.

WA: Both Aisha who was Abu Bakr's daughter, and Umm, the daughter of Abu-Talib, said that Muhammad never left the house. So this trip to Jerusalem must have been a spiritual or dreamt journey. Some Muslims gave up the faith when they heard this story. It was unbelievable for them. In heaven, Moses with the hooked nose and Jesus with the freckles are seen as somewhat less in stature in comparison to Muhammad. In this depiction of Moses and Jesus, Muhammad was establishing himself as the greatest of the prophets. These Qur'anic revelations portrayed the Jews as tyrants, who through Muhammad's trip to Jerusalem would be conquered by Muslims in the future. In Jihad, the Muslims are told to ravage, lay waste, conquer, and bring annihilation to their enemies.[8] This surah established the justification for violence to be used against Jews and Christians.

QUR'AN 72

"The Jinn"

620 AD

SCRIPTURE:

Qur'an 72:1-9, 13-18, 22-23

Ishaq:191-193; Tabari VI:115-118

PREFACE:

This revelation was revealed after Muhammad's unsuccessful trip/missionary journey to Ta'if, where he was seeking a new home for the persecuted Muslims of Mecca. Muhammad's uncle Abu-Talib and his wife Khadijah passed away (619 AD). The Meccans no longer were interested in Muhammad's message. This revelation implies the Jinn ("spirits/demons") were listening to the guidance of Muhammad's preaching.[9]

SURAH:

Qur'an 72:1-9: "[Muhammad] Say: It has been revealed to me that a party of the Jinn listened, so they said: Surely we have heard a wonderful Qur'an, guiding to the right way — so we believe in it. And we will not set up anyone with our Lord. And He — exalted be the majesty of our Lord! — has not taken a consort, nor a son: And the foolish among us used to forge [devise] extravagant lies against Allah: And person from among men used to seek refuge with persons from among the jinn, so they increased them in evil doing: And they thought, as you think, that Allah would not raise anyone: And we sought to reach heaven, but we found it filled with strong guards and flames: And we used to sit in some of the sitting-places thereof [in order] to steal a hearing [concerning what was recited]. But he who tries to listen now finds a flame lying in wait for him."

Qur'an 72:13-18: "And when we heard the guidance, we believed in it. So whoever believes in his Lord, he fears neither loss nor injustice. And some of us are [among] those who submit, and some of us are [among the] deviators. So whoever submits, these aim at the right way. And as to deviators, they are fuel of hell. And whoever turns away from the reminder of his Lord, He will make him enter into an afflicting chastisement: And the mosques are Allah's, so call not upon anyone with Allah."

Qur'an 72:22-23: "[Muhammad] Say: None can protect me from Allah, nor can I find any refuge against Him: Mine is naught [I am only] but to deliver the command of Allah and His messages. And whoever disobeys Allah and his Messenger, surely for him is the Fire of hell to abide therein for ages."

SUNNAH:

DEATH AND REJECTION

Ishaq:191: "Khadijah and Abu Talib died in the same year, and with Khadijah's death troubles followed [...] he used to tell her all his troubles. With the death of Abu Talib he lost [...] a defense and protection against his tribe [...] it was then that the Quraysh began to treat him in an offensive way [...]."

Ishaq:192-193; Tabari VI:115-118: "When Abu Talib died, the Messenger went to Ta'if to seek support and protection against his own people. He spoke to them about the requests which he had come to make, that they should come to his aid in defense of Islam and take his side against those of his own tribe who opposed him. One of them said, 'If Allah has sent you, I will tear off the covering of the Ka'aba.' Another said, 'Couldn't God find somebody better than you to send?' The third added, 'I shall not speak to you, for if you are Allah's messenger as you say, you're too important for me to reply to, and if you're lying, you're too despicable to address.' Muhammad left them, despairing of getting any good out of the Thaqif. I have been told that he said to them, 'If that is your decision, keep it secret and do not tell anyone about it.' for he did not want his tribe to hear about this matter and be emboldened against him. However, they did not comply with his request, and incited against him their ignorant rabble who reviled him, shouted at him, and hurled stones until a crowd gathered and forced him to take refuge in a garden a long distance from town. When the Messenger despaired getting any positive response from the Thaqif, he left Ta'if to return to Mecca. When he was at Nakhlah, he rose in the middle of the night to pray, and, as has told, a number of the Jinn passed by. [...] They listened to him. [...] The Messenger came back to Mecca and found that its people were more determined to oppose him and to abandon his religion, except for a few weak people who believed in him."

SUMMATION:

IL: The power and persuasion of the Prophet's words are on display as his words change the perceptions of some of the Jinn. The Prophet could have been downcast after the events at Ta'if, the death of his wife and uncle. Certainly the persecution of his followers would have left them and him distraught. Despite the bad and sobering news, Allah permitted the revelation which proved the Prophet's power of persuasion.

WA: Muhammad's adult loved-ones were dead. Personal abuse from the Quraysh was increasing. His mission was floundering and his followers were living as outcasts. Amidst all the chaos in Muhammad's life, we are expected to believe that Muhammad could change the mind of evil spirits. In this surah Allah told Gabriel to tell Muhammad what Allah overheard the Jinn saying. Suddenly, after hearing the Qur'an, the Jinn referred to Allah as their Lord and agreed that Allah had no son. Next, we learn that people were responsible for influencing the Jinn to do evil. This view is one-hundred-eighty degrees in contrast with western concepts of evil where devils tempt people. Eventually, we find Muhammad channeling Jinn who were explaining how some of them wanted to listen to the Qur'an in heaven, but there was a flame in heaven that could consume them. Then we are challenged to imagine how a demonic spirit could be fuel for hell. The Jinn who listen to Muhammad will find salvation. Verses 22-23 declare that obedience to Muhammad, who was rejected by almost everyone except the converted Jinn, was necessary to gain paradise.

QUR'AN 46

"The Sandhills"

620 AD

SCRIPTURE:

Qur'an 46:5-12, 20-22, 27-31, 34

Bukhari:V4B55N554

PREFACE:

When the fate of a nation is sealed by Allah, it can be brought about on the sea or on the sand.(10)

SURAH:

Qur'an 46:5-12: "And who is in greater error than he who invokes [another god] such as answer him not till the day of Resurrection, and they are heedless of their call. And when men are gathered together [at the Judgment], they will be their enemies, and will deny their worshipping them. And when Our clear messages are recited to them, those who disbelieve say of the Truth when it comes to them: This is clear enchantment. Nay, they say: He has forged it. Say: If I have forged it, you control naught for me from Allah. He knows best what you utter concerning it. He is enough as a witness between me and you. And he is Forgiving, the Merciful. Say: I am not the first of the messengers, and I know not what will be done with me or with you. I follow naught but that which is revealed to me, and I am but a plain warner. [...] a witness from among the Children of Israel has borne witness of one like him so he believed...Surely Allah guides not the iniquitous people. And those who disbelieve say of those who believe say: [...] It is an old lie. And before it was the Book of Moses [...] this is a

Late Meccan Revelations   211

Book verifying it in the Arabic language, that it may warn those who do wrong, and as good news for the doers of good."

Qur'an 46:20-22: "And on the day when those who disbelieve are brought to the Fire [...] you are rewarded with the chastisement of abasement [a painful doom] because you were unjustly proud in the land and because you transgressed [...] [The prophets of the past said:] Serve none but Allah. Surely I fear for you the chastisement of [that] grievous day. They said: Hast thou come to us to turn us away from our gods? Then bring [to] us that which thou threatenest [hell-fire] [...] He said: The knowledge is with Allah, and I deliver to you that wherewith I was sent [what was sent to me], but I see you are an ignorant people."

Qur'an 46:27-31, 34: "And certainly We destroyed the towns round about [around] you, and We repeat the messages that they may turn [to Islam] [...] A party [some] of the Jinn who listened to the Qur'an; so when they were in its presence, they said: Be silent. Then when it was finished, they turned back to their people warning them. They said: O our people, we have heard a Book revealed after Moses, verifying that which is before it, guiding to the truth, and to a right path. O our people, accept the Inviter to Allah and believe in Him. He will forgive you some of your sins and protect you from a painful chastisement. And on the day when those who disbelieve are brought before the Fire: Is it not true? They will say: Yea, by our Lord! He will say: Then taste the chastisement, because you disbelieved."

SUNNAH:

Bukhari:V4B55N554: "Allah's Apostle said, 'Shall I not tell you about the story of which no prophet told his nation? Someone will bring with him what will resemble Hell and Paradise, and what he will call Paradise will actually be Hell.' The Prophet was going to visit a fair with some Companions. On the way a company of the Jinn happened by [came by]. When they heard the Qur'an being recited, they tarried and listened attentively. This event is described in the Qur'an and shows that the Jinn who heard the Qur'an were polytheists and deniers of the Prophethood of Muhammad. Then, it is confirmed historically that the Prophet was able to convince them to worship Allah alone."

SUMMATION:

IL: Those who accept gods other than Allah, or any god as a partner with Allah, will be damned at the Resurrection and Judgment. The damned call the truth of Islam a lie, but Allah revealed his final truth in Arabic. In doing so, Allah honored Muhammad and the Arabs. This denial of truth will bring a judgment of fire upon the infidels. Allah warns all infidels that their towns will be destroyed just like those who opposed the previous prophets. Even some of the Jinn were reverted by the Qur'anic truth. This means that infidels have no excuse and will be punished.

WA: The horror of hell is continually reinforced. Fear seems to be the driving force, not reason. Muhammad said, "I am not the first of the Prophets and I do not know what will be done with me or with you." (Qur'an 46:9) The Prophet chosen by Allah was told to say that he did not know or have certainty of his eternal fate. This is a troubling realization since the tone of Allah in the Qur'an is one of looking forward to the doom of people who do not believe Muhammad was a prophet.

As we transition to the Sunnah we learn that Hell and Paradise were being confused by someone who Muhammad failed to identify. If that was so, how could Muhammad be sure that he was not confusing one for the other? The Jinn are called polytheist just like the Quraysh. If the Jinn could revert, then was it possible for the Quraysh to also revert to Islam? Finally, we learn that whatever is revealed in the Qur'an to a Muslim is enough confirmation that it is true. At this point in history Muhammad lost everyone who supported and protected him. His mental state could not have been good.

QUR'AN 10

"Jonah"

621 AD

SCRIPTURE:

Qur'an 10:27, 37-38, 64, 68, 94, 99-100

Ishaq:194-195, 197; Tabari VI:120, 124

PREFACE:

This surah gives a warning. The Arabs who believe in Muhammad's revelation mirror the inhabitants of Nineveh who repented by believing Jonah, but those who remain reprobate will be punished. Likewise, all those that heed the warning will benefit. Since this is a late Meccan surah, the abrogation of earlier 'peaceful' verses was established because Muhammad's persecution at the hands of his Quraysh relatives. Those who did not receive Muhammad as the Prophet will be judged and punished, especially those who persecuted Muhammad. Eventually, this persecution would be applied to the People of the Book.[11]

SURAH:

Qur'an 10:27: "And those who earn evil deeds, the punishment of an evil [deed] is the like thereof, and abasement [humiliating disgrace] will cover them [their faces] — they will have none to protect them from Allah — as if their faces had been covered with slices of the dense darkness of night. These are the companions of the Fire; therein they will abide [forever]."

Qur'an 10:37-38: "And this Qur'an is not such as could be forged by those [anyone] besides Allah, but it is a verification of that which is before it and a clear explanation of the Book, there is no doubt in it, from the Lord of the worlds. Or say [some] they: He has forged it? Say: Then bring a chapter like it, and invite whom you can [others] besides Allah, if you are truthful."

Qur'an 10:64: "For them is good news in this world's life and the Hereafter. There is no changing the words of Allah. That is the mighty achievement."

Qur'an 10:68: "They say: Allah has taken a son to Himself. Glory be to him! He is self-sufficient. His is what is in the heavens and what is in the earth. You have no authority for this. Say you against Allah what you know not?"

Qur'an 10:94: "But if thou art in doubt as to that which We have revealed to thee, ask those who read the Book [The Bible] before thee. [...]"

Qur'an 10:99-100: "And if thy Lord had pleased, all those who are in the earth would have believed, all of them. Wilt thou then force men till they are believers? And it is not for any soul to believe except by Allah's permission. And He casts uncleanness on those who will not understand."

SUNNAH:

A CHANGE IN FORTUNE

Tabari VI:120, 124: "The Prophet used to appear [...] before the Arab tribes [...] informing them that he himself was a Prophet sent by Allah, and asking them to believe his words and defend him. [...] When the Prophet completed his speech and his appeal, Abd Al-Uzza Lahab would say, '[...], this man is calling upon you to cast off Al-Lat and Al-Uzza [...] and accept the error of his ways. Do not obey him; do not listen to him.' When Allah wished to make His religion victorious, to render His Prophet mighty, and to fulfill His promise, the Messenger [...] met a group of Ansar at Aqabah, a party of Khazraj."

Ishaq:194-195, 197: "The Apostle offered himself to the Arab tribes whenever an opportunity arose. [...] ask[ing] them to believe in him and protect him. [...] He went to the tents of the Kinda and offered himself to them, but they declined. He went to the Abdullah clan with the same message, but they would not heed. The Apostle went to the Hanifa, where he met with the worst reception of all. He tried the Amir, but one said to him, 'I suppose you want us to protect you from the Arabs with our lives and then if you prevail, someone else will reap the benefits. Thank you, No!' [...] The Prophet heard about Abdul. He asked them if they would like to get something more profitable than their present errand. Their leader took a handful of dirt and threw it in Muhammad's face. [Muhammad said to a group,] 'What tribe are you from?' [They answered,] 'The tribe of the Khazraj.' [...] Allah had prepared them for Islam because they lived next to the Jews, who were people of scripture and knowledge. While the Khazraj were polytheists and idolaters, they had gained mastery over the Jews, raiding them. Whenever any dispute arose the Jews would say, 'A prophet will be sent soon. His time is at hand. We shall follow him and with him as our leader we shall kill you.'"

SUMMATION:

IL: Those who do evil can never hide from Allah. The Qur'an is true because it explains the true meaning of the scripture that preceded it. In doing so, Allah continued to bring verses that clarify the truth. These verses clarify but do not change the meaning of the Qur'an. Christians will have no excuse since Allah repeatedly told them that Allah has no son. Those who will not believe in Allah will be made wretched.

One Arab tribe after another did not respect the Prophet. As a sign of things to come, the Khazraj, who lived among the Jews at Medina, listened to the Prophet. It was through them the Prophet learned the Jews were expecting a Deliverer.

WA: Allah continually appeared to spend more time describing hell than encouraging people to strive towards heaven. Allah also continued His demands. If His demands were not heeded; He then made threats. The challenge offered by Allah through Muhammad insisted that nothing could compare to the Qur'an. It continued to bother Allah that many considered Jesus equal to Allah. Verse 64 states that Allah's words cannot change while in the same surah advocating the concept of abrogation. Verse 94 was an attempt to persuade the Arab polytheists that Jews and Christians of the past had the truth revealed to them. The verses that follow insinuate that Allah does not want everyone to believe. Only those who receive permission can believe. Sadly, those who are not granted permission must suffer in Allah's hell.

In the Sunnah Arabs, for the most part, were not impressed with Muhammad's message. Interestingly, only the Arab Khazraj, who 'gained mastery over the Jews through raids,' had the insight to listen to Muhammad. Since the Jews told the Khazraj that their leader, the Messiah, would kill the Arabs, the Khazraj saw Muhammad as one who would aid them in any future conflict with the Yathrib Jews.

"Hūd"

621 AD

SCRIPTURE:

Qur'an 11:12-14, 17-18, 108

Ishaq:198-199; Tabari VI:125-127

PREFACE:

This surah introduces the readers to Arab Prophets who were not mentioned in the Hebrew Scriptures except for Shu'yeb, who is thought to be Jethro, the Midianite father-in-law of Moses. Those who reject the Qur'anic revelation are challenged to produce ten chapters like it. This surah compares the wrongdoers and righteous of yesteryear with the era in which Muhammad lived. These wrongdoers, the Quraysh who persecuted the Prophet, were assured of punishment. The persecuting nature of the Quraysh made necessary the introduction of abrogating verses which helped justify hostility against the Quraysh. *Taqiyyah* ("Dissimulation") is also sanctioned for use in order to deceive the Meccan enemy.[12]

SURAH:

Qur'an 11:12-13: "[They say:] Why has not a treasure been sent down for him or an angel to come with him? [...] Or, say they: He has forged it. Say [to them]: Then bring ten forged chapters like it, and call upon who you can besides Allah, if you are truthful."

Qur'an 11:14, 17-18: "But if they answer you not, then know that it is revealed by Allah's knowledge, and that there is no God [who may be worshipped] but He. Will you then submit [to Islam]? Is he [Muhammad] like these who has with him clear proof [the Qur'an] from his Lord, and a witness from Him [Allah] recites it, and before it is the Book of Moses, a guide and a mercy? These believe in it but most do not believe. And whoever of the parties disbelieves in it, the Fire is [will be] his promised place. [...] And who is more unjust than he who forges a lie against Allah? These will be brought before their Lord [Allah], and the witnesses will say: These are they who lied against their Lord. Now surely the curse of Allah is on the wrongdoers."

Qur'an 11:108: "And as for those who are made happy, they will be in the Garden abiding therein so long as the heavens and earth endure, *except* [emphasis added] as your Lord please — a gift never to be cut off."

SUNNAH:

Ishaq:198-199; Tabari VI:125-127: "After the Messenger had spoken to the group from Yathrib they said, 'Take note! This is the very Prophet whom the Jews are menacing us with. Don't let them find him before we accept him.' Because of this, they responded to his call and became Muslims. [...]"

SUMMATION:

IL: Since the Qur'an is continually related to the Books of Moses, yet another proof exists that the Qur'an is true. Those who say the Qur'an is not inspired lie against Allah. These people are cursed. Before Muhammad went to Yathrib/Medina, a party of the Khazraj accepted him as a prophet.

WA: We are now eleven years into Muhammad's mission and still Allah must defend Muhammad against the Quraysh who were convinced that Muhammad received his material from another earthly source. This revelation compared Moses to Muhammad. Since those who knew Muhammad could not accept this new faith, they were eternally damned. What should be troubling for Muslims, is verse 108. This verse mentions Islamic salvation with the caveat: *If Allah pleases, a person still may not be saved.* Therefore, without martyrdom there is no assurance. This should cause soul-searching among the Islamic faithful.

The only reason the Khazraj accepted Muhammad was because he used threatening words concerning the Medinan Jews.[13] The Khazraj did not understand the Jewish Messiah could never be a non-Jew. Therefore, they were only interested in Muhammad to the extent they believed he could help them destroy their Jewish enemies.

QUR'AN 12

"Joseph"

621 AD

SCRIPTURE:

Qur'an 12:1-3

Bukhari:V4B56N818

PREFACE:

The retelling of Joseph, who was the son of Jacob, explains that Jacob was aware of the treachery of his other sons. This betrayal foretold what would happen in Muhammad's life. Joseph became a leader in Egypt. Likewise, Muhammad would lead his people, the Arabs. Those who plotted against Muhammad would submit to him. Muhammad would reform the Arabs and then the world.[14]

SURAH:

Qur'an 12:1-3: "I, Allah, am the Seer, These are the verses of the Book that makes manifest [is manifested to you]. Surely We have revealed it — an Arabic Qur'an — that you may understand. We narrate to thee the best of narratives, in that We have revealed to thee this Qur'an, though before this thou wast of these unaware [were unaware]."

SUNNAH:

Bukhari:V4B56N818: "The Prophet said, 'In a dream I saw myself migrating from Mecca to a place having plenty of date trees. I thought it was Yemen or Hajar, but it came to be Yathrib [...]'"

SUMMATION:

IL: The Qur'an was made specifically for the Arabs long before the Arabs had knowledge of it. The Qur'an would become inspiration for most Arabs and all those influenced by the Arabs. Concerning prophethood, Muhammad saw the Muslim migration to Mecca before it happened. This was another proof of his divine mission.

WA: The Arabs of that time were pretty much clueless concerning what the Bible had to say and how Muhammad related to it. Many could not read Arabic let alone Hebrew or Greek. So those who became Muslims trusted Muhammad's words. The problem that must be acknowledged was that Muhammad was unable to read the Bible. It was described to him by someone claiming to be a Christian. Muhammad, being illiterate, could not understand it. Subsequently he declared the Bible must have been corrupted and Muslims did not have to read it. Muhammad also imagined moving to a place with date trees. Many places in Arabia have date trees. It was only after the fact that Arabs interpreted that Muhammad was speaking of Yathrib.

QUR'AN 14

"Abraham"

621 AD

SCRIPTURE:

Qur'an 14:4, 27, 42-43, 47-50

Bukhari:V4B54N524

PREFACE:

This surah announces that Abraham's preference was his firstborn son Ishmael who he established in an uncultivated valley, known as the Wilderness of Par'an or Mecca. This was necessary in order for Abraham to point towards the coming of Muhammad. Moses was mentioned as a Prophet of Islam, but his mission was only to the Israelites, whereas Muhammad's mission was for the world. All those who opposed the prophets will eventually be destroyed. All those who establish the Law of Allah will be rewarded by having all things made subservient to them. The destruction of all forms of polytheism will be brought about by the descendents of Ishmael. All those who oppose the establishment of the Islamic truth will bring about their own ruin and ultimate failure. The plots of those who oppose the establishment of the Islamic truth will be foiled by Allah. Muslims are allowed to dissimulate against the non-believers until Allah's Law is established.[(15)]

SURAH:

Qur'an 14:4: "And We sent no messenger but with the language of his people, so that he might explain to them clearly. Then Allah leaves in error whom He pleases and He guides whom He pleases. And He is the Mighty, the Wise."

Qur'an 14:27: "Allah confirms those who believe with the sure word in this world's life and in the Hereafter; and Allah leaves the wrongdoers in error; and Allah does what he pleases."

Qur'an 14:42-43: "And think not Allah to be heedless [unaware] of what the unjust do. He only respites them [gives them time] to a day when the eyes will stare [long fixed look] in terror, hastening forward [hurrying in fear], their heads upraised, their gaze not returning to them, and their hearts vacant."

Qur'an 14:47-50: "[...] Surely Allah is Mighty, the Lord of retribution. [...] On the day [...] they will come forth to Allah, the One, the Supreme. And thou wilt see the guilty on that day linked together in chains — their shirts are made of pitch, and fire covering their faces."

SUNNAH:

Bukhari:V4B54N524: "The Prophet said, 'A group of Israelites were lost. Nobody knows what they did. I do not see them except that they were cursed and turned into rats [...]'"

SUMMATION:

IL: Initially, Allah's focus was with the Arabs, who—as the descendents of Ishmael—are the truly chosen of Allah. Allah is sovereign regarding who will be granted pardon and who will be eternally punished. Allah, the merciful, gives unbelievers a season to believe before their judgment. The Quraysh suffered the fate of the ancient Israelites who were given the truth and rejected it.

WA: According to the words in the Qur'an, the Arab's were chosen to change the world. We know that most of the West does not practice Islam. Therefore, Muslims can conclude that Allah left non-Muslims in error and led them astray so non-Muslims might feel terror and fear. Those in the West should understand that Allah declared, and Muslim Literalists believe, those who do not recognize the Qur'anic revelation will be linked in chains while being covered in pitch and fire. Specifically, the ancient

Israelites were cursed and turned into rats. Since the ancient Israelites were cursed, one can only imagine what awaits the Jews who have continuously rejected Muhammad the past 1400 years.

QUR'AN 16

"The Bee"

622 AD

SCRIPTURE:

Qur'an 16:15, 21, 25, 27-29, 64, 66, 75, 84, 88, 93, 101, 106, 118, 125-126

Ishaq:203

PREFACE:

This surah warns infidels that rejecting the Islamic message is like rejecting
food and drink. This is because Muhammad collected the best teachings of
all the previous prophets and presented it in the Qur'an. In doing so, the
Qur'an heals the diseases of men. Otherwise, deniers of this truth will meet
their doom. Those who oppose the Qur'anic revelation deserve immediate
disgrace, but because Allah is slow to retribution, their doom will be
delayed. The Qur'an is the final substitute for all previous revelation. All
those who reject this truth are seen as ungrateful by Allah and will meet
their just punishment. Muslims are told to obey the Qur'anic revelation
in order to be successful. Since the previous revelation, as found in the
Tenakh and the New Covenant, have been abrogated by the Qur'an, those
who persist in their false beliefs will be relegated to Dhimmi status because
they persist to believe in books that are corrupted instead of a new Qur'anic
revelation that replaced the former corrupt revelations.[16]

SURAH:

Qur'an 16:15: "And He has cast firm mountains in the earth lest it quake
with you [to prevent quakes], and rivers and roads that you may go aright
[travel]."

Qur'an 16:21, 25: "Dead are they, not living. And they know not when they will be raised. That they may bear their burdens in full on the day of Resurrection, and also of the burdens of those whom they led astray without knowledge. Ah! [E]vil is what they bear."

Qur'an 16:27-29: "Then on the Resurrection day He will bring them to disgrace and will say: Where are My partners, for whose sake you became hostile? Those who are given the knowledge will say: Surely disgrace this day and evil are upon the disbelievers, whom the angels cause to die, while they are unjust to themselves. Then [they would] offer submission [Islam]: We did not do any evil. [...] So enter the gates of hell to abide therein [forever]. Evil indeed is the dwelling place of the proud."

Qur'an 16:64, 66: "And We have not revealed to thee [Muhammad] the Book [Qur'an], except that thou mayest make clear [explain] to them that wherein they differ, and as a guidance and a mercy for a people who believe. And surely there is a lesson for you in the cattle: We give you to drink from what is in their bellies — from betwixt [between] the faeces [feces] and the blood — pure milk, agreeable to the drinkers."

Qur'an 16:75: "Allah sets forth a parable: There is a slave, the property of another, controlling naught, and there is one to whom We have granted from Ourselves goodly provisions, so he spends from it secretly and openly. Are the two alike [equal]? Praise be to Allah! Nay, most of them know not."

Qur'an 16:84: "And on the day when we raise up a witness out of every nation, then permission to offer excuse will not be given to the disbelievers, nor will they be allowed to make amends."

Qur'an 16:88: "Those who disbelieve and hinder men from Allah's way [Jihad], We will add [even more] chastisement to their chastisement because they made mischief."

Qur'an 16:93: "And if Allah please, He would make you a single nation, but He leaves in error whom He pleases and guides whom He pleases. [...]"

Qur'an 16:101: "And when We change a message for [another] message — and Allah knows best what He reveals — they say: Thou art only a forger. Nay, most of them know naught."

Qur'an 16:106: "Whoso disbelieves in Allah after his belief [after accepting faith in Allah] — not he who is compelled while his heart is content with faith [except under duress], but he who opens his breast for disbelief [commit apostasy] — on them is the wrath of Allah, and for them is a grievous chastisement."

Qur'an 16:118: "And to those who are Jews We prohibited what We have related to thee already, and We did them no wrong, but they wronged themselves."

Qur'an 16:125-126: "Call to the way of thy Lord with wisdom and goodly exhortation [beautiful preaching]; and argue with them in the best manner. Surely thy Lord knows best him who strays from the path, for your Lord knows best who has strays from His path, and He knows best those who go aright. And if you take your turn, then punish with the like of that with which you were afflicted. But if you show patience, it is certainly best for the patient."

SUNNAH:

Ishaq:203: "[The chief told Muhammad,] 'Choose what you want for yourself and your Lord. The Messenger recited the Qur'an and made us desirous of Islam. Then he said, 'I will enter a contract of allegiance with you, provided that you protect me as you would your women and children.'"

SUMMATION:

IL: Those who deny or oppose Islam will die by the will of angels. Those who deny Islam when it is offered have done evil and will be damned. The Qur'an will be used to convince the unbelievers and comfort the believing. Slaves are not equal to their masters. After infidels die it will be too late for them. Hell will be terrible for infidels because their unbelief can hinder others from Jihad. In doing so, Allah makes no attempt to guide them to the Islamic truth. To ensure victory, Allah reserves the right to bring verses that will ensure Islam's ultimate victory. Therefore, Allah guides all Muslims to the truth. Those who leave the Islamic truth after receiving it will experience the wrath of Allah and a terrible penalty. The Jews are one such group who are guilty. All are invited to the Islamic *Dawah* ("the call"). In the Sunnah, it was the group from Yathrib who answered the Prophet's Dawah and accepted Islam.

WA: Scientifically I'm still not sure if mountains prevent earthquakes. When tectonic plates come together one slides below the other and pushes up rock that eventually become mountains. The sliding of these plates usually brings about an earthquake. After speaking of geology, the Qur'an again declares that those not accepting Islam are evil and will be punished. Muhammad was supposed to be explaining the Qur'an in plain language, but after eleven years of his mission he had overwhelmingly been rejected. It is hard to believe the Creator of the Universe came up with the cattle analogy. Since Allah will be harsh to unbelievers, Allah's slaves believe they can also maintain the same harsh attitude towards who they term as infidels. The implementation of abrogation was established to give the Prophet the wiggle room needed to change tactics. Islam's willingness to punish those who exercise their free will choice and decide to leave Islam places an exclamation mark next to the term "intolerance." In all of Allah's decrees, he continues to hold the Jews in low esteem. Islamic scholars believe the destiny of the Jews will be filled with humiliation and disgrace.[17]

QUR'AN 6

"The Cattle"

622 AD

SCRIPTURE:

Qur'an 6:20-21, 24, 25, 34, 38, 65-68, 108, 112, 121, 125

Tabari VI:131

PREFACE:

Meccan polytheism was condemned by Allah and His Prophet. Twelve years of preaching by Muhammad produced few converts. Despite this slow progress, triumph was predicted to be accomplished. Christian belief is also compared to Meccan polytheism. Ultimate victory against this 'idolatry' is assured. Divine judgment was also predicted. It is only the worship of Allah that reveals Islam as Abraham's religion. The eventual failure of Islam's enemies is promised. The victory of Islam will be a gradual process. After 12 years of preaching futility in Mecca, this surah—the last surah revealed at Mecca—prepared Muslims for the implementation of abrogation. Abrogating verses were needed to change strategy against the non-Muslims of Arabia.[18]

SURAH:

Qur'an 6:20-21: "Those whom We have given the Book [Bible] recognize him [Muhammad] as they recognize their sons. Those who have lost their souls — they will not believe. And who is more unjust than he who forges a lie against Allah or gives the lie to His messages? Surely the wrongdoers will not be successful."

Qur'an 6:24: "See how they [Christians and Jews] lie against their own souls, and that which they forged [Bible verses] shall fail them."

Qur'an 6:25: "[...] We have cast veils over their hearts so that they understand it not and a deafness into their ears. And even if they see every sign they will not believe in it. [...]"

Qur'an 6:34: "And messengers indeed were rejected before thee, but they were patient when rejected and persecuted, until Our help came to them. And there is none to change the words of Allah. And there has already come to thee some information about the messengers."

Qur'an 6:38: "And there is no animal in the earth, nor a bird that flies on its two wings, but they are communities yourselves. We have not neglected anything in the Book. [...]"

Qur'an 6:65-68: "[Muhammad] Say: He has the power to send on you a chastisement from above or from beneath your feet, or to throw you into confusion, making you of different parties, and make some of you taste the violence [tyranny] of others. [...] And thy people will call it a lie, [but] it is the Truth. [...] For every prophecy is a term, and you will soon come to know it. And when thou seest those who talk nonsense about Our messages withdraw from them until they enter into some other discourse. And if the devil cause thee to forget, then sit not after recollection [don't sit, trying to remember] with the unjust people."

Qur'an 6:108: "And abuse not those who they call upon [other gods] besides Allah, lest, exceeding the limits, they abuse Allah through ignorance. [...]"

Qur'an 6:112: "And thus did We make for every prophet an enemy, the devils from among men and Jinn, some of them inspiring others with gilded speech [using smooth speech] to deceive them. And if thy Lord pleased, they would not do it, so leave them alone with what they forge."

Qur'an 6:121: "[...] And certainly the devils inspire their friends to contend with you; and if you obey them, you will surely be polytheists."

Qur'an 6:125: "So whomsoever Allah intends to guide, He expands his breast for Islam, and whomsoever He intends to leave in error, He makes his breast strait [straight] and narrow as though he were ascending upwards. Thus does Allah lay uncleanness on those who do not believe."

SUNNAH:

Tabari VI:131: "'I shall not turn my back on the Ka'aba and shall pray toward it.' [...] 'By Allah, we have not heard that our Prophet prays in any other direction than Jerusalem, and we do not wish to differ from him.'"

SUMMATION:

IL: The Qur'an testifies that Jews and Christians are full of deceit. The People of the Book knew the Prophet was as identifiable as their forefathers and their own children. In order to hide the Prophet, the People of the Book purposely forged their own scriptures. Now it is too late for them because Allah has now cast blindness on them. All those who came before the Prophet suffered in like manner. All those who make the prophets suffer will be punished. All of this is within the will of Allah. Anyone who opposes Allah's Prophet comes from Satan. Muslims are assured they are the favored of Allah while also being assured that infidels are unclean.

WA: Most Muslims will never touch a Bible and really do not know if Muhammad can be found in the Bible. Christians and Jews are called liars by Islam's god and Islam's prophet. Muslims should read the Bible for themselves to see if the claim is true. Since Allah must know if this is true, Muslims should be able to check this for themselves. Muhammad was unlettered so he never read the Biblical text for himself. Also, for reason of pure certainty, Muslims should have proof the Bible was forged. Saying the Bible does not agree with the Qur'an is not in itself proof of forgery. There must be evidence of change in the Biblical text. In verse 38, Allah spoke through Muhammad and stated, 'We have not neglected anything in the Book,' i.e., the Bible. The Qur'an does not state if the Bible also identified the Jewish Messiah. The Qur'an promises textual inerrancy, but never told Muslims to go and check the veracity of its statements. Those who come to a different conclusion are simply condemned to hell for making their own decisions. Allah clearly does not want Muslims to investigate. The Qur'anic Allah champions blind obedience. When reading verse 65, we must ask ourselves these questions: (1) How can the devil cause believers to forget? and (2) If Allah is all powerful, why was Allah unable to protect his slaves from Satan's powers of induced amnesia? Next, Muslims are told not to abuse non-Muslims unless Allah is abused through ignorance. In other words, Muslims are allowed to abuse non-Muslims. Non-Muslims can be abused when Allah blinds them from coming to Islam. Muslims are told when anyone tries to lead Muslims away from Allah, these unbeliever are of the devil.

On the surface, there also appears to be a problem within the Sunnah. Muhammad claimed he would not turn his back on the Ka'aba, but his followers prayed facing Jerusalem because that was Muhammad's practice. If one prayed in the direction facing Jerusalem while living just northwest of Mecca, they would be turning their back on the Ka'aba because the Ka'aba would be behind them. A Muslim's head was supposed to bow towards Mecca. His posterior was not supposed to be bent towards the Ka'aba.

QUR'AN 22

"The Pilgrimage"

622 AD

SCRIPTURE:

Qur'an 22:5, 17, 19-22, 25, 39-40, 52-53

Ishaq:205, 208, 212-213; Tabari VI:133-134, 136, 138

PREFACE:

Although Muslims were expelled from Mecca, Islam would be taken to the world and would not be confined to the borders of Arabia. Because Mecca was the spiritual center of the Arab polytheists and of those who persecuted the Prophet, it had to be captured by the Muslims. The faithful must be willing to lay down their lives for Islam because Islam must be established in Arabia. Punishment was withheld from the opponents of Muhammad for a time, but the believer is assured that punishment will come. The extirpation of polytheism was assured as well. In preparation for the Islamic decree that permitted fighting, the abrogation of verses would be necessary to justify the use of violence against the enemies of Islam. The violence to be used against them will also bring about their condemnation in the next life. The abrogating verses justify the lesser jihad in order to expand and spread the Dar al-Islam.[19]

SURAH:

Qur'an 22:5: "[...] We created you from the dust, then from a small life-germ, then from a clot, then from a lump of flesh, [...]"

Qur'an 22:17: "Those who believe and those who are Jews and the Sabians and the Christians and the Magians and the polytheists — surely Allah will decide between them on the day of resurrection. Surely Allah is witness over all things."

Qur'an 22:19-22: "These are two adversaries [believers and unbelievers] who dispute about their Lord. So those who disbelieve, for them are cut out garments of fire. Boiling water will be poured out over their heads. With it will be melted what is in their bellies and their skins as well. And for them are whips of iron. Whenever they desire to go forth from it [escape from it], from grief, they are turned back into it, and it is said: Taste the chastisement of burning."

Qur'an 22:25: "Those who disbelieve and hinder men from Allah's way [Jihad] and from the Sacred Mosque, [...] We shall make him taste of painful chastisement."

Qur'an 22:39-40: "Permission to fight is given to those on whom war is made, because they are oppressed. And surely Allah is Able to assist them [to victory] — those who are driven from their homes without a just cause except that they Muslims say: Our Lord is Allah. And if Allah did not repel some people by others, cloisters, and churches, and synagogues, and mosques, in which Allah's name is much remembered, would have been pulled down. And surely Allah will help him who helps Him. Surely Allah is Strong, Mighty."

Qur'an 22:52-53: "And We never sent a messenger or a prophet before thee, but when he desired, the devil made a suggestion respecting his desire; but Allah annuls that which the devil casts, then does Allah establish His messages. And Allah is Knowing, Wise — That He may make what the devil casts a trial [temptation] for those in whose hearts is a disease and [they are] the hard-hearted. And surely the wrongdoers are in severe opposition."

SUNNAH:

Ishaq:205: "'If you are loyal to this undertaking, it will profit you in this world and the next.' They said, 'We will accept you as a Prophet under these conditions, but we want to know specifically what we will get in return for our loyalty.' Muhammad answered, 'I promise you Paradise.'

[...] The following morning, Quraysh leaders came to our encampment saying that they had heard that we invited Muhammad to leave them and that we had pledged ourselves to support him in a war against them. Thereupon members of our tribe swore that nothing of the kind had happened and that we knew nothing of it."

THE AQABAH PLEDGE OF VIOLENCE

Tabari VI:133, 134: "We pledge our allegiance to you and we shall defend you as we would our womenfolk. Administer the oath of allegiance to us, Messenger of Allah, for we are men of war possessing arms and coats of [chain]mail. O Messenger, there are ties between us and the Jews, which we shall have to sever. If we do this and Allah gives you victory, will you perhaps return to your own people and leave us? Muhammad smiled and said, "Nay, blood is blood, and bloodshed without retaliation is blood paid for. You are of me and I am of you. I shall war against whomever you fight. Men of the Khazraj, do you know what you are pledging yourselves to in swearing allegiance to this man.' 'Yes,' they answered. 'In swearing allegiance to him we are pledging ourselves to wage war against all [of] mankind.'"

Ishaq:208: "When Allah gave permission to his Apostle to fight, the second Aqabah [pledge] contained conditions involving war which were not in the first act of submission. [...] We pledged ourselves to war in complete obedience to Muhammad no matter how *evil* [emphasis added] the circumstances. [...]"

Ishaq:212-213: "The Apostle had not been allowed to fight or shed blood before the second Aqabah. He had simply been ordered to call men to Allah, to endure insult and forgive the ignorant. The Quraysh persecuted his followers, seducing some from their religion and exiling others. They [the Quraysh] became insolent towards Muhammad's God [Allah] and rejected His gracious purpose. They accused His Prophet of lying. So He gave permission to His Apostle to fight those who had wronged him.... When they are in the ascendant Muslims will establish the Islamic prayers, pay zakat and institute Islamic law. Then Allah sent down to him: "Fight them so that no Muslim can be seduced from His religion until Allah alone is worshipped."

Tabari VI:136, 138: "When the Quraysh came to recognize what had really happened, they urged one another to torment the Muslims and treat them harshly. [...] The Muslims suffered great hardship. [...] Those present at the oath of Aqabah had sworn an allegiance to Muhammad. It was a pledge of war against all men. Allah had permitted fighting."

SUMMATION:

IL: On the day of Resurrection, Muslims will stand tall over the remainder of unbelief. Jews, Sabians, Christians, Magians, and polytheists are destined to suffer the worst of punishments at the Judgment. What is worse than unbelief? Infidels who prevent Muslims from joining the Jihad or prevent them from going to the mosque should be punished. Allah permitted fighting when Muslims were driven from their homes. In this case, the Meccan Muslims were forced to flee. Allah will always come to the aid of oppressed Muslims. Verse 52 abrogated the events that were captured in Qur'an 53. This removed any blame from the Prophet and placed it on the devil and the Quraysh who suggested the polytheistic agreement with the Prophet. The Quraysh made it impossible for the Prophet and the Meccan Muslims to stay in Mecca. The Quraysh were concerned with the Khazraj who were from Medina because they feared an alliance with Muhammad. Those from Medina were given permission to fight for Islam. This only occurred after the Prophet had endured much hardship from the Quraysh.

WA: Allah's biology lesson is meant to reinforce the belief that Muslims should submit to Allah's will. Once again the details described how non-Muslims are to suffer. These were Muhammad's own words. Non-Muslims will suffer from: burning, boiling, melting, and scourging. This language demeans all non-Muslims. In the eyes of Muslim Literalists, these words give them tacit approval for their behavior. Verse 25 is aimed at Christian missionaries and makes their activities in the Dar al-Islam criminal. This surah also encourages Muslims to fight whenever there is dispute over land possession.[20] Muslims will always be considered the oppressed when there is a dispute over land. The event surrounding verse 52 is an attempt to ease the minds of Muslims who were taken back by Muhammad's agreement three years earlier concerning the goddesses Al-lat, Al-Uzza, and Manat.

In the Sunnah, Muhammad, not Allah, promised the Khazraj Paradise for their loyalty. The Khazraj practiced *Taqiyyah* ("Dissimulation") which they either brought from Medina or learned from Muhammad. They told the Quraysh they had no intent to do violence. The sequence was established:

(1) If one accepted Islam then violence would be permitted to advance Islam.

(2) The Quraysh were to be fought for accusing the Prophet of being a liar; however, it was acceptable for Muhammad's followers to be less than honest.

In the example that involved the Quraysh, Muslims were told to fight those who tried to persuade them to another religion. Optimally, this battle should be engaged with words not blood.[21] However, Islam's global ambitions were vividly expressed; and those ambitions are linked to violence. In the Sunnah dialogue those who told the Quraysh that they knew nothing dissimulated because they were men of war. From the beginning of this discourse, it was not possible to befriend Jews. The Khazraj understood this. Being part of Muhammad's religion meant separation from the Jews. Tangentially, their pledge to Muhammad took on the semblance of the 'Heil Hitler' salutation. The pledge at Aqabah was a pledge of warfare against all non-Muslims. Muhammad and his followers were following their god's permission to fight so they could spread the faith. When the Quraysh realized the men from Yathrib lied to them, they reacted harshly against Muhammad and his followers. War was, and is, inevitable for all who resist Islam.

The allegiance was made provided that Muhammad was protected by the men of Yathrib. Then Muhammad stated that he was one with them and would fight their enemies. He also pledged to be at peace with those who wanted peace with them. In Muhammad's prophetic office this turned out not to be true. The Yathrib Arabs were not at war with the three Jewish tribes at Yathrib, but eventually Muhammad attacked them and defeated them.

QUR'AN 23

"The Believers"

622 AD

SCRIPTURE:

Qur'an 23:5-6, 12-15, 39-41, 82-83, 91, 101-103

Ishaq:221-222; Tabari VI:139-143

PREFACE:

In this surah, the final and future triumph of Islam was foretold. It argues that the life and history of Muhammad mirrored the lives of all previous Prophets. Muhammad's appearance signaled the finality of polytheism. Finally, this surah ends with the promise that the wicked will regret their evil deeds.[22]

SURAH:

Qur'an 23:5-6: "And who restrain their sexual passions [the believers] — except in the presence of their mates or those whom their right hands possess [slave girls], for such surely are not blamable."

Qur'an 23:12-15: "And certainly We create man of an extract of clay, then We make him a small life-germ in a small resting-place, then We make the life-germ a clot, then We make the clot a lump of flesh, then We make in the lump of flesh bones, then We clothe the bones with flesh, then We cause it to grow into another creation. [...] Then after that you certainly die."

Qur'an 23:39-41: "He said: My Lord, help me against their calling me a liar. He said: In a little while they will certainly be repenting. So the punishment overtook them in justice, and We made them as rubbish; so away with the unjust people!"

Qur'an 23:82-83: "They say: 'When we die and become dust and bones, shall we then be raised up? We are indeed promised this, and so were our fathers before. This is naught but of stories of those of old!'"

Qur'an 23:91: "Allah has not taken to Himself a son, nor is there with Him any other god [...]"

Qur'an 23:101-103: "So when the trumpet is blown, there will be no ties of relationship among them that day, nor will they ask of [for] one another. Then those whose good deeds are heavy, those are the successful. And those whose good deeds are light, those are they who have lost their souls, abiding in hell."

SUNNAH:

THE ESCAPE

Tabari VI:139: "After Allah had given His Messenger permission to fight [...], the Messenger of Allah commanded those at Mecca to emigrate to Yathrib [Medina] and join their brethren, the Ansar."

Tabari VI:140-142/Ishaq:221-222: "The Quraysh were now anxious about Muhammad going there as they knew he had decided [...] to make war on them. They deliberated as to what to do [to determine what to do] with Muhammad as [because] they had come to fear him. [...] Let us expel him from among us and banish him from the land. The harm which he has been doing will disappear, and we shall be rid of him. We shall be able to put our affairs back in order and restore our social harmony. [...] [An Arab Shaykh said,] 'If you expel him, I think it likely that he will descend upon some other Arab tribe and win them over with his recitals [words] so that they will follow him and adopt his plans. He will lead them against you. They will attack, crush you, seize your power, rob you, and do with you whatever he wants.' Thereupon Abu Jahl said, 'I think we should take one young, strong, well-born man from each clan and give each [of them] a sharp sword. They should make for him and strike him with their swords as one man and kill him.' Gabriel came to the Messenger and said, 'Do not spend this night in the bed in which you usually sleep.' When the first third of the night had past, the young men gathered at his door and waited for him to go to sleep so that they could fall upon him. When Muhammad saw what they intended to do he said to Ali, 'Lie on my bed and wrap yourself up in my green cloak [...] Nothing unpleasant will befall you from them [happen to you]. [...] If Abu Bakr comes to you, tell him that I have gone to Thawr and ask him to join me. [...]' Then the Messenger went off [...]."

Tabari VI:143: "Among those who had gathered against him was Abu Jahl. He said, while waiting at his door, 'Muhammad alleges if we follow him, we will be kings over the Arabs and the Persians. Then after we die fighting for him, we will be brought back to live in gardens like those in Jordan. He also claims that if we do not submit to him, we shall be slaughtered. After his followers kill us, we shall be brought back to life and thrown into the fires of hell in which we shall burn.' Allah's Messenger came out and took a handful of dust and said, 'Yes, I do say that; and you are one of them.' '[...] This sentence [statement] is justified against most of them, for they do not believe. We will certainly put iron collars on their necks which will come up to their chins so that they will not be able to raise their heads. [...]'"

SUMMATION:

IL: With war on the horizon, Allah granted the Muslims passion with their wives and also with women they captured once the war started. The Quraysh deserved what was about to befall them because for ten years they accused the Prophet of being a liar. Allah assured Muhammad and the Muslims that the Quraysh would pay in this life and the next. Allah's call against the son-ship of the Christians also prepared the Muslims for conflict. This epic struggle would not only be against the Quraysh, but also against those who practiced *shirk*. By following the decrees of Allah, Muslims earn good deeds. Those who reject Allah and Muhammad's prophetic office will not have many good deeds; therefore, they are Allah's enemies and will be damned.

The Hegira was a strategic retreat called by Allah. The Muslims planned to immigrate to the home of the Khazraj and Aws—Medina, of the Hejaz.

As the Quraysh, under Abu Jahl, plotted the murder of the Prophet, Allah ensured the blood of the Quraysh would instead be spilled. Muhammad anticipated their murderous plot and avoided assassination, and once again proved his prophethood. Then Muhammad rightly predicted the fate of the Quraysh.

WA: In verses 5-6, Allah and Muhammad, His spokesperson, sanctioned rape. One cannot assume that slave girls want to have sex with those who capture them. Allah had just created an incentive for Muslims to fight and conquer their foes. Those who knew Muhammad best, his Quraysh relatives, continued to call him a liar. Sometimes where one finds smoke, fire can also be found. Christian dogma concerning Jesus seems to be the main reason why Christians will find themselves, along with many others, on the receiving end of Islamic wrath. These edicts, similar to the previous surahs, promise that non-Muslims will pay dearly.

The Quraysh knew that Muhammad was eventually going to exercise violence against them. Muhammad was their enemy. In retrospect, had Muhammad been killed, history may have been different. When Muhammad told his cousin Ali to sleep in the bed to outwit the assassins, he purposely placed Ali's life in jeopardy to save himself. What if Ali had been murdered? Muhammad placed Ali in a situation where it could have happened. Was this an act of love towards his cousin or self-preservation? Lastly, Muhammad's parting words for his relatives, the Quraysh was the promise they would be taken away in shackles.

QUR'AN 28

"The Narrative"

622 AD

SCRIPTURE:

Qur'an 28:38, 41-43, 85, 88

Ishaq:223; Tabari VI:147

PREFACE:

This revelation was revealed during the flight from Mecca to Yathrib known as Medina. It recalled Moses' expulsion from Egypt, his return to Egypt in victory, and the destruction of Pharaoh and his army. In a similar way, Muhammad departed from Mecca, he would return to Mecca in victory, and the Meccan leadership would meet their doom.[23]

SURAH:

Qur'an 28:38: "And Pharaoh said: O Chiefs, I know no god for you besides myself; so kindle a fire for me, O Haman, on bricks of clay, then prepare for me a lofty [big] building, so that I may obtain knowledge of Moses' God, and surely I think him a liar."

Qur'an 28:41-43: "And We made them leaders who call to the Fire. [...] And We made a curse to follow them in this world, and on the day of Resurrection they will be hideous. And certainly We gave Moses the Book after We had destroyed the former generations — clear arguments for men, and a guidance and a mercy, that they may be mindful."

Qur'an 28:85, 88: "He Who has made the Qur'an binding on thee will surely bring thee back to the place of return [back to this place]. And call not with Allah any other god. There is no God but He. Everything will perish but He. His is the judgment, and to Him you will be brought back."

SUNNAH:

THE HIJRAH

Tabari VI:147: "[…] the Messenger is said to have informed Ali that he was leaving and to have commanded him to stay behind […]"

Ishaq:223: "When the Messenger decided upon departure, he went to Bakr and the two left by a window in the back of Abu's house and went to a cave in Thawr, a mountain below Mecca."

SUMMATION:

IL: Allah revealed the past to assure the Prophet the same type of enemy that confronted him also confronted Moses. This proved that Muhammad was of the stature of Moses. The Quraysh also trusted in fire like the Pharaoh, and so by fire they would be judged. Both thought Allah was a liar. These are all proofs of prophethood. Muslims are warned in this surah the generation that followed Moses was destroyed, so Muslims must be careful to submit.

WA: The "Haman" mentioned in verse 28 can be found in the Book of Esther ("Haddassah") in the Tenakh ("Old Testament"). The event that included both Moses and Pharaoh occurred in the 1300-1250 BC timeframe. Events describing Haman occurred in the 6th Century BC at Babylon. If the large building referred to in this passage was the Tower of Babel then it was constructed by command of Nimrod approx. 3000 years BC. If the Qur'an was referring to these events, then these events were misplaced. Otherwise, we have no biblical account of these events as described or any source other than Allah's declarations, through Muhammad, in the Qur'an. It seems as though a surah does not exist in the Qur'an where Muhammad's relatives, the Quraysh, are not being damned to eternal doom. Polytheism, as well as the belief that Jesus was divine, remain as issues that Muslims are told to avoid and also oppose. Muhammad's departure from Mecca was nothing like Moses' initial departure from Egypt. Muhammad deployed deception to sneak out of town with his followers. Moses was bound and cast out of Egypt into the wilderness. Moses was all alone...or so he thought.

"The Elevated Places"

622 AD

SCRIPTURE:

Qur'an 7:3-4, 27, 41, 44, 123-124, 157, 166-167, 178-179, 182-183, 186, 188

Tabari VI:157; VII:1-3

PREFACE:

This surah was revealed at the close of the Meccan era and at the beginning of the Medinan era. Those who oppose Allah's will and purpose are aligned with Satan. This surah makes the case that all those who opposed the prophets of old met their doom; therefore, all those who oppose the Islamic Prophet will also be doomed. The mission of the Prophet of Arabia resembled the mission Moses. For Moses predicted the coming of a Prophet from Arabia, a son of Ishmael. It also stated that the gospel predicted the coming of Muhammad. Proof that Muhammad revealed the truth was expressed by those who reject the revelation of the Prophets—they will eventually be doomed. According to Islam, the scriptures of the Jews and Christians revealed that Muhammad would come. The Qur'an warned those who did not accept Islam would not only be terrorized by Allah in this life, but will be condemned in the next. Dissimulation was permitted against those who plot against Allah, in this case, the Quraysh.[24]

SURAH:

Qur'an 7:3-4: "[...] little do you mind [remember]! And how many a town [towns] have We destroyed! So Our punishment came to it by night or while they slept at midday."

Qur'an 7:27: "[...] Surely We have made the devils to be the friends of those who believe not [in Islam]."

Qur'an 7:41, 44: "They shall have a bed of hell and over them coverings of it. And thus do We requite [punish] the wrongdoers. And the owners of the Garden call out to the companions of the Fire: We have indeed found that which our Lord promised us to be true; have you, too, that which your Lord promised to be true? They will say: Yes. Then a crier will cry out among them: The curse of Allah is on the wrongdoers."

Qur'an 7:50: "And the companions of the Fire [Hell] call out to the owners of the garden [Paradise]: Pour us some water or some of that which Allah has provided for you. They [the owners of the garden] say: Surely Allah has forbidden them both to the disbelievers [infidels]."

Qur'an 7:65: "And to 'Ad' [A tribe of Arabs near Oman] We sent their brother Hud [Eber]. He said: O my people, serve Allah, you have no god other than Him. [...]"

Qur'an 7:123-124: "[Pharaoh said:] I shall certainly cut off your hands and your feet on opposite sides, then I shall crucify you all together!"

Qur'an 7:157: "Those who follow the Messenger-Prophet, the Ummi ["illiterate"], whom they find mentioned in the Torah and the Gospel. He enjoins them good and forbids them evil, and makes lawful to them the good things and prohibits for them impure things, and removes from them their burden and the shackles which were on them. So those who believe in him and honour him and help him, and follow the light which has been sent down with him — these are the successful."

Qur'an 7:166-167: "So when they [the Jews] revoltingly persisted in that which they had been forbidden, We said to them: Be as apes, despised and hated. [...] [T]hy Lord declared that He would send against them to the day of Resurrection those who would subject them to severe torment. Surely thy Lord is Quick in requiting; and surely He is Forgiving, Merciful."

Qur'an 7:178: "He whom Allah guides is on the right way; and he whom He leaves in error — they are the losers."

Qur'an 7:179: "And certainly We have created for hell many of the jinn and the men — they have hearts wherewith they understand not, and they have eyes wherewith they see not, they have ears wherewith they hear not. They are as cattle; nay, they are more astray [they are even worse than cattle]. These are the heedless ones."

Qur'an 7:182-183: "And those who reject Our messages — We lead them to destruction step by step from whence they know not. And I grant them respite. Surely My scheme is effective."

Qur'an 7:186: "Whomsoever Allah leaves in error, there is no guide for him. And He leaves them alone in their inordinacy, blindly wandering on."

Qur'an 7:188: "Say [Muhammad]: I control not benefit or harm for myself except as Allah please. And had I known the unseen, I should have much of good, and no evil would touch me. I am but a warner and the giver of good news to a people who believe."

SUNNAH:

THE ARRIVAL AT MEDINA

Tabari VI:157: "It is said that when Allah's Prophet came to Medina he ordered the establishment of a new era. They used to reckon time by the number of months after Muhammad's arrival."

Tabari VII:1-3: "The time for the Friday prayer overtook Muhammad while he was in the bed of a wadi [a dry riverbed] This place was used as a mosque that day. This was the first Friday prayer which the Messenger held in Islam. The sermon the Messenger led at the first Friday prayer in a wadi outside of Medina began, 'Praise be to Allah. I praise him, and call on him for help, forgiveness and guidance. I believe in him, do not deny him and I am an enemy of whoever denies him.' I bear witness that there is no deity but Allah, without partner, and that Muhammad is his Messenger whom he has sent after an interval in the appearance of messengers, at a time when knowledge is scarce, men are led astray, time is cut short, the Last Hour is at hand, the End is near. Beware of what Allah has warned you [about] concerning himself. The fear of Allah, for whoever acts according to it in fear and dread of his Lord is a trusty aid to what you desire. Allah says, 'The sentence that comes from me cannot be changed, and I am in no wise a tyrant unto the slaves.' The fear of Allah will ward off Allah's hatred, retribution, and wrath. [...] Be enemies of Allah's enemies and strive in Allah's cause [Jihad] in the way to which He is entitled. He has chosen you and named you Muslims. There is no power but with Allah. Allah pronounces judgment upon men, and because Allah rules men they do not rule him."

SUMMATION:

IL: Allah declared how he commanded Jihad in the past. In the same manner, Muslims will wage Jihad against all those who oppose the establishment of Allah's kingdom. Terror can be used and is sanctioned by Allah to bring repentance to the infidels. This is permitted because all who will not embrace Islam are in league with the devil and must be treated like the devil's allies. At the end of their days, the Muslims will rejoice because they rightly believe and will remind those in torment who did not choose well. The evil infidels, who are damned to hell, will be refused the slightest comfort. Arabs, in particular, have no excuse since Allah sent prophets to them before. Now Arabs must believe in Allah's religion. The Pharaoh threatened the people during the time of Moses; likewise, the evil Quraysh threaten the Muslims. Through Muhammad the miracle of Islam occurred. He was illiterate yet He became the Prophet and brought the Qur'anic revelation to humanity. He can be found in the previous scriptures despite biblical corruption perpetrated by the Jews, who are forever cursed by Allah, the Almighty. Therefore, the Jews are forever misled by Allah so they can all enter damnation. Allah schemes against all unbelievers. They will also be misled to their final destruction. Those who refuse the Prophet's words are worse than animals. As for the holy Prophet, he only did as Allah commanded; therefore, he was blameless in all things.

Muhammad, with the institution of the Hegira, changed time itself. This abrogated the western calendar from the birth of Jesus to the Hegira of Muhammad, because Muhammad was the Seal of the Prophets whereby Jesus was but a Prophet of Islam. Friday Prayers at the Mosque were established because the former time was abrogated to demonstrate that Abraham was a Muslim before Moses and Jesus. Since Islam is the religion of Abraham, Muslims will worship one day before the Jews and two days before the Christians. Whoever denied the Prophet, even though he was mentioned in the Jewish and Christian scriptures, is an enemy of Muslims. [25] Only one who confesses the Shahada proves ones loyalty to Allah and the Prophet. Lastly, it is the will of Allah to accomplish Jihad against all infidels.

WA: It is troubling that Allah rejoiced in the slaughter of his creation while they were at rest. Terror became a recurring theme that Muslim literalists employ to the current day. The concept of Allah associating the devil with Allah's enemies was established. It is still being used today evidenced by their continual references to the Great Satan (United States of America) and the Little Satan (Israel). Why did Allah recall that believers in Allah's paradise will mock those who are in hell? Why is the Islamic Paradise so close to Hell? How else could the inhabitants of both converse? When Allah quoted the Pharaoh, the same quote would once again be found in 5:33, which at that time still had not been revealed. In fact, Allah adopted in 5:33 what the Pharaoh declared in verses 123-124. As for crucifixion, it was not instituted still many years hence. Therefore, historically, it is not likely that the Pharaoh knew about crucifixion. The consistent claim that Muhammad was predicted in the Bible is simply not true. The verses that supposedly speak of Muhammad cannot be located in any historical record. The following Bible verses: Gen. 3:15, 49:10; Deut. 18:15-18; 2 Sam. 7:12; Ps. 2, 22, 110:1, 118:22; Prov. 30:4; Isa 53; Jer. 31; Dan. 7:13-14, 9:24-27; Mic. 5:1-2; Zech. 9:9, 12-10, 14:2, 9; etc., do not describe Muhammad because these scripture describe a descendant of Judah. Muhammad was not a descendant of Jacob/Israel and his son Judah. According to Islam, the Jews of the present must pay for the perceived misdeeds of the Jews of the past. Indubitably, Allah never desired that everyone attain paradise, because He willed, and continues to will, that some be used as fuel for hell.

In this analysis, Muhammad did not fulfill the words of the prophets with the establishment of the Islamic calendar and Friday worship; rather, he created a new faith which was created to replace Judaism and Christianity.

CHAPTER 4 NOTES

1. Ali, p. 586; Pickthall, p. 211
2. Ali, p. 716; Pickthall, p. 259
3. Ali, p. 1255; Pickthall, p. 453
4. Ali, p. 1028; Pickthall, p. 377
5. Zakaria, Muhammad, pp. 12-15
6. Muir, *Life of Mahomet*, pp. 88-89
7. Ali, p. 561; Pickthall, p. 204
8. Peters, *Jihad in Classical and Modern Islam*, p. 29
9. Ali, p. 1140; Pickthall, p. 416
10. Ali, p. 979; Pickthall, p. 357
11. Ali, p. 431; Pickthall, p. 156
12. Ali, p. 453; Pickthall, p. 165
13. Bulandshari, *Illuminating Discourses on the Noble Qur'an*, pp. 98-99
14. Ali, p. 477; Pickthall, p. 174
15. Ali, p. 511; Pickthall, p. 186
16. Ali, p. 535; Pickthall, p. 195
17. Kathir, *Tafsir Ibn Kathir*, Vol. 1, p. 245
18. Ali, p. 285; Pickthall, p. 108
19. Ali, p. 666; Pickthall, p. 241
20. Cook, *Muhammad*, p. 53
21. Al-Ghazali, *Journey through the Qur'an*, p. 547
22. Ali, p. 683; Pickthall, p. 247
23. Ali, p. 766; Pickthall, p. 277
24. Ali, p. 326; Pickthall, p. 121
25. Kathir, *Tafsir Ibn Kathir*, Vol. 4, p. 178

PART II

Muhammad:
Allah's Warlord
and
Conqueror

CHAPTER 5

Early Medinan Revelations

(622-624 AD)

QUR'AN 64

"The Manifestation Of Losses"

622 AD

SCRIPTURE:

Qur'an 64:5, 11, 14-16

Ishaq:228, 231-233, 235

PREFACE:

This surah dealt with how wives and families tried to prevent Muslims from relocating to Medina. It also stated that Muslims will suffer if they do not fulfill their obligations. Muslims will know what to do by listening to Muhammad.[1]

SURAH:

Qur'an 64:5: "Has there not come to you of those who disbelieved before, then tasted the evil consequences of their conduct, and they had a painful chastisement."

Qur'an 64:11: "No calamity befalls [occurs] but by Allah's permission [unless Allah allows it]."

Qur'an 64:14-16: "O you who believe, surely of your wives and your children there are enemies to you, so beware of them. [...] Your wealth and your children are only a trial, and Allah — with Him is a great reward. So keep your duty to Allah as much as you can, and hear and obey, and spend; it is better for your souls. And whoever is saved from the greediness of his soul, these it is that [are those who] are the successful."

SUNNAH:

Ishaq:228: "[...] Finally, he reached the present site of his mosque, and his camel knelt down where the door of his mosque is. [...] The Messenger ordered that a mosque should be built there. [...] It is said that Muhammad bought the site of his Mosque and built upon it, but the correct version in our opinion is this: The site of the Mosque of the prophet belonged to two orphan boys under Najjar's care. It contained palm trees, cultivated land and pre-Islamic graves. The Messenger said, "Ask me a price for it," but they said, "Our only reward shall be from Allah." Muhammad then gave orders concerning the site; the palm trees were cut down, the cultivated land leveled, and the graves were dug up."

CONSTITUTION OF MEDINA ENACTED

Ishaq:231: "This document stated reciprocal obligations: 'In the name of Allah, Ar-Rahman, and Ar-Rahim. This is a treaty from Muhammad the Prophet governing relations between Muslims. They [Muslims] are one Ummah ["Community"] to the exclusion of all men. Believers are friends of one another to the exclusion of all outsiders. No separate peace shall be made when Muslims are fighting in Allah's Cause [Jihad] and Muslims must avenge bloodshed in Allah's cause [Jihad]. [...] Whenever you differ about a matter it must be referred to Allah and Muhammad. [...]' The treaty established the Jews in their religion and gave them rights to their property."

Ishaq:232: "The Jews shall contribute to the cost of war so long as they are fighting alongside the believers [Muslims]. The Jews have their religion, the Muslims have theirs. [...] None of them shall go out to war unless they have Muhammad's permission. The Jews must pay, however, for as long as the war lasts. [...] If the Jews are called to make peace they must, except in the case of Holy War [Jihad]. Allah approves of this document. Fear Allah and Muhammad is the Apostle of Allah."

Ishaq:233: "Allah's Apostle, the Lord of the Muslims, Leader of the Allah Fearing, Messenger of the Lord of the Worlds, the Peerless and Unequalled."

Ishaq:235: "When the Apostle was settled in Medina, and his comrades were gathered to him, the affairs of the workers were arranged, and Islam became firmly established. Prayer [prostration] was instituted, the zakat tax was prescribed, legal punishments were fixed, as were all things permitted and forbidden."

SUMMATION:

IL: The Muslims who came to Medina had to deal with opposition from the Quraysh resistance from their wives and children. Their resistance was at odds with Allah's divine will. Muslims were to obey Allah and spend what they had in order to establish Allah's reign. Muslims who accomplish this are the most favored in the sight of Allah.

Muhammad's divine mission was verified when his camel knelt at the place where the first mosque was built at Medina. Thereafter, Muhammad enacted the Constitution of Medina, which included: (1) Non-Muslim Arabs abiding at Yathrib ("Medina"); (2) Jews; and (3) Muslims from Mecca. Jews were established as partners in the treaty provided they financially supported the Muslims in their hostilities against the Quraysh. Those who signed the treaty also agreed to the implementation of Shari'a... Islamic law.

WA: According to the Qur'an, Allah claimed the Hegira was part of His divine will. When opposition to the movement arose from their women and children, Allah called them "enemies" and "a trial". They dared to express an opinion that went contrary to the will of Allah. Allah and Muhammad clearly did not want the Muslims to accumulate wealth apart from jihad.

In the opening lines of the Constitution of Medina, one can begin to wonder if the non-believers and the Jews even read the treaty, they agreed to abide by, before they acknowledged it. In the Constitution of Medina, Muslims were declared superior and Allah was established as the only God. Also, the Jews were required to finance Muslim raids on Muhammad's enemies. Why would the Jews, who numbered in the tens of thousands, give this much power to Muhammad and his small band of followers? The only explanation is the Jews feared the Muslims from Mecca would convince the Arabs from Yathrib to come against them, so the Jews thought it wise to be partners of the Muslims by signing the treaty.

QUR'AN 2

"The Cow"

623 AD

SCRIPTURE:

Qur'an 2:10, 23-25, 40-43, 61-62, 65, 75, 77, 79, 87, 89-91, 96, 98, 100-101, 105-106, 109, 120, 130, 135, 142-144, 150, 154, 159, 161, 178, 190-191, 193-194, 207, 214, 216-218, 221, 223, 228-230, 256-257, 282, 286

Bukhari:V5B57N119, V5B58N234, V5B58N236, V6B60N7, V7B62N88, V9B87N139-V9B87N140; Ishaq:239-250, 254-259, 262-264, 269, 272, 278, 281-288; Muslim:B31C12N5966; Tabari VII:6-7, 10-13, 15-16, 18-21, 24

PREFACE:

The Jews of Yathrib ("Medina") were bombarding Muhammad with theological questions because they had doubts about his prophetic claim. As a result of these questions, Muhammad, who hoped to be recognized by the Jews as a prophet, decided to change the direction of the *Qiblah* ("Muslim prayer") from Jerusalem to Mecca. Muslims, who already believed Abraham built the Ka'aba with his son Ishmael, viewed this change as acceptable to the Muslim ummah ("community"). This surah describes Jewish stubbornness in light of divine favor, their degenerative tendency towards cow-worship, and their plans against Muhammad. During this period, the Muslims were also preparing to raid Meccan caravans because they had previously received permission to fight them. This occurred at Aqabah near Mecca in 621 AD when they pledged their allegiance to Muhammad. Fighting was permitted to preserve the ummah; however, compulsion, in matters of religion, was not to be forced on the vanquished. For certain, the Islamic code would be established over believer and non-believer. In this surah, the concept of abrogation was put into practice. It allowed for a harsher revelation against the Jews who rejected Muhammad's Qur'anic assertions. Consequentially, the Jews were not only doomed in this world but in the world to come. Warfare, in the cause of Allah (Jihad), was advocated to protect the ummah. Muslims who died as *Shahid* ("martyrs") were assured that this activity pleased Allah. People of the Book, Jews in this instance, were viewed as those who eventually must be subdued just like women submitting to Muslim men.[2]

SURAH:

Qur'an 2:10: "In their [People of the Book] hearts is a disease, so Allah increased their disease, and for them is a painful chastisement because they lie."

Qur'an 2:23: "And if you [Arab pagans, Jews, and Christians] are in doubt as to [concerning] that which We have revealed [sent down, i.e., the Qur'an] to Our servant [Muhammad], then produce a chapter [surah] like it and call on your helpers [supporters and helpers] besides Allah, if you are truthful."

Qur'an 2:24: "But if you do it not [produce a chapter like one in the Qur'an] — and you can never do it — then be on guard against the fire whose fuel is men and stones; it is prepared for the disbelievers."

Qur'an 2:25: "And give good news to those who believe and do good deeds, […] for them therein are pure companions and therein they will abide."

Qur'an 2:40-43: "O Children of Israel […] be faithful to your covenant with Me. […] And believe in that which I have revealed [Qur'an], verifying that which is with you [Hebrew Scriptures], and be not the first to deny it; neither take a mean price for My messages [don't charge Muslims for Bible verses]; ad keep your duty to Me, Me alone. And mix not up truth with falsehood, nor hide the truth while you know. And keep up prayer ["Salat," Islamic prayers] and pay the poor-rate ["Zakat," the tax collected from Muslims to give to poorer Muslims] and bow down with those who bow down [worship Allah]."

Qur'an 2:61: "[…] And abasement and humiliation were stamped upon them [the Jews], and they incurred Allah's wrath. That was so because they disbelieved in the messages of Allah and would kill the prophets unjustly. That was so they disobeyed and exceeded the limits."

Qur'an 2:62: "Surely those who believe [Muslims], and those who are Jews, and the Christians, and the Sabians, whoever believes in Allah [as well as Jews, Christians, and Sabians who turn to Islam] and the Last Day [Day of Judgment] and does good, they have their reward with their Lord, and there is no fear for them, nor shall they grieve."

Qur'an 2:65: "And indeed you know [of] those among you who violated [broke] the Sabbath [the Jews], so We said to them: Be as apes, despised and hated."

Qur'an 2:75, 77, 79: "[…] a party from among them [Jews and Christians] indeed used to hear the word of Allah, then altered it [the Bible] after they had understood it, and they know this. [...] Allah knows what they keep secret and what they make known [...] Woe then to those who write the Book [Bible] with their hands then say, This is from Allah; so that they may take for it a small price. So woe to them for what their hands write and woe to them for what they earn."

Qur'an 2:87: "[…] Is it then that whenever there came to you a messenger with what your souls desired not, you were arrogant? And some you gave the lie to and others you would slay."

Qur'an 2:89: "And when there came to them [Jews] a Book [Qur'an] from Allah verifying that which they have, and aforetime they used to pray for victory against those who disbelieved — but when there came to them that which they recognized [Islam, Abraham's religion] they disbelieved in it; so Allah's curse is on the disbelievers [Jews]."

Qur'an 2:90: "Evil is that for which they [Jews] sell their souls — that they should deny that which Allah has revealed [Qur'an], out of envy that Allah should send down of His grace on whomsoever of His servants He pleases [Muhammad]; so they incur wrath upon wrath. And there is an abasing chastisement for the disbelievers [Jews]."

Qur'an 2:91: "And when it is said to them, Believe in that which Allah has revealed, they say: We believe in that which was revealed to us. [...] Say: Why then did you kill Allah's prophets before this if you were believers?"

Qur'an 2:96: "And thou wilt certainly find them [Jews] the greediest of men for life, greedier even than those [Christians] who set up gods with God [Allah]. One of them [Christians] loves to be granted a life for thousand years and his being granted a long life will in no way remove him further off from the chastisement [being punished]. And Allah is Seer [sees] of what they do."

Qur'an 2:98: "Whosoever is an enemy to Allah and His angels and His messengers and Gabriel and Michael, then surely Allah is an enemy to disbelievers."

Qur'an 2:100-101: "Is it that whenever they [Jews] make a covenant, a party [some] of them cast it aside? Nay, most of them [Jews] have no faith. And when there came to them a messenger from Allah, verifying that which they have, a party [some] of those who were given the Book threw the Book of Allah behind their backs as if they knew nothing."

Qur'an 2:105: "[...] Allah chooses whom He pleases for His Mercy [...]"

Qur'an 2:106: "Whatever message We abrogate or cause to be forgotten, We bring one better that it or one like it [replace it with a better or similar one]. Knowest thou not that Allah is Possessor of power over all things [able to do all things]?"

Qur'an 2:109: "Many of the [P]eople of the Book [Jews and Christians] wish that they could turn you back into disbelievers after you have believed, out of envy from themselves, after truth [was] manifest to them. But pardon and forgive them [for this], till [until] Allah bring[s] about His command."

Qur'an 2:120: "And the Jews will not be pleased with thee [Muslims], nor the Christians, unless thou follow their religion. Say: Surely Allah's guidance — that is the perfect guidance. And if thou [Muslims] follow their desires after the knowledge that has come to thee thou shalt have from Allah no friend, or helper."

Qur'an 2:130: "And [he] who forsakes the religion of Abraham [Islam] [is] he who makes a fool of himself. And certainly We made him [Muhammad] pure in this world and in the Hereafter he is surely among the righteous."

Qur'an 2:135: "And they say: Be Jews or Christians, you will be on the right course. Say [Muhammad]: Nay, We follow the religion of Abraham, the upright one, and he was not one of the polytheists."

Qur'an 2:142-144, 150: "The fools among the people will say: What has turned them from their *Qiblah* which they had? Say: The East and the West belong only to Allah: He guides whom He pleases to the right path. And We did not make that which thou wouldst have to be *Qiblah* [direction of prayer] but [only] that We might distinguish him who follows the Messenger from him who turns back upon his heels. And it was indeed a hard test except for those whom Allah has guided. [...], turn then thy face towards the Sacred Mosque [turn towards Mecca and away from Jerusalem]. And wherever you are turn your faces towards it. And those who have been given the Book [Bible] certainly know that it is the truth from their Lord. And from whatsoever place thou comest forth turn thy face towards the Sacred Mosque."

Qur'an 2:154: "And speak not of those who are slain in Allah's way [Jihad] as dead. Nay, they are alive, but you perceive not. [This verse may have been revealed after the first Muslim casualties were made known.]"

Qur'an 2:159: "Those who conceal the clear proofs and the guidance that We revealed after We have made it clear in the Book [Bible] for men, these it is [are] whom Allah curses, and those who curse, curse them too."

Qur'an 2:161: "Those who disbelieve and die while they are disbelievers, these it is on whom is the curse of Allah and the angels and men."

Qur'an 2:178: "O you who believe [Muslims], retaliation is prescribed for you in the matter of the slain [retaliate when one of you is slain]. If the murderer is free, a slave or a female they shall be slain. If the injured family member forgives the murderer then blood-money can be exchanged for one's life.

Qur'an 2:190: "And fight in the way of Allah against those who fight against you, but be not aggressive [do not initiate hostilities]. Surely Allah loves not the aggressors."

Qur'an 2:191: "And kill [slay] them wherever you find them, and drive them out from where they drove you out, and [because] persecution is worse than slaughter. And fight not with them at the Sacred Mosque [place of worship] until they fight with you [unless they attack first] in it [the place of worship]; so if they fight with you in it, slay them. Such is the recompense of the disbelievers."

Qur'an 2:193-194: "And fight them until there is no persecution, and religion is only for Allah. But if they desist, then there should be no hostility except against the oppressors. [...], and retaliation is allowed in sacred things. Whoever then acts aggressively against you, inflict injury on him according to the injury he has inflicted on you and keep your duty to Allah, and know that Allah is with those who keep their duty."

Qur'an 2:207: "And of men [a man] is he who sells himself [his life] to seek the pleasure of Allah. And Allah is Compassionate to the[se] servants."

Qur'an 2:214: "Or do you think that you will enter the garden [Paradise] while there has not yet befallen you the like of what befell those who have passed away before you. Distress and affliction befell them and they were shaken violently, so that the Messenger and those who believed with him said: When will the help of Allah come? Now surely the help of Allah is nigh [not coming]!"

Qur'an 2:216: "Fighting is enjoined on you [warfare is ordained for you], though it is disliked by you; and it may be [happen] that you dislike a thing while it is good for you, and it may be that you love a thing while it is evil [bad] for you; and Allah knows, while you know not."

Qur'an 2:217: "They ask thy about fighting in the sacred month. Say: Fighting in it is a grave offence. And hindering men from Allah's way [Jihad] and denying Him and the Sacred Mosque and turning [forcing] its people out of it, are still graver with Allah; and persecution is graver than slaughter. And they will not cease fighting you until they turn you from your religion, if they can. And whoever of you turns back from his religion [leave Islam], then he dies while an unbeliever — these it is whose works go for nothing in this world and the Hereafter. And they are the companions of Fire: therein they will abide."

Qur'an 2:218: "Those who believed and those who fled their homes [to escape Meccan persecution] and strove hard Allah's way [fighting in Jihad] — these surely [have] hope for the mercy of Allah. [...]"

Qur'an 2:221: "And marry not the idolatresses until they believe [...]. Nor give believing women [Muslim women] in marriage to idolaters until they believe [...]."

Qur'an 2:223: "Your wives are a tilth [field] for you [to cultivate], so go into your tilth [field] when you like, and send good [deeds] beforehand for yourselves. And keep your duty to Allah, and know that you will meet Him [one day]. And give good news to the believers."

Qur'an 2:228: "And the divorced women should keep themselves in waiting for three courses [women must wait three months—to ensure that she is not pregnant from the previous husband]. And it is not lawful for them to [try to] conceal that which Allah has created in their wombs, if they believe in Allah and the Last Day. And their husbands have a better right [would do better] to take them back in the meanwhile [in that case] if they wish for reconciliation. And women have rights similar to those against them [who are placed above them] in a just manner [in kindness], and [but] men are a degree above them. And Allah is Mighty, Wise."

Qur'an 2:229: "Divorce may be pronounced twice; then keep them [women] in good fellowship or let them [women] go with kindness. And it is not lawful for you to take any part of what you have given them, unless both fear that they cannot keep within the limits of Allah. Then if you fear they cannot keep within the limits of Allah, there is no blame on them for what she gives up to become free thereby. These are the limits of Allah, so exceed them not; and whoever exceeds the limits of Allah, these are the wrongdoers. ["[...] in that case, it is no sin for either of them if the woman pays ransom for herself [...]"] (3)

Qur'an 2:230: "So if he divorces her the third time, she shall not be lawful to him afterwards until she marries another husband. If he divorces her, there is no blame on them both, if they return to each other by marriage [to the original husband], if they think that they can keep within the limits of Allah. [...]"

Qur'an 2:256: "There is no compulsion in religion — the right way is indeed clearly distinct from error. So whoever disbelieves in the devil and believes in Allah, he indeed lays hold on the firmest handle which shall never break. And Allah is Hearing, Knowing."

Qur'an 2:257: "Allah is the Friend of those who believe — He brings them out of darkness into light. And those who disbelieve, their friends are the devils who take them out of light into darkness. They are the companions of the Fire; therein they will abide."

Qur'an 2:282: "And call from among your men two witnesses, but if there are not two men, then one man and two women from among those whom you choose to be witnesses, so that if one of the two errs, the one may remind the other."

Qur'an 2:286: "Allah imposes not on any soul a duty beyond its scope. For it, is that which earns of good, and against it that which it works of evil. [...]"

SUNNAH:

Bukhari:V6B60N7: 'Abdullah bin Salam heard the news of the arrival of Allah's Apostle (at Medina) while he was on a farm collecting its fruits. So he came to the Prophet and said, "I will ask you about three things which nobody knows unless he is a prophet. Firstly, what is the first portent of the Hour? What is the first meal of the people of Paradise? What makes a baby look like its father or mother?" The Prophet said, "Just now Gabriel has informed me...Abdullah said, "He, among the angels is the enemy of the Jews." On that the Prophet recited this Holy Verse-- "Whoever is an enemy to Gabriel (let him die in his fury!); because he brought it [i.e., the Qur'an] down to your heart by Allah's permission."(Qur'an 2:97) "As for the first portent of the Hour, it will be a fire that will collect the people from the East to West. And as for the first meal of the people of Paradise, it will be the extra lobe of the fish liver. If a man's discharge comes before the discharge of the woman then the child resembles the father. If the woman's discharge came before the discharge of the man the child would resemble the mother." On hearing that, Abdullah said, "I testify that none has the right to be worshipped but Allah, and that you are the Apostle of Allah." "O, Allah's Apostle; the Jews are liars, and if they should come to know that I have embraced Islam, they would accuse me of being a liar…"

THE CHILD BRIDE

Tabari VII:6: "In May 623 AD [1 AH], Allah's Messenger consummated his marriage to Aisha."

Bukhari:V5B58N236: "When the Prophet married Aisha, she was very young [six-years-old] and not yet ready for consummation."

Bukhari:V5B58N234: "[Aisha is speaking] My mother came to me while I was being swung on a swing between two branches and got me down. My nurse took over and wiped my face with some water and started leading me. When I was at the door she stopped so I could catch my breath. I was brought in while Muhammad was sitting on a bed in our house. My mother made me sit on his lap. The other men and women got up and left. The Prophet consummated his marriage with me at my house when I was nine years old."

Bukhari:V9B87N139, V9B87N140: "Allah's Apostle told Aisha, 'You were shown to me twice in my dreams. I beheld a man or angel carrying you in a silken cloth. He said to me, "She is yours, so uncover her." And behold, it was you. (It was Aisha the nine years old). I would then say to myself, "If this is from Allah, then it must happen" ' […]"

Tabari VII:7: "Aisha replied, 'The angel brought down my likeness; the Messenger married me when I was seven; my marriage was consummated when I was nine; he married me when I was a virgin, no other man having shared me with him; inspiration came to him when he and I were in a single blanket; I was one of the dearest people to him; a verse of the Qur'an was revealed concerning me when the community [ummah] was almost destroyed […]."

Bukhari:V5B57N119: "The people used to send presents to the Prophet on the day of Aisha's turn [to have sex with Muhammad]. Aisha said,

'His other wives gathered in the apartment of Um Salama [another wife of Muhammad in Medina] and said, "Um, the people send presents on the day of Aisha's turn and we too, love the good presents just as much as she does. You should tell Allah's Apostle to order the people to send their presents to him regardless of whose turn it may be." [...] After the third time [telling Muhammad her request], the Prophet said, "Um, don't trouble me by harming Aisha, for by Allah, the Divine Inspiration [Qur'an] never came to me while I was under the blanket [having sex] of any woman among you except her.""""

Bukhari:V7B62N88: "The Prophet wrote the marriage contract with Aisha while she was 6 years old and consummated his marriage to her when she was 9 years old and she remained with him for 9 years [Until he died at age 62]."

Muslim:B31C12N5966: "Muhammad said, '[...] the excellence of Aisha as compared to women is that of Tharid [a dish of very thin bread soaked in broth of meat and some vegetables] over all other foods.'"

THE RAMADAN RAID

Tabari VII:10: "In Ramadan, seven months after the Hijrah, Muhammad entrusted a white war banner to Hamza with the command of thirty Emigrants [Those who came with Muhammad from Mecca]. Their aim was to intercept a Quraysh caravan."

Tabari VII:11-13: "In this year the Messenger entrusted Sa'd a white war banner for the expedition to Kharrar. [...] Those who were with Sa'd were all Emigrants. The Messenger of Allah went out on a raid as far as Waddan, searching for Quraysh. [...] he sent Ubaydah at the head of sixty horseman from the Emigrants [...] He got as far as a watering place in Hijaz, below the pass of Marah. There he met a greater band of Quraysh, but there was no fighting except Sa'd shot an arrow. Then the two groups separated from one another, the Muslims leaving a rearguard. Muhammad led an expedition [...] in search of Quraysh. He went as far as Buwat, in the region of Radwa, and then returned without any fighting. Then he led another expedition in search of the Meccans. He took the mountain track and crossed the desert, halting beneath a tree in Batha. He prayed there. After a few days the Prophet went out in pursuit of the Kurz."

Tabari VII:15-16: "In this year, according to all Sira writers, the Messenger personally led the Ghazwa [an Islamic invasion in Allah's cause] of Alwa. He left Sa'd in command of Medina. On this raid his banner was carried by Hamza. [...] In this year Muhammad sent forth the Emigrants to intercept a Quraysh caravan en route to Syria. His war banner was carried by Hamza. Ali and I were with the Messenger on the Ghazwa [invasion] of Ushayrah. [...]"

Tabari VII:18-19: "[...] A Meccan caravan went past them carrying raisins, leather, and other merchandise, which the Quraysh traded. When they saw the Muslims they were afraid of them. [...] They hesitated and were afraid to advance on them, but then they plucked up courage and agreed to kill as many as they could and to seize what they had with them. Waqid ibn Abd Allah shot an arrow at Amr and killed him [Meanwhile, the others escorting the caravan either surrendered or fled]. Then Abd Allah and his companions took the caravan and the captives back to Allah's Apostle in Medina."

Tabari VII:20-21: "Abd Allah told his Companions, 'A fifth of the booty we have taken belongs to the Apostle.' This was before Allah made surrendering a fifth of the booty taken a requirement. [...] He set aside a fifth of the booty for Allah's Messenger and divided the rest between his Companions. [...] When they reached the Prophet he said, 'I did not order you to fight in the sacred month.' He impounded the caravan and the two captives and refused to take anything from them. [...] When Allah's Messenger said this they were aghast and thought that they were doomed. The Muslims rebuked them severely for what they had done. They said, 'You have done what you were not commanded to do, and have fought in the sacred month.' The Quraysh said, 'Muhammad and his Companions have violated the sacred month, shed blood, seized property, and taken men captive.' The polytheists [the Quraysh] spread lying slander concerning him, saying, 'Muhammad claims that he is following obedience to Allah, yet he is the first to violate the holy month and to kill our companion in Rajab.' The Muslims who were still in Mecca refuted this." [Meccan Muslims disagreed with the accusations and conclusions of the Quraysh. They refused to believe that Muhammad and his men violated the sacred month]

CHANGING THE QIBLAH

Tabari VII:24: "Allah changed the Muslim Qiblah from Jerusalem to the Ka'aba in the second year of residence in Medina. The people used to pray toward Jerusalem. [...] This was abrogated in favor of the Ka'aba."

Ishaq:239: "About this time Jewish rabbis showed hostility to the Apostle in envy, hatred, and malice, because Allah had chosen His Apostle from [among] the Arabs. The Jews considered the Prophet a liar and strove against Islam. The Aus and Khazraj joined the Jews by obstinately clinging to their heathen religion. They were hypocrites. When Islam appeared and their people flocked to it, they were compelled to pretend to accept it to save their lives. [...] Jewish rabbis used to annoy the Apostle with questions, introducing confusion. [...] Qur'ans [Qur'anic revelations] used to come down in reference to their questions."

Ishaq:240: "Labid bewitched Allah's Apostle [with impotency] so that he could not come at his wives. These Jewish rabbis opposed the Apostle. They asked questions and stirred up trouble against Islam trying to extinguish it. I [Abd Allah ibn Salam] concealed the matter from the Jews and then went to the Apostle and said, 'The Jews are a nation of liars, and I want you to give me a house and hide me from them. If they learned I've become a Muslim, they'll utter slanderous lies against me. So the prophet gave me a house, and when the Jews came, I emerged and said, 'O Jews, fear Allah and accept what He has sent you. For you know that he is the Apostle of Allah. You will find him described in your Torah and even named.' They accused me of lying and reviled me. I told Muhammad, 'The Jews are a treacherous, lying and evil people.'"

Ishaq:241: "Mukhayriq was a learned rabbi, owning much property in date palms. He recognized the Apostle by his description and felt a predilection for his religion. He violated the Sabbath to fight on behalf of Islam and was killed in battle. I am told the Prophet used to say, 'Mukhayriq is the best of the Jews.' The Apostle took his property."

Ishaq:242: "Julas the Jew used to say, 'If Muhammad is right we are worse than donkeys' [...] The Apostle ordered Umar to kill him, but he escaped to Mecca."

NON-ARABS AND NON-MUSLIMS

Ishaq:243: "I have heard the Apostle say: 'Whoever wants to see Satan should look at Nabtal!' He was a sturdy black man with long flowing hair, inflamed eyes, and dark ruddy cheeks. [...] Nabtal said, 'Muhammad is all ears. If anyone tells him anything he believes it.' [...] Gabriel came to Muhammad and said, 'If a black man comes to you, his heart is more gross than a donkey's [heart].' [...] [One of Muhammad's Companions said,] 'Muhammad promised that we would enjoy the treasures of Chusroes [the Persians] and Caesar [the Romans] [...].'"

Ishaq:244-245: "Hatib was a sturdy man steeped in paganism. Yazid, his son, was one of the best Muslims when he was disabled by wounds. At the point of death, Muslims said, 'Rejoice, son of Hatib, in the thought of Paradise!' Then his father's hypocrisy showed itself. He [Hatib's father] said, 'Humph! It is a Garden of Rue. You have sent my son to his death by your deception.' [...] The Apostle used to say, 'He [Yazid] belongs to the people of hell.' Yet he had fought valiantly and killed many polytheists. [...] When the pain of his wounds became unbearable he took an arrow from his quiver, slit his wrist and committed suicide. He was suspected of hypocrisy and love of Jews. This poem was written of him: 'Who will tell him that by cutting his vein he won't be glorified in Islam? Do you love Jews and their religion, you liver-hearted ass, and not Muhammad? Their religion will never march with ours.'"

Ishaq:246: "These Hypocrites used to assemble in the mosque and listen to the stories of the Muslims and laugh and scoff at their religion. So Muhammad ordered that they should be ejected. They were thrown out with great violence. Abu went to Amr, who was a custodian of the gods. He took his foot and dragged him out of the mosque. Another Muslim slapped a man's face while dragging him forcefully. 'Keep out of the Apostle's Mosque, you Hypocrite,' he said. Another was punched in the chest and knocked down. One was pulled violently by his hair. 'Don't come near the Apostle's mosque again for you are unclean.' The first hundred verses of the Cow surah [Qur'an 2] came down in reference to these Jewish rabbis and Hypocrites."

Ishaq:247-248: "It is a guide for those who fear Allah's punishment. It is for those who believe in the unseen, perform prostrations, share what Allah provides the Apostle, and pay the zakat tax expecting a reward. [...] Allah has sealed their hearts and their hearing, blinding them so that they will never find guidance. And that is because they have declared you a liar and they do not believe in what has come down from their Lord to you even though they believe in all that came down before you. For opposing you they will have an awful punishment. [...] Allah increases their sickness. A tormented doom awaits the Jews. [...] Allah said, 'They are mischief makers. They are fools. The Jews deny the truth and contradict what the Apostle has brought.' Allah said, 'I will mock them and let them continue to wander blindly.'"

Ishaq:249-250: "[...] Fear hell whose fuel is men and stones prepared for the infidels. [...] "Stand in awe of Me lest I bring down on you what I brought down on your fathers. The vengeance that you know of, the bestial transformation and the like." [...] Fear me and do not mingle truth with falsehood or hide the truth which you know. [...] You are readers of scripture. Why do you forbid men to believe in the prophecy you have and in the covenant of the Torah. You must pronounce My Apostle to be true. [...] the bestial transformation occurred when Allah turned Jews into apes."

Ishaq:254: "[...] We will not remove a Jew from punishment. The Jew knows the shameful thing that awaits him in the next life because he has wasted the knowledge he has."

LOSING JEWISH SUPPORT

Ishaq:255-256: "Jewish rabbis came to the apostle and asked him to answer four questions saying, 'If you do so we will follow you, testify to your truth, and believe in you.' They began, 'Why does a boy resemble his mother when the semen comes from the father?' Muhammad replied, 'Do you not know that a man's semen is white and thick and a woman's is yellow and thin? The likeness goes with that which comes to the top.' [...] [T]he rabbis [after asking their four questions and receiving their four answers] said, 'But Muhammad, your spirit is an enemy to us, an angel who comes only with violence and the shedding of blood, and were it not for that we would follow you.' [...] The Apostle wrote a letter to the Jews at Khaybar. [...] Allah says to you, 'O Scripture folk, and you will find it in your scripture "Muhammad is the Apostle of Allah. Those with him are severe against the unbelievers. You see them bowing, falling prostrate, seeking bounty, and acceptance. The mark of their prostrations is on their foreheads." That is their likeness in the Torah and in the Gospels.' [...] If you do not find that [proof of Muhammad's prophethood] in your scripture then there is no compulsion upon you."

Ishaq:257-258: "'O Jews, fear Allah and submit, for you used to hope for the Messiah's help against the Arabs when we were pagans. You told us that he would be sent.' A Jew responded, 'Muhammad has not shown us anything we recognize as prophetic. He is not the one we spoke to you about.' So Allah revealed, 'We confirmed what they had, and We sent one they recognized, but they rejected him so We are cursing them.' The Jews replied, 'No Covenant was ever made with us about Muhammad. Muhammad, you have not brought anything we recognize. And God has not sent down any sign or miracle suggesting that we should believe you.' So Allah said, 'We have sent down to you plain signs and only evildoers disbelieve them.' The Jews used to turn men away from Islam. [...]"

Ishaq:259: "When the direction of prayer was changed from Syria (Jerusalem) to the Ka'aba, the seventeenth month after the Prophet's arrival [...], a number of others from among the Jews of Medina [...] asked the Prophet why he changed the Qiblah when he alleged he followed the religion of Abraham. If he would return to the Qiblah in Jerusalem, they would follow him and declare him to be true."

Ishaq:262-263: "[...] Some Muslims remained friends with the Jews, so Allah sent down a Qur'an [Qur'anic verse] forbidding them to take Jews as friends. From their mouths hatred has already shown itself and what they conceal is worse. [Muhammad said,] 'You believe in their Book while they deny your book, so you have more right to hate them than they have to hate you. [...] Abu Bakr went into a Jewish school and found many pupils gathered around Finhas, a learned rabbi. Bakr told the Jews to fear Allah and submit. He told them that they would find that Muhammad was an Apostle written in the Torah and Gospels. Finhas [the learned rabbi] replied, 'We are rich compared to Allah. We do not humble ourselves to Allah. He humbles himself to us. We are independent of him, while he needs us. Why does your god ask us to lend him money as your master pretends?' [Abu] Bakr [who would become the first Caliph] was enraged and hit Finhas hard in the face. [Abu Bakr said,] 'Were it not for the treaty between us, I would cut off your head, you enemy of Allah.'"

Ishaq:264: "Allah revealed concerning Finhas and the other rabbis: '[...] they cast the Torah behind their backs and sold it for a small price. Wretched was their exchange. They will therefore receive a painful punishment.' [Next,] Muhammad said, 'The Torah confirms what Muhammad brought.'[Then] Rifa'a, a notable Jew, spoke to the Apostle, twisting his tongue, 'Give us your attention, Muhammad, so that we can make you understand.' Then he attacked Islam and reviled it. [...] The Jewish rabbis knew that Muhammad had brought them the truth, but they denied that they knew it. They were obstinate. So Allah revealed, 'People of the Book, believe in what we have sent down in confirmation of what you had been given before or We will efface your features and turn your face into your ass, cursing you.'"

Ishaq:269: "[The Jews said,] 'Tell us when the Day of Doom will be, Muhammad, if you are a prophet as you say.' [Muhammad said,] '[...] only Allah knows of it. None but He will reveal it at its proper time.' [The Jews said,] 'How can we follow you, Muhammad, when you have abandoned our Qiblah? And you do not acknowledge that Uzayr [Either Ezra from the Tenakh Book of Ezra or Azariah from the Book of Daniel] is the son of God.' [...] [The Jews said,] 'For our part we do not see how your Qur'an recitals are arranged anything like our Torah is.' [Muhammad said,] 'You know quite well that the Qur'an is from Allah. You will find it written in the Torah which you have.' [...] [Finhas,] the rabbi said, 'When God sends a Prophet, He provides for him, so bring us a book that is divinely inspired that we may read it and determine if you are telling the truth. We can produce *our* book.' [...]"

AN ENCOUNTER WITH CHRISTIAN DOCTRINE

Ishaq:272: "A group of Christians including a bishop came from Najran... they differed among themselves in some points saying Jesus is God, He is the son of God, He is the third person of the Trinity which is the doctrine of Christianity [...] after they told Muhammad they submitted to God, Muhammad stated, "You lie. You assert that God has a son, you worship the cross, and your pork-eating holds you back from Islam (submission)."

HANIFIYYAH OR ISLAM

Ishaq:278: "[...] Abu Amir came to the Prophet in Medina to ask him about the religion he had brought. 'The Hanifiyyah, the religion of Abraham,' [Muhammad responded]. [Abu Amir replied,] 'That is what I follow.' [Muhammad stated,] 'You do not.' [Abu Amir answered,] 'But I do. You, Muhammad, have introduced into the Hanifiyyah things which do not belong to it.' [Muhammad answered,] 'I have not. I have brought it white and pure.' [Abu Amir said,] 'May God let the liar die a lonely, homeless, fugitive!'"

JIHAD AND THE QURAYSH

Ishaq:281-282: "The Raid on Waddan was the first Maghazi [military expedition]. The expedition of Ubayda Harith was [the] second. The Apostle sent Ubayda out on a raid with sixty to eighty riders from the Emigrants, thee not being a single Ansar among them. He encountered a large number of Quraysh in the Hijaz. Abu Bakr composed a poem about the raid: '[...] When we called them to the truth, they turned their backs and howled like bitches. Allah's punishment on them will not tarry. I swear by the Lord of Camels that I am no Perjurer. A valiant band will descend upon the Quraysh which will leave [their] women husbandless. It will leave men dead, with vultures wheeling around. It will not spare the infidels as Ibn Harith did [...] And every infidel who is trying to do evil; If you assail my honor in your evil opinion I will assail yours.' [Another Companion replied] [...] In the hands of warriors dangerous as lions, wherewith we deal with the conceited, are you here to quench your thirst for vengeance? No, they withdraw in great fear and awe [...]."

Ishaq:283-284: "Hamza's expedition to the seashore comprised thirty riders, all Emigrants from Mecca. He met Abu Jahl who had three hundred riders. Amr intervened, for he was at peace with both sides. [...] We called them to Islam but they treat it as a joke. They laughed until I threatened them. [Abu Jahl said,] '[...] They abandoned our fathers' ways. They come with lies to twist our minds. But their lies cannot confound the wise. If you give up your raids we will take you back for you are our cousins our kin. But they [Muslims militants] chose to believe Muhammad and became obstinately contentious. All their deeds became evil."

Ishaq:285-286: "Then the Apostle went raiding [...] making for the Quraysh. He returned to Medina without fighting. Then he raided the Quraysh by way of Dinar. [...] Meanwhile the Apostle sent Sa'd on the raid of Abu Waqqas. The Prophet only stayed a few nights in Medina before raiding Ushayrah and then Kurz."

Ishaq:287-288: "The Messenger sent Abd Allah out with a detachment of eight men of the Emigrants without any Ansari or Helpers, among them. He wrote a letter, but ordered him not to look at it until he had traveled for two days. [...] When Abd Allah opened the letter it said, 'March until you reach Nakhlah between Mecca and Ta'if. Lie in wait for the Quraysh there, and find out for us what they are doing.' [...] [Abd Allah then said,] 'The Prophet has forbidden me to compel you [to fight], so whoever desires martyrdom, let him come with me. If not, retreat. I am going to carry out the Prophet's orders.' [...] His companions went with him; not one of them stayed behind. [...] The Muslim raiders consulted one another concerning them, this being the last day of Rajab. One of the Muslims said, 'By Allah, if we leave these people alone tonight, they will get into the Haram [sacred territory] and they will be safely out of our reach. If we kill them we will have killed in the sacred month.' The Jews [...] said, 'Muslims killing Meccans means war is kindled.' There was much talk of this. However, Allah turned it to their disadvantage. When the Muslims repeated what the Jews had said, Allah revealed a Qur'an to His Messenger: 'They question you with regard to warfare in the sacred month. Say, "War therein is serious, but keeping people from Islam, from the Sacred Mosque, and driving them out is more serious with Allah."'[Qur'an 2:217] The Muslims now knew that seduction was worse than killing. When the Qur'an passage concerning this matter was revealed, and Allah relieved Muslims from their fear and anxiety, Muhammad took possession of the caravan and prisoners. The Quraysh sent him a ransom [...] and the Prophet released the prisoners on payment of ransom. When the Qur'an authorization came down to Muhammad, Abd Allah and his Companions were relieved and they became anxious for an additional reward. They said, 'Will this raid be counted as part of the reward promised to Muslim combatants?' So Allah sent down this Qur'an: 'Those who believe and have fought in Allah's Cause may receive Allah's mercy.' Allah made the booty permissible. He divided the loot; awarding four-fifths to the men He had allowed to take it. He gave one-fifth to His Apostle."

SUMMATION:

IL: In answering the questions posed by Abdullah bin Salam, Muhammad proved to his new hosts that he was indeed the Prophet who received divine guidance from Gabriel by answering the questions to Salam's total satisfaction. The episode that involved the betrothal, marriage, and consummation of the Prophet's third marriage was strictly the result of the Divine will of Allah. It was Allah's will that Aisha played an important part in Islamic history.

Long before the Quraysh began to treat the Prophet badly, it was forbidden to attack an enemy during the month of Ramadan. The Quraysh rejected the Qur'anic revelation which was offered to them by the Prophet, and as a consequence, it was made permissible for the Muslims to attack them during Ramadan.[4]

About this time the Jews, unjustifiably, reviled the Prophet in every possible way. They turned on him after they agreed to the Constitution of Medina. As a result, Allah revealed this surah. The Jews were condemned for abusing the Prophet, denying Allah, disrespecting Islam, and trying to turn Muslims from Islam. Although the Qur'anic revelation forbade Islamic war that was not defensive, Jewish actions directed against the Prophet justified an Islamic reaction against the Jews.[5] According to Al-Misri:

> "A person should not speak of anything he notices about people besides that which benefits a Muslim to relate or prevent disobedience."

> —Al-Misri, *Reliance of the Traveller*, r3.1

WA: Let's now take a look at the farmer Salam. First, what were his qualifications to determine if Muhammad was a Prophet? How did he know the angel Gabriel was the enemy of the Jews when Gabriel appeared to the Prophet Daniel, a Jew, and Mary, the mother of Jesus, who was also Jewish?

In the brief encounter with the Christians, Muhammad accused them of being liars, cross worshippers, and pork-eaters. He was wrong to think that only some Christians believed Jesus one with the triune God, when in reality, only heretical professing Christians refused to believe that Jesus was not part of the God-head.

What followed was Muhammad's reply to Salam's query: (1) The first response to Salam's question was, "a fire that will collect the people from the East to West"; (2) The second response was, "extra lobe of the fish liver"; and (3) the third response to Salam's question was, "if a man's discharge comes before the discharge of the woman, then the child resembles the father." The first response by Muhammad made no sense. The second answer could never have been proven by the Medinan farmer, and the third response from Muhammad was just scientifically nonsensical. It seemed that Salam was given a platform and considered reputable because he hated Jews, considered them liars, and accepted Muhammad.

The story of Muhammad's marriage to Aisha could never be condoned by biblically based Judeo-Christians for the following reasons: (1) Muhammad admitted dreaming about this young girl; (2) He attributed these dreams to Allah and believed that Allah wanted him to marry and have sex with a nine-year-old girl who was forty-four years his junior; and (3) In order to solidify his relations with her, Muhammad said that he experienced divine revelation during intercourse with Aisha. Muhammad acknowledged this revelation to justify to others that Allah permitted this union. Something was not right. Aisha acknowledged Muhammad's Divine revelation, during his intercourse, with her. There seemed to be an explanation in this case. Aisha may have confused Muhammad's Divine revelation with his orgasm, which, understandably, could have been misinterpreted as Divine revelation, given their comparable characteristics and trance-like reaction. Also, it must be understood that one does not love little girls be having sex with them. Little girls are loved by allowing them to be little girls. A grown man's private parts inserted into a prepubescent child could never, and should never, be considered holy or sanctified. By Western standards, Muhammad would've been incarcerated.

Allah's war, through Muhammad, had begun. Although the early raids were not successful, Muslims were shedding the blood of non-Muslim Arabs, taking their possessions, and taking captives.[6] The fact that Arabs were attacked and killed in the pagan month of Ramadan violated an Arab taboo. If Ramadan was invented by the Muslims, then the Quraysh in Mecca would not have cared that it was violated. The earlier raids were failures, so Muhammad prayed to Allah for the success of future raids. Muhammad understood that an Arab taboo was breached, but since the Muslims returned with booty and prisoners, the victory must have been Allah's will.[7]

The Jews of Yathrib turned on Muhammad when they realized he was not holy, sanctified, or a prophet of their God Yahveh. They could not find Muhammad in the Jewish scriptures and his actions towards other non-Muslim Arabs proved to them the Quraysh were correct about him. The Jews questioned Muhammad. Without a Divine revelation, Muhammad was stumped. To make matters worse, he was told by Abu Amir the Hanif that Muhammad's religion was not the religion of Abraham because Muhammad added foreign elements to Islam. Muhammad then disagreed with Abu Amir, an expert on Hanifiyya.

In response to the Jews, Muhammad changed the Qiblah, direction of prayer, from Jerusalem to Mecca. He was so confused by their learned questions that he was unable to perform sexually. The Jews were also blamed for his temporary inability. However, one Jew did accept Muhammad. Muhammad called him the best of the Jews after he was killed fighting Arabs. For his sacrifice, Muhammad took his property. Yazid, son of Habib and convert to Islam, killed himself when his wounds became unbearable. His father told Muhammad the truth about his son's death. Muhammad did not have a rebuttal. The Jews scoffed at Muhammad because, in their mind, Muhammad was clueless when it came to their religion. The Muslims then became violent with them because they so ridiculed Muhammad. The Jews were troubled by Muhammad's spirit and condonation of violence against others. Every oral defense the Jews mounted against Muhammad was met with beatings, threats, and cursing. The Jews were proven right in their discourse when Muhammad told them they believed Uzayr was the son of God. Biblical Jews have never held this belief. Muhammad lost any credibility he had with the Jews when he made that statement.

Muhammad then began to channel Allah. It was revealed the Jews were stubborn, doomed, liars, had diseased hearts, would be fuel for hell, would be humiliated, were responsible for biblical corruption, were cursed by Allah, greedy, faithless, envious of Muslims, and were hated apes. Does this sound like the God who made an everlasting covenant with the children of Israel?

Allah told the Muslims to break their friendship with Jews. They were told Muhammad was righteous and pure, Islam was the religion of Abraham, Muslim martyrs live, and non-Muslims are cursed by Allah. When Muslims understood the nature of Allah's enemies, Allah told the Muslims they could fight them. They could slay them and slaughter them because warfare was now ordained by Allah. According to Allah, Muslims were to fight until only Islam remained.

In the final part of this surah, Allah forbade Muslim women to marry non-Muslims.[8] Men are always to be above women. Then 2:256, the verse that Muslims frequently quote, was revealed: "There is no compulsion in religion." Muslim apologists say this proves that Islam is tolerant, but they never quote the very next verse, 2:257, to the Western audience, which states that non-Muslims are the friends of devils and will be their companions in hell.

QUR'AN 8

"Voluntary Gifts"

624 AD

SCRIPTURE:

Qur'an 8:7, 12, 14-16, 30-31, 39, 41, 57-61, 67, 72

Bukhari:V5B59N702; Ishaq:289-290, 295-298, 300, 303-311, 313, 315-316, 322-324, 326-327, 341, 344, 349, 357; Muslim:B1C9N33, B19C50N4472; Tabari VII:26, 28-30, 32, 52-56, 59, 61-65, 71, 80-81

PREFACE:

This surah was revealed after the Battle at Badr when the Muslims attacked a Meccan caravan. Allah revealed that all booty confiscated after a Muslim victory, belonged to Allah and his Prophet. Muhammad intended to attack the caravan because the revelation in this surah granted Allah and Muhammad the spoils of Jihad. Muhammad went into a trance during the Battle at Badr as he listened to Gabriel. These revelations encouraged the outnumbered Muslims onto victory and announced that Muslims would eventually be masters of Mecca. As a consequence, non-Muslims would no longer have access to it. The victory at Badr was proof that all of Muhammad's predictions would come true. To achieve the ultimate victory, Muslims would be tested to fight armies that were much larger. They were also encouraged to enter treaties to preserve the ummah. The victory at Badr was proof that the Prophet's mission was from Allah. The verses in this surah, especially in 8:39, abrogated other verses that would not have permitted a more violent approach to spreading Islam among the non-believers. Dissimulation was permitted to make treaties with the powerful until Muslim numbers began to increase. Eventually, all unbelievers, to include the People of the Book, will be subdued by Muslims.[9]

Qur'an 8:7: "And when Allah promised you one of the two parties that should be yours, and you loved that the one not armed would be yours, and Allah desired to establish the Truth by is words, and to cut off the root of the unbelievers [Kill the infidels to the last man]."

Qur'an 8:12: "[...] I will cast *terror* [emphasis added] into the hearts of those who disbelieve. So smite above the necks and smite every finger-tip of them [cut off their heads and cut off every fingertip]."

Qur'an 8:14-16: "This — taste it, and know that for the disbelievers is the chastisement of the Fire. O you who believe [Muslims], when you meet those disbelieve marching for war, turn not your backs to them. And whoso turns his back to them that day — unless maneuvering for battle or turning to join a company [retreating to one's own troops] — he, indeed, incurs Allah's wrath and his refuge is hell. And an evil destination it is."

Qur'an 8:30-31: "And when those who disbelieved devised plans against thee [Muhammad] that they might confine thee [Muhammad] or slay thee [Muhammad] or drive thee away [Muhammad] — they devised plans [plots] and Allah, too, had arranged a plan [plot]; and Allah is the best of the planners [schemers]. And when our messages are recited to them, they say: We have heard. If we wished, we could say the like of it [same thing]; this is nothing but the stories of the ancients."

Qur'an 8:39: "And fight with them until there is no more persecution, and all religions are [only] for Allah. But if they desist, then surely Allah is Seer of what they do [sees what they do]."

Qur'an 8:41: "And know that whatever you acquire in war, a fifth of it is for Allah and for the Messenger and for the near of kin [for relatives] and the orphans and the needy and the [pilgrim] wayfarer [...]."

Qur'an 8:57: "So if thou overtake them in war [gain mastery over them in battle], scatter by them those who are behind them [inflict such a defeat as would terrorize them], that they may be mindful [so that they would learn a lesson and be warned]."

Qur'an 8:58: "And if thou fear treachery on the part of the people [from anyone], throw back to them their treaty [Muslims can cancel treaties with non-believers if Muslims come to fear that the non-believers will violate the treaty] on terms of equality. Surely Allah loves not the treacherous."

Qur'an 8:59-60: "And let not those who disbelieve think that they can outstrip [escape] Us. Surely they cannot escape. And make ready for them whatever force you can [...] to frighten thereby [terrorize] the enemy of Allah and your enemy and others besides them, whom you know not — Allah knows them. And whatever you spend in Allah's way [Jihad], it will be paid back to you fully and you will not be wronged."

Qur'an 8:61: "And if they incline to peace, incline thou also to it, and trust in Allah. Surely He is the Hearer, the Knower."

Qur'an 8:67: "It is not for a prophet to take captives unless he has fought and triumphed in the land. You desire the frail goods [the lure] of this world, while Allah desires for you the Hereafter. And Allah is Mighty, Wise."

Qur'an 8:72: "Surely those who believed and fed [left] their homes and struggled hard in Allah's way [Jihad] with their wealth and their lives, and with those who gave shelter and helped — these are friends of one another. [...]"

SUNNAH:

THE BATTLE OF BADR

Muslim:B1C9N33: "Muhammad said, 'I have been commanded to fight against people, until they testify to the fact that there is no god but Allah, and believe in me that I am the Prophet, and in all that I have brought. When they do it their blood and riches are guaranteed protection on my behalf except where it is justified by Shari'a, and their affairs rest with Allah.'"

Bukhari:V5B59N702: "[...] Allah's Apostle had only gone out in search of the Quraysh caravan so that he could rob it. But Allah arranged for the Muslims and their enemies to meet by surprise. I was at the Aqabah pledge with Allah's apostle when we gave our lives in submission, but the

Badr battle is more popular amongst the people. I was never stronger or wealthier than I was when I followed the Prophet on a Ghazwa [raid]."

Muslim:B19C50N4472: "The Messenger of Allah set out for Badr. When he reached Harrat-ul-Wabara (a place four miles from Medina) a man met him who was known for his valor and courage. The Companions of the Messenger of Allah were pleased to see him. He said: I have come so that I may follow you and get a share from the booty. The Messenger of Allah said to him: Do you believe in Allah and His Apostle? He said: No. The Messenger of Allah said: Go back I will not seek help from a Mushrik [polytheist] [...]. The man returned and overtook him at Baida?' He asked him as he had asked previously: Do you believe in Allah and His Apostle? The man said: Yes. The Messenger of Allah said to him: Then come along with us.

Tabari VII:26: "In this year Muhammad ordered people to pay the zakat tax. [...] In this year the great battle of Badr took place between the Messenger of Allah and the Quraysh unbelievers in the month of Ramadan."

Tabari VII:28-29: "Abd al-Rahman said, 'Muhammad celebrated the night of 17 Ramadan. In the morning traces of sleeplessness would be on his face. He would say, "On this morning Allah distinguished between truth and falsehood, revealing the Qur'an. On this morning he made Islam mighty, humbling the leaders of unbelief at Badr."' [...] The Apostle heard that Abu Sufyan was coming from Syria with a large Quraysh caravan containing their money and their merchandise. He was accompanied by only thirty men. [...] This was after fighting had broken out between them, and people had been killed and taken captive at Nakhlah. [...] This incident had provoked a state of war between the Prophet and the Quraysh and was the beginning of fighting in which they inflicted casualties upon one another. When Allah's Apostle heard about them he called his companions together and told them of the wealth they had with them and the fewness of their numbers. The Muslims set out [...]. They did not think this raid would be anything other than easy booty. [...] When Abu Sufyan heard that Muhammad's Companions were on their way to intercept his caravan, he sent a message to the Quraysh. [...] When the Quraysh heard this, the people of Mecca hastened to defend their property and protect their men as they were told Muhammad was lying in wait for them."

Ishaq:289 "Muhammad summoned the Muslims and said, 'This is the Quraysh caravan containing their property. Go out and attack it. Perhaps Allah will give it to us as prey. The people answered the Prophet's summons [call]; some eagerly, some reluctantly.

Ishaq:290: Sitting around the mosque [Ka'aba], they [Meccans] wondered why they had allowed this evil rascal to attack their men.

Ishaq:295: A young man was brought to the Apostle and beaten. When the Muslims were displeased with his answers they beat him soundly. Watching the interrogation while performing two prostrations, the Prophet interrupted the proceedings and said, 'Mecca has thrown us pieces of its liver.'

Tabari VII:30: "A body of Meccan men was drawn from the clans. Neither the Prophet nor his Companions heard about this force until they reached Badr. [...] While the Prophet was standing in prayer some Quraysh water-carriers came to the well. Among these was a black slave. Muhammad's men seized him [...]. They questioned him [...]. When the slave began to tell them about the protecting force, it was unwelcome news, for the object of their raid was Abu Sufyan and his caravan. [...] When the slave told them that the Quraysh had come to meet them, they began to beat him and call him a liar. [...] They beat him severely and continued to interrogate them but they found that he had no knowledge of what they were looking for. [...] When the Prophet saw what they were doing he stopped his prayer. He said, 'By Him in Whose Hand my soul rests, you beat him when he tells the truth and leave him alone when he lies.'"

Ishaq:296-300: When [Abu] Sufyan saw that he had saved his caravan he sent word to the Quraysh. [...] [Others said, 'We came out to protect our property and defend our men. There is no point of staying to fight.' So they returned to Mecca. When the Apostle saw them he cried, 'Allah, they called me a liar. Destroy them this morning.' [...] Utba rose to speak. [Utba said,] 'Let us turn back and leave Muhammad to the rest of the Arabs. If we fall on him, we will be haunted for having slain a son or brother of our kin.' [...] Then the Apostle went forth to the people and incited them saying, 'By God [Allah] in whose hand is the soul of Muhammad, no man will be slain this day fighting against them with steadfast courage advancing and not retreating but God [Allah] will cause him to enter Paradise. [Umayr said,] 'I am fighting in Allah's service. This is piety and a good deed. In Allah's war I do not fear as others should. For this fighting is righteous, true and good.'

Tabari VII:32: "[…] Allah gave victory to His Messenger, shamed the unbelievers, and satisfied the Muslims' thirst for revenge on them."

Tabari VII:52-54: "Aswad, an ill-natured man, took to the field, and Hamza came out to meet him. In the encounter Hamza cut off Aswad's foot and half [of] his leg…Hamza pursued him and struck a blow, killing Aswad. After this Utbah took to the field and issued a challenge to single combat. Three young Ansar Muslims came forward to meet him. Muhammad commanded, 'Arise Ubaydah, Hamza, and Ali.' It was no time before Hamza had killed Shaybah and Ali had killed Walid. Ubaydah and Utbah each inflicted a blow upon his adversary. Hamza and Ali then turned on Utbah with their swords and finished him off. They lifted up their companion Ubaydah to safety. His foot had been cut off and the marrow was flowing out. When they brought him to Muhammad, Ubaydah said, 'Am I not a martyr, O Messenger of Allah?' 'Yes indeed,' the Prophet replied. Muhammad turned toward his new Qiblah and said, 'Allah, if this band perishes today, you will be worshipped no more.' […] Abu Bakr picked up his cloak, grasping him from behind. [Abu Bakr, the next caliph, said,] 'O Prophet whom I value more than my father and mother, this constant calling on your Lord is annoying.' […]"

Tabari VII:55: "Mihaja, the mawla [slave] of Umar was struck by an arrow and killed. He was the first Muslim to die. Allah's Messenger went out to his men and incited them to fight. He promised, 'Every man may keep all the booty he takes.' Then Muhammad said, 'By Allah, if any man fights today and is killed fighting aggressively, going forward and not retreating, Allah will cause him to enter Paradise.' Umayr, who was holding some dates in his hand and eating them, said, 'Fine, fine. This is excellent! Nothing stands between me and my entering Paradise except to be killed by these people!' He threw down the dates, seized his sword, and fought until he was slain."

Tabari VII:56: "'O Messenger of Allah, what makes the Lord laugh with joy at his servant?' He replied, 'When he plunges his hand into the midst of an enemy without armor.' So Auf took off the coat of mail he was wearing and threw it away. Then he took his sword and fought the enemy until he was killed. [...] Muhammad picked up a handful of pebbles and faced the Quraysh. He shouted, 'May their faces be deformed.' He threw the pebbles at them and ordered his companions to attack. The foe [Quraysh enemy] was routed [killed or in full retreat]. Allah killed Quraysh chiefs and caused many of their nobles to be taken captive. While the Muslims were taking prisoners, the Messenger was in his hut. [...] As the Muslims were laying hands on as many prisoners as they could catch, the Prophet, I have been told, saw disapproval in the face of Sa'd. He [Muhammad] said, 'Why are you upset by the taking of captives [prisoners]?' Sa'd replied, 'This was the first defeat inflicted by Allah on the infidels. Slaughtering the prisoners would have been more pleasing to me than sparing them.'"

Tabari VII:59: "At Badr I passed Umayyah was standing with his son Ali, holding his hand. I had with me some coats of mail which I had taken as plunder. Umayyah said, Abd al-llah, would you like to take me as a prisoner? I will be more valuable to you as a captive to be ransomed than the coats of mail that you are carrying. I [Abd al-llah] said, 'Yes. Come here then.' I flung away the armor and bound Umayyah and his son Ali, taking them with me. The Muslims encircled us. Then they restrained us physically. One of the Muslims drew his sword and struck Ali in the leg, severing it so that he fell down. Umayyah [the father] gave a scream the like of which I have never heard. I said, 'Save yourself, for there is no escape for your son. By Allah I cannot save him from these men.' Then the Muslims hacked Ali to pieces.' Abd al-Rahman [Abd al-llah] said, 'May Allah have mercy on Bial! I lost my coats of mail, and he deprived me of my captives.'"

Ishaq:303: I was pursuing one of the Meccan Polytheists in order to smite him, when his head suddenly fell off before my sword touched him. Then I knew that someone other than I killed him.

Tabari VII:61-62: "When the Prophet had finished with the enemy, he gave orders that Abu Jahl should be found among the dead. He said, 'O Allah, do not let him escape!' The first man who encountered Jahl yelled out and I made him my mark. When he was within my reach, I attacked him and struck him a blow which severed his foot and half his leg. Then [Abu] Jahl's son hit me [Abd al-llah] on the shoulder and cut off my arm. It dangled at my side from a piece of skin. The fighting prevented me from reaching him after that. I fought the whole day, dragging my arm behind me. When it began to hurt me, I put my foot on it and stood until I pulled it off. [...] Then Mu'awwidh passed by Abu Jahl, who was now crippled and laying there helpless. He hit him until he could no longer move, leaving Jahl gasping for his last breath. But then Mu'awwidh was killed. Abu Allah bin Mas'ud [then] passed by Jahl right when the Messenger ordered us to search for him among the corpses. [...] I cut off Abu Jahl's head and brought it to the Messenger. I said, 'O Allah's Prophet, this is the head of the enemy of Allah [Abu Jahl].' Muhammad said, 'Is this so, by Allah, than whom there is no other deity [This is a reaffirmation that Allah is the only god]?' This used to be the Messenger of Allah's oath. I said, 'Yes.' Then I threw down his head before the Prophet's feet. He said, 'Praise be to Allah!'"

Ishaq:304: Abd Allah bin Mas'ud said, 'I found Abu Jahl at his last gasp [near death]. I put my foot on his neck because he had grabbed me once at Mecca and had hurt me, and said to him, 'Has God [Allah] put you to shame, you enemy of God [Allah]?' He [Abu Jahl] replied, 'How has He [Allah] shamed me? Am I anything more remarkable than a man you have killed?' [i.e., 'You should not be proud that you have killed me.]"[(10)]

ADDRESSING THE DEAD

Ishaq:305-306: "Ukkasha fought until he broke his sword. [...] These were his dying words: 'What do you think about when you kill people? Are these not men just because they are not Muslims.' [...] Allah's Prophet said, '70,000 of my followers shall enter Paradise like the full moon,' Ukkasha asked if he could be one of them. Then a lesser Ansari asked to be included, but the Prophet replied, 'Ukkasha beat you too it and my prayer is now cold' [After the fighting] The Prophet ordered all the dead to be thrown into a pit. All were thrown in except Umayyah. He had swollen up in his coat of mail and filed it. They went to move him, but he fell apart, so they left him where he was and flung some rocks over him. As the dead were being thrown in [the pit] Muhammad stood over them and said, 'O people of the pit, have you found what your Lord promised you to be true? For I have found what my Lord promised me to be true.' [...] The Apostle's Companions heard him get up in the middle of the night. He went to the pit and said, 'O people of the pit,' enumerating all who had been thrown into the dirty well. 'I have found what my Lord promised me to be true.'"

Tabari VII:63: "The Messenger uttered these words, 'O people of the pit, you were evil fellow tribesman to your Prophet. You disbelieved me when other people believed me. You drove me out when other people gave me shelter. You fought me when others came to my aid.'"

Ishaq:307: "The 'Spoils of War' surah came down from Allah to His Prophet concerning the distribution of the booty when the Muslims showed their evil nature. Allah took it out of their hands and gave it to the Apostle."

BLESSED BOOTY

Tabari VII:64: "The Messenger of Allah gave orders concerning the contents of the camp which the people had collected, and it was all brought together. Among the Muslims, however, there was a difference of opinion concerning it. Those who collected said, 'It is ours. Muhammad promised every man that he could keep the booty he took.' Those who were fighting said, 'If it had not been for us, you would not have taken it. We distracted the enemy from you so that you could take what you took.' Those who were guarding the Prophet for fear that the enemy would attack him said, 'By Allah, you have no better right to it than we have. We wanted to kill the enemy when Allah gave us the opportunity and made them turn their back, and we wanted to take property when there was no one to protect it; but we were afraid that the Meccans might attack the Prophet. We protected him so you have no better right to it than we have.' [...] He [Muhammad] divided it equally among the Muslims. In this matter there can be seen fear of Allah, obedience to His Messenger, and the settling of differences."

Tabari VII:65: "Allah's Messenger came back to Medina, bringing with him the booty which had been taken from the polytheists. [...] There were forty-four captives in the Messenger of Allah's possession. There was a similar number of dead."

Tabari VII:71: "Among the captives was Abu Wada. Muhammad said, 'He has a son who is a shrewd merchant with much money.' [...] [The son of Abu Wada] slipped away at night, went to Medina, [and] ransomed his father [Abu Wada] for 4000 dirhams. The Prophet said, 'Abbas you must ransom yourself, your two nephews, Aqil and Nawfal, and your confederate Utbah, for you are a wealthy man.' 'Muhammad,' Abbas said, 'I was a Muslim, but the people compelled me to fight against my will.' 'Allah knows best concerning your Islam,' Muhammad said, 'If what you say is true, Allah will reward you for it. As for your outward appearance, you have been against us, so pay to ransom yourself.' The Messenger had previously taken twenty ounces of gold from him following the battle, so Abbas said, 'Credit me with this amount towards my ransom.' 'No,' Muhammad replied, 'That money Allah has already taken from you and given to us.'"

Tabari VII:80-81: "Abu Bakr said, 'O Prophet of Allah, these are your people, your family; they are your cousins, fellow clansmen and nephews. I think that you should accept ransoms for them so that what we take from them will strengthen us.' 'What do you think Khattab?' Muhammad asked. 'I say you should hand them over to me so that I can cut off their heads. Hand Hamza's brother over to him so that he can cut off his head. Hand over Aqil to Ali so that he can cut off his brother's head. Thus Allah will know that there is no leniency in our hearts towards unbelievers.' The Messenger liked what Abu Bakr said and did not like what I said, and accepted ransoms for the captives. The next day I went to the Prophet in the morning. He was sitting with Abu Bakr and they were weeping. I said, O Messenger of Allah, tell me, what has made you and your companion weep? If I find cause to weep, I will weep with you, and if not, I will pretend to weep because you are weeping. The Prophet said, 'It is because of the taking of ransoms which has been laid before your companions. It was laid before me that I should punish them instead.' Allah revealed: 'It is not for any prophet to have captives until he has made slaughter in the land.' After that Allah made booty lawful for them."

APPLYING THE NEW CODE

Ishaq:308: "When the Apostle was in Sufra, Nadr was assassinated by Ali because he said he told better stories than Muhammad [Ishaq:136]. When Muhammad reached Irq al-Zabyah, he killed Uqbah [a Meccan who was captured at Badr]. When the Holy prophet ordered him to be killed, Uqbah said [to Muhammad], 'Who will look after my children, Muhammad?'

'Hell-Fire,' the Apostle replied, and he was killed. After Uqba was slain Muhammad replied, "Wretch that you were and persecutor; Unbeliever in Allah and his Prophet [Sir William Muir, The Life of Mohamet, Vol. 3, Ch. XII, p. 115-116]."

Ishaq:309: "Sawdah [Muhammad's second wife] said: 'I went to my house and the Messenger was there with Abu Yazid [Meccan prisoner]. His hands were tied to his neck. I could not restrain myself when I saw Abu Yazid like that and I shouted out to him. So Muhammad asked, "Sawdah, are you trying to stir up trouble against Allah's Messenger?" This brought me back to my senses.'"

Ishaq:310-311: "A [captured] Meccan said, 'As soon as we were confronted by the raiding party, we turned our backs and they started killing and capturing us at their pleasure. [...].' When the Quraysh began to bewail [cry over] their dead, consumed in sorrow, one said, 'Do not do this [Show fear to the Muslims] because Muhammad and his Companions will rejoice over our misfortune.'"

Ishaq:313: "The Muslims told Abu Safyan to pay them a ransom to free his son, Amr. He replied, 'Am I to suffer the double loss of my blood and my money? After you have killed my son Hanzala, you want me to pay you a ransom to save Amr?'"

Ishaq:315: "[Abdallah recited this poem:] 'It was so criminal, men could hardly imagine it. Muhammad was ennobled because of the bloody fighting. I swear we shall never lack soldiers, nor army leaders. Driving before us, infidels, until we subdue them with a halter above their noses and a branding iron. We will drive them to the ends of the earth. We will pursue them on horse and on foot. We will never deviate from fighting in our cause. We will bring upon the infidels the fate of Ad and Jurhum [Destruction]. Any people that disobey Muhammad will pay for it. If you do not surrender to Islam, you will live to regret it. You will be shamed in Hell, forced to wear a garment of molten pitch forever!'"

INTRODUCING TERROR

Ishaq:316: "Following Badr, Muhammad sent a number of raiders with an order to capture some of the Meccans and burn them alive. But on the following day he sent word to us, 'I told you to burn these men if you got hold of them. But I decided that none has the right to punish by fire save [except] Allah. So if you capture them, kill them.'"

Ishaq:322: "Allah said, 'Do not turn away from Muhammad when he is speaking to you. Do not contradict his orders. And do not be a hypocrite, one who pretends to be obedient to him, then disobeys him. Those who do so will receive My vengeance. You must respond to the Apostle when he summons you to war. [...] I will cast terror into the hearts of those who reject Me. So strike off their heads and cut off their fingers. All who oppose Me and My Prophet shall be punished severely.' "

Ishaq:323: "[Allah said,] 'I am the best of plotters. I deceived them with My guile so that I delivered you from them.'"

Ishaq:324: "Allah said, 'Leave Me to deal with the liars. I have fetters and fire and food which chokes. I will smote the Quraysh at Badr.' [...] Allah taught them how to divide the spoil. He [Allah] made it lawful and said, 'A fifth of the booty belongs to the Apostle [...] Muslims must fight against infidels until only Allah is worshipped."

Ishaq:326: "If you come upon them, deal so forcibly as to terrify those who would follow them that they may be warned. Make a severe example of them by *terrorizing* [emphasis added] Allah's enemies. [...] If they ask you for peace on the basis of Islam [Submission], make peace on that basis. Be of one mind by His religion. [...] O Prophet exhort the believers to fight. If there are twenty good fighters they will defeat two hundred for they are a senseless people. They do not fight with good intentions nor for truth. [...] when this verse came down it was a shock to the Muslims who took it hard. They were afraid, as the odds were too great. So Allah relieved them and cancelled the verse with another: 'Now has Allah relieved you and He knows that there is a weakness among you. So if there are 100 [instead of 20] they shall vanquish 200.' [...] Muhammad said, 'I was made victorious with *terror* [emphasis added]. The earth was made a place for me to clean. I was given the most powerful words. Booty was made lawful for me. I was given the power to intercede. These five privileges were awarded to no [other] prophet before me.'"

Ishaq:327: "Allah said, 'A prophet must slaughter before collecting captives.

A slaughtered enemy is driven from the land. Muhammad, you craved the desires of this world, its goods and the ransom captives would bring. But Allah desires killing them to manifest the religion.' [...] Allah made booty lawful and good. He used it to incite the Muslims to unity of purpose. So enjoy what you have captured."

Ishaq:341: "[Ali said:] Have you seen how Allah favored His Apostle and how He humiliated the unbelievers? They were put to shame in captivity and death. [...] Their women wept with burning throats for the dead were lying everywhere. But now they are all in Hell."

Ishaq:344: "[...] The impious met death. They became fuel for hell. All who aren't Muslims must go there. [...]"

Ishaq:349: "[...] I am a Muslim. I will exchange my life for the one with virgins fashioned like the most beautiful statues."

Ishaq:357: "Their leaders were left prostrate. Their heads were sliced off like melons. Many an adversary have I left on the ground to rise in pain, broken and plucked. When the battle was joined I dealt them a vicious blow. Their arteries cried aloud, their blood flowed. This is what I did on the day of Badr."

SUMMATION:

IL: The Prophet, who was now in possession of fighting men, was given permission by Allah to be merciless towards the enemies of Allah. Allah staged the Badr raid to prove that Muslims could defeat a larger force. In the Battle at Badr, Allah instructed the Muslims to kill the infidels to the last man, because Allah would send them to hell. Allah assured the Prophet that He was countering the plots of the Quraysh by plotting against them. Allah revealed Shari'a when He shared that Prophet Muhammad was entitled to 1/5 of the booty captured from the infidels. Allah understood that Muhammad, as an orphan, never enjoyed what should have been his among the Quraysh. The Prophet was promised material gain, but he and the Muslims understood they must first psychologically terrorize Allah's enemies and slaughter them in battle. The Badr victory was proof the Muslims heeded Allah's revelation through the Prophet. Those who supported the Muslim warriors in battle were also recognized in Allah's

Qur'an.[(11)] Allah's distain for the infidels was so great that he offered the infidels not a single kindliness, as displayed from Al-Misri:

"It is not permissible to give *Zakat* ["alms"] to a non-Muslim […]"

—Al-Misri, *Reliance of the Traveller*, h8.24

WA: One must look at this surah through the prism of eleven years of Qur'anic condemnation of Muhammad's polytheistic Islam-rejecting relatives, the Quraysh. Armed with the anointed right to wage a merciless war against these infidels and Qur'anic permission to engage in hostilities during Ramadan, the opportunity became reality. The following events described cannot be interpreted as being religious or spiritual: (1) The beating a black slave; (2) Muslim calls for revenge; (3) Abu Bakr's sense of annoyance at listening to Qur'anic revelations from Muhammad; (4) The promise that faces of the Quraysh would be deformed by Allah; (5) Sa'd's slaughter of the prisoners; (6) Muhammad's insistence on ransom for the captives; (7) Umar's wish that all the prisoners would be executed; (8) Muhammad's tears of weeping because he ransomed the captives when Allah really wanted them all slaughtered; (9) Allah's declaration that the taking of others property, or booty, was now lawful; (10) Muhammad's recognition of the opportunity to raid the Meccan caravan at Badr and calling the caravan "prey"; (11) Muhammad's desire to have them, the Meccans, destroyed; and (12) Muslim treatment of their own kinsman as sub-human.

After the Muslim victory at Badr, Muhammad promised that 70,000 Muslims would enter Paradise. Today, there are over 1.5 billion Muslims on earth. The veracity of this statement would mean that most Muslims will, in fact, not gain Paradise. While Muhammad made this statement, he was addressing the dead Quraysh as if they could hear him. Muhammad realized that he was now justified; therefore, permission was given to kill Nadir and Uqba. The unbelievers were to be fought and bound in humiliating fashion. In the afterlife, these enemies of Islam will wear molten pitch. Muhammad wanted to burn his foes alive, but Allah helped arrest his zeal by declaring that burning was reserved for Allah alone. Muhammad plotted his next move and was granted permission by Allah to use terror against his enemies in order to psychologically handicap them and bring about Muslim victory for the sake of Allah.

QUR'AN 59

"The Banishment"

624 AD

SCRIPTURE:

Qur'an 59:2-4, 6-8, 11, 13-14

Ishaq:363-364; Muslim:B19C20N4363; Tabari VII:85-88

PREFACE:

Although revealed prior to the Hudabiyah armistice, the instruction provided to Muslims dictated that they must fight in ranks in order to protect the ummah ("Muslim community"). This injunction was given because Moses and Jesus both predicted the advent of Muhammad. Therefore, fighting was permitted to allow for the fulfillment of the Prophecy. An additional prophecy predicted the triumph of Islam over the religions of Moses and Jesus. Muslims were told to strive hard in this endeavor to provide Islam's victory over the Quraysh and the other religions of the world. Jihad was advocated as the means by which Islam would conquer its enemies and the other religions. It is clear that Islam will triumph as long as Muslims wage Jihad.[12]

SURAH:

Qur'an 59:2-3: "He [Allah] it is Who caused those who disbelieved of the People of the Book [Jews] to go forth from their homes [into exile] at the first banishment. You deemed that they would go forth, while they thought [imagined] their fortresses [strongholds] would defend them against Allah. But Allah came to them from a place they expected not and cast terror into their hearts — they demolished their house [homes] with their own hands and the hands of the believers. So take a lesson [listen to my warning], O you who have eyes. And had it not been that Allah had decreed for them [the Jews] the exile, He certainly would have chastised them in this world [Allah would have punished them]; and for them in the Hereafter is the chastisement of the Fire."

Qur'an 59:4: "That is because they were opposed to Allah and His Messenger, and whoever is opposed to Allah, surely Allah is Severe in retribution."

Qur'an 59:6: "And whatever Allah restored to His Messenger from them, you did not press forward against it any horse or any riding-camel, but Allah gives authority to His messengers against whom He pleases. And Allah is Possessor of power over all things."

Qur'an 59:7: "Whatever Allah restored to His Messenger from the people of the towns, it is for Allah and for the Messenger, and for the near of kin and the orphans and the needy and the wayfarer, so that it be not taken by turns by the rich among you. And whatever the Messenger gives you, accept, and whatever he forbids you, abstain therefrom; and keep your duty to Allah. Surely Allah is Severe in retribution."

Qur'an 59:8: "It is for the poor who fled, who were given from their homes and their possessions, seeking grace of Allah and His pleasure, and helping Allah and His Messenger. These it is that are truthful."

Qur'an 59:11: "Hast thou not seen the hypocrites? They say to their brethren who disbelieve from among the People of the Book: If you are expelled, we certainly will go forth with you, and we will never obey anyone concerning you; and if you are fought against, we will certainly help you. And Allah bears witness that they surely are liars."

Qur'an 59:13: "Your fear in their hearts is indeed greater than Allah's. That is because they are a people who understand not."

Qur'an 59:14: "They will not fight against you in a body save [except] in fortified towns or from behind walls. Their fighting between them is severe. Thou wouldst think them united, but their hearts are divided. That is because they are a people who have no sense."

THE JEWS REJECT MUHAMMAD

Muslim:B19C20N4363: "We were (sitting) in the mosque when the Messenger of Allah came to us and said: (Let us) go to the Jews. We went out with him until we came to them. The Messenger of Allah (may peace be upon him) stood up and called out to them (saying): O ye assembly of Jews, accept Islam (and) you will be safe...he added: You should know that the earth belongs to Allah and His Apostle, and I wish that I should expel you from this land those of you who have any property with them should sell it, otherwise they should know that the earth belongs to Allah and His Apostle (and they may have to go away leaving everything behind)."

Tabari VII:85-86: "After Muhammad killed many Quraysh polytheists at Badr, the Jews were envious and behaved badly toward him [...]. They also infringed the treaty in various ways. [...] What happened to the Banu Qaynuqa was that Muhammad assembled them in the marketplace and said, 'Jews, beware lest Allah bring on you the kind of vengeance which He brought on the Quraysh. Accept Islam and become Muslims. You know that I am a Prophet. You will find me in your scriptures and in Allah's Covenant with you.' The Jews of the Banu Qaynuqa replied, 'Muhammad, do you think that we are like your people? Do not be deluded by the fact that you met a people with no knowledge and you made good use of your opportunity.' [...] Gabriel brought down [a] verse [Qur'an 8:58] to the Prophet [...]. When Gabriel finished delivering this verse, the Prophet said, 'I fear the Banu Qaynuqa.' It was on the basis of this verse that Muhammad advanced upon them. Allah's Apostle besieged the Banu Qaynuqa until they surrendered at his discretion unconditionally."

THE BANU QAYNUQA ARE EXPELLED

Ishaq:363: "Say to those who do not believe you: 'You will be vanquished and gathered into Hell, an evil resting place. You have already had a sign by way of the two forces which met, the Apostle's Companions and the Quraysh. One side fought in Allah's cause. Verily [Truly], that was an example for the discerning.' [...] The Banu Qaynuqa were the first Jews to infringe the agreement between them and the Messenger. The campaign of the Prophet against the Banu Qaynuqa was in Shawwal [early spring] in the second year of the Hijrah. [...] Abd Allah rose up when Allah had put them in his power, [After the Banu Qaynuqa surrendered] and said, 'Muhammad, treat my ally well, for the Qaynuqa are a confederate of the Khazraj.' The Prophet ignored him, so Abd Allah repeated his request. The Prophet turned away from him so Abd Allah put his hand on the collar of the Messenger's robe. Muhammad said, 'Let go of me!' He [Muhammad] was so angry his face turned black. Then he [Muhammad] said, 'Damn you, let me go!' Abd Allah replied, 'No, by God, I will not let you go until you treat my ally humanely. There are seven hundred men among them, some with mail, who defended me from my foes when I needed their help. And now, you would mow them down in a single morning? By God I do not feel safe around here anymore. I am afraid of what the future may have in store.' So the Messenger said, 'You can have them.'"

Tabari VII:87: "The Prophet said, 'Let them go; may Allah curse them, and may He curse Abd Allah with them.' So the Muslims let them go. Then Muhammad gave orders to expel the Jews. Allah gave their property as booty to His Messenger. The Qaynuqa did not have any farmland, as they were goldsmiths. The Prophet took many weapons belonging to them and the tools of their trade. The person who took charge of their expulsion from Yathrib along with their children was Ubadah. He accompanied them as far as Dhubab, saying: 'The farther you go the better.'"

Tabari VII:88: "Some say there were three Ghazwa [Muslim raids] led by the Messenger himself and one maghazi raiding party which he dispatched between his expedition to Badr and the campaign against the Qaynuqa."

HEZBOLLAH: THE PARTY OF ALLAH

Ishaq:364: "[Allah said:] Muslims, take not Jews and Christians as friends. Whoever protects them becomes one of them, they become diseased, and will earn a similar fate. [...] [Abd Allah replied,] 'I fear this change of circumstance may end up overtaking us.' So Allah replied, 'He will be sorry for his thoughts. True believers perform prostrations, they pay the tax, they bow in homage, and renounce their agreements with the Jews. They are Hezbollah—Allah's Party.'"

SUMMATION:

IL: Once the Jews of Banu Qaynuqa were found to have violated the Constitution of Medina, Muhammad was permitted by Allah to lay siege and terrorize their community. This surah was revealed after the siege as a warning to the next Jewish tribe the Banu Nadir. They were reminded that the Banu Qaynuqa were destined for hell and the same fate awaited the Banu Nadir unless they acknowledged Allah and accepted Muhammad as their Prophet. They were reminded that these Jews, only by the mercy of Allah, were allowed to live when they deserved to die. Their Arab allies in Yathrib could not help these Jews against Allah's justice. Rightfully, the possessions of the Banu Qaynuqa were divided between the Muslims, especially among the Muslims who migrated from Mecca.

WA: Allah addressed the Banu Nadir (Jewish tribe) and told them to recall the fate of the Banu Qaynuqa (Another Jewish tribe who were to be expelled from Medina). Allah permitted migration or the Banu Qaynuqa would have been punished. Allah opposes all who oppose Muhammad and Allah. So Allah gave the belongings of the Banu Qaynuqa to Muhammad, the Muslims, and the needy who were the families of the Muslims who were forced to leave Mecca. What the Prophet gave and kept was left to his discretion (Qur'an 59:7) The Banu Nadir should not think that the Arab hypocrites (those who refuse to fight) would be any aid to them for they were of no aid to the Banu Qaynuqa. The consequences for both, (the Arab hypocrites and Jewish tribes) will be an abode in the fire, the rightful reward for evildoers.

The Sunnah is clear that Muhammad's intention regarding the Banu Qaynuqa was to expel them and confiscate their possessions. These Jews knew about Muhammad's victory at Badr. They also knew the intent and capabilities of Muhammad and his Muslims. The pretext for the siege was the Jews' violated the Constitution of Medina. The only proof we have of their violation was their bad behavior and they believed Muhammad was nothing more than a warlord seeking the wealth of others. The truth came to the surface when Muhammad admitted that he feared these Jews. After the encounter in the marketplace, the Muslims, in short order, came upon the Jews. These Jews were not initially killed, because the Arab Abdallah begged for their lives to be spared. Muhammad grudgingly complied, but not before he damned Abdallah. Abdallah knew that Muhammad wanted to kill every Jew. Frustrated, Muhammad forbade Muslims to have Jewish or Christian friends. Muhammad did not want the People of the Book to have an Arab or Muslim advocate. Muhammad then stated that *true* Muslims: (1) bow to Allah; (2) pay the zakat tax; and (3) renounce any agreements with the Jews. He declared that true Muslims are *Hezbollah* ("Party of Allah"). The behavior of Islamic Literalists, from this point forward, was now fully defined.

QUR'AN 57

"Iron"

624 AD

SCRIPTURE:

Qur'an 57:10, 19, 27, 29

Bukhari:V5B59N369; Ishaq:365, 368-369; Tabari VII:94-95, 97

PREFACE:

This surah was revealed before the Meccan conquest. Muslims were assured of conquest but not without great sacrifice. Muslims were warned that a time would come when the mentality of the hypocrites will harden the hearts of the true believers. Worldly enjoyments will blind Muslims from the truth for a time, but Allah promised that all those who take up the sword against Islam will be punished with a great punishment. The onward march of Islam was assured. The eventual demise of the religion of Jews and Christians was declared by Allah. The truth of Islam must and will be established.[13]

SURAH:

Qur'an 57:10: "What reason have you that you spend not [money] in Allah's way [Jihad]? [...] Those of you who spent before the Victory and fought are not on a level with others [the same level with others]. They are greater in rank than those who spent and fought afterwards. [...]"

Qur'an 57:19: "And those who believe in Allah and His messengers, they are the truthful and the faithful ones with their Lord. They have their reward and their light. And those who disbelieve and reject Our messages, they are the inmates of hell."

Qur'an 57:27, 29: "[…] We made Jesus son of Mary to follow, and We gave him the Gospel. And We put compassion and mercy in the hearts of those who followed him. And as for monkery [Monks], they innovated [changed] it […]. So We gave those of them who believed their reward, but most of them are transgressors. That the People of the Book [Jews and Christians] may know that they control naught of the grace of Allah, and that grace is in Allah's hand. He gives it to whom he pleases [chooses]. And Allah is the Lord of mighty grace."

SUNNAH:

ASSASSINATION

Ishaq:365: "Ka'b bin Ashraf was from the Jewish clan Banu Nadir. When he heard the news, he said, 'Can this be true? Did Muhammad actually kill these people? These were fine men. If Muhammad has slain them, then the belly of the earth is a better place for us than its surface.' When the enemy of Allah became convinced the report was true, he set out for Mecca. He began to arouse people against Muhammad. […] Ka'b Ashraf composed the following poetic lines: 'The blood spilled at Badr calls to its people. They cry and weep. The best men were slain and thrown into a pit.' […] [Ka'b urged the people, saying,] 'Drive off that fool of yours so that you may be safe from talk that makes no sense. Why do you taunt those who mourn over their dead? They lived good lives, and as such we must remember them. But now you have become like jackals.' […] The Prophet said, 'Who will rid me of Ashraf?' Maslama said, 'I will deal with him for you. O Apostle, I will kill him.' Muhammad said, 'Do so if you can.'"

Bukhari:V5B59N369: "Allah's Apostle said, 'Who is willing to kill Ka'b bin Ashraf who has hurt Allah and His Apostle?' Thereupon Muhammad bin Maslama got up saying, 'O Allah's Apostle! Would you like me to kill him?' The Prophet said, 'Yes.' Maslama said, 'Then allow me to say false things in order to deceive him.' The Prophet said, 'You may say such things.'"

Tabari VII:94: "The Prophet said, 'Who will rid me of Ashraf?' Muhammad bin Maslama, said, 'I will rid you of him, Messenger of Allah. I will kill him.' 'Do it then,' he [Muhammad] said, 'If you can.' [...] The Prophet summoned him [Maslama] and said, 'Why have you given up food and drink?' 'O Prophet, I said something and do not know if I can fulfill it.' 'All that is incumbent on you is to try,' Muhammad replied. [...] Muhammad bin Maslama said, 'O Messenger, we shall have to tell lies.' 'Say what you like,' Muhammad replied. 'You are absolved, free to say whatever you must.' [...] Before they went to him, they sent Abu ahead. [...] Then Abu said, 'Ka'b, I have come to you about a matter which I want you to keep secret.' 'Go ahead,' he [Ka'b] replied. 'The arrival of Prophet Muhammad has been an affliction for us.' Abu said, 'Most Arabs are now hostile to us. We cannot travel along the roads, and the result is that our families are facing ruin. We are all suffering.' Ka'b replied, 'I warned you, Abu, that things would turn out like this.' Abu said, 'I would like you to sell us some food. We will give you some collateral and make a firm contract. Please treat us generously.'"

Tabari VII:95: "[...] Abu wanted to fool the Jew so that he would not be suspicious about the weapons when they came bearing them. [...] Abu went back to his companions, informed them of what had happened. He told them to grab their swords and join him. Before leaving, they went to the house of the Messenger. Muhammad walked with them as far as Baqi al-Gharqad. Then he sent them off, saying, 'Go in Allah's name; O Allah, help them!'"

Tabari VII:97: "He spoke to them for a while. Then they said, 'Would you like to walk with us, Ka'b, so that we can talk?' [...] 'We carried Ka'b's head and brought it to Muhammad during the night. We saluted as he stood praying and told him that we had slain Allah's enemy. When he came out to us we cast Ashraf's head before [at] his feet. The Prophet praised Allah that the poet had been assassinated and complemented us for the good work we had done in Allah's cause. Then he spat upon our comrade's wounds and we returned to our families. Our attack upon Allah's enemy cast *terror* [emphasis added] among the Jews, and there was no Jew in Medina who did not fear for his life.'

Ishaq:368: "Then Abu called out to him. He had recently married, and he leapt up in his bed. His wife took hold of the sheets, and said to the strange voice, 'You are a fighting man; as only a man of war leaves his house [home] at an hour like this' [...] Their swords rained blows upon him, but did not kill him. Muhammad bin Maslama said, 'When I saw that they were ineffective, I remembered a long, thin dagger which I had in my scabbard. I took hold of it. By this time the enemy of Allah had shouted so loudly lamps had been lit in the homes around us. I [Maslama] plunged the dagger into his breast and pressed upon it so heavily that it reached his pubic region. Allah's enemy fell to the ground. [...] Sword in hand we cut him down. By Muhammad's order we were sent secretly by night. Brother killing brother. We lured him to his death with guile. Traveling by night, bold as lions, we went into his home. We made him taste death with our deadly swords. We sought victory for the religion of the Prophet."

Ishaq:369: "The next morning, the Jews were in a state of fear on account of our attack upon the enemy of Allah. After the assassination, the Prophet declared, 'Kill every Jew.' Thereupon Mas'ud leapt upon Sunayna, one of the Jewish merchants with whom his family had social and commercial relations and killed him. The Muslim's brother complained, saying, 'Why did you kill him? You have much fat in your belly from his charity.' Mas'ud answered, 'By Allah, had Muhammad ordered me to murder you, my brother, I would have cut off your head.' Wherein the brother said, 'Any religion that can bring you to this is indeed wonderful!' He accepted Islam."

SUMMATION:

IL: After the Badr victory and the banishment of the Banu Qaynuqa, Allah revealed his displeasure with those Muslims who failed to participate in Jihad. Those who contributed financially were recognized, but not considered at the same level as those who spilled their blood in Jihad. Allah assured the Muslims; those who resist Islam will burn. The Prophet Isa was mentioned for his mercy, but his followers followed a crooked course that departed from the straight path. The majority of the People of the Book are transgressors.[14]

WA: Ka'b Ashraf, an influential Jew of the Banu Nadir, set out to warn the Meccans. Ashraf found it hard to comprehend what Muhammad did at Badr and what he perpetrated against the Banu Qaynuqa. After Muhammad heard what he was doing, he demanded Ashraf's assassination. Through guile and lies, of which Muhammad approved, Ashraf was stabbed and beheaded in his home. Ashraf's severed head was then laid at Muhammad's feet. Muhammad rejoiced at the assassination and made a declaration that every Jew should be killed. The murders of Ashraf, the influential Jew from Banu Nadir, and Sunayna, the Jewish merchant, were considered victories for Islam.[15] This is what we must learn from their actions. The price for speaking against Muhammad was death. Muhammad prayed to Allah for the assassination to be successful. Muhammad praised the assassins and Allah, upon confirmation of their successful mission. Henceforth, Muhammad stated that terror should be used against the perceived enemies of Islam. Muhammad asked for the death of Ka'b Ibn Ashraf, a Jew who spoke against him. Maslama, given permission to lie by Muhammad, devised a plan to deal with the influential Jew. After Ashraf's head was presented to Muhammad he declared "Allah Akbar Kill every Jew whom you come across."

QUR'AN 62

"The Congregation"

624 AD

SCRIPTURE:

Qur'an 62:2, 5-6

Ishaq:482-483; Tabari VII:98-101

PREFACE:

Muslims are told that they will meet the same fate as the Jews if they ever behave like them. The Jews gave themselves up to worldly possessions and; thus, experience the wrath of Allah.[(16)]

SURAH:

Qur'an 62:2: "He it is Who raised among the illiterates a Messenger from among themselves, who recites to them His messages and purifies them, and teaches them the Book and the Wisdom — although they were previously in grave error."

Qur'an 62:5-6: "The likeness of those who were charged with the Torah, then they did observed it not, is as the likeness of [an] ass carrying books. Evil is the likeness of the people [in this instance the Jews] who reject the messages of Allah. And Allah guides not the iniquitous people. Say: O you who are Jews, if you think you are the favorites of Allah to the exclusion of other people, then invoke death [If you are so sure that you are right put your life on the line], if you are truthful."

BLEEDING THE QURAYSH

Tabari VII:98: "The Messenger ordered Zayd [Muhammad's adopted son] out on a raid in which he captured a Quraysh caravan led by Abu Sufyan at a watering place in Najd. [...] Zayd captured the caravan and its goods but was unable to capture the men. He brought the caravan to the Prophet. The reason for this expedition was that the Quraysh said, 'Muhammad has damaged our trade and sits astride our road. If we stay in Mecca we'll consume our capital.' [...] The news of the caravan reached the Prophet, as did the information that it contained much wealth and silver vessels. Zayd therefore intercepted it and made himself master of their caravan. The fifth [of the capture money] was twenty thousand dirhams; Allah's Prophet took it [Muhammad took the 1/5th or 20,000 dirhams, for himself] and divided the other four-fifths [of the captured money] among the members of the raiding party. Furat was taken captive. They said to him, 'If you accept Islam the Messenger will not kill you.'"

KILLING THE JEWS

Tabari VII:99: "In this year, it is said, the killing of Abu Rafi the Jew took place. The reason for his being killed, it is said, that he used to take the part of Ka'b bin Ashraf against the Messenger. The Prophet is said to have sent Abd Allah bin Atik against him in the middle of Jumada [Fifth or sixth month of the Islamic calendar]. Abu Rafi used to injure and wrong the Prophet [verbally]."

Tabari VII:100: "When I reached [Abu] Rafi he was in a dark room with his family. As I did not know where he was in the room, I said, 'O Abu Rafi.' When he replied, I proceeded toward the voice and gave him a blow with my sword. He shouted and I came back, pretending to be a helper. I said, 'O Abu,' changing the tone of my voice. He asked me, 'I don't know who came to strike me with his sword.' Then I drove my sword into his belly and pushed it forcibly till it touched the bone. I hit him again and covered him with wounds, but I could not kill him, so I thrust the point of my sword into his stomach until it came out through his back. At that, I knew that I killed him. [...] I came to my companions and said, 'By

Allah, I will not leave until I hear the wailing of their women.' So, I did not move until I heard them crying for the Jewish merchant [Abu Rafi]. I said, 'Deliverance! Allah has killed Abu Rafi.' I got up, feeling no ailment, and proceeded till we came upon the Prophet and informed him."

Tabari VII:101: "[…] The Aws had killed Ka'b Ashraf on account of his enmity to the Messenger and inciting people against him, so the Khazraj asked the Prophet for permission to kill Sallam Huqayq, who was in Khaybar. He granted this."

Ishaq:482-483: "One of the favors which Allah conferred on His Prophet was that these two tribes of the Ansar, the Aws and the Khazraj, used to vie with one another like stallions to carry out the will of Muhammad. […] His [Huqayq's] wife came out and we told her that we were Arabs in search of supplies. When we entered, we bolted the door on her so she gave a shout to warn him of our presence. We rushed upon him with our swords as he lay in his bed. He took his pillow and tried to fend us off. Abd Allah thrust his sword into his stomach and transfixed him while he was shouting, 'Enough! Enough!' At once we went out but Abd Allah had bad eyesight, and he fell off the stairway, bruising his leg or arm. 'How shall we know that the enemy of Allah is dead?' one of us asked. 'I will go and look,' one replied. He set off and mingled with the people. He said, 'I found him with the men of the Jews, and with his wife, who had a lamp in her hand, peering into his face. She [Huqayq's] wife said, 'By the God of the Jews [Yahveh], he is dead.' I never heard any more pleasing words than these. We went to the Messenger of Allah and told him that we had killed the enemy of Allah. We disagreed in his presence about the killing of Salaam, each of us claiming to have done it. The Prophet said, 'Bring me your swords.' We did and he looked at them. He said, 'This sword of Abd Allah killed him. I can see the marks left by bones on it.' […] [The Aws and Khazraj sang about their accomplishments:] Allah, what a fine band you have, one willing to kill Salaam and Ashraf! We went with sharp swords, like fighting lions. We came upon their homes and made them drink death with our swift-slaying swords. Looking for the victory of our Prophet's religion, we ignored every risk."

SUMMATION:

IL: Allah's miracle in Islam is His choice of Muhammad, who was raised illiterate, as His Prophet. Because he was chosen by Allah, the Prophet's words were able to purify others and the words of the Qur'an were able to save the infidels from their infidelity. The Qur'an is clear. Any Jew who rejected the Qur'anic revelation violated the Torah. Anyone who rejected the Qur'anic revelation was evil [...] anyone. Death to those infidels who believe they are chosen by the Almighty. They are the most sinful. They will all receive the painful chastisement, the Fire. All Praise to Allah!

WA: The Muslim tactic against the Quraysh was difficult to defend. The Quraysh realized that Muhammad and his Muslims were out to deprive the Quraysh of their wealth. The Muslim war was fought on two fronts. It was fought against the Meccan polytheists and against the Jews of Medina. The Jew, Ka'b Ashraf, was assassinated for speaking against the Islamic prophet. Muhammad then sent another death squad against Ashraf's friend Abu Rafi. The details of Abu Rafi's assassination included: guile, trickery, deceit, brutality, and the lack of any compassion. Abu Rafi also spoke against Muhammad, but did not try to physically harm him. The murderous episode ended with Allah being credited with Abu Rafi's death, though the slaughter was absent of any righteousness and holiness. The next victim was Sallam Huqayq of Khaybar. Lying, trickery, lack of compassion, and rejoicing at the demise of another, became righteous deeds for Muhammad's assassins. Nothing should resonate more to a Western audience than these words, "Allah, what a fine band you have, one willing to kill Sallam and Ashraf!"

CHAPTER 5 NOTES

1. Ali, p. 1097; Pickthall, p. 401
2. Ali, p. 6; Pickthall, p. 32
3. Esposito, *Women in Muslim Family Law*, pp. 29-30
4. Peters, *Muhammad and the Origins of Islam*, p. 211
5. Asad, *The Message of the Qur'an*, p. 51
6. Warraq, *Why I am not a Muslim*, p. 92
7. Watt, *Muhammad: Prophet and Statesman*, p. 112
8. Al-Misri, *Reliance of the Traveller*, p. 529
9. Ali, p. 374; Pickthall, p. 137
10. Davis, *100 Decisive Battles*, pp. 97-98
11. Caner, *Unveiling Islam*, p.50
12. Ali, p. 1074; Pickthall, p. 392
13. Ali, p. 1058; Pickthall, p. 387
14. Qutb, *In the Shade of the Qur'an*, p. 73
15. Spencer, *The Politically Incorrect Guide to Islam*, p. 12
16. Ali, p. 1091; Pickthall, pp. 398-399

CHAPTER 6

Middle Medinan Revelations

(625-627 AD)

QUR'AN 65

"The Divorce"

625 AD

SCRIPTURE:

Qur'an 65:4

Bukhari:V4B52N260, V9B84N57, V9B84N59; Muslim:B19C37N4420, B19C47N4457

PREFACE:

This surah was revealed to amend the divorce statute after the Muslim Ibn Umar made a mistake in the divorce process. A waiting period of generally three months was required after a woman was divorced before she could remarry. This amendment also applied to those who had not menstruated—girls who were age nine and up.[1]

SURAH:

Qur'an 65:4: "And those of your women who despair of menstruation, if you have a doubt, their prescribed time is three months [the waiting period is three months], and of those, too, who have not [menstruated] had their courses [Little girls can also be married and divorced as well]."

SUNNAH:

INTOLERANCE

Bukhari:V4B52N260: "Ali burnt some people and this news reached Ibn

'Abbas, who said, 'Had I been in his place I would not have burnt them, as the Prophet said, "Don't punish (anybody) with Allah's Punishment." No doubt, I would have killed them, for the Prophet said, 'If somebody (a Muslim) discards his religion, kill him.'".

Bukhari:V9B84N57: "Some Zanadiqa (atheists) were brought to Ali and he burnt them. The news of this event, reached Ibn Abbas who said, 'If I had been in his place, I would not have burnt them, as Allah's Apostle forbade it, saying, "Do not punish anybody with Allah's punishment [fire]." I would have killed them according to the statement of Allah's Apostle, "Whoever changed his Islamic religion, then kill him."'"

Bukhari:V9B84N59: "Allah's Apostle said, 'I have been ordered to fight the people till they say: "None has the right to be worshipped but Allah." Whoever says this will save his property and his life from me.'"

Muslim:B19C37N4420: "The Prophet said: 'Great is the wrath of Allah upon a people who have done this to the Messenger.' At that time he was pointing to his front teeth. The Apostle said: 'Great is the wrath of Allah upon a person who has been killed by me in Allah's Cause [Jihad].'"

Muslim:B19C47N4457: "The Messenger of Allah (may peace be upon him) used not to kill the children, so you should not kill them *unless* [emphasis added] you could know what Khadir had known about the child he killed, or you could distinguish between a child who would grow up to be a believer (and a child who would grow up to be a non-believer), so that you killed the (prospective) non-believer and left the (prospective) believer aside.'"

SUMMATION:

IL: Muhammad, through divine direction, turned his attention to administrative matters after Allah willed that His Jewish enemies die by the sword. Regarding men and women, women were instructed to wait three months after a divorce in order to make sure they were not pregnant with the previous husband's child. It was also stated by Al-Misri:

> "Circumcision is obligatory [...] for both men and women."[2]

—Al-Misri, *Reliance of the Traveller*, e4.3

WA: Muhammad announced his expectations for Muslims after shocking the Quraysh, expelling a group of Jews, threatening another Jewish group, and assassinating a few other Jews. Muslims were ordered to kill any Muslim who departed from the Islamic faith. After this decree was given, it appeared that Ali either did not get the memo or he chose to ignore it when he burned some atheists to death. In order to sidestep the issue, Muhammad reasserted that all who oppose Islam would be fought until Allah's reign was supreme. He also did not hide the fact that he wanted to confiscate the property of his enemies.

In these instances, the Quraysh and the Jews insulted Muhammad. Muslims therefore believed, with Muhammad's sanction, that raiding caravans and political assassinations were justified. The last hadith is also hair-raising. It tells Muslims that children should not be killed in battle *unless* the Jihadi can determine if he or she will grow up to be a non-believer. The hadith espousing this stance is impossible to determine for no one can determine the course of anyone's life from childhood. This is used to justify the killing of Jewish and Christian children and advocates honor killing in the Muslim community.

QUR'AN 3

"The Family Of Amran"

625 AD

SCRIPTURE:

Qur'an 3:2-3, 10, 21-22, 28, 32, 52, 54-56, 61-62, 67, 75, 77-78, 85, 95, 110, 112, 118, 120, 132, 140-141, 145, 151, 157-158, 169-171, 178, 181, 183, 195

Bukhari:V5B59N377; Ishaq:372-375, 379-380, 383-386, 388-400, 403, 405, 407, 414-415, 422; Muslim:B19C7N4318, B20C41N4678; Tabari VII:105-106, 112, 120-121, 124, 126-127, 129, 133, 139

PREFACE:

This surah makes the case that Imran was the grandfather of Jesus whereas the Torah declared that Imran was the Father of Moses. The   Gospel of Matthew claimed that Jacob begat Joseph. Luke's Gospel stated, "Joseph, which was the son of Heli." It does not state that Heli begat Joseph; therefore, Joseph could have been the adopted son of Heli. According to Exodus 6:20, Amran was the father of Moses. As this surah unfolds, Jewish defiance to Muhammad's revelation continued in its stubbornness. The Meccans also came to Uhud and defeated the Muslims in battle. The Muslim defeat was caused by fifty archers and others who abandoned the battlefield because they did not want to fight and wanted to position themselves to get the Meccan booty.[3] As the wives of the victors mutilated the dead Muslims on the battlefield, Muhammad vowed revenge until another revelation prohibited mutilation. This surah also reveals how Jews and Christians try to discredit Islam. The surah assured Muslims that the new spiritual center would be the Ka'aba at Mecca. Muslims were warned by Allah that even if Jews are outwardly friendly, they are inwardly hostile towards Islam. Therefore, Muslims are permitted to fight against those who threaten Islam. This surah announces judgment against the People of the Book. Allah is against those who pervert the truth. Terror and dissimulation are permitted against those who threaten Islam. True Muslims who die in this struggle are promised the reward of a *Shahid* ("martyr").[4]

SURAH:

Qur'an 3:2-3: "Allah, there is no but He, the Ever Living, the Self-subsisting [the One Who sustains] by Whom all subsist [and protects all that exists]. He has revealed to thee [Muhammad] the Book [Qur'an] with truth, verifying that which is [came] before it, and He revealed [sent down] the Torah [Taurat] and the Injil [Gospel]."

Qur'an 3:10: "Those who disbelieve, neither their wealth nor their children will avail them aught [in the least] against Allah. And they will be fuel for fire."

Qur'an 3:21-22: "Those [the Jews] who disbelieve in the messages of Allah and would slay the prophets unjustly and slay those among men who enjoin justice, announce to them a painful chastisement. Those [the Jews] are they whose works will be of no avail in this world and the Hereafter, and they will have no helpers."

Qur'an 3:28: "Let not the believers take the disbelievers for friends rather than [in preference to] believers. And whoever does this has no connection with Allah — except [unless] that you guard yourselves against them, guarding carefully."

Qur'an 3:32: "Say [Muhammad]: Obey Allah and the Messenger; but if they turn back [from Islam], Allah surely loves not the disbelievers [infidels]."

Qur'an 3:52: "But when Jesus perceived disbelief on their part, he said: Who will be my helpers in Allah's way [Jihad]?' The disciples said: We are Allah's helpers: we believe in Allah, and bear thou witness that we are submitting ones [Muslims]."

Qur'an 3:54: "And the Jews planned [conspired] and Allah also planned [conspired]. And Allah is ["Khayrul-Makireen," the greatest of all deceivers] the best of planners." [*Makara* ("conniving")]

Qur'an 3:55: "And remember when Allah said: O Jesus! I am gathering you and causing you to ascend to Me, and am cleansing you of those who disbelieve and am setting those who follow you above those who disbelieve until the Day of Resurrection. Then to Me you will all return, and I shall judge between you as to that in which you used to differ."

Qur'an 3:56: "Then as to those who disbelieve, I shall chastise [punish] them with severe chastisement [a severe punishment] in this world and the Hereafter and they will have no helpers."

Qur'an 3:61-62: "Whoever then disputes with thee [Muhammad] in [concerning] this matter [Jesus as Son of God] after the knowledge that has come to thee [Muhammad], say: [...] let us [...] invoke the curse of Allah on the [all] liars. Surely this is the true account, and there is no god but Allah [...]"

Qur'an 3:67: "Abraham was not a Jew nor a Christian, but he was an upright man, a Muslim; and he was not one of the polytheists."

Qur'an 3:75: "And among the People of the Book [...] they say there is no blame on us in the matter of the unlearned people and they forge a lie against Allah while they know [the truth]."

Qur'an 3:77-78: "Those who take a small price [took money] for the covenant of Allah [Allah's words in the Bible] and their own oaths — they have no portion in the Hereafter, and Allah will not speak to them, nor will He look upon them on the day of Resurrection, nor will He purify them, and for them is a painful chastisement. And there is certainly a party of them [some of them] who lie about the Book [Bible] that you may consider it to be a part of the Book [Qur'an] while it is not a part of the Book (Mother of the Book in Paradise with Allah); and they say, It [The corrupted Bible] is from Allah, while it is not from Allah; and they forge a lie against Allah whilst they know [the truth]."

Qur'an 3:85: "And whoever seeks a religion other than Islam, it will not be accepted from him [by Allah], and in the Hereafter he will be one of the losers."

Qur'an 3:95: "And: Allah speaks the truth; so follow the religion of Abraham, the upright one. And he was not one of the polytheists."

Qur'an 3:110: "You [Arab Muslims] are the best nation [that were] raised up for men: you enjoin good and forbid evil and you believe in Allah. And if the People of the Book [Jews and Christians] had believed [in Islam], it would have been better for them. Some of them are believers [Jews and Christians who have converted to Islam], but most of them are transgressors [evil-doers]."

Qur'an 3:112: "Abasement will be their lot wherever they are found, except under a covenant with Allah and a covenant with men, and they shall incur the wrath of Allah, and humiliation will be made to cling to them. This is because they disbelieved in the messages of Allah and killed the prophets unjustly. This is because they disobeyed and exceeded the limits."

Qur'an 3:118: "O you who believe, take not for intimate friends others than your own people: they spare no pains to cause you loss [they do not fall short of inflicting loss upon you]. They love that which distresses you. Vehement hatred has already appeared from out of their mouths, and that which their hearts conceal is greater still. Indeed We have made the messages clear to you, if you [will] understand."

Qur'an 3:120: "If good befalls you, it grieves them, and if an evil afflicts you, they rejoice at it. […]"

Qur'an 3:132: "And obey Allah and the Messenger, that you may be shown mercy."

Qur'an 3:140-141: "If a wound has afflicted you [if you have received a blow and have been wounded], a wound like it has also afflicted the disbelieving people [be sure a similar wound has hurt the infidels]. And We bring these days we give to men by turns, that Allah may know those who believe, and [that He may] take witness [martyrs] from among you [to Himself]. And Allah loves not the wrongdoers, and that He may purge those who believe and deprive the disbelievers of blessings."

Qur'an 3:145: "And no soul can die but with Allah's permission — the term [the time] is fixed. And whoever desires the reward of this world, We give him of it, and whoever desires the reward of the Hereafter, We give him of it. And We shall reward the grateful."

Qur'an 3:151: "We will cast terror into the hearts of those who disbelieve because they set up with Allah [ascribe partners to Allah] that for which he has sent down no authority [has not been revealed], and their abode is the hellfire. And is the abode [place] of the wrongdoers."

Qur'an 3:157-158: "And if you are slain in Allah's way or you die, surely Allah's protection and His mercy are better than what they amass. And if you die or you are slain, to Allah you are gathered."

Qur'an 3:169-171: "And think not of those who are killed [slain] in Allah's way [Jihad] as dead. Nay, they are alive, being provided sustenance from their Lord, rejoicing in what Allah has given them [bounty] out of His grace, and they rejoice for the sake [with regard to] of those who, being left behind them, have not yet joined them [in their bliss], that they [the martyrs] have no fear, nor shall they grieve. They rejoice for Allah's favour and His grace, and that Allah wastes not the reward of the believers."

Qur'an 3:178: "And let not those who disbelieve think that our granting them respite is good for themselves. We grant them respite only that they may add to their sins; and for them is a humiliating chastisement."

Qur'an 3:181: "Allah has certainly heard the saying of those [the Jews] who said: Allah is poor and we are rich. We shall record what they say, and their killing the prophets unjustly, and We shall say: Taste the chastisement of burning [Hell]."

Qur'an 3:183: "Say [Muhammad]: Indeed there came to you messengers before me with clear arguments and with that which you demand. Why then did you try to kill them, if you are truthful?"

Qur'an 3:195: "So their Lord accepted their prayer [...]. So those who fled and were driven forth from their homes and persecuted in My way and who fought and were slain, I shall truly remove their evil and make them enter gardens [with virgins] wherein flow rivers — a reward from Allah. And with Allah is the best reward."

SUNNAH:

THE BATTLE OF UHUD

Tabari VII:105: "In this year there was an expedition of the Prophet to Uhud. In year three of the Islamic era, the Quraysh were provoked against the Prophet because he had killed their nobles and Chiefs at Badr. [...] Muhammad has bereaved us and killed our best men. So help us defend ourselves against him and perhaps we will obtain vengeance for those he has slain.

Tabari VII:106: "Abd Allah Al-Jumahi had been treated kindly by the Messenger on the day of Badr, being a poor man with daughters. He was among the captives, and said, 'Muhammad, I am a poor family man with needs of which you are aware; so treat me well.' The Prophet treated him kindly."

Tabari VII:112: "When he [Mirba, a blind Jew] became aware of the presence of the Messenger and the Muslims he rose and threw dust in their faces, saying, 'Even if you are a prophet, I will not allow you into my garden!' I was told that he took a handful of dirt and said, 'If only I knew that I would not hit anyone else, Muhammad, I would throw it [the dirt] into your face.' The people rushed up to kill him, but the Prophet said, 'Do not do so, for this man is blind of sight and blind of heart.' But Sa'd rushed in before the Messenger had forbidden this and hit him in the head with his bow and split the Jew's head open. [...] The polytheists numbered [3000] and their cavalry numbered [200]. [...] Among the polytheists there were [700] men wearing coats of mail, while among the Muslims there were only [100]. The Muslims had no cavalry."

Ishaq:372: "The opinion of Abd Allah bin Ubayy was the same as the Prophet. He should not go out to meet the Meccans camped near Uhud. Yet some Muslims whom Allah ennobled with martyrdom on the day of Uhud and others who had missed Badr jumped at the chance to fight. [...] When he went out, Abd Allah bin Ubayy came back with 300 men, saying, 'We do not know why we should get ourselves killed here.' So he went back to Medina with the Hypocrites, and doubters who followed him. Abd Allah bin Amr said, 'Allah curse you, enemies of Allah. Allah will let us manage without you.'"

Ishaq:373: "The Prophet, wearing two coats of mail, drew up his troops for battle, about 700 men. There were 50 archers. Muhammad said, 'Keep their cavalry away with your arrows.' Then he asked, 'Who will take my sword with its right and use it as it deserves to be used?' Abu Dujana asked, 'What is its right, Apostle?' [The Apostle said,] 'That you should smite the enemy with it until it bends.'"

Ishaq:374: "The black troops and slaves of the Meccans cried out and the Muslims replied, 'Allah destroy your sight, you impious rascals.'"

Tabari VII:120: "When the enemy overwhelmed the Holy Prophet he said to the Ansar, 'Who will sell his life for me?' [...] [Muhammad, during the battle, said,] 'May Allah's anger be intense against those who have bloodied the face of His Prophet. [...] By Allah, I never thirsted to kill anyone as I thirst to kill a Meccan.'"

Ishaq:375: "[Hamza shouted,] 'Come here you son of a female circumciser.' His mother was Umm Anmar, a female circumciser in Mecca. Hamza smote and killed him."

Tabari VII:121: "I saw Hamza cutting down men with his sword, sparing no one. He yelled out to us, 'Come here, you son of a cutter-off of clitorises.' He hit Siba so swiftly, his sword could not be seen striking his head. So I balanced my javelin until I was satisfied. Then I hurled it at Hamza. It struck him in the lower part of the belly with such force it came out between his legs. He came toward me, but was overcome and fell. I waited until he was dead and recovered my javelin. I returned to the camp since there was nothing else I wanted."

Tabari VII:124: "Abd Manat came and threw a stone at Muhammad, breaking his nose and his lateral incisor [a tooth], splitting his face open, and stunning him. His Companions dispersed and abandoned him, some of them going to Medina and some climbing up Uhud and standing there. The Messenger cried out to his men, 'To me! To me!'"

Ishaq:379-380: "[...] They slew the enemy with the sword until they cut them off from their camp and there was an obvious rout [slaughter coupled with an enemy retreat]. We attacked them thrusting, slaying, chastising, and driving them before us with blows on every side. Had not women seized their war banner they would have been sold in the markets like chattel. [...] The Muslims were put to the fight and the Meccans slew many of them. It was a day of trial and testing in which Allah honored several with martyrdom. [...] The enemy got at the Apostle who was hit with a stone so that he fell on his side and one of his teeth was smashed, his face scored [cut], and his lip injured [split]. [...] When the enemy hemmed him in, the Apostle said, 'Who will sell his life for me?' Five Ansar arose. All were killed. Abu Dujana made his body into a shield for the Prophet. Arrows were falling and sticking into his back as he leaned over him. [...] Muhammad cried out, 'How can a people prosper who have stained their Prophet's face with blood while he summoned them to their Lord?'"

Tabari VII:129: "[Abu Sufyan, the Meccan leader, said,] 'If you had seen what they did at the pit of Badr you would have been *terror struck* [emphasis added] for as long as you lived. [...] Hind [a Meccan woman who lost her family at Badr] stopped to mutilate the Muslim dead, cutting off their ears and noses until she was able to make anklets and necklaces out of them. Then she ripped open Hamza's body for his liver and chewed it, but she was not able to swallow it and spit it out. [...] Then she climbed a rock and screamed rajaz poetry at the top of her voice, taunting us. 'We have paid you back for Badr. A war that follows a war is always violent. I could not bear the loss of Utba or my brother, his uncle, or my first-born son. I have slaked [satisfied] my vengeance and fulfilled my vow.' Umar recited these verses back to her: 'May Allah curse Hind [...]. Her backside and her genitals are covered with ulcers [...]. [...] Woe to you Hind, the shame of the age.'"

Tabari VII:126-127: "Allah spoke of Abu Sufyan's approach [...]. The first grief was that victory and booty that eluded them. The second grief was the enemy's approaching them. They were not to grieve for the booty or the men they lost. [...] The Messenger said, 'Hamza is being cleansed by the angels. He went into battle in a state of ritual impurity [Failed to observe Islamic rituals] when he heard the call to arms. That is why the angels are cleansing him.'"

Tabari VII:133: "When Muhammad saw Hamza he said, 'If Allah gives me victory over the Quraysh at any time, I shall *mutilate* [emphasis added] 30 of their men.' When the Muslims saw the rage of the Prophet they said, 'We shall *mutilate* [emphasis added] them in a way which no Arab has ever *mutilated* [emphasis added] anybody.' [...] Allah revealed concerning this threat made by His Messenger, 'If you have to retaliate and punish them, do so to the extent you have been injured.'"

Ishaq:383: "The Prophet went up the mountain. He had become stout and heavy with age. He was wearing two coats of mail. When he tried to climb up, he could not manage on his own. Talba Ubaydullah squatted beneath him and lifted him up until he settled comfortably on a rock. During Uhud, Quzman fought hard and killed seven to nine polytheists with his own hands being brave, gold, and strong. But he got wounded so seriously, he had to be carried off [the battlefield] by his comrades. They [his comrades] said, 'Rejoice, you fought valiantly.' He replied, 'For what have I fought?' When the pain of his [Quzman's] wounds became too severe he [Quzman] decided to bring about his death more quickly [Quzman leaned on his sword]. [...] That day I heard the Prophet saying, 'Talha earned paradise when he did what he did for the Apostle.' [...] [Some Companions of Muhammad said,] 'Perhaps Allah will grant us martyrdom.' So they took their swords and sailed out until they mingled with the enemy. One was killed by the Meccans, the other [was killed] by his fellow Muslims who failed to recognize him. One of the young men's fathers confronted Muhammad and said, 'You have robbed my son of his life by your deception and brought great sorrow to me.'"

Ishaq:384-385: "Upon hearing this, Muhammad proclaimed, 'I testify that I am truly the Messenger of God, Allah's Apostle.' Amr Jamuh was a very lame man. [...] At Uhud he came to the Prophet and told him that his sons wanted to keep him back and prevent his joining the army. [Amr Jamuh said,] 'Yet, by Allah, I hope to tread in the Heavenly Garden of Paradise despite my lameness.' The Apostle said, 'Allah has excused you, and Jihad is not incumbent on you.' Then Muhammad turned to his sons and said, 'You need not prevent him. Perhaps Allah will favor him with martyrdom.' So the lame old man went into battle and was killed."

Bukhari:V5B59N377: "On the day of the battle of Uhud, a man came to the Prophet and said, 'Can you tell me where I will be if I should get martyred?' The Prophet replied, 'In Paradise.' The man threw away some dates he was carrying in his hand, and fought till he was martyred."

Muslim:B19C7N4318: "The Messenger of Allah said on the day of the Battle of Uhud: 'O Allah, if Thou wilt (defeat Muslims), there will be none on the earth to worship Thee.'

Muslim:B20C41N4678: "Jabir [said] that a man said: 'Messenger of Allah, where shall I be if I am killed?' He replied: 'In Paradise.' The man threw away the dates he had in his hand and fought until he was killed."

Ishaq:386: "[…] When Abu Sufyan wanted to leave he went to the top of the mountain shouted loudly saying, 'You have done a fine work; victory in war goes by turns. Today is in exchange for the day [of Badr]. Show your superiority, Hubal.' [i.e., vindicate your religion] […] When he came Abu Sufyan said, 'I adjure thee by God [Allah], Umar, have we killed Muhammad?' 'By God, you have not, he is listening to what you are saying now,' he [Umar] replied. […]"

DISSIMULATION

Ishaq:388-389: "Some Muslims wanted to bury their dead in Medina. The Apostle forbade this and told them to bury them where they lay. […] When the Apostle came home he handed his sword to his daughter Fatima, saying, 'Wash the blood from this, daughter, for by Allah it has served me well today.'"

Ishaq:390: "[…] Abu Sufyan said [to Ma'bad, a polytheist, sent out by Muhammad to deceive the Meccans], 'We have killed the best of Muhammad's companions. Shall we go back and exterminate the rest of them?' Ma'bad said [to Abu Sufyan], 'Muhammad has come out with his Companions to pursue you with an army whose like I have never seen. They are burning with anger against you. You'd better go home before his cavalry gallops upon you.' […]"

MUSLIM HYPOCRITES

Ishaq:391: "[…] [Abd Allah Ubayy, the Ansar leader who retreated with a third of the Muslim army before the battle started, spoke to Muslims in the Mosque—trying to reconcile himself with them.] But the Muslims in attendance took hold of his garments and said, 'Sit down, you enemy of Allah. You are not worthy of that, having behaved as you did.' [...] The day of Uhud was a day of trial, calamity, and heart-searching on which Allah tested the believers. He put the hypocrites on trial, those who professed faith with their tongue and hid unbelief in their hearts. And it was a day in which Allah honored with martyrdom those whom He willed."

Ishaq:392: "It is not your affair whether Allah changes His attitude to them or punishes them, for they are evildoers. You are not to be bothered with My judgment of My slaves except in so far as I give you orders concerning them. I may change My mind toward them. Punishing them is my prerogative. They deserve this for their disobedience to Me."

Ishaq:393: "Fear Allah that you may be prosperous. Obey Allah and *perhaps* [emphasis added] you may escape from His punishment of which He has warned you [...]. And fear the fire which He has prepared for the disbelievers, a resort for those who disbelieve Me. [...] Then Allah said: 'Obey Allah and the Apostle and *maybe* [emphasis added] you will attain mercy.' '[...] They have wronged themselves by disobedience. But they must not continue disobeying me for I have prohibited the worship of any but Myself.' [...] Allah loves the steadfast. [...] They did not show weakness toward their enemies and were not humiliated when they suffered in the fight for Allah and their religion. That is steadfastness, and Allah loves the steadfast. [...]"

Ishaq:394: "Allah said, '[...] But We cause days like this so that Allah may know those who believe and may choose martyrs from among you. Allah must distinguish between believers and hypocrites so that He can honor the faithful with martyrdom."

Ishaq:395: "No soul can die but by Allah's permission in a term that is written. [...] Practice your religion as they did, and be not renegades, turning back on your heels, retreating. Those who retreat and turn away from battle are losers in this world and in the next. [...] Muslims, if you listen to the unbelievers you will retreat from the enemy and become losers. Ask Allah for victory and do not retreat, withdrawing from His religion.

'We will *terrorize* [emphasis added] those who disbelieve. In that way I will help you against them.'"

Ishaq:396: "Allah pardoned the great sin in that He did not destroy you for having disobeyed your Prophet. I did not exterminate all for the debt you owed Me. You suffered for disobeying Me. [...]"

Ishaq:397: "It was by the mercy of Allah that you Muhammad were lenient to them. [...] So overlook their offence and ask pardon for them and consult with them about the matter. [...] They have the duty to obey their Prophet. [...] Then Allah said, "It is not for any prophet to deceive. There is no escape from death, so death for Allah's sake in battle is better than all one can amass in life while holding back from fighting in fear of death. [...] Let fighting and the reward which Allah holds out for you be the most important thing."

Ishaq:398: "Show them that you listen to them and ask them for their help. Thereby make the religion of Islam agreeable to them. And when you are resolved in the matter of religion concerning fighting your enemy you will have the advantage. [...] Allah sent you an Apostle of your own, reciting to you His verses concerning what you did, and teaching you good and evil that you may know what is good and do it, and know what is bad and refrain from it, and so that you might gain much by obeying Him and avoid His wrath proceeding from disobedience and thereby escape His vengeance and obtain the reward of His Garden of Bliss."

Ishaq:399: "You had smitten your enemy with a double dose of torment at Badr, slaying them and taking prisoners. Yet you disobeyed your Prophet's orders and brought the defeat of Uhud on yourselves. [...] The hypocrites stopped fighting for Allah's sake [in Jihad] eager to survive, fleeing death. So Allah said to His Prophet to make the Muslims wish to fight and to desire battle: 'And do not think that those who were killed for Allah's sake are dead. Nay, they are alive with their Lord being nourished [...].'"

ISLAM MEANS SUBMISSION

Ishaq:400: "'If our fellow Muslims knew what Allah has done for us they would not dislike fighting or shrink from war!' [...] One whom I do not suspect told me that he was asked about these verses and he said, 'We asked Muhammad about them and we were told that when our brothers were slain at Uhud Allah put their spirits in the crops of green birds which come down to the rivers of the Garden and eat of its fruit.' In the shade of the Throne of Allah the Lord takes one look at them and says three times: 'O My slaves, what do you wish that I should give you more?' They said, 'We should like our spirits to return to our bodies and then return to earth and fight for You until we are killed again.' [...] The Apostle swore that there was no believer who had parted from the world and wanted to return to it for a single hour even if he could possess it with all it has except the martyr who would like to return and fight for Allah and be killed a second time."

Ishaq:403, 405: "Allah killed twenty-two polytheists at Uhud. [...]"

Ishaq:405: "It is your folly to fight the Apostle, for Allah's army is bound to disgrace you. We brought them to the pit. Hell was their meeting place. We collected them there, black slaves, men of no descent, and leaders of infidels. [...]"

Ishaq:406-407: "Among us was Allah's Apostle whose command we obey. When he gives an order we do not examine it. The spirit descends on him from his Lord. We tell him about our wishes and our desires which is to obey him in all that he wants. Cast off fear of death and desire it. Be the one who barters his life. Take your swords and trust Allah. With a compact force [...] we plunged into a sea of men [...] and all were made to get their fill of evil. We are men who see no blame in him who kills."

A WIN-WIN SCENARIO

*Ishaq:410: "O Christians, you know right well that Muhammad is a prophet sent by Allah and he has brought a decisive declaration about the nature of your master. You also know that a people has never invoked a curse on a prophet and seen its elders live and its youth grow up. If you do this [curse Muhammad] you will be exterminated [...]"

Ishaq:414-415: "If you kill us, the true religion is ours. And to be killed for the truth is to find favor with Allah. [...], know that the opinion of those who oppose Islam is misleading. We are men of war who get the utmost from it. We inflict painful punishment on those who oppose us. [...] If you insult Allah's Apostle, Allah will slay you. [...]"

Tabari VII:139: "On the following day [...], the Messenger of Allah's crier called out to the people to go in pursuit of the enemy. [...], he [Muhammad] wanted to give the impression that [...] the Muslim casualties had not weakened their ability to engage in fighting."

SUMMATION:

IL: The Qur'an is the fulfillment of the Jewish and Christian scriptures and corrects the errors of the Jewish authors. Nothing in this world can help non-Muslims from hell-fire. Since the Jews killed the prophets, who were righteous Muslims, nothing they do will help them. For this reason, Muslims should not take infidels as friends nor should they ever have love for them. Jesus, himself, advocated holy Jihad. His true disciples, who were Muslims, understood this truth. Allah deceived all those who denied this truth. Disbelief must be punished just as those who worship Jesus must be punished as liars and blasphemers. Christians and Jews are without excuse because they know that Abraham was a Muslim. To hide this truth they forged the Bible because they know Islam is the religion of Abraham. Since it is the religion of Abraham, Islam is the only religion accepted by Allah. This final message came to the Arabs. In receiving it, they became the best of people, while the People of the Book, who deny the truth, are evil doers. Since Arabs and Muslims are the best of people, Muslims know that any misfortune that befalls Muslims can be attributed to the infidels. [5] Therefore, the wrath of Allah is against those who killed the prophets. It is the Jews who hate Muslims so Muslims must be prepared to become martyrs. They must understand that Allah controls death so there should be no fear of it. In doing so, slain Muslims receive forgiveness, mercy, and live forever. This must happen because the People of the Book, Christians and Jews, deserve to be terrorized.

As an exclamation point to what has previously been stated, the following Islamic source, the *Reliance of the Traveller*, records the following:

> "Retaliation is obligatory against anyone who kills a human being purely intentionally and without right. The following are not subject to retaliation: (1) A child or

insane person under any circumstances; (2) a Muslim for killing a non-Muslim; (3) a Jewish or Christian subject of the Islamic state for killing an Apostate from Islam; (4) a father or mother (or their fathers or mothers) for killing their offspring [children] or offspring's offspring [grandchildren]; (5) nor is retaliation permissible to a descendent for killing someone whose death would otherwise entitle the descendent to retaliate, such as when his father kills his mother."

—Al-Misri, *Reliance of the Traveller*, o1.1-2

Regarding Muslims who live in the Dar-al-Harb; they can show loyalty to non-Muslims with their tongue, while at the same time, they are permitted to harbor inner animosity towards them. Allah has forbidden believers from being friendly or being on intimate terms with the infidels instead of believers — except when infidels are above them in authority. In such a scenario, they may act friendly towards them.

WA: The claim that Jesus advocated Jihad is an attempt to Islamize the Jesus of history. In essence, the argument follows two paths: (1) Your Jesus is really our Jesus; and (2) his followers were really our co-religionists, not yours. At the same time, Allah admitted in the 54th verse that he "is the greatest of all deceivers." This is a very troubling admission because it equates Allah with, what westerners know about, El Diablo. Allah, by his own admission, is the greatest of all deceivers who advocates terror against Christians. He also promises eternal life through Islamic martyrdom, and declares the damnation of all Jews. Islam appears more and more at odds with Christianity, evidenced by the following quote: "We are men who see no blame in him who kills." Even though the Jews also believe that Jesus was crucified, Muhammad denied it. In this analysis, the gospel accounts, according to the first Muslims, were false. If anyone opposed or insulted Muhammad, they were slain.[6]

In the Sunnah, we see that Abd Allah bin Amr was wrong for believing that Muslims could manage without the hypocrites who returned to Mecca. They left because they did not want to get killed at Uhud. The battle went very badly. Muhammad was bloodied as he shouted for his men to protect him. This theme remained constant. Muslims earned paradise by sacrificing their life on the battlefield for Allah's cause, Jihad. Muhammad took no responsibility for the death of so many young men and even sent a lame man to die in battle. In addition to fighting, Allah promised to punish those who would not fight. Interestingly, Allah gave nothing definitive to those who obeyed the call to fight using the words "perhaps" and "maybe." Allah honored his followers by letting them die on the field of battle. Most Westerners would want no such honor from a deity. Therefore, Muslims who turn from battle withdraw from Islam. Those who do not terrorize unbelievers are *not* faithful. Fighting is part of Islamic ideology. Allah wants fighting to be what is most important to Muslims. Muhammad did not try to kill the hundreds of Muslims who fled, because he would have lost much of his viable fighting force. At this juncture, Muhammad's task was to get them to *want* to fight. Martyrdom then became the preferred way for a Muslim to die.

Muhammad, leading up to the battle at Uhud, thirsted to kill Meccans. In the battle, Abu Manat got credit for hitting Muhammad in the face with a rock. The mutilation of dead Muslims by Hind was followed by calls for Muslims to mutilate the Meccans. In reading this material Muslim literalists are assured they will be married to the Houris of Paradise by dying for Muhammad's religion.

QUR'AN 63

"The Hypocrites"

625 AD

SCRIPTURE:

Qur'an 63:1-4, 6-7, 10

Ishaq:426, 434; Tabari VII:145-152

PREFACE:

The hypocrites were the Arabs from Yathrib ("Medina") who were adverse to the concept of Jihad. Muslims from Mecca were told not to be influenced by the love of wealth and children. This surah was revealed in response to the Muslim defeat at Uhud when the Muslim hypocrites refused to fight. (7)

SURAH:

Qur'an 63:1-4: "When the hypocrites come to thee and say: We bear witness that thou art indeed the Allah's Messenger. [...] And Allah bears witness that the hypocrites are surely liars. They take shelter [hide] under their oaths, thus turning men from Allah's way [Jihad]. Surely evil is that which [what] they do. That is because they believed, then disbelieved, thus their hearts are sealed, so they understand not. [...] They are the enemy, so beware of them. May Allah destroy [Muslims who chose not to fight] them! How they are turned back!"

Qur'an 63:6-7: "[...] Allah will never forgive them. Surely Allah guides not the transgressing people. They it is who say: Spend not on those who are with the Messenger of Allah [...]."

Qur'an 63:10: "And spend out of that which [what] We have given you before death comes to one of you, and he says: My Lord, why didst Thou not respite me to a near term [take me so soon], so that [because] I should have given alms and been of the doers of good deeds?"

SUNNAH:

MISFORTUNE AFTER UHUD

Ishaq:426: "After Uhud, a group of men from Adal and Qarah came to the Messenger of Allah and said, 'O Prophet, we are good Muslims and have accepted Islam. Please send us some of your Companions to instruct us in the religion. Teach us to recite the Qur'an, and teach us the laws of Islam. The Muslims bivouacked for the night and were taken by surprise. So the Muslims took up their swords to fight them, but the Lihyans said, 'We don't want to kill you. We only want to get some money by selling you to the Meccans. We swear by Allah's Covenant that we will not kill you.' 'By Allah,' Asim said, 'we will never accept an agreement from an unbelieving infidel.' They fought until they [the Muslims] were killed."

Tabari VII:145: "The tribe of Lihyan [were] seeking vengeance for the killing of their chief [...] Khubayb gave himself up and became a prisoner. They took him to Mecca and handed him over to the sons of al-Harith, as Khubayb had killed their father at Uhud. [...] They took Khubayb out of the Haram [A sacred sanctuary] to kill him. [...] Khubayb said, 'My death is for Allah [...] he will bless the limbs of my mangled corpse.' "They took him out and beheaded him."

Tabari VII:146: "The Messenger sent Amr to the Quraysh as a spy. He said, 'I came to the cross on which Khubayb was bound and untied him. He fell to the ground, and I withdrew a short distance [It appears they may have tied his beheaded body to a cross for all to see].'"

A BLESSED KILLER

Tabari VII:147-150: "Amr [Umayyah] was sent by Muhammad to kill [assassinate] Abu Sufyan [the Quraysh leader]. The Prophet said, 'Go to Abu Sufyan and kill him.' [...] When I entered Mecca [...] my Ansar companion [...] kept pestering me until in the end we went to the Ka'aba, circumambulated it seven times, and prayed. One of the Meccans recognized me and shouted, 'That is Amr!' They rushed after us, saying, 'By Allah, Amr has not come here for any good purpose! He has come for some evil reason.' Amr had been a cutthroat and a desperado before accepting Islam. [...] We left at full speed, took to the hills, hiding in a cave. In this way we gave them the slip [e escaped]. [...] I was still in the cave when Uthman bin Malik came riding proudly on his horse. He reached the entrance to the cave [...]. So I went out and stabbed him with my dagger. He gave out a shout and the Meccans came to him while I went back to my hiding place. [...] The death of their companion impeded their search for us, for they carried him away. [...] On the way I went into a [another] cave with my bows and arrows. While I was in it a one-eyed man from the Banu Bakr came in driving some sheep. He said, 'Who is there?' I said, 'I am Banu Bakr.' [...] Then he laid down next to me, and raised his voice in song: 'I will not be a Muslim and will not believe in the faith of the Muslims.' I said, 'You will soon see.' Before long the Bedouin went to sleep and started snoring. So I killed him in the most dreadful way that anybody has ever [been] killed. I leant over him, struck the end of my bow into his good eye, and thrust it down until it came out the back of his neck. After that I rushed out like a wild beast and took flight. I came to the village of Naqi and recognized two Meccan spies. I called for them to surrender. They said, 'No,' so I shot an arrow and killed one, and then I tied the other up and took him to Muhammad. [...] The Messenger of Allah looked at him and laughed so that his back teeth could be seen. Then he questioned me and I told him what had happened. Well done he said, and prayed for me to be blessed.

REPRISAL

Tabari VII:151-152: "Abu Bara, the Chief of the Banu Amir, came to the Prophet and presented a gift. Muhammad said, 'I do not accept presents from pagans, so become a Muslim if you want me to accept it.' Muhammad expounded Islam to Abu Bara and invited him to accept it. [...] [Abu] Bara did not accept Islam. [...] The Apostle was afraid to send his people to Abu's tribe for fear that they would kill him. But Chief Abu gave Muhammad a surety [collateral] so he sent Mudhir with forty to seventy riders. After halting at B'ir Ma-unah, they sent Haram [a Muslim] to Amir Tufayl with a letter from Muhammad. When Haram arrived Amir killed him. Then he set out and took the Muslims by surprise, surrounding them while they were encamped. On seeing them, the Muslims snatched up their swords and fought until they were all killed except Ka'b. The enemy left him at the point of death."

Ishaq:434: "[...] Amr and an Ansari were out grazing camels and saw vultures circling around the camp. They went to investigate and saw their Companions lying in their blood. The Ansari said, 'What do you think that we should do?' Amr answered, 'Go tell the Prophet.' [...] when he [Amr] was at Qarqarah, two Banu Amir men halted near him in the shade. They had a compact of protection with Allah's Messenger which Amir knew nothing. Amr waited until they were asleep. Then he killed them, thinking that he had taken vengeance for the Muslims who had been slain. When he came to the Messenger, he told him what had happened. The Prophet said, 'You have killed men for whom I shall have to pay blood-money.'"

SUMMATION:

IL: Muslims must know that consequences for disobeying Allah can be dreadful. Allah's plan at Uhud was perfect, but the hypocrites behaved improperly. Loving the wealth of this world more than longing for death, in Allah's cause, brings the wrath of Allah. In the aftermath of the battle at Uhud, more Muslim blood was spilled by unbelieving Arabs. The embodiment of a true Muslim was Khubayb. He gave himself up to death in obedience to Islam. The death of the Bedouin in the cave was justified because he was offered Islam and rejected it. The proof of his righteous deed was the blessing that Amr Umayyah received from the Prophet. The non-Muslim Banu Amir killed Muslims after they rejected Islam when it was offered by the Prophet. Considering non-Muslim hatred of Islam, Allah's pronouncements against non-Muslims in the Qur'an was warranted.

WA: Islamic ideology established that Muslims who want no part of violent Jihad are to be considered: hypocrites; disbelieving; an enemy, those who are never to be forgiven; sinful; and evil. Why would Allah say, 'May Allah destroy them?' Since these words came out of Muhammad's mouth, it seems as though his personal feelings once again entered into the Qur'an. This surah concluded with Allah encouraging the faithful to spend their money for Jihad. In the Sunnah, the point cannot be made that non-Muslim Arab behavior was any better than Muslim behavior. This bloodletting appeared to resonate from the root of 7th century Arab culture. As for Muhammad, he was more concerned about paying blood money than all of the people who were dead on the battlefield. One cannot consider the actions of Amr Umayyah as being righteous. He was sent out as an assassin by Muhammad. He murdered Uthman bin Malik and drove an arrow through the eye of a sleeping Bedouin, murdering him. He then killed one Meccan spy and kidnapped another, whom he brought to Muhammad. Amr Umayyah was known as a cutthroat by his own people before he accepted Islam. Muhammad must have known about Amr's past or he would not have tasked him with the assassination of Allah's enemies. When Amr arrived with the kidnapped Meccan spy, Muhammad looked at the spy and laughed so hard his back teeth could be seen. He then proceeded to pray for Amr to be blessed by Allah.

QUR'AN 4

"The Women"

626 AD

SCRIPTURE:

Qur'an 4:3-4, 11, 13-18, 24-25, 34, 46-48, 56, 59, 69, 74, 76, 80, 89, 91, 95, 100-101, 104, 115, 142, 145, 152, 155, 157-161, 163, 171

Bukhari:V1B2N28, V1B2N35, V1B4N231, V3B48N826, V4B52N54; Dawud:B11N2141-B11N2142; Muslim:B1C35N142, B8C38N3467

PREFACE:

This surah describes the rights of Muslim women. This surah also dealt with the aftermath of the defeat at Uhud where many Muslims died. Included is a renewed disdain for Muslim hypocrites. These revelations also accused the Jews of supporting the Meccans, the enemies of Islam. The Jews at this point preferred Arab polytheism to Islam. According to the Qur'anic revelation, this justified warfare against the Jews. The Jews were seen as having departed from purity by harboring envy for the Muslims. This made them side with the Meccans against Muslims. Allah predicted the doom of the Jews in Arabia because they rejected Muhammad. Allah stated that the Jewish Prophets of old could not save them. The Qur'an claimed that Muhammad was good to the Jews even while they were disrespectful to him. Punishment for those who murder Muslims is described in this surah. The final decrees against the hypocrites are also detailed in this revelation. The Christians are criticized for believing in the crucifixion and the deity of Jesus. The Qur'an declares that all previous prophesy points to Muhammad, not Jesus. The place of women in Muslim society is codified. Then judgment, or condemnation, is declared against the People of the Book. Jihad was authorized against them which would result in their

Dhimmitude. Dissimulation was permitted during this struggle as were more abrogating verses. These new verses were introduced to counter the hostile attitude of the Jews. The martyrdom of vanquished Muslims was emphasized once again to assure that those fighting in Jihad will continue sacrificing their lives in this struggle ordained by Allah.[8]

SURAH:

Qur'an 4:3-4: "And if you fear that you cannot do justice to orphans [young females who do not have a family], marry such women as seem good to you, two, or three, or four; but if you fear that you will not do justice, then marry only one, or that which your right hands possess [a slave]. This is more proper that you may not do injustice. And give the women their dowries as a free gift. But if they of themselves be pleased [of their own good pleasure] to give you a portion thereof [remit any part of it to you], consume it with enjoyment and pleasure."

Qur'an 4:11: "Allah enjoins you [directs you] concerning your children [inheritance]: for the male is the equal of the portion of two females [...]. This [the portions of inheritance] is an ordinance from Allah. [...]"

Qur'an 4:13: "These are Allah's limits. And whoever obeys Allah and His Messenger, He will admit him to [the] Gardens wherein rivers flow, to abide in them. And this is the great achievement."

Qur'an 4:14: "And whoever disobeys Allah and His Messenger and goes beyond His limits, He will make him enter [the] fire to abide in it, and for him is an abasing chastisement."

Qur'an 4:15: "And as for those of your women [wives] who are guilty of an indecency [of lewdness], call to witness against them four witnesses [take the evidence of four witnesses] from among you; so if they bear witness [testify], confine them to houses until death [by starvation] takes them away [claims them] or Allah opens a way for them [If they change their behavior they regain their liberty]."

Qur'an 4:16-17: "And as for the two of you who are guilty of it, [indecency, i.e., fornication], give them both a slight punishment; then if they repent and amend, turn aside from them. Surely Allah is [often merciful].

Repentance with Allah is only for those who do evil in ignorance, then turn to Allah soon [quickly], so these it is whom Allah turns mercifully. And Allah is ever Knowing, Wise."

Qur'an 4:18: "And repentance is not [accepted] for those who go on doing evil deeds, until when death comes to one of them, he says: Now I repent; nor [is repentance] for those who die while they are disbelievers [infidels]. For such We have prepared a painful punishment."

Qur'an 4:24-25: "And all married women *except* [emphasis added] those whom your right hands possess [slaves; single or married women captured by Muslim victors] are forbidden. [...] And whoever among you cannot afford to marry free believing women, let him marry such of your believing maidens [slave girls] as your right hands possess. And Allah knows best your faith. [...] So marry them with the permission of their slave masters. [...]"

Qur'an 4:34: "So the good women are obedient, guarding the unseen as Allah has guarded [a husband's right]. And as to those on whose part fear desertion admonish, them, and leave them alone in the beds [make them sleep in separate beds] and chastise them [beat them]. So if they obey you, seek not a way against them. Surely Allah is ever Exalted, Great."

Qur'an 4:46: "Some of those who are Jews alter words from their right places and say: We have heard and we disobey; and say: Hear without being made to hear [hear nothing]; and say: *Raina,* distorting with their tongues and slandering [the] religion [of Islam]. And if [only] they had said: We hear and obey, and hearken, and *unzurna* ["Do make us understand"], it would have been better for them and more upright [proper]; but Allah has cursed them on account of their disbelief, so they believe not but a little [except a few]."

Qur'an 4:47-48: "O you who have been given the Book [Christians], believe in what We have revealed, verifying that which you have, before We destroy the leaders and turn them on their backs, or curse them as We cursed the Sabbath-breakers. And the command of Allah is ever-executed. Surely Allah forgives not that a partner should be set up with Him, and forgives all besides that to whom He pleases. And whoever sets up a partner with Allah, he devises indeed [is guilty of] a great sin."

Qur'an 4:56: "Those who disbelieve in Our messages, We shall make them enter Fire. As often as their skins are burned, We shall change them for other skins, that they may taste the chastisement. Surely Allah is every Mighty, Wise."

Qur'an 4:59: "O you who believe, obey Allah and obey the Messenger [...] then if you quarrel [disagree] about anything, refer it to Allah and the Messenger, if you believe in Allah and the Last Day."

Qur'an 4:69: "And whoever obeys Allah and the Messenger, they are with those upon whom Allah has bestowed favours [...]."

Qur'an 4:74: "So let those fight in the way of Allah [Jihad] who [would] sell this world's life for the Hereafter. And whoever fights in the way of Allah [Jihad], be he slain or be he victorious, We shall grant him a mighty reward."

Qur'an 4:76: "Those who believe fight in the way of Allah, and those who disbelieve fight in the way of Devil. So fight against the friends of the devil; surely the struggle [plotting] of the devil is ever weak."

Qur'an 4:80: "Whoever obeys the Messenger, he indeed obeys Allah. [...]."

Qur'an 4:89: "They long that you should disbelieve as they have disbelieve so that you may be on the same level [as them]; So take not from among them friends until they flee [forsake] their homes in the Allah's way. Then if they turn back to hostility [to enmity], seize them and kill them wherever you find them. [...]"

Qur'an 4:91: "You will find others who desire to be secure from you [Muslims] and secure from their own people. Whenever they are made to return to hostility, they are plunged into it. So if they withdraw not from you, nor offer you peace and restrain their hands, then seize them and kill them wherever you find them. And against these we have given you a clear authority."

Qur'an 4:95: "The holders-back from among the believers [Those who do not fight from among the believers], not disabled by injury, and those who strive hard in Allah's way with their property and their persons, are not equal. Allah has made the strivers with their property and their persons to excel [above] the holders-back [those who hold back] to a high degree. And to each Allah has promised good. And Allah has granted to the strivers above the holders-back [those who hold back] a mighty reward."

Qur'an 4:100: "And he who [his home] in Allah's way [Jihad], he will find in the earth many a place of escape [refuge] and abundant resources. And whoever goes forth from his home fleeing to Allah and His Messenger, then death overtakes him, his reward is indeed with Allah. And Allah is ever Forgiving, Merciful."

Qur'an 4:101: "And when you journey in the earth, there is no blame on you if you shorten the prayer [curtail worship], if for fear that those who disbelieve will give you trouble [attack you]. Surely the disbelievers are an open enemy to you."

Qur'an 4:104: "And be not weak-hearted [do not relent] in [your] pursuit of the enemy. If you suffer they too suffer as you suffer, and you [have] hope from Allah what they hope not. And Allah is ever Knowing, Wise."

Qur'an 4:115: "And whoever acts hostilely to the Messenger after guidance has become manifest to him [from Allah] and follows other than the way of the believers [and does not follow Islam] We turn him [appoint him] to that to which he himself turns and make him enter hell; and it is an evil resort."

Qur'an 4:142: "The hypocrites seek [strive] to deceive Allah, and He will requite their deceit to them [retaliate by deceiving them]. […]"

Qur'an 4:145: "The hypocrites are [will be] surely in the lowest depths of the Fire; and thou wilt find no helper for them."

Qur'an 4:152: "Those who believe in Allah and His Messengers and make no distinction between any of them [Muhammad must be accepted], to them He will grant their rewards. And Allah is ever Forgiving, Merciful."

Qur'an 4:155: "Then for their breaking their covenant and their disbelief in the messages of Allah and their killing the prophets wrongly […] Allah has sealed them owing to their disbelief, so they believe but a little."

Qur'an 4:157-158: "And for their saying: We have killed the Messiah, Jesus, son of Mary, the messenger of Allah, and they killed him not, nor did they cause his death on the cross, but he was made to appear to them as such. And certainly those who differ are in doubt about it. They have no knowledge about it, but only follow a conjecture, and they killed him not for certain. Nay, Allah exalted him [raised *Isa* ("Jesus") up with his body and soul] in His presence [unto Himself in the heavens]. And Allah is ever Mighty, Wise."

Qur'an 4:159: "And there is not one of the People of the Book [Jews and Christians] but will believe in this before his death; and on the day of Resurrection he [Jesus] will be a witness against them."

Qur'an 4:160-161: "So for the iniquity of the Jews, We forbade [made unlawful] them the good things which had been lawful for them, and for their hindering many people from Allah's Way. And for their taking [of] usury [interest] — though indeed they were forbidden it — and their devouring the property of people falsely. And We have prepared for the disbelievers from among them a painful chastisement."

Qur'an 4:163: "Surely We have revealed to thee as We revealed to Noah and the prophets after him, and We revealed to Abraham, and Ishmael, and Isaac, and Jacob and the tribes, and Jesus, and Job, and Jonah, and Aaron, and Solomon, and We gave to David a scripture."

Qur'an 4:171: "O People of the Book, exceed not the limits in your religion nor speak anything about Allah, but the truth. The Messiah, Jesus, son of Mary, is only a messenger of Allah and His word which he communicated to Mary and a mercy from Him. So believe in Allah and His messengers. And say not, three [Trinity]. Desist, it is better for you. Allah is only one God. Far be it from His glory to have a son. […]"

SUNNAH:

MARTYRDOM

Bukhari:V1B2N35: "The Prophet said, 'The person who participates in (Holy battles) in Allah's cause and nothing compels him to do so except belief in Allah and His Apostles, will be recompensed by Allah either with a reward, or booty (if he survives) or will be admitted to Paradise (if he is killed in the battle as a martyr). Had I not found it difficult for my followers, then I would not remain behind any sariya [army unit] going for Jihad and I would have loved to be martyred in Allah's cause and then made alive, and then martyred and then made alive, and then again martyred in His cause.'"

Bukhari:V4B52N54: "The Prophet said, 'By him in Whose Hands my life is! Were it not for some among the believers who dislike to be left behind me [do not want me to leave them] and whom I cannot provide means of conveyance, I would certainly never remain behind any Sariya [army unit] setting out in Allah's Cause. By Him in Whose Hands my life is! I would love to be martyred in Allah's Cause and then get resurrected and then get martyred, and then get resurrected again and then get martyred and then get resurrected again and then get martyred.'"

MUSLIM WOMEN

Bukhari:V1B2N28: "The Prophet said: 'I was shown the Hell-Fire and the majority of its dwellers were women who were ungrateful.' It was asked, 'Do they disbelieve in Allah or are they ungrateful to Allah?' He replied, 'They are ungrateful to their husbands and are ungrateful for their favors and good (charitable deeds) done to them. If you have always been good (benevolent) to one of them and then she sees something in you (not of her liking), she will say, 'I have never received any good from you.'"

Bukhari:V1B4N231: "I asked Aisha [the nine-year-old wife of Muhammad] about the clothes soiled with semen. She replied, 'I used to wash it [the semen] off the clothes of Allah's Apostle and he would go for the prayer ["Salat"] while water spots were still visible.'"

Bukhari:V3B48N826: "The Prophet said, 'Isn't the witness of a woman equal to half of that of a man?' The women said, 'Yes.' He said, 'This is because of the deficiency of a woman's mind.'"

Dawud:B11N2141, B11N2142: "Many women have gone around Muhammad's family complaining against their husbands. They are not the best among you. A man will not be asked as to why he beat his wife.

Muhammad was told that women have become emboldened towards their husbands, whereupon he gave permission to beat them.'"

Muslim:B1C35N142: "'O womenfolk, you should give charity and ask [for] much forgiveness for [because] I saw you in bulk amongst the dwellers of Hell.' A wise lady among them said: 'Why is it, Messenger of Allah, that [women] our folk [comprise the] bulk [of the inhabitants] in Hell? The Prophet observed: 'You curse too much and are ungrateful to your spouses. You lack common sense, fail in religion and rob the wisdom of the wise.' Upon this the woman remarked: What is wrong with our common sense? Upon this [question] the Holy Prophet observed [replied]: 'You curse too much and are ungrateful to your spouses. I have seen none lacking in common sense and failing in religion but (at the same time) robbing the wisdom of the wise, besides you [besides women]. Upon this the woman remarked: What is wrong with our common sense and with religion. He (the Holy prophet) observed: Your lack of common sense (can be well be judged from the fact) that the evidence of two women is equal to one man. That is a proof of the lack of common sense, and you spend some nights (and days) in which you do not offer prayer and in the month of Ramadan (during the days) you do not observe fast; that is a failing in religion. [...]"

Muslim:B8C38N3467: "Woman has been created from a rib and will in no way be straightened for you; so if you wish to benefit by her, benefit by her while crookedness remains in her. And if you attempt to straighten her, you will break her, and breaking her is divorcing her."

SUMMATION:

IL: In Islam, if a child has a mother and no father and there is a fear the child could become an orphan, then the believer should marry the woman. Muslims may marry up to four women. They may also add women to their harem. This will ensure the child will be raised a Muslim. When the parents die the male children will get double the amount of the female because the male will have added financial responsibilities and the female will eventually have a male to support her. Women who do not appreciate the support they receive from their husbands and who are seen by four witnesses committing lewdness can be confined to their homes until they repent and submit. Should they not recant then they would not be suitable mothers or wives in the Islamic community and, in this case, they could be starved.[9] If Muslims commit sexual sin, they must repent quickly. If Muslims do not repent quickly, they will not be forgiven and will inherit hell. Muslims may not sleep with another Muslim's wife, but can sleep with a non-believing married woman who becomes a slave after a successful conquest. Muslims can sleep with or marry slave girls with the permission of their master. A wife can be beaten if a Muslim fears that she may abandon him.[10] If a Muslim does not treat his wives equitably, it will not be held against him in the next life.[11]

As for Jews and Christians, they are doomed, condemned, and cursed. The Christians, especially, will be burned in hell. Allah will then give them new skin so that they can be burned again and again. Muslims must obey Allah and Muhammad in all things. Muslims who give their life as a martyr will live forever.[12] Those who do not fight in the name of Allah always fight for Satan. Jews and Christians conspire to convert Muslims, so Muslims must be aware of their schemes. If the Jew or Christian continues in hostility, then they should be killed where they are found.[13] Muslims have been given authority over non-Muslims who are not equal with Muslims. Muslims who refuse to fight in Jihad are not equal to Muslims who fight in Jihad. Muslims do not have to say their prayers if they fear an attack. According to the Qur'an, those who reject Muhammad are open enemies of all Muslims. Therefore, Muslims are never to stop their pursuit of the infidels.

As for Muslim hypocrites, they are bound for hell because they do not obey the Prophet. It not only applied to the hypocrites, but also to the Jews who killed the prophets. The Jews also claim to have crucified, but this is not true.[14] He was taken up into heaven by Allah. At the end of time, Jesus will return, but the Jews and Christians will not believe who he is until he dies [According to Islam, Jesus has not died but will return during the period of the last Caliphate/Imamate, to confirm Islam, subjugate all non-Muslims, get married, die, and be buried at Muhammad's tomb]. At that time it will be too late, because Jesus will bear witness before Allah and condemn the Jews for not believing in him and condemn the Christians for making him equal with Allah. The Jews are condemned for not believing any of the prophets and the Christians are doomed because they believe in the Trinity and believe Jesus is the Son of God.

WA: For Westerners, believing in Muhammad's example and words can only happen if the truth about him is hidden from them. Allah's decree concerning any form of wife beating will also be rejected. Women are to be loved not beaten. They are not to be taken as sex slaves for western armies. The Qur'an makes it impossible for Muslims to like, or even make a lasting peace with, the Jews. Cursing Christians and describing their fate in hell also ensures that peace will not be possible with literalist Islam. The assurances of reward for martyrdom make modern-day suicide bombers a reality. Verse 76 enables the Mullah's of Iran to call Israel the 'Little Satan' and American the 'Great Satan.' Jews and Christians are portrayed as forever conspiring against Muslims which means that Muslims must pursue them and not be merciful towards them. Muslims who refuse to pursue Jihad against Jews and Christians—because they are decent and good people—are repeatedly condemned by their own holy book.

As for the crucifixion, one must ask why the Jewish leadership at that time sought the death of Jesus. Wasn't the charge blasphemy? If so, then Jesus must have said that he was the Son of God. If he would have renounced this, then why was he sentenced to die? Muslims do not deny that there was a crucifixion, but Allah and Muhammad state that Jesus was taken away and another was crucified.[15] There are many problems with this view. If another was made to look like Jesus, why was he killed? The other person would not have said he was the Son of God. Also, Mary and John were present at the crucifixion. Are we to believe that John, who was with Jesus for three years, could not recognize him or his words from the cross? Are we to believe that Mary, who is mentioned often in the Qur'an, could not recognize her own son from the cross? Was Mary in a position to tell authorities that Jesus never said that he was the Son of God? If Mary knew that Jesus was not the Son of God, she would not have stood by and watched her son die for something she knew was untrue. She was at the foot of the cross, yet she kept silent. She knew it was true and the dialog from the cross proved that Jesus of Nazareth was being crucified. If Jesus was not buried, who then removed the stone from the tomb? The Jewish Temple guards who were there to ensure that no one stole the body? Why did the faith of Jesus' apostles explode after the crucifixion? Why did they all claim Jesus as the Son of God, if not for the resurrection? They all gained nothing in this world by accepting Jesus as the Son of God except persecution and death from Jewish leaders and the Romans.

Finally, in the hadith, Muhammad claimed that women have a deficient mind and are also ungrateful. They curse, lack common sense, are inferior to men, fail in religion, and are not intelligent. Muhammad would have sex with many women but did not love any of them. Muhammad, like the modern-day Mullahs, sent others to their deaths, but gave lip service to actual martyrdom. Women are ungrateful and hell-bound. Muslims must be baffled why Bukhari included passages about Muhammad's semen-soiled clothes after intercourse with a very young Aisha. The hadith goes on to say that Muhammad himself gave permission for husbands to beat their wives. One must wonder if Muslim women would still choose Muhammad over the Jesus of the New Testament if they could read the New Testament and make up their own mind without fear of being beaten or killed.

QUR'AN 61

"The Ranks"

626 AD

SCRIPTURE:

Qur'an 61:4

Ishaq:437-438, 440-442; Tabari VI:157-159

PREFACE:

This surah comments on the expulsion of the second Jewish tribe, the Banu Nadir. According to Islam, they were expelled because of their 'secret' plans against Muhammad. Therefore, the Muslims were permitted to expel them and confiscate their property. The Muslims who sided with the Jews, but did not help them or go into exile with them, were deemed hypocrites by Allah. In order to attack the Banu Nadir, abrogating verses were once again introduced because a treaty with this Jewish tribe already existed. These new verses also had to grant permission for the taking of their property. In order to defeat the Banu Nadir and their 'secret' plot, Allah permitted the use of terror against them.[16]

SURAH:

Qur'an 61:4: "Surely Allah loves those who fight in His way [Jihad] in ranks, as if they were a solid wall."

THE BANU NADIR ARE EXPELLED

Ishaq:437: "[…] Amr killed two men to whom had been given a promise of protection by the Apostle. Their chief wrote Muhammad asking him for blood money. So the Prophet turned towards the [Jews of] Nadir to seek their help in the payment of the blood money. With him were Bakr, Umar, and Ali. […] When the Prophet came to ask for their help in the payment of the blood-money, the Jews said, 'Yes, Abu al-Qasim [Muhammad]. Of course, we will give you the help you want in the way you want it.' Then they spoke privately with one another. […] Muhammad has gone outside and was sitting by a house wall. The Jews said, 'Who will go on the roof of this house and drop a stone, relieving us of him?' […] Amr Jihash, who was one of the Jews, came forward and said, 'I am your man.' […], and the news of what the people intended came to him [Muhammad] from Heaven.' […] The Prophet [got up] went back to his home. When his Companions thought that he had been gone a long time they got up to look for him. On the way they [Muhammad's companions] told a man the story of the treachery intended by the Jews and ordered them to get ready to fight and march against them.' […] Muhammad personally led his men against the Nadir […]. The Jews took refuge against him in their homes, so he ordered their date palms to be cut down and burnt. They shouted, 'Muhammad you have forbidden wonton destruction of property and have blamed those who perpetrated it. Why are you doing this?' […] So Allah cast terror into the hearts of the Jews. Then the Prophet said, 'The Jews have declared war.' […] A number of the al-Khazraj […] said, 'Stand firm and protect yourselves, for we will not betray you. If you are attacked we will fight with you and if you are turned out, we will go with you. Accordingly they [the Banu Nadir] waited for the help they [the al-Khazraj] promised, but they [the al-Khazraj] did nothing and God cast terror into [the] hearts [of the Banu Nadir]. They [the Banu Nadir] then asked the Apostle to deport them and to spare their lives […]"

Tabari VII:157: "Amr went up to the roof to roll the stone. News of this came to the Prophet from Heaven and he [Muhammad] got up as if he wished to relieve himself. His Companions waited for him but was gone a long time. The Jews began to say, 'What has delayed Abu al-Qasim

[Muhammad]?' Muhammad's companions left and Kinana said, 'News of what you intended has reached him.'"

Tabari VII:158: "They [Muhammad's companions] said, 'O Prophet, we waited for you but you did not come back.' 'The Jews intended to kill me,' he [Muhammad] replied, 'and Allah informed me of it. Call Muhammad bin Maslama to me.' When Muhammad [bin Maslama] came, he was told to go to the Jews and say, 'Leave my country. You have intended treachery.' He [Muhammad bin Maslama] went and said, 'The Messenger orders you to depart from his country.' They replied, 'We never thought that an Aws would come with such a message.' 'Hearts have changed,' Muhammad [bin Maslama] said, 'Islam has wiped out our old covenants.' [...] Salaam, a Qurayza Jew, said, 'We shall not break our compact for as long as I am alive. We are eminent among the Jewish people by virtue of our wealth.' Continuing to speak to the Nadir Jews the Qurayza leader said, 'Accept what Muhammad has proposed before you have to accept what is worse.' What could be worse?' Huyayy, the Nadir chief, asked. 'The seizure of your wealth, the enslavement of your children, and the killing of your men,' the Qurayza Jew replied. Huyayy refused to accept his advice. He told a Muslim courier, 'We will not leave our homes and farms; so do what you see fit.' [...] The Messenger of Allah besieged the Nadir Jews for fifteen days. In the end they made peace with him on the condition that the Prophet would not kill them and that their property and coats of mail would be his [Muhammad's]."

Ishaq:438: "The Jews loaded their camels with their wives, children, and property. [...] They went to Khaybar [...]. The Nadir left their property to Muhammad and it became his personal possession, to do with it as he wished. He divided it among the Emigrants, to the exclusion of the Ansar. [...] Allah wrecked His vengeance on the Jews and gave His Apostle power over them and control to deal with them as he wished. Allah said, 'I turned out those who disbelieve of the Scripture People from their homes. You did not think that they would go but I came upon them and terrorized them. And in the next world I will torment them again with a painful punishment in Hell.' The palm trees you cut down were by Allah's permission; they were uprooted on My order. It was not destruction but it was vengeance from Allah to humble the evildoers. The spoil which Allah gave the Apostle from the Nadir belongs to him.'"

Ishaq:440: "Helped by the Holy Spirit [Jibril] we smited [killed] Muhammad's foes. He is a true Messenger from the Compassionate, an Apostle reciting Allah's Book. He became honored in rank and station. So the Apostle sent a message to them with a sharp cutting sword."

Ishaq:441-442: "[…] A sharp sword in the hand of a brave man kills his adversary. The rabbis were disgraced for they denied mighty Lord Allah. […] Sword in hand we brought down the Nadir. By Muhammad's order we beguiled them."

Tabari VII:159: "The Prophet fought them until he made peace with them on the condition that they evacuate Yathrib [Medina]. He expelled them to Syria, but allowed them to keep what their camels could carry, except for their coats of mail and weapons."

SUMMATION:

IL: Allah loves those who fight because if all Muslims would fight then the whole world would be Muslim. Infidels must be fought because they will never understand or accept Islam. The Banu Nadir had a treaty with Muhammad so it was lawful for the Prophet to ask them to pay the blood money requirement. The Jews initially agreed, then became treacherous, conspiring to murder the Prophet. The Prophet punished them for their deeds with the siege, taking their possessions.

WA: It is clear that Allah loves those who fight, not those who love. As for the Banu Nadir, they agreed to pay the blood money and then met in secret. This meant the Jews knew what they were talking about. Knowledge of their conversation came from Allah's revelation to Muhammad. No one heard the Jews plot the murder of Muhammad. So Muhammad either heard the revelation or made it up to get rid of the Jews. These Jews were then terrorized when Muhammad decided to destroy their livelihood. Amazingly, in the Sirah, the word "compassionate" and the phrase "sharp cutting sword" were used to describe Muhammad. The message became clear: If you deny the Lord Allah, the sword will descend on your people collectively, specifically, on one's neck. In Tabari, Maslama revealed that Islam dissolved the previous treaty. The Muslims believed what Muhammad told them because they also wanted the possessions of the Banu Nadir. By Muhammad's order the Muslims "beguiled" the Jews of the Banu Nadir. These words are as true today, concerning Islamic Literalists, as they were to their co-religionists 1400 years ago.

QUR'AN 58

"The Pleading Woman"

626 AD

SCRIPTURE:

Qur'an 58:22

Bukhari:V4B51N72, V6B60N116; Muslim:B17C5N4206; Tabari VII:162, 164, 167

PREFACE:

This surah was revealed after a woman complained that her husband got rid of her according to the pagan tradition. She asked Muhammad for a remedy to the situation. The revelation contained in this surah was Allah's response. The remainder of this surah warns true Muslims not to trust Muslim hypocrites and Jews because they are hidden enemies of Islam. Muslims are not to be friends with them. Muslims were promised that they will ultimately conquer them.[17]

SURAH:

Qur'an 58:22: "Thou wilt not find a people who believe in Allah and the latter [last] day [Muslims] loving those who oppose Allah and His Messenger [Jews and Christians], even though [even if] they be [they are] their fathers, or their sons, or their brothers, or their kinsfolk [relatives]. [...] Allah is well-pleased with them and they are well-pleased with Him. These are Allah's party. Now surely it is Allah's party who are the successful!"

THE RAIDS CONTINUE

Tabari VII:162: "[...] Muhammad remained in Yathrib for two months before leading a raid on Najd, directed against the Banu Muharib and Tha'labah. As the armies approached one another, no fighting took place, because our army was afraid of theirs. [...] The rules of the Prayer of Fear was revealed during the raid. The Messenger of Allah divided the Companions into two groups; one stood facing the enemy while the other stood behind the Prophet. He magnified Allah by shouting, 'Allah Akbar.' [...]"

Bukhari:V4B51N72: "[...] Umar asked the Prophet, 'Is it not true that our men who are killed go to Paradise and those of the Pagan's will go to (hell) fire? The Prophet said, 'Yes.'"

Tabari VII:164: "We went out with the Messenger on a raid to Dhat Riqa in the neighborhood of Nakhal. At one point, a Muslim killed a polytheist woman. When Muhammad was on his way back to Yathrib, her husband swore he would not rest until he had wrought bloodshed among the Prophet's Companions. [...] Muhammad set up guards at night, an Ansar and an Emigrant. [...] The woman's husband saw them and shot an arrow. The Ansari pulled it out, put it down, and remained standing in prayer. The man shot a second and third arrow at him, but exactly the same thing happened. Finally the Ansari, after bowing and prostrating himself, woke his companion. [The Ansari said,] 'Sit Up. I have been wounded.' The Emigrant leapt to his feet. When the woman's husband saw the two of them there, he fled. Then the Emigrant, seeing the Ansari's blood-stained condition, exclaimed, 'Allah Almighty! Why didn't you wake me the first time he shot you?' 'I was in the middle of reciting a surah and I did not want to stop without finishing it.'"

Bukhari:V6B60N116: "Ibn Um Maktum came [up] while the Prophet was dictating [...] and said, 'O Allah's Apostle! By Allah, if I had the power to fight (in Allah's Cause), I would,' and he was a blind man. So Allah revealed to his Apostle [...], '[Muslims must fight in Jihad] except those who are disabled.'"

SCRIPTURE AND ISLAMIC JUSTICE

Tabari VII:167: "The Messenger married Umm Salama. In this year also, The Prophet commanded Zayd bin Thabit to study the Book of the Jews, saying, 'I fear that they may change my Book.' [...]"

Muslim:B17C5N4206: "[...] There came to him [Muhammad] a woman of Ghamid and said: Allah's Messenger, I have committed adultery, so purify me. He turned her away. On the following day she said: Allah's Messenger, why do you turn me away? Perhaps, you turn me away as you turned away Ma'iz [another who committed adultery] By Allah, I have become pregnant. He [Muhammad] said: Well, if you insist upon it, then go away until you give birth to the child. When she was delivered she came with the child wrapped in a rag and said: He is the child whom I have given birth to. He said: Go away and suckle him until you wean him. When she had weaned him she came to him with the child who was holding a piece of bread in his hand. He entrusted the child to one of the Muslims [took the child from her] and then pronounced [her] punishment. And she was put [cast] into a ditch [pit] and he commanded people [to kill her] and they stoned her [to death]. [...]"

SUMMATION:

IL: True Muslims will never hold any affection for non-Muslims. Muslim dedication to the words found in the Qur'an is what will always be required. The woman of Ghamid was stoned because sex outside of Islamic stipulations was never permitted. This consistency was also displayed in the stoning of the adulterous couple. This strictness was enforced to stop un-Islamic sexual activity.[18] According to Al-Misri:

> "A woman may not leave the city without her husband or a member of her unmarriageable kin [...] accompanying her, unless the journey is obligatory, like the hajj. It is unlawful for her to travel otherwise, and unlawful for her husband to allow her."

> —Al-Misri, *Reliance of the Traveller*, m10.3

WA: Allah is well-pleased with Muslims who want nothing to do with non-Muslims. Muhammad's Muslim army wanted nothing to do with fighting when they knew they could not win. Muhammad was forced to create a new prayer, the Prayer of Fear, as a contingency. Muhammad's commission for a literate Muslim to read the *Tenakh* ("Old Testament") meant that Muhammad did not know what was in the Tenakh despite telling the Jews that he could be found in their book. How could the Jews change his book, the Qur'an, unless Muhammad was also claiming the Tenakh as his book? If so, he could accuse the Jews of corruption when no evidence of him was found in the Jewish scriptures. As for the woman at Ghamid, she came seeking forgiveness. The message taken from this incident is that once one violates an Islamic law, there is no forgiveness. Muhammad made the child an orphan. There was a serious problem with stoning people for unlawful sex. This punishment was *never* prescribed in the Qur'an.[19]

QUR'AN 33

"The Allies"

627 AD

SCRIPTURE:

Qur'an 33:21, 23, 26-27, 37, 50-52, 59, 64

Bukhari:V5B59N401, V5B59N459; Ishaq:450-451, 456-457, 459, 461-473, 475, 479-481; Muslim:B19C7N4315, B19C21N4368, B19C21N4370; Muwatta:B29S32N99; Tabari VIII:1-4, 6-7, 13, 15-19, 22-23, 25-30, 34, 38-40

PREFACE:

This surah revealed that the Jews conspired with the Quraysh at Mecca to come to Yathrib ("Medina") to destroy the Muslims. The Quraysh came to Medina but they were stopped at the trench built by Muslims. The Jews displayed no treachery during the siege, yet the Muslims laid siege to the Jews. The Medinan Arab tribe Aws counseled for leniency. Muhammad appointed Sa'd Muad'h, who was wounded in the fighting, to make a judgment concerning the Jews. His pronouncement declared death to Jewish male adults and slavery for their women and children. Up to 900 Jewish males were decapitated. Also described in this surah was how Muhammad arranged the marriage of his female cousin to his adopted son. His adopted son then divorced his wife and Muhammad married his cousin, the former wife of his adopted son. Muhammad was also granted permission through revelation to marry as often as he wanted as well as having slave girls as concubines. In this surah, traditional norms concerning marriage were abrogated. The Jews were to be subjugated and the Quraysh were condemned for opposing Islam. Muslim martyrs in these conflicts against the Quraysh and the Jews were adulated. Allah continued to sanction the use of terror against the Jews. Revelation also stated that Muslim men could marry up to four wives, a limitation that was not imposed on Muhammad.[(20)]

SURAH:

Qur'an 33:21: "Certainly you have in the Messenger of Allah an excellent exemplar [model] for him who hopes in Allah and the Latter day and remembers Allah much.

Qur'an 33:23: "Of [Among] the believers are men who are [have been] true to the covenant they made with Allah; so of them is he who has accomplished his vow [fulfilled his obligations to Allah, i.e., they have been killed in Allah's Cause, Jihad], and of them is he who yet waits [to be killed and martyred], and they have not changed in the least."

Qur'an 33:26-27: "And He [Allah] drove down [took down] those of the People of the Book [Jews, in this case] who backed them from their fortresses and He cast awe [terror] into their hearts; some you killed and you took captive some [others were made prisoners]. And He made you heirs to their land and their dwellings and their property, and [given] to [you] a land which you have not yet trodden [never traversed before]."

Qur'an 33:37: "[...] We gave her to thee as a wife, so that there should be no difficulty for the believers about the wives of their adopted sons, when they have dissolved their marriage-tie. And Allah's command is ever performed."

Qur'an 33:50: "O Prophet, We have made lawful to thee [for you] thy wives whom thou hast given their dowries, and those whom thy right hand possesses [slave girls] out of those whom Allah has given thee as prisoners of war [...]"

Qur'an 33:50-51: "Thou mayest put off whom thou pleases of them, and take to thee whom thou pleasest [Muhammad may marry as many women as he wishes, including first cousins, and he may have as many concubines as he wants]."

Qur'an 33:52: "It is not allowed [it is prohibited] to thee [Muhammad] to take wives [marry more women] after this [from this point forward], nor to change them [divorce wives] for other wives [to marry more women], though their beauty be pleasing to him [though they are pleasing to him], except those whom thy right hand possesses [Muhammad can still have sex with concubines and add more female captives as concubines]. And Allah is ever Watchful over all things."

Qur'an 33:59: "O Prophet, tell thy wives and thy daughters and thy women of believers to let down upon them their over-garments [covering themselves completely except for one or two eyes to see the way and enabling the wearing of the hajab, chador, and burqa]. This is more proper, so that they may be known, and not be given trouble. [...]"

Qur'an 33:64: "Surely Allah has cursed the disbelievers and prepared for them a burning Fire [flaming Hell]."

SUNNAH:

COUSIN, DAUGHTER-IN-LAW, AND WIFE

Tabari VIII:1-2: "In this year the Messenger married Zaynab bint Jahsh [Muhammad's first cousin]. [...] Allah's Prophet came to the house of Zayd bin Muhammad [Muhammad's adopted son]. Perhaps the Messenger missed him at that moment Zaynab, Zayd's wife, rose to meet him. Because she was dressed only in a shift, the holy Prophet turned away from her. She said, 'He is not here. Come in, you are as dear to me as my father and mother!' Muhammad refused to enter. Zaynab had dressed in haste when she heard the Prophet at her door. She jumped up eagerly and excited the admiration of the Allah's Messenger, so that he turned away murmuring something that could scarcely be understood. However, he did say overtly, 'Glory be to Allah Almighty, who causes hearts to turn!' [...] So Zayd went to Muhammad, saying, 'Prophet, I have heard that you came to my house. Why didn't you go in? Perhaps Zaynab has excited your admiration, so I will leave her.'"

Tabari VIII:3-4: "Zayd left her, and she became free [To please his step-father Muhammad]. While the Messenger of Allah was talking with Aisha, a fainting overcame him. When he was released from it he smiled and said, 'Who will go to Zaynab to tell her the good news? Allah has married her to me.' Then the Prophet recited [the Qur'an] to the end of the passage [to the end of Qur'an 33]. Aisha said, 'I became very uneasy because of what we heard about her beauty, and another thing, the loftiest of matters—what Allah had done for her by personally giving her to him in marriage. I said that she would boast of it over us. [...] One day Muhammad went out looking for Zayd. Now there was a covering of Haircloth in the doorway, but the wind had lifted the covering so that the doorway was uncovered. Zaynab was in her chamber, undressed, and admiration for her entered the heart of the Prophet. After that Allah made her unattractive to Zayd.'"

BATTLE OF THE TRENCH

Tabari VIII:6-7: "What brought on the battle, according to what has been reported, was related to the expulsion of the Banu Nadir from their settlements by Allah's Apostle. [...] The Quraysh said: 'Jews, you are the people of the first Scripture, and you have knowledge about the subject on which we and Muhammad have come to differ. Is our religion better or his?' 'Your religion is better,' they said, 'You are closer to the truth than he.' [...]"

Muslim:B19C7N4315: "The Messenger of Allah cursed the tribes [who had marched upon Medina with a combined force in 5 Hegira, i.e., 627AD] and said: 'O Allah, Revealer of the Book, swift in (taking) account [delivering judgment on Islam's enemies], put the tribes to rout. O Lord, defeat them and shake them.'"

Ishaq:450: "The account of the trench is as follows. A group of Jews were the ones who assembled parties against the Messenger. They went to the Quraysh in Mecca and invited them to rid themselves of Muhammad. They said, 'We will be with you against him until we root him out.' [...] When Muhammad received word of them and what they had determined to do, he laid out a trench to protect Medina. He encouraged the Muslims to dig it with promises of Heavenly reward. The person who advised him about the trench was Salman. [...] Certain men of the hypocrites slacked off and disobeyed the Messenger. They pretended to be too weak to work, slipping away to their families without the knowledge or permission of the Prophet."

Ishaq:451: "[There are] some stories about the digging of the trench in which there is an example of Allah justifying His Prophet and confirming his prophetic office. [...] Muhammad spat on a rock, sprinkled water on it, and it crumbled. Then the Prophet said, 'I struck the first blow and what you saw flash out was Iraq and Persia [who] would see dog's teeth. Gabriel informed me that my nation would be victorious over them. Then I struck my second blow, and what flashed out was for the pale men in the land of the Byzantines to be bitten by the dog's teeth. Gabriel informed me that my nation would be victorious over them. Then I struck my third blow and Gabriel told me that my nation would be victorious over Yemen. Rejoice, victory shall come. Praise be to Allah. He has promised us victory after tribulation.' And this increased the Muslims faith and submission."

Tabari VIII:13: "[...] When Allah's Apostle finished the trench, the Quraysh came and encamped near streams with 10,000 men from many tribes. The Messenger went out with 3,000 Muslims. The enemy of Allah, Huyayy bin Akhtab, came to Ka'b bin Asad, who had formed a treaty with the [Jews of] Qurayza [the last remaining Jewish settlement in Medina]. Ka'b made a truce with Muhammad on behalf of his people. [...]

Tabari VIII:15-16: "Ka'b said, 'Leave me alone to deal with Muhammad.' But Huyayy kept wheedling and twisting until Ka'b yielded. Huyayy promised, 'If the Quraysh and Ghatafan [Tribe located north of Medina that aligned with the Quraysh] retreat without having killed Muhammad, I will enter your fortress so that whatever happens to you shall happen to me.' So Ka'b broke his treaty and renounced the bond. When news reached Muhammad, he sent Sa'd, chief of the Aws to Ka'b. 'If it is true, speak to me in words that we can understand that will be unintelligible to others.' So he went out and found them engaged in the worst of what had been reported. They slandered the Messenger and said, 'There is no treaty between us.' Sa'd reviled them, and they reviled him. Sa'd was a man with a sharp temper. He told the Jews, 'Stop reviling him for the disagreement between us is too serious for an exchange of taunts.' [...] Soon the trial became great for the Muslims and fear intensified. Their foe came at them from above and below, so that the believers were beset with fear. The hypocrisy of the hypocrites became evident. One said, 'Muhammad was promising us that we should [would] eat up the treasures of Chusroes [the Persians] and Caesar [the Byzantines], and now none of us even can go out to relieve himself [go to the toilet]!'"

Tabari VIII:17-18: "The Muslims and polytheists stayed in their positions for twenty nights with no fighting except for the shooting of arrows and the siege. When the trial became great [...], the Messenger sent for the leaders of the Ghatafan. He offered them a third of the date harvest of Medina [which did not belong to Muhammad] on [the] condition that they leave. The truce between the sides progressed to the point of drawing up a written document, but there was no witnessing or firm determination to make peace; it was only a matter of maneuvering [deception]. [...] The Quraysh rode out on their horses and said, 'Get ready for warfare. Today you shall know the real horseman.' Then they advanced towards the trench and halted by it. When they saw it, they said, 'By Allah, this is a stratagem that the Arabs have never employed' [...] I summon you to Allah, to His Messenger and to Islam.' Amr replied, 'I have no use for these [Allah, Muhammad, and Islam].' So Ali said, 'Then I summon you to fight.' Amr replied, 'Why, son of my brother? By Allah, I do not want to kill you.' Ali shouted, 'But I, By Allah, want to kill you.' Amr jumped from his horse and advanced towards Ali. The two fought until Ali killed Amr. He [Ali] shouted, 'Allah Akbar!'"

Tabari VIII:19: "Naufal plunged into the trench and became trapped in it. The Muslims pelted him with stones. He said, 'Arabs, a slaying is better than this.' So Ali went down and killed him. The Muslims took his corpse. They asked the Messenger to sell them his body. The Prophet said, 'We have no need for his body or its price. Do with it as you like.'"

Ishaq:456-457: "As he [Ali] returned to the Prophet smiling with joy [after having killed his Uncle Amr], Jumar asked him if he had stripped Amr of his armor. 'No,' Ali answered, 'I saw his private parts and was ashamed.' Sa'd was hit by an Arab arrow and the median vein of his arm was cut. He said, 'Allah make your face sweat in the hellfire, grant me martyrdom, and do not let me die, until I see my desire done to the [Jews of] Qurayza.'"

Tabari VIII:22: "Hassan was with the women and children. A Jew passed by and began to walk around the settlement. There was no one around to protect them while the Apostle and his Companions were at the Meccans' throats. So I said: 'Hassan, this Jew is walking around. I fear he will point out our weaknesses while the Muslims are too busy to attend to us. So go down to him and kill him.' [...] '[May] Allah forgive you, daughter of

Abd al Muttalib,' Hassan said, 'You know that I am not the man to do it.' When he [Hassan] said that ['You know that I am not the man to do it.'] to me, I saw that nothing could be expected of him. I girded myself, took a club, and, having gone down from the fortress to the man [the Jew walking by], I struck him with the club until I killed him. When I had finished with him, I returned to the fortress and said, 'Hassan, go down to him and strip him—only his being a man kept me from taking his clothes.' Hassan replied, 'I have no need of his spoils.'"

Ishaq:459: "Nu'aym said, 'Then know the Jews regret what they did regarding relations with Muhammad. They [the Qurayza Jews] told him, "Will you forgive us if we take nobles from the Quraysh and give them to you, so that you can behead them?" If the Jews ask for hostages, don't comply.' [...] Allah disrupted their unity and sowed distrust."

Tabari VIII:23: "[...] Then Nu'aym came to the Prophet and said, 'I have become a Muslim, but my tribe does not know of my Islam; so command me whatever you will.' Muhammad said, 'Make them abandon each other if you can so that they will leave us; for war is deception.' [...] Nu'aym went to the Qurayza. He had been their drinking companion in the Time of Ignorance. He said, 'You know my affection for you and the special ties between us.' 'Yes,' they said. 'You are not a person whom we doubt.' Nu'aym said, 'The Quraysh and [the] Ghatafan have come to make war on Muhammad, and you have aided them against him.' The position of the Quraysh is not like yours. This is your land. Your wealth, your children, and your women are in it. You can't move. The Quraysh live elsewhere. If they see an opportunity and booty, they will take it. If it turns out otherwise, they will return home and leave you exposed to Muhammad. You will lose if you have to deal with him alone. So don't support the Quraysh until you take hostages from them that as assurance they'll stay.' They said, 'You have given good advice.'"

Tabari VIII:25-27: "We will not fight on your side until you give us hostages for we fear that war tests your mettle. When fighting becomes difficult you will go to Mecca, leaving us alone with this man. We do not have the strength to fight with Muhammad. [...] The Prophet asked, 'Who will go and spy on the enemy?' The Messenger stipulated that should he come back, Allah would cause him to enter paradise. But no one stood up. The Prophet prayed then offered the same words, but no one volunteered. Again he asked, 'Whoever goes may be my companion in Paradise.' Yet no one stood [...]. The next morning, the Prophet left the trench and went back to Medina with the Muslims, and they laid down their weapons. [...]"

THE BANU QURAYZA

Tabari VIII:28: "When the Messenger approached the Jews, he said, 'You brothers of apes! Allah [has] shamed you and cursed you!'"

Ishaq:461: "Just before the noon prayers, Gabriel came to the Apostle wearing a gold turban. He was riding a mule. He said, 'Have you laid down your weapons and stopped fighting, Muhammad?' 'Yes,' he replied. Gabriel said, 'The angels have not laid down their arms! I've just returned from pursuing the enemy. Allah commands you to march to the Qurayza [Jews]. I, too, will attack the Jews and shake them out of their homes.' [...] The Prophet sent Ali ahead with his war banner against the Jews, and the Muslims hastened to it. Ali advanced toward their homes and heard insulting language from the Jews about Allah's Messenger. Ali ran back and told the Prophet that the Jews were rascals and that there was no need for him to go near those wicked men. 'Why?' Muhammad asked, 'Have you heard them insult me?' 'Yes,' Ali answered. Allah's Apostle replied, 'Had they seen me, they would not have said anything of the sort.' Before reaching the Qurayza, Muhammad greeted his Companions. 'Has anyone passed you,] he asked. 'Yes, Prophet,' they replied, 'Dihyah ibn Khalifah passed us on a white mule with a brocade-covered saddle.' Allah's Prophet said, 'That was Gabriel. He was sent to the Qurayza to shake their homes and *terrorize* [emphasis added] them.' [...] Muhammad besieged them for twenty-five nights. When the siege became too severe, Allah *terrorized* [emphasis added] them. Then they were told to submit to the judgment of Allah's Messenger. [...] After the siege exhausted and *terrorized* [emphasis added] them, the Jews felt certain that the Apostle would not leave them until he had exterminated them. So they decided to talk to Ka'b Asad. [...] He [Ka'b Asad] said, 'Swear Allegiance to this man and accept him; for, by Allah it has become clear to you that he is a Prophet sent by Allah. It is he that you used to find mentioned in your scripture book. Then you will be secure in your lives, your property, your children, and your wives.'"

Ishaq:462: "The Jews said, 'We will never abandon the Torah or exchange it for the Qur'an.' Asad said, 'Since you have rejected this proposal of mine, then kill your children and your wives and go out to Muhammad and his Companions as men who brandish swords, leaving behind no impediments to worry you. If you die, you shall have left nothing behind; if you win, you shall find other women and children.' The Jews replied, 'Why would we kill these poor ones? What would be the good of living after them?' [...] The Jews asked Muhammad, 'Send us Abu Lubaba, one of the Aws,' for they were allies, 'so that we can ask his advice.' The Prophet complied and the Jews grabbed hold of him. The women and children were crying, so he felt pity for them. They said, 'Abu [Lubaba], do you think we should submit to Muhammad's judgment? Abu said, 'Yes.' But he pointed with his hand to his throat, indicating that it would be slaughter. Abu later said, As soon as my feet moved, I knew that I had betrayed Allah's Apostle.' [...] He [Abu] cried, 'I will not leave this spot until Allah forgives me for what I've done. I betrayed His [Allah's] Apostle. [...] I heard Allah's Apostle laughing at daybreak, so I said, 'Why are you laughing, Prophet? May Allah make you laugh heartily!' He [Muhammad] said, '[Abu] Lubaba has been forgiven.'"

Tabari VIII:29: "Muhammad pitched a round tent over Sa'd in the Mosque. He laid down his sword, having just returned from the Trench. Then Gabriel came to him and said, 'Have you abandoned the fight? By Allah, the angels have not yet put down their weapons! Go out and fight the Jews!' So he called for his breastplate and put it back on. Then he went out and the Muslims followed him. [...] The Holy Prophet said, 'No one should pray the afternoon prayer until they are in the territory of the Qurayza because warfare against the Jews is incumbent upon Muslims [Muslims are obligated fight the Jews because it is the duty of Muslims to make warfare with the Jews]. ...Abu Lubaba gave a sign that it would mean slaughter. So they [Jews] said, 'We will submit to the judgment of Sa'd.' The Holy Prophet said, 'Submit to his judgment.' So they [the Jews] submitted. [...]"

Tabari VIII:30: "The Jews said, 'We will not profane our Sabbath [Make war on the day Yahveh commanded us to rest].'"

THE VERDICT

Ishaq:463: "[...] In the morning, the Jews submitted to the judgment of Allah's Messenger. The Aws leapt up and said, 'Muhammad, they are our allies [...].' The Messenger said, 'People of the Aws, will you not be satisfied if one of your own men passes judgment on them?' 'Yes,' they proclaimed. So the Prophet said, 'It [passing judgment] shall be entrusted to Sa'd Mu'adh.' [...] Then the Prophet appointed him [Sa'd] judge over the Qurayza Jews [...] En route to Muhammad, the Aws said, 'Treat our client well for the Prophet has put you in charge of this matter.' [...] Sa'd said, 'The time has come for Sa'd, in the Cause of Allah [Jihad], not to be influenced by anyone's reproach.' Some of the people who heard him, announced the impending death of the Qurayza before Sa'd Mu'adh reached them because of the words he had said. Then Muhammad said, 'Pass judgment on them.' Sa'd replied, 'I pass judgment that their men shall be killed, their women and children made captives, and their property divided.' Allah's Apostle proclaimed, 'You have passed judgment on the Jews with the judgment of Allah and the judgment of His Messenger.'"

Muslim:B19C21N4368: "[...] The Messenger of Allah sent for Sa'd who came to him riding a donkey. When he approached the mosque, the Messenger of Allah said to the Ansar: 'Stand up to receive your chieftain.' Then he [Muhammad] said [to Sa'd]: 'These people have surrendered accepting your decision.' He [Sa'd] said: 'You will kill their fighters and capture their women and children.' [Hearing this], the Prophet said: 'You have adjudged by the command of God.'"

Tabari VIII:34: "Sa'd replied, 'I pass judgment that the men shall be killed, their women and children made captives [slaves], and their property divided.' Allah's Apostle proclaimed, 'You have passed judgment on the Jews with the judgment of Allah and the Judgment of His Messenger.'"

Muslim:B19C21N4370: "Sa'd was wounded on the day of the Battle of the Ditch. A man from the Quraysh called Ibn al-Ariqah shot at him an arrow which pierced the artery in the middle of his forearm. The Messenger of Allah (May peace be upon him) pitched a tent for him in the mosque and would inquire after him being in close proximity. When he returned from the Ditch and laid down his arms and took a bath, the angel Gabriel appeared to him and he was removing dust from his hair (as if he had just returned from the battle). The latter said: You have laid down arms. By God, we haven't (yet) laid them down. So march against them. The Messenger of Allah (May peace be upon him) asked: Where? He pointed to [the] Banu Qurayza. So the Messenger of Allah (may peace he upon him) fought against them. They surrendered at the command of the Messenger of Allah (may peace be upon him), but he referred the decision about them to Sa'd who said: I decide about them that those of them who can fight be killed, their women and children taken prisoners and their properties distributed (among the Muslims)."

GENOCIDE OF THE JEWS

Tabari VIII:38: "The Messenger of Allah commanded that all the Jewish men and boys who had reached puberty should be beheaded. Then the Prophet divided the wealth, wives, and children of the Qurayza Jews among the Muslims. [...] On that day Muhammad made known the shares of the horseman and the shares of the foot soldiers, and he deducted from these shares his fifth. [...] According to this example, the procedure of the Messenger of Allah in the divisions of booty became a precedent which was followed in subsequent raids. [...] The Prophet selected for himself from among the Jewish women of the Qurayza, Rayhana bint Amr. She became his concubine. When he [died in 632 AD], she was still in his possession. When the Messenger of Allah took her as a captive, she showed herself averse to Islam [she did not convert to Islam] and insisted on Judaism."

Tabari VIII:39: "He [Sa'd] passed judgment on the Jews and prayed saying, 'O Allah, You know there are no men whom I would rather fight and strive to kill than men who called Your Messenger a liar.' [...] Then the Messenger of Allah sent Sa'd bin Zayd with some of the Qurayza captives to Najd, and in exchange for them he purchased horses and arms."

Ishaq:464: "The Jews were made to come down, and Allah's Messenger imprisoned them. Then the Prophet went out to the marketplace of Medina, and he had trenches dug in it. He sent for the Jewish men and had them beheaded in those trenches. They were brought out to him in batches. [...] some put the figure as high as 800 to 900 [boys and men]. [...] The affair continued until the Apostle [of Allah] made an end to them [had killed all of them]. [...] Huyayy [b. Akhtab, a Jewish leader] was brought out [before Muhammad] [...] with his hands bound to his neck with a rope. When he saw the Apostle, he [Huyayy b. Akhtab] said, 'By God, I do not blame myself for [regret] opposing you, but he who forsakes God

Middle Medinan Revelations

365

will be forsaken.' Then he [Huyayy b. Akhtab] went to the men and said, 'Gods command is right. A book and a decree, and massacre have been written against the Sons of Israel" Then he [Huyayy b. Akhtab] sat down and [at the signal from Muhammad to kill him] his head was struck off. [...] Aisha said, 'Only one of their women [their Jewish women] was killed. She was actually with me [by my side] and talking with me and laughing immoderately [nervous laughter from not being able to accept the evil spectacle] as [while] the Apostle was killing her men in the market when suddenly an unseen voice called her name [...] She said, 'I am going to be killed,' [...] 'because of something I did?' [...] She was taken away and beheaded. [...]'"

Tabari VIII:40: "The Messenger of God commanded that furrows should be dug in the ground for the Qurayza. Then he sat down. Ali and Zubayr began cutting off their heads in his presence. [...] Aisha, the Mother of the faithful, was asked, 'How did the Messenger of God behave? She replied, 'His eye did not weep for anyone.'

Bukhari:V5B59N401: "Allah's wrath became severe on anyone the Prophet killed during Allah's Cause [Jihad]."

Ishaq:465: "When their wrists were bound with cords, the Apostle was a sea of generosity to us. [...] Then the Apostle divided the property, wives, and children of the Qurayza among the Muslims. Allah's Messenger took his fifth of the booty."

TAKING LIBERTIES WITH THE VANQUISHED

Ishaq:466: "The Apostle chose one of the Jewish women for himself. Her name was Rayhana. She remained with him until she died, in his power. The Apostle proposed to marry her and put the veil on her but she said, 'Leave me under your power, for that will be easier.' She showed a repugnance towards Islam [she was repulsed by Islam] when she was captured. ...Allah sent down [a surah] concerning the Trench and Qurayza raid. [...] In it He mentions their trial and His kindness to the Muslims. [...]"

Bukhari:V5B59N459: "I entered the Mosque, saw Abu, sat beside him and asked about sex. Abu Sa'd said, 'We went out with Allah's Apostle and we received female slaves from among the captives. We desired women and we loved to do coitus interruptus.'"

Muwatta:B29S32N99: "He [Ibn Fahd] said, 'Abu Sa'd! I have slave girls. None of my wives in my keep are more pleasing to me than them, and not all of them please me so much that I want a child by them, shall I then practice coitus interruptus?' [...] I [Al-Hajjaj] said, 'She is your field, if you wish, water it, and if you wish, leave it thirsty.' [...]"

LACKING HUMILITY

Ishaq:467-469: "Allah addressed the believers and said, 'In Allah's Apostle, you have a fine example for anyone who hopes to be in the place where Allah is.' [...] Then Allah said, 'Some of you have fulfilled your vow to Me by dying; you have finished your work and returned to Me like those who sought martyrdom in prior battles. And some of you are still waiting to capitalize on Allah's promise of martyrdom. You do not hesitate in your religion and never doubt.' [...] Allah brought down the People of the Scripture Book [Jews]. I forced the Qurayza from their homes and cast *terror* [emphasis added] into their hearts. Some you slew [killed], and some you took captive [as slaves]. You killed their men and enslaved their women and children. And I caused you to inherit their land, their dwellings, and their property. Allah can do all things.' Gabriel came to the Apostle when Sa'd was taken. He visited him in the middle of the night wearing an embroidered turban and said, 'O Muhammad, who is this dead man for whom the doors of heaven have been opened and at whom the throne shook?' [...] Muhammad said, 'He had angelic pallbearers because the angels rejoiced when Sa'd's spirit shook Allah's throne.' [...] An Ansar recited this poem: 'The throne of Allah shook for only one man: Sa'd the brave the bold, a glorious leader, a knight ever ready. Stepping into the battle, he cut heads to pieces.'"

Ishaq:469: "The Apostle said, 'Every wailing woman lies except those who wept for Sa'd.' On the day the [Jews of] Qurayza were slain, one Muslim was martyred. A stone was thrown on him and it inflicted a shattering wound. The Apostle said, 'He will have the reward of two martyrs.'"

Ishaq:470-473: "We attacked them fully armed, sharp swords in hand, cutting through heads and skulls. [...] We were steadfast trusting in Him.

We have a Prophet by whom we will conquer all men. [...] Muhammad's companions are the best in war. [...] Muhammad and his Companions humiliated every doubter. [...]"

Ishaq:475: "[...] We obeyed our Prophet's orders when he called us to war. When he called for violent efforts we made them. The Prophet's command is obeyed for he is truly believed. He will give us victory, glory and a life of ease. Those who call Muhammad a liar disbelieve and go astray. They attacked our religion and would not submit. [...]"

Ishaq:479: "Slain in Allah's religion, Sa'd inherited Paradise with the martyrs. His was a noble testimony. When he pronounced his verdict on the Qurayza, he did not judge on his own volition. His judgment and Allah's were one. Sa'd is among those who sold his life for the Garden of Bliss."

Ishaq:480: "The Qurayza met their misfortune. In humiliation they found no helper. A calamity worse than that which fell upon the Nadir, befell them. On that day Allah's Apostle came to them like a brilliant moon. We left them with blood upon them like a pool. They lay prostrate with the vultures circling round."

Ishaq:481: "The Apostle slew them [Jews of Qurayza] in their own town. With our troops he surrounded their homes. We shouted out cries in the heat of battle. The Jews were given the Scripture and wasted it. Being blind, they strayed from the Torah. You Jews disbelieved the Qur'an and yet you have tasted the confirmation of what it said. May Allah make our raid on them immortal [never-ending]. May fire burn in their quarter. They will no longer ruin our lands. You [Jews] have no place here, so be off!"

SUMMATION:

IL: In this revelation, Muslims come to know that Muhammad is Allah's model for a perfect human being. He is the one Muslims should strive to imitate. Muslims must always be ready to lay their life down to spread Allah's religion. When Muslims act according to Allah's will, Allah promises to terrorize the enemies of Islam. In doing so, Allah awards Muslims the possessions of their enemies as in the case of the Qurayza Jews. Muhammad was a perfect example of Allah's mercy because he obeyed the commands of Allah. Muhammad's obedience was rewarded with his marriage to Zaynab, and with unlimited wives and concubines from Islamic conquests. Verses 50-52 should be interpreted in the following manner: Muhammad can marry and divorce whom he pleases, but he cannot divorce women he marries without cause. If the women are pleasing to him he cannot divorce them or leave women without means of support. This was a mercy given by Allah as was permission to continue to add concubines. However, in order for Muslim men not to be carried away with Allah's mercy, concerning women, Muslim women were commanded by Allah to cover themselves completely, except for their eyes. Those, from among the kuffar [infidels], who question or disagree with the commands of Allah, are cursed and will go into the flaming hell already prepared for them by Allah.

Lastly, the fate of the Banu Qurayza was settled when they broke the treaty with the Prophet by assisting the Azhab at the Battle of the Trench. Muhammad, therefore, was justified in declaring war against the Banu Qurayza.[21]

WA: Muhammad adopted a son because the sons born to his first wife, Khadijah, all died in infancy. Muhammad's adopted son, Zayd, married Muhammad's cousin, Zaynab. One day, Muhammad saw her not fully dressed and was attracted to his sons' wife, his female cousin. The adopted son, after learning of Muhammad's attraction, offered to divorce her in order to make her available to his father, the Islamic Prophet. While talking to his child bride Aisha, Allah chose to tell Muhammad that he could marry his cousin and daughter-in-law. This made Aisha feel terrible because she knew she had to share Muhammad with yet another woman. The admiration that entered his heart was nothing more than his longing to have carnal relations with his cousin and daughter-in-law.

It cannot be understated that the events related to the Battle of the Trench changed the course of history. Tabari reported the Quraysh marched over 200 miles because the Jewish tribe, Banu Nadir, was expelled. The one remaining Jewish tribe in Yathrib (Medina), the Banu Qurayza, were seen as complicit with the polytheistic Quraysh from Mecca. In fact, the Jews were accused of playing both sides. Eventually, the Jews yielded to Quraysh pressure and were seen as betraying the Muslims. Thus, the Jews were blamed for the fear that came into the Muslim camp at the trench that protected Yathrib from the advancing Quraysh. Muhammad, who was now fearful, tried to buy off Quraysh allies with produce from the property the Muslims took from the Banu Nadir. In a telling encounter, uncle Amr, a Meccan, did not want to harm Ali, his nephew, but Ali, on the other hand, wanted very much to kill Amr. After Ali stated his desire to kill his uncle, they fought and Ali killed his uncle. After the encounter, Ali shouted, "Allahu Akbar." Ali rejoiced at the killing of his uncle. After Naufal was also killed by Ali, Muhammad told the Muslims they could do what they wished with his corpse. Why not just say, bury it? The death of the Jewish man in the settlement revealed that Ali's son, Hassan, wanted to kill this innocent Jewish man. So his Aunt, daughter of Abd al-Muttalib, Ali's sister clubbed the Jewish man to death. Hassan also wanted to strip the dead man of his modesty. Are both of these folks considered righteous Muslims?

Outnumbered, Muhammad had only trickery to use, so he sent out misinformation to try to divide the Quraysh and Ghatafan. What he needed was more intelligence concerning their intentions. Three times he asked Muslims to leave the trench to spy on Allah's enemy. These offers were always accompanied with the guarantee of Paradise, but none of the Muslims answered his call. Neither the promise of paradise nor martyrdom was enough to entice these Muslims into action. Faced with faithless Muslim followers, Muhammad left the trench, knowing the Meccans could not breach it. He needed to find a scapegoat for his losing situation, so he went full throttle against the Qurayza Jews. Muhammad claimed he received a new revelation from Allah concerning the Jews. Allah wanted Muhammad to continue his onslaught against the Jews. So the Muslims initiated a fight they knew they could win. Surrounded, the Jews had no option but to submit. The Jews could not accept Muhammad as their Prophet. They believed Muhammad was a liar. As a result, Sa'd developed a hatred for the Jews. Muhammad, undoubtedly, knew this about Sa'd, so Muhammad appointed Sa'd to preside over the fate of the Qurayza Jews. Sa'd then rendered his verdict upon the Qurayza Jews: Death.

When Sa'd gave his death verdict, Muhammad said it came from Allah. He then ordered that all males with pubic hair suffer decapitation. Trenches were dug in Medina for their execution. Muhammad then sat down and watched the decapitation of 800–900 Jewish males. Ali and Zubayr performed the majority of the butchery, which lasted all day—it

The Dawn of Islamic Literalism

finally ended, far into the night.[(22)] Muhammad, who was unmoved by the genocide of these Jews, then proceeded to enslave their families. When Muhammad arrived at Medina, the Jewish community numbered from 36,000-42,000. The Jewish community, within five years, was either evicted or slaughtered.[(23)] They were sold for provisions. If that was not enough, he picked Rayhana as his concubine. She had just witnessed Muhammad put her husband, father, and brothers to death. Muhammad had relations with her that evening. Islamic scholar, William Muir, stated the following:

> "[…] The men and women were penned up for the night in separate yards; […]. During the night, graves or trenches sufficient to contain dead bodies of the men were dug in the chief market-place of the city. When these were ready in the morning, Mohamet [Muhammad], himself a spectator of the tragedy, gave command that the captives be bought forth in companies of five or six at a time. Each company was made to sit down by the brink of the trench destined for its grave, and there beheaded. Party after party were led out and butchered in cold blood, till the whole were slain. […] Having sated his revenge, and drenched the marketplace with the blood of 800 [to 900] victims, and having given command for the earth to be smoothed over their remains, Mohamet [Muhammad] returned from the horrid spectacle to solace himself with the charms of Rayhana, whose husband and all her male relatives had just perished in the massacre. […]" [(24)]

Nothing increased the faith of Muhammad's Muslim followers like Gabriel telling Muhammad that they would conquer their enemies. In Ishaq's account, Sa'd wanted the Jews to be destroyed before Muhammad appointed him as the 'impartial' judge. Allah was given all the credit for personally terrorizing these Jews. During this slaughter, Aisha, Muhammad's child-bride, said when Muhammad was killing the Jews, one woman was beheaded along with the men. The Muslims rejoiced because Allah was generous, giving to them the property of the Qurayza Jews.

Ishaq:467-468 proves conclusively that Allah cannot be equated with the

God of the Jews and the Christians, nor could Muhammad, the Prophet of Islam, ever be considered a prophet by the Jews or Christians. These verses are mutually exclusive with any biblical teaching. Sa'd, whose verdict ensured the slaughter of hundreds of Jews was welcomed into heaven? Furthermore, Ishaq:475 contradicts Tabari VIII:15-16, 25-27. How can Muhammad's Muslims be confident of Muhammad's promises in one account and then be fearful and not cooperate with him in the other account? Another example of this incompatibility is Ishaq:479 where this account, related to Sa'd, violated any semblance of love and compassion. Sa'd's actions would have been condemned in Judaism and Christianity, yet in Islam, he inherited the "Gardens of Bliss." Other Muslims raped many of the Jewish female slaves.[25] In conclusion; these verses have sealed Islamic hatred of Jews into eternity.

CHAPTER 6 NOTES

1. Ali, p. 1101; Pickthall, p. 403
2. Al-Misri, *Reliance of the Traveller*, p. 59
3. Caner, *Unveiling Islam*, p. 51
4. Ali, p. 132; Pickthall, p. 061
5. Spencer, *The Truth About Muhammad*, p. 52
6. Kathir, *Tafsir Ibn Kathir*, Vol. 2, p. 158
7. Ali, p. 1094; Pickthall, p. 400
8. Ali, p. 190; Pickthall, p. 78
9. Al-Misri, *Reliance of the Traveller*, p. 638
10. Bulandshahri, *Illuminating Discourses on the Noble Qur'an*, Vol. 1, pp. 550-551
11. Kathir, *Tafsir Ibn Kathir*, Vol. 2, p. 375
12. Khan, *The Legacy of Prophet Muhammad*, Ijtihad
13. Kathir, *Tafsir Ibn Kathir*, Vol. 3, p. 376
14. Ibid., Vol. 3, pp. 26-27
15. Bulandshahri, *Illuminating Discourses on the Noble Qur'an*, Vol. 2, p. 8
16. Ali, p. 1086; Pickthall, p. 397
17. Ali, p. 1061; Pickthall, p. 390
18. Al-Misri, *Reliance of the Traveller*, p. 610
19. Cook, *Muhammad*, p. 50
20. Ali, p. 823; Pickthall, pp. 299-301
21. Peters, *Muhammad and the Origins of Islam*, p. 224
22. Guillaume, *Islam*, pp. 47-48
23. Ahmad, *Muhammad and the Jews*, pp. 42-43
24. Muir, *Life of Mahomet: From Original Sources*, pp. 329-331
25. Bulandshahri, *Illuminating Discourses on the Noble Qur'an*, Vol. 1 p. 502

*Ishaq:410 was found in *The Complete Infidel's Guide to the Koran* by Robert Spencer on page 148*

CHAPTER 7

Late
Medinan
Revelations

(628-632 AD)

QUR'AN 24

"The Light"

628 AD

SCRIPTURE:

Qur'an 24:2, 6, 31, 40, 52, 56

Bukhari:V2B23N413, V4B56N829, V7B71N660, V7B72N715, V8B82N816, V8B86N6830; Ishaq:485-486, 489-492; Muslim:B4C203N2127, B17C4N4194, B33C6N6435, B17C8N4226, B19C2N4294; Tabari VIII:42, 44, 46, 48, 52, 55-58, 62-63

PREFACE:

After the campaign against the Banu Mustaliq, Aisha, the Prophet's child-bride, rode upon the camel of a young Muslim. Rumors circulated that she was having an affair. Ali was also in accord with this point of view. Since Islam is the manifestation of divine light, the Islamic home is also to be pure and free of adultery. Once the kingdom of Islam is established, this surah warns against the evils inherent in the establishment of a Kingdom. Therefore, preventative measures against adultery must be taken. Slander is another target of this surah, based on the accusations against Aisha. In anticipation of the establishment of the Muslim Kingdom, abrogating verses were continually introduced to ensure its success. After the establishment of the Kingdom, the ease of life that results could tempt Muslims into slander and adultery. Countermeasures were introduced, specifically targeted at women, to dissuade anyone from future temptation.[1]

SURAH:

Qur'an 24:2: "The adulteress and adulterer, flog each of them with a hundred stripes [lashes], and let not pity for them detain [withhold] you from obedience to Allah, if you believe in Allah and the Last Day, and let a party of believers witness their chastisement."

Qur'an 24:6: "And those who accuse [charge] their wives and [but] have no witnesses [or evidence] except themselves [and what they themselves say], let one of them testify four testimonies [swearing four times], bearing Allah to witness, that he is of those speaking the truth."

Qur'an 24:31: "And say to the believing women that they lower their gaze and restrain their sexual passions and do not display their adornment except what appears thereof [except what is apparent]. And let them wear their head-coverings over their bosoms. And they should not display their adornment except to their husbands or their fathers, or the fathers of their husbands [their father-in-laws], or their sons, or their brothers, or their brothers' sons [nephews], or their sisters' sons, or their women, or those whom their right hands possess [their servants and slaves], or guileless male servants [little children] who know not women's nakedness. [...]"

Qur'an 24:40: "[...] And to whom Allah gives not light, he has no light.

Qur'an 24:52: "And he who obeys Allah and His Messenger, and fears Allah and keeps duty to Him, these it is that are the achievers."

Qur'an 24:56: "And keep up prayer and pay the poor-rate [zakat tax] and obey the Messenger, so that mercy may be shown to you."

SUNNAH:

RETRIBUTION

Tabari VIII:42: "Allah's Messenger set out six months after the conquest of the Qurayza. He went to Lihyan, seeking vengeance for the men betrayed at Faji. To take the enemy by surprise, he pretended to go north. Then veered to the left and, having passed Yayn, his route led him directly by the main road of Mecca."

Ishaq:485-486: "[...] Allah's Messenger said, 'Give your allegiance, for Islam does away with all that preceded it, as does the Hijrah.' [...]

Muhammad found that the Lihyan had been warned. [...] After he failed to take them by surprise as he intended, he said, 'If we go down to Usfan, the Meccans will think we have come to terrorize them.' [...], and then he returned to Medina. [...] If the Lihyan had remained in their homes they would have met bands of fine fighters, audacious warriors who *terrorize* [emphasis added]. [...]"

Ishaq:489: "War is kindled by passing winds. Our swords glitter; cutting through pugnacious heads. [...] Do the bastards think that we are not their equal in fighting? We are men who believe there is no shame in killing. We don't turn from piercing lances. We smite the heads of the haughty with blows that squash the zeal of the unyielding [disbelievers]. We're heroes, protecting our war banner. We are a noble force, as fierce as wolves. We preserve our honor and protect our property by smashing heads."

Tabari VIII:44: "Salam said, 'Tell the Messenger that the polytheists have raided his camels.' Standing on a hill, I faced Medina and shouted, 'A raid!' Then I set out after the enemy, shooting arrows and saying rajaz verses: Today the mean [cruel] ones will receive destruction.'"

Tabari VIII:46: "[Salama continued] If you believe in Allah and know that Paradise is real and that the Fire is real, do not stand between me and martyrdom! But Abd-Rahman dismounted and thrust his spear into Akram. So I shot Abd-Rahman with an arrow, and said, 'Take that!'"

Tabari VIII:48: "[...] Then he set out after the enemy—he was like a beast of prey. [...]"

Tabari VIII:52: "[...] Abdallah bin Ubayy [the leader of the Ansar, Medinan Muslims] became enraged and said, 'Why are they [Meccan Muslims] doing this [fighting the Ansar]? Are they trying to outrank us and outnumber us in our own land? [...]'"

Tabari VIII:55: "Messenger of Allah, I have been told that you want to kill Abdallah bin Ubayy [another Muslim]. If you are going to do it; command me and I will bring you his head. I will kill a believer to avenge an unbeliever and thereby enter the Fire of Hell.' [...] Miqyas came to Mecca, pretending to have become a Muslim, and said, 'Muhammad, I have come to you as a Muslim to seek blood money for my brother who was killed by mistake. The Prophet ordered him to be paid blood money for his brother and he stayed briefly with Muhammad. Then he attacked his brother's slayer, killing him. He left for Mecca as an apostate."

RUINATION OF THE BANU MUSTALIQ

Ishaq:490: "When Allah's Messenger heard about the Mustaliq gathering against him, he set out and met them at one of their watering holes near the coast. [...] Allah caused the Mustaliq to fight and killed some of them. Allah gave the Apostle their children, women, and property as booty."

Tabari VIII:56-57: "[Aisha said,] 'A great number of [the] Mustaliq [people] were wounded. The Messenger took many captives, and they were divided among all the Muslims. Juwayriyah was one of the slaves. When the Prophet divided the captives by lot, Juwayriyah fell to the share of Thabit, Muhammad's cousin. She gave him a deed for her freedom which he did not accept. Juwayriyah was the most beautiful woman and she captivated anyone who looked at her. She came to the Apostle seeking his help. As soon as I saw her at the door of my chamber, I took a dislike to her [Jealousy], and I knew what he would see in her what I saw.' [...] Muhammad said, 'Would you like something better than that? I will discharge your debt and marry you.' [...] A hundred families of the Mustaliq were freed as a result of the marriage. I know of no woman who was a greater blessing to her people than she."

Bukhari:V9B93N506: "That during the battle with Bani Al-Mustaliq they [Muslims] captured some females and intended to have sexual relations with them without impregnating them. So they asked the Prophet about coitus interruptus. The Prophet said, 'It is better that you should not do it, for Allah has written whom He is going to create till the Day of Resurrection.' Qaza'a said, 'I heard Abu Sa'd saying that the Prophet said, "No soul is ordained to be created but Allah will create it."'"

AISHA'S DILEMMA

Bukhari:V7B71N660: "[Aisha recalled,] 'Magic was worked on Allah's Apostle so that he used to think that he had sexual relations with his wives while he actually had not. [Sufyan said,] "That is the hardest kind of magic as it has such an effect."""

Tabari VIII:58: "Aisha said, 'When the raid on the Mustaliq took place, Muhammad had his wives draw lots as he used to do to see who would accompany him. My lot came out over theirs, and he took me along. Women in those days used to eat only enough to stay alive; they were not bloated with meet so as to become heavy. [...] I had just lain down when Safwan al-Sulami passed by. He had lagged behind attending to a need of his. He had not spent the night with the troops [i.e., Muhammad was having sex]. [...] He used to look at me before the veil and hijab was imposed on us. When he saw me, he exclaimed in astonishment, 'The Apostle's wife!' He asked why I was alone, but I did not speak. Then he brought his camel near and said, 'Mount!' I mounted and he came. He took hold of the camel's head and set out with me, hastening in pursuit of the party. He told me to ride it while he kept behind. So I rode it.'"

Tabari VIII:60: "The story reached the Prophet and I missed the attention he once showed me. [...] One day while I was out with the girls, one said, 'Daughter, take it lightly. Whenever a beautiful woman married to a man has rival wives, they always gossip about her, and people do the same. [...] [Usayd said,] 'Even if they are brothers [Muslim companions speaking ill of the Prophet's wife Aisha], give the command. I will rid you of them because they deserve to have their heads cut off!'"

Tabari VIII:62: "Ali said, 'Prophet, women are plentiful. You can get a replacement, easily changing one for another. [...] Ask the slave girl; she will tell you the truth.' So the Apostle called Burayra to ask her. Ali got up and gave her a violent beating first, saying, 'Tell the Apostle the truth.'"

Bukhari:V7B72N715: "Aisha said, 'I have not seen any woman suffering as much as the believing women.'"

Tabari VIII:63: "When Muhammad came into my room, my parents were with me. I was crying. I waited for my mother and father to reply to the Apostle, but they did not speak. I asked my parents why they were afraid to defend me, but they said nothing. My weeping broke out afresh. I swear, I considered myself to lowly and unimportant for Allah to reveal a Qur'an about me to be recited in Mosques and used in worship But I was hoping that the Prophet would see something in a dream from Allah which would clear me of this. Before Allah's Messenger left the place he was sitting, there came over him from Allah what used to come over him. He began wiping the perspiration [sweat] from his brow and said, 'Good news, Aisha! Allah has sent down word about your innocence.' [...] He recited the Qur'an Allah had revealed concerning me and gave orders concerning Mistah, Hassan, and Hamnah who were the most explicit in their slander. They received their prescribed flogging of eighty lashes. They were beaten to the boundary of death [to the point of death] for their crime against the religion of Islam."

Muslim:B4C203N2127: "[Aisha said,] 'He [Muhammad] struck me on the chest which caused me pain and then said, "Did you think that Allah and His Apostle would deal unjustly with you?"'"

DISCORD AMONG MUSLIMS

Ishaq:491-492: "Abdallah bin Ubai [Medina Muslim leader of the Ansar] became enraged [Medina and Meccan Muslims were quarreling over access to a watering hole] and said, 'Why are they doing this? Are they trying to outrank us and outnumber us in our own land? The proverb "Feed a dog and it will devour you" fits these Quraysh vagabonds [...] Then he turned to his tribe and said, [...] you have allowed them to settle in your land and divide your wealth [...] "Umar said, 'Tell someone to go kill him.' The Apostle answered, 'But what will men say about me if I start killing Muslims?'" [...] Abdullah [another Muslim] came to the Apostle saying, saying ' I heard that you want to kill Abdallah bin Ubai [...] [Abdallah told Muhammad], "If you really want him killed, command me to do it and I will bring you his head...but if you order another to kill him, I am afraid if you order another to kill him my soul will be unable to bear the sight of his murderer...I shall kill him and then I shall have killed one of the faithful for an infidel, and I shall go to hell."

SCOURGING OR STONING

Bukhari:V2B23N413: "The Jew brought to the Prophet a man and a woman from amongst them who have committed illegal sexual intercourse [adultery]. He ordered both of them to be stoned to death, near the place of offering the funeral prayers beside the mosque."

Bukhari:V4B56N829: "The Jews came to Allah's Apostle and told him that a man and a woman from amongst them had committed illegal sexual intercourse. Allah's Apostle said to them, "What do you find in the Torah (old Testament) about the legal punishment of Ar-Rajm (stoning)?" They replied, (But) we announce their crime and lash them." Abdullah bin Salam said, "You are telling a lie; Torah contains the order of Rajm." They brought and opened the Torah and one of them solaced his hand on the Verse of Rajm and read the verses preceding and following it. Abdullah bin Salam said to him, "Lift your hand." When he lifted his hand, the Verse of Rajm was written there. They said, "Muhammad has told the truth; the Torah has the Verse of Rajm. Muhammad ordered the couple to be stoned to death (Rajm). [Another Muslim remembered], "I saw the man leaning over the woman to shelter her from the stones."

Muslim:B17C4N4194: "[...] Stoning is a duty laid down in Allah's book for married men and women who commit adultery when proof is established, or if there is pregnancy, or a confession."

REWARD AND PUNISHMENT

Muslim:B33C6N6435: "Aisha, the mother of the believers, reported that a child died and I said: There is happiness for this child who is a bird from amongst the birds of Paradise. Thereupon Allah's Messenger said: Don't you know that Allah created the Paradise and He created the Hell and He created the dwellers for this (Paradise) and the denizens for this (Hell)?"

Muslim:B17C8N4226: "Anas b. Malik reported that a person who drank wine was brought to Allah's Apostle. He gave him forty stripes with two lashes. Abu Bakr also did that, but when Umar assumed the responsibilities of the Caliphate, he consulted people and Abd al-Rahman said, 'The mildest punishment for drinking is eighty stripes and Umar their [then] prescribed this punishment.'

THE DEMANDS OF ISLAMIC FUNDAMENTALISM

Muslim:B19C2N4294: "[...] He [Muhammad] would say [when he appointed a commander], 'Fight in the name of Allah and in way of Allah. Fight against those who disbelieve in Allah. [...] When you meet your enemies who are polytheists, invite them to three courses of action. [...] Invite them to accept Islam, if they respond to you, accept it from them and desist from fighting against them. [...] If they refuse to accept Islam, demand from them the Jizya [penalty tax]. If they agree to pay, hold off your hands [do not harm them]. If they refuse to pay the tax, seek Allah's help and fight them.' [...]"

SUMMATION:

IL: Public punishment is ordered by Allah for those guilty of adultery. Whipping is prescribed to deter others from committing what is forbidden. In order to protect women against false accusations, four witnesses are needed. Allah prescribed this in light of the accusations that occurred against Aisha. To ensure this does not occur, as in the past, Muslim women are to be covered and bridle their passions. Allah restated if he withheld the light of truth, no one could find it. Therefore, the light of truth is found in all of those who obey Allah and Muhammad. Obedience to the Prophet occurs when one says their prayers and pays the zakat. This is how a Muslim attains mercy. According to Al-Misri:

> "A woman has no right to custody of her child from a previous marriage when she remarries because married life will occupy her with fulfilling the rights of her husband and prevent her from tending the child."[2]

—Al-Misri, *Reliance of the Traveller*, m13.4

WA: The lashing of wayward men and women contradicted Muhammad's previous edict to stone adulterers. The problem with the four-witness rule, was that four people could lie, which would doom the innocent. Allah's solution was to have women covered from head to toe.[3] This surah concluded by telling Muslims their salvation was dependent on obeying Muhammad, who was not God. So, he-who-must-be-obeyed, was seeking vengeance on others only six months after he committed Muslim forces to commit genocide against a Jewish community that they obliterated.

Once again, we see the most violent acts of Muslims being adulated. These violent Muslims even agreed to kill one another.

In the raid on the Mustaliq, Aisha accompanied the Prophet. After the Muslims killed the men of the Mustaliq, Muhammad took a beautiful woman as another wife. Since Muhammad wanted to be with her, Aisha was left alone. Another Muslim offered to give Aisha a ride back to Medina. This started an alleged slander. Ali was one who joined in and told the Prophet to get rid of her. Others also joined in with contention, but Aisha was cleared, because Allah told Muhammad she did nothing wrong. This meant that Muhammad still wanted her to be around. He then had three Muslims beaten to the point of death. The crime wasn't against Aisha, it was against Islam. A question presents itself here. Did Ali also sin against Islam? Ali wasn't punished to the point of death like the other three Muslims, but he slandered as well. Ali wasn't beaten because Muhammad needed him as a cousin, a son-in-law, and a violent Muslim warrior.

Westerners must notice that the Sirah declares Islam wants allegiance and does away with all that preceded it. Muslim warriors terrorize, glorify war, brandish swords, behead (according to Islamic law), have no shame in killing, are as fierce as wolves, smash heads, sell women and children for provisions, and justify rape.[4]

After the events related to the Mustaliq concluded, Aisha spoke of Muhammad's imaginary sexual fantasy and his battery against her. The seeming contradiction between lashing and stoning for sexual infidelity was emphasized in this portion of the Qur'an and Sunnah. Either the Qur'an or the Hadith was wrong concerning this issue.

QUR'AN 48

"The Victory"

628 AD

SCRIPTURE:

Qur'an 48:16, 18-20, 27-29

Ishaq:498-500, 502-504; Tabari VIII:71, 75-77, 82, 85-86

PREFACE:

This surah claims that the treaty at Hudabiyah between Muhammad and the Quraysh was the greatest victory of all. The Muslims sought pilgrimage to Mecca, but were prevented by the Quraysh. Muhammad then sent a representative into Mecca who was detained by the Quraysh. The ten-year Hudna made between the Meccans and Muslims contained favorable terms for the Meccans. A treaty that is favorable towards ones enemy is seen as better than a military victory because it is seen as a moral victory. Through these moral victories, Islam will gain advantage over the other religions. The moral victory of the Hegira and the moral victory of the Hudna will ensure future victories on the battlefield. Victory over all religions of the world is seen as a future certainty. In order for Islam's moral victories to turn into military victories, abrogating verses must appear to remove constraints from Jihadists. This global Jihad will eventually defeat the religions of the world and subjugate the Jews and Christians who reject the call of Islam.[5]

SURAH:

Qur'an 48:16: "You will soon be called [invited] against [to fight] a people of [possessing] mighty prowess to fight against them until they submit.

Then if you obey, Allah will grant you a good reward; but, if you turn your back as you turned back before, He will chastise you with a painful chastisement."

Qur'an 48:18: "Allah indeed was well pleased with the believers, when they swore allegiance to thee under the tree, and He knew what was in their hearts, so he sent down tranquility [a piece of reassurance] on them and rewarded them with a near victory."

Qur'an 48:19-20: "And many gains which they will acquire [They will capture much booty]. And Allah is ever Mighty, Wise. Allah promised you many gains which you will acquire [much booty], then He Hastened this on for you [has given this to you in advance], and held back the hands of men from you [has withheld men's hands from you]; and that it may be a sign [token] for the believers and that He may guide you on a right path."

Qur'an 48:27: "[...] You shall certainly enter the Sacred Mosque, if Allah [permits] please [...]. But He knows what you know not, so He has ordained a near victory before that."

Qur'an 48:28-29: "He it is Who has sent His messenger with the guidance and the Religion of Truth [Islam] that He may make it prevail over all religions. And Allah is enough for a witness. Muhammad is the Messenger of Allah, and those with him are [fierce to the unbelievers] firm on the heart of the disbelievers, [but they are] compassionate among themselves [to one another]. [...]"

SUNNAH:

COMPENSATION

Tabari VIII:71: "Umar said, 'Messenger, will you without arms or horses enter the territory of people who are at war with you?' So the Prophet sent men back to Medina and they gathered all of the horses and weapons they could find. When they approached Mecca, they [Quraysh] prohibited him from entering, so they marched to Mina. Muhammad's spy brought him word that Ikrimah was coming out with five hundred men. Muhammad said, 'Khalid, your paternal uncle's son is coming against you.' Khalid [Al-

Walid] replied, 'I am the sword of Allah and the sword of His Messenger! Direct me to whatever you wish!' Muhammad sent him in command of horseman and he met Ikrimah [Khalid's cousin] in the canyon and routed him — driving him back into Mecca. Regarding him, Allah revealed: [Qur'an 48:24]."

Ishaq:498-499: "Safwan smote Hassan with his sword and tied his hands to his neck. [When Muhammad asked why, Safwan replied,] 'He insulted and satirized me and I became enraged. So I smote him.' The Apostle said, 'Hassan, did you look on my people with an evil eye [wish them harm and ill will] because Allah had guided them to Islam?' [...] The Apostle provided some compensation that included a castle, some property, a portion of the zakat tax, and a Copt [Christian] slave girl."

AN ACCOMMODATION

Ishaq:499-500: "The Prophet set out to make the lesser pilgrimage, not intending to make war [...] Many Bedouins were slow in coming to him. So the Messenger set out with the Emigrants [Muslims from Mecca] and Ansar [migrants from Mecca]. [...] his purpose was to visit the shrine and venerate it."

Tabari VIII:75-76: "The Prophet said, 'We have not come to fight anyone; we have come to make the lesser pilgrimage. War has exhausted and harmed the Quraysh. If they wish, we will grant them a delay and they can leave me alone to deal with the Arabs. If they refuse the delay, I shall fight them for the sake of this affair of mine as long as I live.' [...] Urwah went to the Prophet [and said,] 'Muhammad, tell me, if you exterminate your tribesmen—have you ever heard of any of the Arabs who has destroyed his own race before you?'"

Ishaq:500: "The Messenger said, 'Woe to the Quraysh! War has devoured them! [...] If the Arabs defeat me, that will be what they want. If Allah makes me prevail over the Arabs, the Quraysh can enter Islam en masse. Or they can fight. By Allah, I shall not cease to fight against them for the mission which Allah has entrusted [to] me until Allah makes me victorious or I perish.' [...] [Muhammad then said,] 'Who will take us out by a way in which we will avoid the Quraysh?' [Muhammad then said,]

'[...] bring the army out over Murar Pass to the descent of Hudabiyah below Mecca.' [...]"

ILL WILL PERSISTS

Tabari VIII:77: "Urwah began looking at the Companions of the Prophet. He said, 'If Muhammad coughs up a bit of phlegm and it falls onto the hand of one of them, he rubs his face in it [Perception that the Prophet's waste was considered sanctified]. If he gives them an order, they vie with each other to carry it out [because both good deeds and martyrdom are virtuous].'"

Ishaq:502: "[Urwah said,] 'Muhammad, you have collected a mix group of people and brought them to your kin to destroy them. By Allah, I see both prominent people and rabble who are likely to flee, deserting you tomorrow.' Now Abu Bakr [Future Caliph], who was standing behind the Apostle, said, 'Go suck the clitoris of Al-Lat!' [...] Whenever Urwah extended his hand toward the Prophet's beard, Mughira struck his hand with the lower end of his scabbard and said, 'Take your hand away from his beard before you lose it!' Urwah raised his head and said, 'Who is this?' They said, 'Mughira.' Urwah said, 'Rude man, I am trying to rectify your act of treachery.' During the Time of Ignorance [Jahiliyyah] Mughira had accompanied some men and killed them, taking their money. [...] The Apostle just smiled [at the verbal exchange between Mughira, the murderer, and Urwah]."

Tabari VIII:82: "Allah's Messenger summoned Uthman and sent him to Abu Sufyan and the dignitaries of the Quraysh to inform them that they had come not for war but merely to visit the House [Ka'aba] and venerate its sanctity. When Uthman delivered the message, the Quraysh said, 'If you wish to circumambulate the Temple [Ka'aba], do so.' He replied, 'I will not do it until the Messenger does.' So the Quraysh imprisoned him. [...] When Muhammad received a report that Uthman had been killed, he said, 'We will not leave until we fight it out with the enemy.' He summoned the people to swear allegiance. The Prophet's crier announced: 'People, an oath of allegiance! The Holy Spirit has descended!'"

HUDNA: A TEMPORARY TRUCE

Ishaq:503: "On the day of Hudabiyah we swore allegiance to Messenger while Umar was holding his hand under the acacia tree. It was a pledge unto death. [...] Allah saw what was in their hearts so He rewarded them with victory and with as much spoil [booty] they could take. Allah promised that they would soon capture a great deal of [even more] booty."

Ishaq:504: "The Quraysh intended peace when they sent Suhayl to Muhammad. He spoke for some time. He spoke for some time and they negotiated with each another. When the matter had been arranged and only the writing of the document remained, Umar jumped up and went to Abu Bakr and said, 'Isn't he the Messenger of Allah?' 'Yes,' Bakr replied. 'And are we not Muslims?' Umar asked. 'Yes,' answered Abu Bakr. 'And are they not polytheists?' he [Umar] asked. 'Yes,' [Abu Bakr replied.] 'Then why,' asked Umar, 'should we grant what is demeaning to our religion?' Umar jumped up and went to the Prophet [and said,] 'Are you not the Messenger of Allah?' 'Yes,' Muhammad replied. 'Are we not Muslims?' Umar asked the Prophet. 'Yes,' Muhammad replied. 'Then why should we grant what is detrimental to our religion,' Umar asked. He [Muhammad] replied, 'I am Allah's Messenger. I will not disobey and He will not allow me to perish.' [...] Suhayl said [after completing the treaty of Hudabiyah], 'You shall go back, leaving us this year and not enter Mecca. When the next year comes, we will go out, and you shall enter Mecca with your companions and stay for three nights. Your swords must remain in scabbards. You shall not enter with [any] other weapons.'"

Tabari VIII:85: "The Prophet summoned me [Ali] and said, 'Write: "In the name of Allah, Ar-Rahman and Ar-Rahim."' Suhayl said, 'I do not know Ar-Rahman or Ar-Rahim. Should I write rather, "In Thy name, O Allah"?' So Muhammad said, 'Write: "In Ty name, O Allah."' So I wrote it. [...] He said, 'Write: "Muhammad, the Messenger of Allah, has made peace with Suhayl."' Suhayl said, 'If I testified that you were the Messenger of Allah, I wouldn't fight you. Why not write your name and the name of your father.' So Muhammad said, 'Write: "Muhammad bin Abdullah has made peace with Suhayl."'"

Tabari VIII:86: "They agreed to terms: Warfare shall be laid aside for ten years [Hudna], during which men can be safe and refrain from hostilities.

[...] During this time whoever comes to Muhammad from the Quraysh without permission [...], Muhammad shall return him to them; and whoever shall come to the Quraysh from those who are with Muhammad [Muslims], they shall not return him to Muhammad. There shall be neither clandestine theft nor betrayal."

SUMMATION:

IL: The Hudna was signed. The hypocrite Muslims were warned in revelation that they would gain great riches from future conquests. So with their allegiance to Muhammad confirmed, Allah promised them there would be much booty to collect in the battles, wars and subsequent conflicts. Allah restated the goal of Islam: Islam will prevail over all other religions. In order to accomplish this goal, Muslims must be fierce to non-Muslims, but considerate to one another.

WA: This section starts with another murder. In order to make it right, Muhammad agreed that compensation must be paid which included: (1) Property the Muslims gained from others in Jihad; and (2) a Christian slave girl. Think about these gifts. Muhammad gave stolen property and a slave girl to another person as appropriate measures of just compensation. In the march towards Mecca, Muhammad's goal was to defeat his relatives. He knew if Mecca fell, all of Arabia would be his for the taking. In his encounter with the Meccan Urwah, Abu-Bakr's language relieved the Muslims of any sanctity. Mughira, who reverted to Islam, was a murderer before he entered Islam. This meant that his life was meaningless. As a Muslim, his intention was still set on violence.

Muslims were then confronted at Hudabiyah by the Quraysh; so Muhammad was ready to bide his time. In verse 27 Muhammad injected himself into the Qur'anic revelation when he declared, "If Allah permits...He knows... He has ordained." Allah wouldn't say "If Allah permits or speak, He knows..." Why would Allah speak in the third person?[6] Muhammad then promised, those eager to fight with him, more booty. Khalid, the Muslim who declared himself the "Sword of Allah," won the initial encounter, but the Muslims could not take Mecca. During negotiations, a Meccan asked Muhammad how he could justify the killing of his own kinsman. Afterward, a ten-year Hudna was ratified. In the agreement they promised not to attack one another.

QUR'AN 60

"The Woman Who Is Examined"

628 AD

SCRIPTURE:

Qur'an 60:8-9

Bukhari:V4B52N41-V4B52N43, V4B52N50, V4B50N317; Ishaq:505, 508, 752; Tabari VIII:87, 89-97

PREFACE:

In the original Hudabiyah treaty, Muslims were required to return any women who came to them and wanted to leave the Quraysh. In this surah, Allah arbitrarily changed the conditions of the original treaty, stating if the women coming to the Muslims were sincere reverts to Islam, then the Muslims did not have to return them. This rationale is as follows; the Quraysh, the other party to the Hudabiyah treaty, really wanted Islam to be destroyed, because they were in a state of war with the Muslims. Therefore, Muslims should not enter treaties with those who seek Islam's destruction. Based on this, Allah could amend the treaty without the consent of the Quraysh. Women who were shown to revert to Islam were to be kept in the Muslim camp. Also, the amendment was allowed because the treaty, i.e. armistice, did not negate the original call for Jihad; furthermore, the armistice [Hudna] could not last more than 10 years.[7]

SURAH:

Qur'an 60:8-9: "Allah forbids you not respecting those who fight you not for religion [Allah allows you to respect an enemy who does not fight you for religion], nor drive you forth from your homes [or try to drive you from your homes], that you show them kindness and deal with them justly. Surely Allah loves the doers of justice. [However,] Allah forbids you only respecting those who fight you for religion [Allah forbids you from respecting an enemy who fights you for religion], and drive you forth from your homes and help others to your expulsion [or drives you forth from your homes and helps others in order to expel you], that you make friends of them; and whoever makes friends of them, these are the wrongdoers."

SUNNAH:

Ishaq:505: "[...], when they [the Companions] saw the negotiations for peace, the retreat, and the obligations [conditions] the Messenger agreed to—the Muslims felt so grieved about it that they were close to despair. Some were depressed to the point of death. [...] Umar jumped up, walking beside Jandal, and saying, 'Be patient. They are only pagans, and the blood of any of them is no more than the blood of a dog!' Umar held the hilt of his sword close to him. He said, 'I hoped he would take the sword and kill his father with it.' But Jandal was too attached to his father to kill him. [...]" "When the Prophet finished the document...the Prophet was encamped in the profane territory [...]. When the peace was concluded he slaughtered his victims and sat down and shaved his head [...]."

Tabari VIII:87: "[...] Abu Jandal, the son of Suhayl, came in shackles. He had escaped to the Muslims. When Suhayl saw Jandal, he struck him and grabbed his garment. He [Suhayl] said, 'Muhammad, the pact was ratified between me and you before he came to you.' 'You are right,' He [Muhammad] replied. Suhayl began dragging his son by his robe. Jandal began screaming at the top of his voice, 'Muslims, shall I be returned to the polytheists so that they can entice me from my religion?' The Messenger said, 'Abu Jandal, count on a reward, Allah will give you a way out. We have made a treaty, and we will not act treacherously toward them.' [...]"

INTENT ON VIOLATING THE TREATY

Ishaq:508: "Abu Jandal, Suhayl's son, escaped and joined Abu Basir. Nearly seventy Muslim men gathered around them and they harassed the Quraysh. Whenever they heard of a Meccan caravan setting out for Syria, they intercepted it, and killed everyone they could get hold of. They tore every caravan to pieces and took the goods. [...]"

THE MURDER OF UMM QIRFAH

Tabari VIII:89-90: "When the Messenger had finished his pact, he said to his Companions, 'Arise, sacrifice, and shave.' Not a man stood even after he had said it three times. When no one stood up, Muhammad went into Umm's tent and told her what he had encountered from the Muslims. She said, 'Do you approve of this? Go out, and speak not a word to any of them until you have slaughtered your fattened camel and summoned your shaver to shave you.' When they [the Muslims] saw this, they rose, slaughtered, and shaved until they almost killed each other in grief. [...] Abu Basir was a Muslim confined in Mecca. He escaped and headed to Medina. There, the Prophet told Basir, 'We have given these people our word. Breaking a promise is not right in our religion.' Abu Basir went out with his Companions. When they stopped to rest, he [Abu Basir] asked one of them, 'Is this sword of yours sharp.' 'Yes,' he replied. 'May I look at it,' Basir asked. Basir unsheathed the sword, attacked the man, and killed him. The other Muslim ran back to the Messenger, saying, 'Your Companion has killed my friend.' While the man was still there, Abu appeared girded with the sword. He [Basir] halted before Muhammad and said, 'Messenger, your obligation has been discharged.' The Prophet said, 'Woe to his mother—the kindler of war's fire.'"

Tabari VIII:91: "When word of how Abu Basir killed his companion reached Suhayl, he leaned his head back against the Ka'aba and said, 'I will not move until they pay blood money for this man.' 'By Allah,' a Quraysh man said, 'they will never pay.'"

INSHALLAH...JIHAD

Tabari VIII:92: "On that day Umar divorced two women who had been his wives in polytheism. Thus, he forbade them to send the women back, but commanded them to return the bride price. Then Mu'ayt emigrated to the Messenger. Her brother went to the Prophet and asked him to return her to them according to the treaty of Hudabiyah. But he did not do so. Allah rejected it."

Bukhari:V4B52N41-V4B52N43: "I asked Allah's Apostle, 'O Allah's Apostle! What is the best deed?' He replied, 'To offer the prayers at their early stated fixed times.' I asked, 'What is next in goodness?' He replied, 'To be good and dutiful to your parents.' I further asked, 'What is next in goodness?' He replied, 'To participate in Jihad in Allah's Cause.' [...] Allah's Apostle said, 'There is no Hijrah [i.e., migration] (from Mecca to Medina) after the Conquest (of Mecca), but Jihad and good intention remain; and if you are called (by the Muslim ruler) for fighting, go forth immediately.' Aisha said, 'O Allah's Apostle! We consider Jihad as the best deed. Should we not fight in Allah's Cause?' He said, 'The best Jihad for women is Hajj-Mabrur (i.e., Hajj which is done according to the Prophet's tradition and is accepted by Allah).'"

Bukhari:V4B52N50: "The Prophet said, 'A single endeavor (of fighting) in Allah's Cause in the forenoon or in the afternoon is better than the world and whatever is in it.'"

Tabari VIII:93: "[...], the Messenger sent out Ukkashah with forty men to raid Ghamr. He traveled quickly, but the enemy became aware and fled. He sent out scouts and they captured a spy who guided them to some of their cattle. They took two hundred head [of cattle alive] back to Medina. [...] The Messenger sent out Muhammad Maslama with ten men. The enemy lay in wait for them until he and his companions went to sleep. Before they suspected anything, the Muslims were killed; Muhammad escaped, wounded. [...] The Messenger dispatched the raiding party of Abu Ubaydah with forty men. They [...] reached Qassah just before dawn. They raided the inhabitants [...]. They took cattle, clothes and a man. [...] a raiding party led by Zayd went to Jamum. He captured a Muzaynah woman named Hamilah. She guided them to an encampment of the Banu Sulaym where they captured cattle, sheep, and prisoners. Among the captives was Hamilah's husband. When Zayd brought back what he had taken, the Prophet granted the woman and her husband their freedom."

Tabari VIII:94: "In this year a raiding party led by Zayd went to al-Is. During it, Abu As'b's property was taken. [...] A fifteen-man raiding party led by Zayd went to Taraf against the Banu Tha'labah. The Bedouins fled, fearing that Allah's Messenger had set out against them. Zayd took twenty camels from their herds. He was away four nights.

Tabari VIII:95: "In this year a raiding party led by Abd al-Rahman bin Awf went to Dumat. The Messenger said to him, 'If they obey you, marry the king's daughter. [...] In this year a raiding party led by Ali went to Fadak with a hundred men against the clan of the Banu Sa'd. This was because the Prophet received information that a force of theirs intended to aid the Jews of Khaybar. [...]"

Tabari VIII:96: "A raiding party led by Zayd set out against Umm in the month of Ramadan. During it, Umm suffered a cruel death. [...] She was a very old woman. [...] Umm's story is as follows. Allah's Messenger sent Zayd to Wadi Qura where he encountered the Banu Fazarah. Some of his Companions were killed, and Zayd was carried away wounded. [...] When Zayd returned, he vowed that no washing should touch his head until he has raided the Banu Fazarah. After he recovered, Muhammad sent him with an army against the Fazarah settlement. He met them in Qura and inflicted casualties on them and took Umm Qirfah prisoner. He also took one of Umm's daughters and Abdallah bin Mas'adah prisoner. Zayd bin Harithah ordered Qays to kill Umm, and he killed her cruelly. He tied each of her legs with a rope and tied the ropes to two camels, and they split her in two. Then they brought Umm's daughter and Abdallah to the Messenger. Umm's daughter belonged to Salama who had captured her. Muhammad asked Salama for her, and Salama gave her to him."

IGNORING THE TREATY

Bukhari:V4B52N317: "When the Prophet returned (from Jihad), he would say Takbir thrice and add, 'We are returning, if Allah wishes, with repentance and worshipping and praising (our Lord) and prostrating ourselves before our Lord. Allah fulfilled His Promise and helped His Slave, and He alone defeated the (infidel) clans.'"

Tabari VIII:97: "The Messenger appointed Abu Bakr as our commander, and we raided some of the Banu Fazarah. When we came near the watering place, we went down to the watering hole and there we killed some people. I saw some women and children among them, who had almost outstripped us [...] Among them was a woman of the Banu Fazarah. [...] With her was her daughter, among the fairest of the Arabs. Abu Bakr gave me her daughter as booty. [...] When I returned to Medina, the Prophet met me in the market and said, 'Salama—how excellent the father who begot you! Give me the women.' I said, 'Holy Prophet of Allah, I like her, and have not uncovered her garment.' Muhammad said nothing to me until the next day. He again met me in the market and said, 'Salama, give me the woman.' I said, 'Prophet, I have not uncovered her garment but she is yours.' Muhammad sent her to Mecca, and with her he ransomed some Muslim captives who were in the hands of the Quraysh."

SLAUGHTERING THE JEWS

Ishaq:752: "[…] when [after] the Apostle got the better of the sons of the Qurayza [the last Jewish tribe of Medina], he seized [400] men from the Jews who had been allies of [the] Aus [an Arab tribe in Medina] against [the] Khazraj [Arab enemies of the Aus], and ordered that they should be beheaded. Accordingly Khazraj began to cut off their heads with great satisfaction. The Apostle saw that the faces of [the] Khazraj showed pleasure but there was no such indication on the part of [the] Aus, and he [Muhammad] suspected that was because of the alliance that had existed between them and the B. Qurayza. When there were only [12] of them [Jews] left he gave them over to [the] Aus, assigning one Jew to every two of Aus, saying, 'Let so-and-so [one of you] strike him and let so-and-so [the other] finish him off.'

SUMMATION:

IL: Those who do not fight or oppose Muslims for their religion can be respected; however, if an enemy rejected Islam and drove Muslims from the land, a Muslim may never be friendly with them. Although the treaty was signed, Allah's revelation showed that Muslims could not honor a treaty against this Quraysh enemy which was hostile towards Islam and was guilty of driving the Muslims from their homes.

WA: When the vast majority of Muslims came to understand the terms of the Hudabiyah treaty, they clearly did not like it or want peace it was supposed to provide. Why? They believed a pagan's blood was worth no more than the blood of a dog. This is why Muslim literalists can kill others so easily. Their victims are not their equals and deserve death. Umar, the future Caliph, desired that a son murder his father. This could never be considered righteous behavior in Western society. Next, other Muslims went out to raid every caravan they could find and then bragged they killed everyone in their search for the property of those murdered.

The Muslims moved to a non-Meccan profane area after the treaty was signed. There, they came in contact with non-Meccan non-Muslims. Muhammad decided to slaughter them. Afterward he shaved his head. This behavior could only mean that Muhammad did not have peace in his heart. Obviously those not obliged by the treaty were still fair game. As for his companions, they followed the example of their Prophet. The treaty was just signed and immediately a Muslim, who was not in favor of it, murdered a polytheist who wanted to become Muslim. Rather than allow Muhammad to return him, Badir stabbed the captive to death. Suhayl wanted blood money paid. Not only was it not paid, but the Muslim Badir was not punished for killing a non-Muslim. After Umar divorced two wives, Allah decided He was not going to honor the treaty. So Muslims set out against other Arabs. Over and over again, Muslims killed and took the booty of those who resisted them. Against the Fazarah, an old woman, Umm Qirfa, was captured. Umm Qirfa had an especially cruel death. Her legs were tied with rope and the rope attached to each leg was tied to two camels [...] then she was split in two. Afterwards, her daughter was given to another Muslim and then to Muhammad. Muhammad demanded her in order to exchange her for Muslim prisoners the Quraysh had in their possession. Muhammad, knowing full well that a peace treaty was signed, stated Jihad was the holiest endeavor in which a Muslim could participate.

Ishaq then records another massacre of Jews. Some think that this is another rehash of the slaughter of the Banu Qaynuqa; however, if that is true, then Ishaq:752 and Ishaq:464 contradict each other. These accounts, which are from the same source, give different details, including the victims, who differ in count by 500 murdered Jews. Let's put it this way. If Muhammad could participate in the beheading of 900 Jews, could he also be capable of directing Arab tribes to butcher another 400 Jews who escaped the earlier slaughter? In his campaign, he forced people who wanted no part of the slaughter to strike decapitating blows against defenseless Jews.

QUR'AN 49

"The Apartments"

628 AD

SCRIPTURE:

Qur'an 49:15

Bukhari:V8B82N794, V8B82N797; Tabari VIII:98, 100, 104, 108-110

PREFACE:

This surah dealt with the phenomena of Arabs who came from the four corners of Arabia to pledge their allegiance to Muhammad. Muslims are admonished to make peace among themselves. Living in ease and comfort in civilized societies are denounced as vices. Finally, Muslims were to perform good manners towards the Prophet.[8]

SURAH:

Qur'an 49:15: "The believers are those only who believe in Allah and His Messenger, [and] then they doubt not, and struggle hard with their wealth and their lives in the way of Allah [Jihad]. Such are the truthful ones."

SUNNAH:

RADICAL ISLAMIC JUSTICE

Bukhari:V8B82N794, V8B82N797: "Eight Muslims from the clan of Uraynah were brought to Muhammad for murdering a camel Shepherd. Their eyes were gouged out with hot irons; their feet and hands were chopped off on opposite sides. Their remaining limbs were nailed to the desert floor, water was withheld until death. Some people of the Uraynah tribe came to Medina. When Muhammad learned that they did not like the climate. So Muhammad ordered them to drink the milk and urine of camels […]. They killed the shepherd of the Prophet and drove away the camels. When the news reached Muhammad he sent men to capture them. After they were captured and returned to Muhammad he ordered that their hands and feet be cut off on opposite sides. After this was done their eyes were branded with hot irons. They were crucified at Al-Harrah [Qur'an 5:33] and water was withheld from them until they died."

INVITING INFIDELS TO ISLAM

Tabari VIII:98: "[…] a raiding party led by Kurz set out against the members of the Banu Uraynah with twenty horsemen. […], the Messenger dispersed some of his Companions to the kings of the Arabs and the foreigners to call them to Allah. He sent a letter to Ibn Shihab. The letter stated: 'I have been sent as a mercy and for all. Therefore, convey the message from me, and Allah shall have mercy on you. Do not become disobedient to me as the Disciples became disobedient to Jesus. He called them to the like of what I called you to. […] Jesus complained of their behavior to Allah, and when they awoke the next morning, each [of them] could speak the language of the people to whom he had been sent. Then Jesus said, 'This is an affair that Allah has determined for you; so go forth.'"

Tabari VIII:100: "The Prophet sent Hatib to Muqawqis, the ruler of Alexandria. Hatib delivered the letter of the Prophet, and Muqawqis gave Allah's Apostle four slave girls. The Messenger sent Dihyah to Caesar who was Heraclius, the king of the Romans [Byzantines] When Dihyah brought him the letter, he looked into it and then placed it between his thighs and his flanks. [Meanwhile, in Mecca,] Abu Sufyan said, 'We were merchants but the fighting between us and Muhammad has prevented us from journeying, so our wealth is [now] depleted. Even after the truce with the Muslims, we fear that we still are not safe. Nevertheless, I will set out with a group of merchants for Gaza.'"

Tabari VIII:104: "Heraclius received the following letter from the Messenger: 'In the name of Allah, Ar-Rahman, Ar-Rahim. From Muhammad, the Messenger of Allah, to Heraclius, the ruler of the Romans

[Byzantines]. Peace to whoever follows the right guidance! To proceed; Submit yourself, and you shall be safe.'"

Tabari VIII:108-110: "'In the name of Allah, Ar-Rahman, and Ar-Rahim. From Muhammad, the Messenger of Allah, to Negus, king of the Ethiopians. May you be at peace. […] I bear witness that Jesus son of Mary […] whom Allah created from His Spirit and breathed into him, even as He created Adam by His hand and breathed into him. I call you to Allah alone, Who has no partner, to continued obedience to Him, and that you follow me and believe in what has come to me; for I am the Messenger of Allah. I call you and your armies to Allah.' [After Muhammad married a slave girl sent by the Ethiopians Abu Sufyan commented] When Abu Sufyan learned that the Prophet married her, he said, 'That stallion's nose is not to be restrained!'"

SUMMATION:

IL: A true Muslim acknowledges Allah, Muhammad, spends their wealth for Jihad, and is willing to die for Islam. Muhammad, the Prophet, then sent and invited Arab Christians, Coptic Christians, Orthodox Christians, and Ethiopian Christians to faith in Allah alone. None of these unbelievers answered the Dawah to Islam. Rejecting Islam placed them against Islam. Those who are against Islam are the enemies of Muslims.

WA: One cannot take issue that Muhammad put murderers to death; however, one can take issue in how he desired to achieve their execution. Chopping off limbs, crucifixion, blinding with hot irons, and withholding water, go beyond the realm of capital punishment and turns into grievous torture. We do not know if the camel shepherd was tortured, but how can one call himself "a mercy to all humanity" and inflict this kind of punishment onto another human being? The one who considered himself a mercy continued to send raiding expeditions. Muhammad's actions and his references to Jesus and the disciples continued to part ways with the New Testament. Muhammad seemed to have another motive attached to his invitations to join Islam. Muhammad continued to accept slave girl concubines. It was obvious that Abu Sufyan and the Meccans knew that Muhammad desired many women.

"The Shaking"

628 AD

SCRIPTURE:

Qur'an 99:6-8

Bukhari:V4B55N547; Ishaq:510-512, 514-515, 517-519, 521, 522, 524; Muslim:B8C14N3329; Tabari VIII:116-117, 119, 124-125, 128-130; Dawud:B14N2482

PREFACE:

This surah speaks of the "earthquake" in Arabia that would not only transform Arabia but the world. Muhammad was establishing the Kingdom of Heaven on earth. Those who oppose this reality face doom because of their lack of belief. Islamic belief was promised to rise and all efforts to oppose it would fail. The disgrace that the opponents of Islam must face is eventual subjugation...to the Muslim world.[9]

SURAH:

Qur'an 99:6-8: "On that day mankind will come forth in sundry bodies [scattered groups] that they make be shown their works [to be shown their deeds]. So he who does an atom's weight of good will see it. And he who does an atom's weight of evil will see it."

DESTROYING THE JEWS AT KHAYBAR

Ishaq:510: "After his return from Hudabiyah, Allah's Messenger marched against Khaybar. He halted with his army in a valley between the people of Khaybar and the Ghatafan tribe to prevent the latter from assisting the Jews. [...] When the Apostle looked down on Khaybar he told his Companions, 'O Allah, Lord of the heavens and what they overshadow, and the Lord of Devils and what error they throw, and Lord of the winds and what they winnow, we ask Thee for the booty of this town and its people. We take refuge in Thee from its evil and the evil of its people. [Go] forward in the name of Allah.' He used to say this of every town he raided."

Ishaq:511: "When the Apostle raided a people he waited until morning, and then he attacked. [...] We met the workers of Khaybar coming out in the morning with their spades and baskets. When they saw the Prophet and our army, they [...] turned tail and fled. The Apostle yelled, 'Allahu Akbar! Khaybar is destroyed.' When we arrive at a people's square, it is a bad morning for them [...] The Prophet took some of its people captive including Safiyah, the wife of Kinana and her two cousins [...] The Prophet traded for Safiyah (wife of Kinana) by giving Dihiyah her two cousins. The women of Khaybar were distributed among the Muslims.

Ishaq:512: "The Apostle prohibited [a number of] things the morning of the Khaybar raid: Intercourse with captured pregnant women, mingling his seed with another man's [i.e., a Muslim could not have sex with a captured women right after another Muslim had her]; nor is it lawful for him to take [have sex with] her [a captured woman] until she is in a state of cleanliness [not while she is menstruating]; nor can a Muslim eat the flesh of donkeys, nor eat a carnivorous animal; nor sell any booty before it has been duly allotted. [...]"

Ishaq:514: "Encamped at their fortress, Muhammad presented his war banner to Abu Bakr and sent him against the Jews. He fought but he retreated, suffering losses. The following morning the same thing happened to Umar. When they returned to Muhammad, Umar's companions accused him of cowardice, and he accused them of the same. [...] The next day

Bakr and Umar vied for the war banner, but the Prophet called Ali, who was suffering from inflamed eyes, and, having spat on his eyes, gave him the war banner. Ali advanced against the people of Khaybar. [...] he fought until Allah gave Muslims the victory. [...]"

Tabari VIII:116-117: "[...] So Muhammad began seizing their herds and their property bit by bit. He conquered Khaybar home by home. The first stronghold defeated was Naim. Next was Qamus, the community of Abi Huqayq. The Messenger took some of its people captive including Safiyah, the wife of Kinana and her two cousins. The Prophet chose Safiyah for himself. [...] Dihyah had asked the Messenger for Safiyah when the Prophet chose her for himself. Muhammad gave Dihyah her two cousins instead. [...] The Banu Sahm of Aslam came to the Messenger and complained, 'Muhammad, we have been hurt by drought and possess nothing.' Although they had fought for the Prophet they found he had nothing to give them. The Apostle said, 'O Allah, You know their condition—I have no strength and nothing to give them. So conquer for them the wealthiest of the Khaybar homes, the ones with the most food and fat meat.' [...] The next morning Allah opened the township of Sa'ib bin Mu'adh for them to conquer. There was no stronghold [community] in Khaybar more abounding in food. After the Prophet had defeated some of their settlements and taken their property, they reached the communities of Watib and Sulalim, which were the last of the Khaybar neighborhoods to be conquered. Muhammad besieged the inhabitants between thirteen and nineteen nights."

Tabari VIII:119: "The Messenger often had migraines and would remain a day or two without coming out. When Muhammad encamped at Khaybar, he came down with a migraine and did not come out. Bakr took the Prophet's war banner and fought vigorously. Next, Umar took it, and fought with even more ferocity than the first fighting."

THE TORTURE AND DEATH OF KINANA

Ishaq:515: "[...] Ali struck the Jew with a swift blow that split his helmet, neck protector, and head, landing on his rear teeth. And the Muslims entered the city. Muhammad conquered Qamus, the Jewish neighborhood of Abi Huqayq. Safiyah [...] was brought to him, and another woman with her. Bilal led them past some of the Jews we had slain including the woman's dead husband. When she saw them, the woman with Safiyah cried out, slapped her face, and poured dust on her head. When Allah's Prophet saw her, he said, 'Take this she-devil away from me!' [...] Muhammad commanded that Safiyah should be kept behind him and he threw his cloak over her. Thus, the Muslims knew that he had chosen her for himself.

Abi Huqayq [Safiyah's father] held the treasure of the Nadir [the second Jewish tribe expelled from Medina]. He was brought to Allah's Messenger, and he questioned him. But Huqayq denied knowing where it was. So the Prophet questioned the other Jews. One said, 'I have seen Kinana [Safiyah's husband] walking around a ruin.' Muhammad had Kinana brought to him and said, 'Do you know that if we find it, I shall kill you.' 'Yes,' Kinana answered. [...] The Prophet commanded that the ruin be dug up. Some treasure was extracted from it. Then Muhammad asked Kinana for the rest. He refused to surrender it; so Allah's Messenger gave orders concerning him to Zubayr, saying, 'Torture him until you root out and extract what he has.' So Zubayr kindled a fire on Kinana's chest, twirling it with his fire stick until Kinana was near death. Then the Messenger gave him to Maslama, who beheaded him. [...] Allah's Apostle besieged the final [Jewish] community of Khaybar until they could hold out no longer. Finally, when they were certain that they would perish, they asked Muhammad to banish them and spare their lives, which he did. The Prophet took possession of all their property. [...] When the people of Fadak heard what had happened, they sent word to the Messenger, asking him to banish them and spare their lives, saying they too would leave him their property. When the people [Jews] of Khaybar surrendered on these conditions, the survivors asked Muhammad to employ them on their farms for half share of whatever they produced. So Muhammad made peace with them for a half share, provided that: 'If we want to expel you, we may.' He made a similar arrangement with Fadak. So Khaybar became the prey of the Muslims, while Fadak belonged exclusively to the Messenger of Allah, becoming his personal property, because the Muslims had not attacked its people with cavalry."

TAKING THE WIFE OF A MURDERED MAN

Muslim:B8C14N3329: "Safiyah fell to the lot of Dihya in the spoils of war, and they praised her in the presence of Allah's Messenger and said:

We have not seen the like of her among the captives of war. He sent (a messenger) to Dihya and he gave him whatever he demanded. He then sent her to my mother and asked her to embellish her. Allah's Messenger then got out of Khaybar until when he was on the other side of it, he halted, and a tent was pitched for him. When it was morning Allah's Messenger (may peace be upon him) said: He who has surplus of provision with him should bring that to us […] Anas said that that constituted the wedding feast of Allah's Messenger […] And Safiyah was at his back, and Allah's Messenger had seated her behind him. The camel of Allah's Messenger stumbled and he (the Holy Prophet) fell down and she also fell down. And none among the people was seeing him and her, until Allah's Messenger stood up and he covered her, and we came to him and he said: We have received no injury. We entered Medina and there came out the young ladies of the household. They saw her (Hadrat Safiyah) and blamed her for falling down."

Ishaq:517: "When the Apostle married Safiyah on his way out of town, she was beautified and combed, putting her in a fitting state for the Messenger. The Apostle passed the night with her in his tent. Abu Ayyub, girt with his sword, guarded the Apostle, going round the tent until he saw him emerge in the morning. Abu said, 'I was afraid for you with this woman for you have killed her father, her husband, and her people. [The following is a poem about Khaybar:] Khaybar was stormed by the Apostle's squadron, fully armed, powerful, and strong. It brought certain humiliation with Muslim men in its midst. We attacked and they met their doom. Muhammad conquered the Jews in fighting that day as they opened their eyes to our dust."

COMPASSION FOR FALLEN MUSLIMS

Dawud:B14N2482: "A veiled women came to Muhammad as she was looking for her son who had been killed on the battlefield. Muhammad asked her, 'You have come here asking for your son while veiling your face?' She replied, 'If I am afflicted with the loss of my son, I shall not suffer the loss of my modesty.' Muhammad responded, 'You will get the reward of two martyrs for your son, because the People of the Book [Jews] have killed him.'"

Ishaq:518: "Mas'ud was one of those who found martyrdom at Khaybar. Muhammad said, 'He has with him now his two dark-eyed virgins. When a martyr is slain, his two virgins pet him, wiping the dust from his face. They say, "May Allah throw dust on the face of the man who did this to you, and slay him who slew you!'"

TRUTH IS OPTIONAL

Ishaq:519: "Hajjaj said to the Apostle, 'I have money scattered among the Meccan merchants, so give me permission to go and get it.' Having got Muhammad's permission, he said, 'I must tell lies.' The Apostle said, 'Tell them.'"

POISONING THE PROPHET

Tabari VIII:123: "When the Messenger rested from his labor, Zaynab, the wife of Sallam, served him a roast sheep. She had asked what part Muhammad liked best and was told that it was the shoulder and foreleg. So she loaded it with poison, also poisoning the rest. Then she placed it before him. He took the foreleg and chewed it, but he did not swallow. With him was Bishr, who like the Prophet, took some, but he swallowed it. The Prophet spat out the lamb saying, 'This bone informs me that it has been poisoned.' ...Muhammad summoned the woman, and she confessed. He asked, 'What led you to do this?' She said, 'You know full well what you have done to my people.'"

Ibn Sa'd:N249: "The Apostle of Allah and his companions ate from it. It [the goat] said: 'I am poisoned.' He [Muhammad] said to his companions, 'Hold your hands! It has informed me that it is poisoned!' They withdrew their hands, but Bishr Ibn al-Bara expired. The Apostle of Allah sent for her (the Jewess) and asked her, 'What induced you to do what you have done? She replied, 'I wanted to know if you are a prophet, in that case, it will not harm you, and if you are a king, I shall relieve the people of you.' He gave orders and she was put to death."

Tabari VIII:124: "The Messenger during the illness from which he died, said to Bishr's mother, 'Umm, at this very moment I feel my aorta being severed because of the food I ate with your son at Khaybar.' [...] The Muslims believed that in addition to the honor of prophethood, the Messenger died a martyr.' [...] Having finished with Khaybar, the

Apostle went to Wadi Qura and besieged its people for a while. Then we headed back to Medina. [...] With Muhammad was a slave lad of his [...]. Suddenly, as we were setting down the saddle of the Prophet, a stray arrow came and struck the slave boy killing him. We congratulated him, saying, 'May he enjoy Paradise!' But Allah's Apostle said, 'Certainly not! The sheet of cloth on his back is now being burnt on him in Hell Fire! He pilfered [stole] it from the booty of the Muslims following the Khaybar raid before it was duly distributed.'"

JEWISH WEALTH BECOMES BOOTY FOR MUSLIMS

Tabari VIII:128: "Khaybar was divided among the people who had been at Hudabiyah."

Ishaq:521: "Khaybar was apportioned among the men of Hudabiyah without regard to whether they were present at Khaybar or not. The spoil was divided into 1,800 shares. [...] When the spoil of Khaybar was apportioned, the settlements of Shaqq and Nata were given to the Muslims while Katiba was divided into five sections: Allah's fifth; the Prophet's fifth; a fifth for Muhammad's relatives, a fifth for the maintenance of the Prophet's wives, a fifth for the men who acted as intermediaries in the peace negotiation with Fadak."

Ishaq:522: "Then the Apostle distributed the booty between his relatives, his wives, and other men and women. [...] Muhammad, the Apostle of Allah, gave his wives from the dates and wheat of Khaybar: 180 loads [in total]."

Ishaq:524: "[...] We cannot accept the oaths of Jews. Their infidelity is so great they swear falsely. [...]"

Bukhari:V4B55N547: "The Prophet said, 'But for the Israelis [If it were not for the Israelis], meat would not decay and but for Eve [if not for Eve], wives would never betray their husbands.'"

Tabari VIII:129: "After the Messenger had finished with the Khaybar Jews [most of the males were executed], Allah cast *terror* [emphasis added] into the hearts of the [Jews of] Fadak when the received news of what Allah had brought upon Khaybar [...] Fadak became the exclusive property of Allah's Messenger."

Tabari VIII:130: "The Messenger said during his final illness, 'Two religions cannot exist in the Arabian Peninsula.' Umar investigated the matter, then sent to the Jews [of Fadak], saying: 'Allah has given permission for you to be expelled; for I have received word that the Prophet said that two religions cannot coexist in Arabia.'"

SUMMATION:

IL: The Jewish perversion of Allah's intentions lead to global decay. The Jews are responsible for this global calamity. Eve, the first woman, betrayed her husband and brought a curse on all women. Muhammad's kingdom will come and usher a great judgment. This judgment against the Jews occurred at Khaybar and fulfilled Allah's promise found in 48:19-20. This prediction was given after the Hudabiyah treaty.

WA: Although the Jews were defeated in Arabia, they continued to be dehumanized by their Muslim victors. Deeds determine ones fate and those deeds must conform to Islamic principles. All people will be judged by the Islamic order. The implementation of this Islamic order is the proximate motivation of contemporary Islamists.

At Khaybar Muhammad was still worried about the Ghatafan, who were allied with the Quraysh, so he placed his army between the Jews at Khaybar and the Ghatafan. At this juncture the displaced Jews from Medina were no threat to Muhammad. Muhammad's diatribe against them and the others he raided included calling those who opposed him evil. According to his definition, if one opposed him or rejected Islam, they were evil and an attack against them was justified. Muhammad's headaches, possibly his conscience, prevented him from leading the attack. Ali was credited with breaking through the Jewish defenses after Muhammad spit in his eyes. After the fall of Khaybar, Muhammad made some new rules. Muslims could have sex with married Jewish women and widowed Jewish women, but not pregnant Jewish women. The Muslims could not have sex with women who were menstruating. Also, Muslims could not have sex with a Jewish woman right after another Muslim had sex with her. In other words, Muhammad regulated the ravishing of Jewish women at Khaybar.

This also showed why the Muslims looked forward to raiding. They would kill the men and then rape their women. Where can love be found in any of this? Sadly it cannot. As for Muhammad, he chose Safiyah. Her father and husband were killed by Muhammad's order. Her husband Kinana was the treasurer accused of hiding the money that belonged to the Banu Nadir. They were booted from Medina a few years earlier and escaped with what Muhammad said they could have, but now Muhammad wanted it for himself. Kinana would not talk, so Zubayr built a fire on his chest until Kinana was near death. When he still would not talk, Maslama decapitated him. Muhammad then took Kinana's wife with him on the very day her husband and father were murdered by the Muslims. He had sex with her that evening.

After the conquest, the Muslims used the Jewish sex slaves to cook for them. Zaynab poisoned the meat in an attempt to kill Muhammad. Earlier she witnessed her husband, father, and uncle put to death.[10] All Zaynab had to look forward to, after all the men in her life were killed, was being forced to have sex with Arabs, who she detested. Under these circumstances, it is understandable—not justifiable, but understandable—why she tried to kill Muhammad. Muhammad forgave her for what she did to him, but executed her for poisoning to death his Companion. In Tabari VIII:123, he spat out the meat. In Tabari:124, thinking better of it, he claimed he swallowed it. In this way, the Prophet of Islam could claim martyrdom when he eventually died.

After these events concluded, Muhammad stated the virgins in Paradise chant they want the people who kill Muslims during Jihad to be slain. He also told Hajjaj that he could lie to remove his wealth from Mecca. Great detail was given to the division of booty; including how much the Muslims would get from the slain Jews. With little rest, the Muslims attacked Wadi Qura. On the way back from fighting, Muhammad's slave boy was killed by an arrow. Muhammad said afterward; the boy was burning in hell. The reason was the boy stole booty from the Muslims who stole from the Jews. So stealing stolen goods can be damning to Muslims. With more Jews being targeted, the Fadak Jews gave their wealth to Muhammad in hope that he would leave them alone. In addition, the authoritative sources state that Allah terrorized these Jews into compliance.

QUR'AN 13

"The Thunder"

629 AD

SCRIPTURE:

Qur'an 13:5, 7, 11, 27, 31-33, 38-39, 41, 43

Bukhari:V8B73N28

PREFACE:

Reward and punishment will be based upon those who obey Islamic Law and those who disobey, or reject, Islamic Law. More specifically, those who oppose the teaching of Muhammad will be punished. Through the implementation of Shari'a, the idolatrous nations will fall and the Islamic nation will rise. There will be no miracles in Islam except those that work inside of a person. The reading of the Qur'an will transform the person and these people will transform the world. Those who oppose the spread of Islam champion falsehood, but the truth of the Qur'an will triumph over them. The process spreading Islam will be slow but steady. In order for Islam to expand to the world, new abrogating verses had to be introduced. These verses would allow those who have been transformed by the Qur'an to dissimulate among those who live in falsehood in order to establish Shari'a in the lands of the idolaters.[11]

SURAH:

Qur'an 13:5: "[…] These are they who disbelieve in their Lord, and they have chains on their necks, and they are the companions of the Fire; in it they will abide."

Qur'an 13:7: "And those who disbelieve say: Why has not a sign been sent down to him from his Lord? Thou art only a warner and for every people a guide."

Qur'an 13:11: "Surely Allah changes not the condition of a people, until they change their own condition. And when Allah intends evil to a people, there is no averting it, and besides Him they have no protector."

Qur'an 13:27: "[...] Allah leaves in error whom He pleases [...]."

Qur'an 13:31-33: "[...] Do not those who believe know that, if Allah please [wanted], He would certainly guide all the people? And as for those who disbelieve, disaster will not cease to afflict them because of what they do [...]. And messengers [Allah's prophets] were certainly mocked [before you], but I gave respite to those who disbelieve [I endured those who disbelieve], then [finally] I seized them. How awful was then my requital [punishment]! [...], their plan is made fair-seeming [to seem reasonable] to those who disbelieve, and they are kept back from the path [truth]. And whom Allah leaves in error, he has no guide."

Qur'an 13:38: "[...] And it is not in the power of a messenger to bring a sign except by Allah's permission. [...]"

Qur'an 13:39: "Allah effaces [erases] what He pleases and establishes what He pleases, and with Him is the basis of the Book.

Qur'an 13:41, 43: "See they not that We are visiting the land, curtailing it of its sides [encircling it on all sides]? And Allah pronounces a doom — there is no [one who can repel] His decree. And He is Swift in calling to account. And those who disbelieve say: Thou [Muhammad] art not a Messenger. Say [Muhammad]: Allah is sufficient for a witness between me and you and whoever has knowledge of the Book [Bible]."

SUNNAH:

A SELFLESS SLAVE IS BELITTLED

Bukhari:V8B73N28: "Some Sabi (i.e., war prisoners, children and woman only) were brought before the Prophet and behold, a woman amongst them was milking her breasts to feed and whenever she found a child amongst the captives, she took it over her chest and nursed it (she had lost her child but later she found him) and the Prophet said to us, 'Do you think that this lady can throw her son in the fire?' We replied, 'No, if she has the power not to throw it (in the fire).' The Prophet then said, 'Allah is more merciful to His slaves than this lady to her son.'"

SUMMATION:

IL: By this time, all in the region heard of Islam's truth; therefore, the pronouncements were harsh on those who stubbornly resisted. Since they still questioned the resolve of the Prophet, they were encircled. When this happened their fate was sealed.

WA: Allah's Qur'an is, if anything, consistent. Those destined for hell will go there in chains. How can Allah intend evil and be a protector at the same time? There is no mention that Allah wanted to save all people; rather, Allah can lead anyone astray. Allah has no intention to guide all people. Why? Disaster must be visited upon all those who decide that Islam must be resisted. Knowing this, Allah will leave people in error. As abrogation was affirmed, the stage was set for the eventual onslaught at Mecca. The Meccan resistance was based on knowing Muhammad. He could not produce a miracle and craved the wealth of his relatives. Muhammad was not an abolitionist. All of his enemies, especially the Meccans, understood the possibility that they could eventually become Muhammad's slaves.

QUR'AN 55

"The Beneficent"

629 AD

SCRIPTURE:

Qur'an 55:33, 35, 41, 43, 56-58

Muslim:B37C4N6638

PREFACE:

This speaks of the rewards of those who favor what is pleasing to Allah and do not deny Allah's religion, Islam. It promises that Allah will look after one's physical welfare but will also guard and provide spiritual care. Finally, the guilty will be judged for rejecting the spiritual benefits that Allah has provided. Those who do rightly will receive those benefits. The subtlety being described is for the *Shahid* ("martyr"). This pleases Allah and, this obedience to Allah's law will bring spiritual benefits, i.e., "Gardens of Delight", for the Shahid.[12]

SURAH:

Qur'an 55:33, 35, 41, 43: "O assembly of Jinn and men, if you are able to pass through the regions of the heavens and the earth, then pass through. You cannot pass through but with authority [except with permission]. The flames of fire and sparks of brass will be sent upon you, then you will not be able to defend yourselves. The guilty will be known by their marks, so they shall be seized by the forelocks and the feet. This is the hell which the guilty deny."

Qur'an 55:56-58: "Therein are those restraining their glances [bashful virgins], whom no man nor jinn has touched before them."

SUNNAH:

PARADISE IS NOT GUARANTEED

Muslim:B37C4N6638: "Abu Huraira reported Allah's Messenger (May peace be upon him) as saying that a person committed sin beyond measure and when he was going to die, he left this will: '(When I die), burn my dead body and then cast them (the ashes) to the wind and in the ocean. By Allah, if my Lord takes hold of me, He would torment me as He has not tormented anyone else.' They did as he had asked them to do. He (the Lord) said to the earth: 'Return what you have taken.' And he was thus restored to his (original form). He (Allah) said to him: 'What prompted you to do this?' He said: 'My Lord, it was Thine fear or Thine awe, and Allah pardoned him because of this.' Abu Huraira reported Allah's Messenger (May peace be upon him) as saying that a woman was thrown into Hell-Fire because of a cat whom she had tied and did not provide it with food. Nor did she set it free to catch insects of the earth until it died inch by inch. Zuhri said: '(These two hadiths) show that a person should neither feel confident (of getting into Paradise) because of his deeds, nor should he lose (all hopes) of getting into Paradise.'"

SUMMATION:

IL: Islam offers the truth. This truth benefits the believer physically and spiritually. Since it is offered through the graciousness of Allah and His Prophet, a rejection of Allah's truth will have the most severe consequences. These consequences will be experienced in this life and the next. The desire of one's heart will be granted to those who submit and are obedient to their death.

WA: In Mecca, the march towards absolutism and intolerance was solidified. Both jinn (demons) and men are constrained in the heavens. For humankind this occurs after death. The guilty are dragged to hell and those who practice true Islam experience a sensual eternity. How does this part of Islam please Allah? The hadith reinforces the notion that Muslims who fear Allah can be forgiven, but Allah will not assure Muslims of their eternal destination. Muslims can never know where they are going to go short of martyrdom.

QUR'AN 76

"The Man"

629 AD

SCRIPTURE:

Qur'an 76:1, 4, 7, 11, 19, 23, 28, 31

Bukhari:V1B3N111

PREFACE:

These are the stages of attaining perfection: suppress all evil, sacrifice, and fight in the way of Allah. Allah promises to replace Muslims who do not obey the Qur'an, because the Qur'an is the perfect revelation. The sacrifice that Allah revealed in the Qur'an was the desire for Muslims to sacrifice and be obedient to death. This fulfills Qur'anic perfection.[13]

SURAH:

Qur'an 76:1: "Surely there came over man a time when he was nothing that could be mentioned."

Qur'an 76:4: "Surely We have prepared for the disbelievers chains and shackles and a burning Fire."

Qur'an 76:7: "They fulfill vows and fear a day, the evil of which is widespread."

Qur'an 76:11: "So Allah will ward off from them the evil of that day, and cause them to meet with splendor and happiness."

Qur'an 76:19: "And round about them will go youths, never altering in age; when thou seest them thou wilt think them to be scattered pearls."

Qur'an 76:23: "Surely We have revealed the Qur'an to thee, in portions."

Qur'an 76:28: "We created them and made firm their make, and, when We will [when we want], We can bring in their place [replace] the like [man] of them by change [by substituting another in his stead]."

Qur'an 76:31: "He admits whom He pleases to His mercy; and [to] the wrongdoers — He has prepared for them a painful chastisement."

SUNNAH:

Bukhari:V1B3N111: "[...] Abu Juhaifa said, 'I asked Ali, "What is written in this sheet of paper?" Ali replied, "It deals with blood money paid by the killer to the relatives of the victim, the ransom for the releasing of the captives from the hands of the enemies, and the law that no Muslim should be killed in Qisas [according to the law of reciprocity] for the killing of a disbeliever.""

SUMMATION:

IL: Man is nothing except what Allah desires from the believers life. What we know is the punishment of non-Muslims is a certainty. True Muslims will be protected by Allah. In the next life adolescents will surround them. This is part of the revelation that came to the Prophet little by little, so the faithful could comprehend it. Allah determined who were faithful to Him. All others are doomed.

WA: Instead of mankind being the greatest creation of the Almighty, Allah revealed man was really nothing. Not even worth mentioning. Why would Allah think that people want to see youths as scattered pearls in the life to come? Wouldn't most people want to see their loved ones in the next life? Since the revelation came from Muhammad, perhaps he was void of any loved ones or family members who he wanted to see. Perhaps his adolescent years were very painful for him. By replacing humankind, it suggested that Allah had no value for human life. Since it appeared that Allah had little value for human life, it explains why Muhammad also had very little compassion for human life. Allah was most certain when he damned the unbelievers; however, when it came to the salvation of Muslims, he stated, "He admits whom He pleases to His mercy." In other words: salvation is up to Allah. Muslims should be very concerned about this.

The West also needs to be mindful of the hadith. When it stated that Muslims are not to be killed for killing an infidel, it meant there was no blind justice in Islam or equality. All non-Muslims are considered of less value than Muslims, and even if it came to cold-blooded murder, a Muslim will never pay with his/her life for murdering a non-Muslim.

QUR'AN 47

"Muhammad"

629 AD

SCRIPTURE:

Qur'an 47:4, 20, 35

Ishaq:530-535, 538; Tabari VIII:131-133, 138-139, 141-143, 145, 149-151, 158-159

PREFACE:

This surah addressed the eventual fate of Muhammad's enemies in Mecca, the Quraysh. It predicted that war would bring demise to the leaders of the Quraysh. War, in Allah's cause brings about an Islamic spiritual awakening. Through this spiritual awakening, Mecca was conquered. Conflict will also separate Muslims who embrace Jihad from the hypocrites who reject it. Islam, with Allah's help, will conquer the world. The defeat and conversion of Mecca was assured as was the defeat and eventual dhimmitude of the Jews. Both were assured through Jihad.[14]

SURAH:

Qur'an 47:4: "So when you meet in battle those who disbelieve, smite them on the neck; then, when you have overcame them, make them prisoners, and afterwards set them free as a favour or for ransom till the war lay down its burdens. [...] And those who are slain in the way of Allah [during jihad], He will never allow their deeds to perish [their actions will not be in vain]."

Qur'an 47:20: "And those who believe say: Why is not a chapter revealed?

But when a decisive chapter is revealed, and fighting is mentioned therein, thou seest those in whose hearts is a diseased look [bad demeanor] to thee with the look of one fainting at death. So woe to them!"

Qur'an 47:35: "And be not slack [do not falter] so as to cry for peace — and you are the utmost [when you have the upper hand] — and Allah is with you, and He will not bring your deeds to naught [nothing]."

SUNNAH:

MUHAMMAD'S HAJJ

Ishaq:530: "When the Apostle returned from Khaybar he sent out raiding parties and expeditions before he made the hajj. When the Meccans heard of it they got out of the Muslim's way. Gathering at the door of the assembly house to look at them, they said, 'Muhammad and his Companions are in poverty and misery; they are covetous and miserly.' The Prophet stroked and kissed the Black Stone. Then he went out trotting around the Ka'aba as did his Companions. When the Temple concealed Muhammad from the Meccans and he had *istalama* [stroked and kissed] the southern corner of the Ka'aba, he walked to *istalama* [stroked and kissed] the Black Stone a second time. Then he *harwala* [trotted] similarly for three circumambulations. He walked the remainder of them. The Apostle only did this to show off in front of the Quraysh. [...] [A poem from that day:] 'Get out of his way you infidel unbelievers. Every good thing goes with His Apostle. O Lord, I believe in his word. We will fight you about its interpretations as we have fought you about its revelation with strokes that will remove heads from shoulders. And we will make enemies of friends.'"

SACRED VIOLENCE

Tabari VIII:131-132: "Allah's Apostle sent Umar with thirty men against the rear of Hawazin. They traveled by night and hid by day. However, word reached Hawazin and they fled. [...] According to Waqidi, a thirty-man raiding party led by Bahir went to the Banu Murrah. His companions were killed and he was carried away wounded with the dead. They returned to Medina. [...] The Messenger sent Abdallah al-Kalbi to the land of the Murrah. During the raid, Usama and one of the Ansar killed Mirdas.

When they overcame him, Usama said, 'I testify that there is no god but Allah,' but we killed him anyway."

Tabari VIII:133: "The raiding party led by Ghalib went to Abd Tha'labah. One of Muhammad's slaves, said, 'Prophet, I know where the Abd can be taken by surprise.' So Muhammad sent him with Ghalib and 130 men. They raided Abd, and drove off the camels and sheep, bringing them back to Medina. [...] A raiding party led by Bahir went to Yumn. What prompted this raiding party was that Hussayl [...] the guide of the Prophet at Khaybar [...] claimed that the Ghatafan had been summoned to march against him. The Muslims went out and captured camels and sheep. A slave belonging to Uyaynah met them, and they killed him. Then they encountered Uyaynah's army which retreated."

Tabari VIII:138: "[...] Muhammad carried arms, helmets, and spears. He led one hundred horses [...]. When the Quraysh received word of this, it frightened them. The Prophet said, 'Young or old, I have never been known but for keeping a promise. I do not want to bring in weapons against you, but the weapons will be close to me.'"

Tabari VIII:139: "In this year the Messenger of Allah commanded Ghalib Abdallah to go on a raid to Kadid against the Mulawwih. They traveled until they encountered Harith. Ghalib said, 'We captured Harith,' but he said, 'I came only to become a Muslim.' Ghalib replied, 'If you have come as a Muslim, it will not harm you to be bound for a day. If you have come for another purpose, we shall be safe from you.' So he [Ghalib] secured him with a rope and left a little black man in charge, saying, 'If he gives you any trouble, cut off his head.'"

Tabari VIII:141: "[...] After they had milked their camels and set them out to rest, we launched our raid. We killed some of them, drove away their camels, and set out to return. [...] Reinforced, the villagers were too powerful for us. But Allah sent clouds, and there was a torrent that no one could cross so we eluded the tribesmen with what we had taken. The battle cry of the Companions of the Messenger of Allah that night was: 'Kill! Kill! Kill!'"

Tabari VIII:142: "The Messenger made peace with them on [the] condition that the Zoroastrians should be required to pay the Jizya tax and that one [a Zoroastrian] should not marry their [Muslim] women. The Prophet exacted the Zakat tax [2.5%] on the wealth of two men who believed in him and collected the Jizya [50%] from all of the Zoroastrians."

Tabari VIII:143: "In this year a twenty-four man raiding party led by Shuja went to the Banu Amir. He launched a raid on them and took camels and sheep. The shares of booty came to fifteen camels for each man. Also a raid led by Amr went to Dhat. He set out with fifteen men. He encountered a large force whom he summoned to Islam. They refused to respond so he killed all of them."

Tabari VIII:145: "The Prophet said, 'Amr, swear allegiance; for acceptance of Islam cuts off what went before.' So I swore allegiance to him."

Tabari VIII:149-150: "Abdallah married a woman but could not afford the nuptial gift. He came to the Prophet and asked for his assistance. [...] Muhammad said, 'I have nothing with which to help you. Go out and spy on the Jusham tribe,' he [Muhammad] asked. He gave me an emaciated camel and a companion. We set out armed with arrows and swords. We approached the encampment and hid ourselves. I told my companion, 'If you hear me, shout Allahu Akbar and [if you] see me attack, you should shout Allah is Greatest ["Allahu Akbar"] and join the fighting.' [...] When their leader, Rifa'ah, came within range, I shot an arrow into his heart. I leaped at him and cut off his head. Then I rushed toward the encampment and shouted, 'Allahu Akbar!' [...] We drove away a great herd of camels and many sheep and goats and brought them to the Messenger. I brought him Rifa'ah's head, which I carried with me. The Prophet gave me thirteen camels from that herd as booty, and I consummated my marriage."

Tabari VIII:151: "The Prophet sent Ibn Abi out with a party of sixteen men. [...] Their share of booty was twelve camels for each man, [...]. When the people they raided fled in various directions, they took four women, including one young woman who was very beautiful. She fell to Abu Qatadah. The prophet asked Abu about her. Abu said, 'She came with the spoils.' The Messenger said, 'Give her to me.' So Abu gave her to him [Muhammad] and the Prophet gave her to Mahmiyah. [...] Allah's Apostle sent us to Idam. This was before the conquest of Mecca. As Adbat passed us, he greeted us with the greeting of Islam, 'Peace be upon you.' So we held back from him. But Muhallim attacked him because of some quarrel, and he [Muhallim] killed him [Adbat]. Then he took his camel and his food. [...]"

THE FIRST MUSLIM RAID AGAINST CHRISTIANS

Ishaq:531-532: "When the Prophet made his farewell pilgrimage he adhered to the practice making it required Sunnah to be carried out forever. While the polytheists supervised the hajj pilgrimage, the Prophet sent out his expedition to Syria. It met with disaster at Mu'ta. They equipped themselves and set out with 3,000 men [...] [Muslims then sang this song:] 'I ask the Merciful One for a pardon and for a sword that cuts wide and deep, creating a wound that shoots out foaming blood. I ask for a deadly thrust by a thirsty lance held by a zealous warrior that pierces right through the guts and liver, slitting the bowels. People shall say when they pass my grave, "Allah guided him, a fine raider that he was, O warrior, he did well."' [...] The men journeyed on and encamped at Mu'an in [the land of] Syria. They heard that Heraclius had come with 100,000 Greek and [100,000] Byzantines joined with 100,000 Arabs. [...]"

Ishaq:533: "Abdallah Rawahah encouraged the men, saying, 'By Allah, what you loathe is the very thing you came out to seek—martyrdom. We are not fighting the enemy with number, strength, or multitude, but we are fighting them with this religion with which Allah has honored us. So come on! Both prospects are fine: victory or martyrdom.' So they went forward."

Ishaq:534: "The men journeyed on and were met by Heraclius' armies of Romans and Arabs. When the enemy drew near, the Muslims withdrew to Mu'ta, and the two sides encountered each other. Zayd fought with the war banner of the Messenger until he perished among the enemy's javelins. Ja'far took it next, but could not extricate himself from difficulties. He fought until he was killed. Abdallah took up the banner, urging his soul to obey. He hesitated and said, 'Soul, why do you spurn Paradise?' He took up his sword, advanced, and was killed. Then Thabit took the banner. He said, 'O Muslims, agree on a man from among yourselves.' They said, 'You.' I said, 'No.' So they gave it to Khalid. He deflected the enemy in retreat, and escaped."

MUSLIM WARRIORS NEVER LOSE

Ishaq:535: "The women began to cry after learning about Ja'far's death. Disturbed, Muhammad told Abd-Rahman to silence them. When they wouldn't stop wailing, Allah's Apostle said, 'Go and tell them to be quiet, and if they refuse throw dust in their mouths.'"

Tabari VIII:158-159: "The Prophet ascended his pulpit and said, 'A gate to good fortune. I bring you news of your campaigning army. They have set out and have met the enemy [Christians]. Zayd has died a martyr's death.' He prayed for his forgiveness. He said, 'Ja'far has died a martyr's death.' He prayed for his forgiveness. [...] The people began to throw dust at the army, saying, 'You retreating runaways. You fled the Cause of Allah!' But the Messenger said, 'They are not fleers. Allah willing, they are the ones who will return to fight another day.'"

Ishaq:538: "[...] Allah bless the martyrs lying dead at Mu'ta. Refresh their bones for they fought for Allah's sake like good Muslims. Stallions clad in armor. Their ranks were trapped and now they lay prostrate. The moon lost its radiance at their death. The sun was eclipsed and it became dark. We are a people protected by Allah to whom he has revealed His Book, excelling in glory and honor. Our enlightened minds cover up the ignorance of others. They would not embark on such a vicious enterprise. But Allah is pleased with our guidance and the victorious good fortune of our apostolic Prophet."

SUMMATION:

IL: When the enemies of Islam make war, Muslims are to separate their heads from their bodies. Although Allah commanded this many times in the Qur'an, the hypocrites were always looking for an excuse not to participate in Jihad. Allah knew what was in their hearts. As for those who rightly believe, Muslims were commanded never to want or desire peace when they have the upper hand in battle. The martyr was promised Paradise and the victor in Jihad was promised a good deed from Allah.

WA: In violation of the Hudabiyah treaty, the Muslims sent out raiding parties. This was done to intimidate the Meccans. It worked. The Meccans cleared out as the Muslims came to perform rights that the Arabs performed under Jahiliyyah. Pagan rites like circumambulation were now made into Islamic practices by the Prophet of Islam himself. Muhammad's "showing off" displayed a lack of humility. His kissing and stroking of the black stone was a throw-back to Allah, the polytheistic moon-god. Muhammad did not come to make peace. He threatened his Quraysh relatives with decapitation and slaughter upon his return. While Muhammad trusted the Meccans to abide by the treaty, he sent 3000 Muslims to fight the Byzantines at Mu'ta. The Muslims were seriously overmatched. This was perhaps their worst defeat. Upon arriving at Medina, Muhammad was greeted with the sounds of wailing women mourning their dead. This disturbed Muhammad because he knew that once again he needed an explanation of why Allah permitted this to happen. He needed the mourning to stop in order to redirect the believers. So the "Model of human behavior" told other Muslims to throw dirt in the faces of these grieving Muslim women. Ishaq:538 was pure spin. What Westerners need to see is that good Muslims [according to the authoritative Islamic texts] fight and die in Jihad. Referring to his moon-god deity, Muhammad spoke about the moon, not the sun, losing its brilliance. The only brilliance that comes from the moon is reflected from the sun. Otherwise, the moon is dark, cold, and dead.

Desperate to recapture momentum, Muhammad sent out small bands of Muslim raiding parties. They killed some of those they attacked and those they attacked killed some of them. After the fighting subsided they returned to Medina with booty, contraband of war, and prisoners. The treaty with the Meccans was now fully violated, yet Muhammad said that he was always known as a promise keeper. Muhammad invoked the battle cry during raids where Muslims would yell their objective: Kill! Kill! Kill! How can Islam call itself a religion of peace when the Islamic texts prove otherwise? When these captured male Arabs did not respond to the call of Islam they were all slaughtered. No tolerance here. The Zoroastrians were extorted for money. Other raids that were sanctioned by Muhammad managed to violate most, if not all, of the Ten Commandments given by Moses at Sinai.

In the example of Abdallah, Muhammad told him to spy on another tribe. Abdallah knew the drill. Returning with the chieftain's head and the possessions of their "prey" were usually enough to secure the blessing of the Islamic Prophet. Right after Abdallah shot an innocent man through the heart and chopped off his head, he was able to return and have sex with his new wife. Tabari VIII:151 is another example of theft, sexual slavery, corruption, and murder committed by these Muslims. Numerous successful raids after their defeat at Mu'ta enabled Muhammad to put a favorable spin on, what was otherwise, a military mismatch.

QUR'AN 9

"The Immunity"

630 AD

SCRIPTURE:

Qur'an 9:1, 3, 5, 12, 14, 19-20, 23, 29-30, 34-36, 41, 44, 61, 73, 89, 111, 120, 123

Bukhari:V3B39N72, V4B52N46, V4B52N53, V5B52N63, V4B52N182, V4B52N184, V4B52N256, V4B52N260, V4B52N269, V4B53N374-V4B53N375, V7B62N136; Dawud:B2N2150; Ishaq:540-541, 543-544, 546, 548, 550-552, 554-555, 557-558, 560-561, 564-572, 574, 576, 578, 580, 583-584, 586-590, 592-595, 597, 601; Muslim: B19C9N4321, B19C18N4360, B19C30N4395, B19C30N4396; Tabari VIII:160-161, 163-165, 168, 170-171, 173, 175-176, 178-183, 187; IX:1, 3, 6-8, 10-15, 18, 20-22, 25, 28, 31, 36-37

PREFACE:

This surah was revealed after the Jews were defeated and the Muslims set their sights on Mecca. Eventually, the Muslims would seek revenge against the Christian Byzantines at Tabuk. As at Uhud, the Muslim "hypocrites" were responsible for the previous defeat. This surah claimed that the Meccans violated the Hudabiyah treaty. Therefore, the Muslims had immunity and were free to attack Mecca. The goal was the destruction of all idolatry. This surah also predicts the final triumph against the Christians who are also guilty of idolatry. The ultimate goal of Islam is defined: *World Domination*. This is a global conquest in which every Muslim community is expected to provide men to wage Jihad for Islam. This surah not only focused on the eventual defeat of the Meccans, but also on the defeat of the People of the Book. By the time this surah was revealed to Muhammad, the Jews were already vanquished. Only the Christians in Arabia remained to be defeated since the Jews and the Christians will be subjugated and endure *Dhimmitude*. The struggle will be long and hard, so many Muslim martyrs will fall in battle, but their salvation is assured. The verse of the Sword also had to be revealed in order to abrogate the earlier Meccan "peaceful" verses.[15]

SURAH:

Qur'an 9:1: "A declaration of immunity [freedom from obligation] from Allah and His Messenger [is proclaimed] to those of the idolaters with whom you made an agreement [a treaty]."

Qur'an 9:3: "[...] Allah is free from liability [obligations] to the idolaters, and so is His Messenger. [...]"

Qur'an 9:5: "So when the sacred months have passed, slay the idolaters, wherever you find them, and take them captive and besiege them and lie in wait for them in every ambush. But if they repent and keep up prayer, and pay the poor-rate [Zakat tax], leave their way free."

Qur'an 9:12: "And if they [Polytheistic Arabs and Christians] break their oaths [their agreement to pay the Jizya, a tax on Dhimmis] after their agreement [was made] and revile your religion [Islam], then fight the leaders of disbelief — surely their oaths are nothing — so that they may desist."

Qur'an 9:14: "Fight them: Allah will chastise them at your hands and bring them to disgrace, and assist you against them and relieve [heal] the hearts of a believing people."

Qur'an 9:19-20: "Do you hold the giving of drink to the pilgrims and the maintenance of the Sacred Mosque [are] equal to the service of one who believes in Allah and the Last Day and who strives hard in Allah's way [Jihad]? They are not equal in the sight of Allah. And Allah guides not the iniquitous people. Those who believed [Muslims] and fled their home, and strived hard in Allah's way [Jihad] with their wealth and lives, are much higher [greater] in rank [worth] in the sight of Allah. And Allah guides not the iniquitous people."

Qur'an 9:23: "O you who believe, take not your fathers and your brothers for friends if they love [take pleasure in] disbelief above faith [rather than faith]. And whoever of you takes them for friends, such are the wrongdoers."

Qur'an 9:29: "Fight [against] those who believe not in Allah [Jews and Christians], nor in the Last Day, nor forbid that which Allah, and His Messenger have forbidden have forbidden nor follow the Religion of Truth [Islam], out of those who have been given the Book, until they pay the [Jizya] tax [penalty] in acknowledgement of [the] superiority [of Islam] and [in acknowledgement that] they are [subdued] in a state of subjection."

Qur'an 9:30: "And the Jews say: Ezra is the son of Allah; and the Christians say: The Messiah is the son of Allah. These are the words of their mouths. They imitate the saying of those who disbelieved before [what the unbelievers of old used to say]. Allah's curse be on them! How they are turned [deluded] away [from the truth]!"

Qur'an 9:34-35: "[...] And those who hoard up gold and silver and spend it not in Allah's way [Jihad] — announce to them a painful chastisement. On the day when it will be heated in the Fire of hell, then their foreheads and their sides and their backs will be branded it: This is what you hoarded up for yourselves, taste what you used to hoard."

Qur'an 9:36: "Surely the number of months with Allah is twelve months by Allah's ordinance, since the day when He created the heavens and the earth — of these four are sacred. That is the right religion; so wrong not yourselves therein. And fight the polytheists all together as they fight you all together. And know that Allah is with those who keep their duty."

Qur'an 9:41: "Go forth, light or heavy [armed], and strive hard in Allah's way [Jihad] with your wealth and your lives. This is better for you, if you know."

Qur'an 9:44: "Those who believe in Allah and the Last Day ask not leave of thee to stay away from striving hard with their wealth and their persons [in Jihad]. And Allah is [the] Knower of those who keep their duty."

Qur'an 9:61: "And of them are those who molest [interfere with, vex] the

Prophet and say, He is all ear [believes everything he hears]. [...] And those who molest the Messenger of Allah, for them is a painful chastisement."

Qur'an 9:73: "O Prophet, strive hard against the disbelievers and the hypocrites and be firm against them. And their abode is hell, and evil is the destination."

Qur'an 9:89: "Allah has prepared for them [the martyrs] Gardens wherein flow rivers, to abide therein. This is a great achievement."

Qur'an 9:111: "Surely Allah has bought from the believers their persons [lives] and their property [wealth] — theirs in return will be the Garden. They fight in the Allah's way, so they [shall] slay and be slain. [...]"

Qur'an 9:120: "It was not proper for the people of Medinah [Medina] and those round about them of the desert Arabs to remain behind the Messenger of Allah, nor to prefer their own lives to his life. That is because there afflicts them neither thirst, nor fatigue, nor hunger in Allah's way [Jihad], nor tread they a path which enrages the disbelievers, nor cause they any harm to an enemy, but a good work is written down for them on account of it. [...]"

Qur'an 9:123: "O you who believe, fight those of the disbelievers who are near to you and let them find firmness [harshness] in you. And know that Allah is with those who keep their duty."

SUNNAH:

JUSTIFYING THE SIEGE OF MECCA

Ishaq:540-541: "After sending his expedition to Mu'ta, the Messenger learned that the Banu Bakr assaulted the Khuza'ah while the later were at a watering place in lower Mecca. [...] That night the [Banu] Bakr attacked the Khuza'ah and killed a man named Munabbih. [...] The others ran away and escaped. [...] When the Quraysh leagued together with the [Banu] Bakr against the Khuza'ah and killed some men, they broke the treaty because of the pact the Khuza'ah had with Muhammad. This was one of the things that prompted the conquest of Mecca."

Tabari VIII:160-161: "Allah's Apostle set out on the expedition against the people of Mecca in the month of Ramadan. [...] The [Banu] Bakr entered into a pact with the Quraysh, and the Khuza'ah entered into a pact with the Muslims. The truce having been concluded, the Banu Bakr took advantage of it [the truce] against the Khuza'ah. To retaliate, they wanted to kill the persons responsible for killing their men. So the [Banu] Bakr killed a Khuza'ah man. The Quraysh aided the Bakr with weapons, and some Quraysh fought on their side under the cover of darkness until they drove the Khuza'ah into the sacred territory."

Tabari VIII:163-164: "Khuza'ah men came to the Messenger and told him how the Quraysh had backed the [Banu] Bakr against them. The Prophet replied, 'I think you will see Abu Sufyan come to strengthen the pact and extend the term.' [...] Sufyan went to Abu Bakr and asked him to intercede, but he refused. When Sufyan asked Umar to help, he replied, 'No way. By Allah, if I only had ant grubs, I would fight you with them.' [...] Ali said, 'Woe to you, Sufyan. When the Messenger has determined a thing it is useless for anyone to talk to him.'"

Ishaq:543-544: "Abu Sufyan went to Muhammad in Medina to affirm the peace treaty. Upon arrival, he visited his own daughter Umm. When he was about to sit on the caret bed of the Prophet, she folded it up to stop him. He said, 'My daughter, I do not know if you think that I am too good for this or if this carpet [bed] is too good for me. Umm replied, 'You are an unclean polytheist.' Abu answered, 'My daughter, by Allah, evil came over you after you left me. You have gone bad.' Then Abu Sufyan went to Allah's Messenger, but he refused to speak to him. [...] Fatima said, 'No one can provide any protection against Allah's Apostle.' [...] Muhammad commanded the people to prepare for the foray [raid]. The Messenger informed his troops that he was going to Mecca. He ordered them to prepare themselves and ready their equipment quickly. He said, 'O Allah, keep spies and news from the Quraysh until we take them by surprise in their land.' [...] Hassan incited the men, reciting, 'This is the time for war. Don't feel safe from us. Our swords will open the door to death.'"

Ishaq:546: "[...] The Apostle punched him [Abu Sufyan] in the chest [after he was captured]."

Tabari VIII:165: "There is nothing you can do to make peace with him.

So Abu Sufyan, stood in the mosque and said, 'People, I came to make peace. I promise protection between men.' [...] He mounted his camel and departed. [...]When Abu Sufyan reported back to the Quraysh that Muhammad had given him no reply, they said, 'Woe to you! By Allah, he did no more than play with you.'"

Ishaq:548: "Finally, the squadrons of the Messenger composed of Emigrants and Ansar in iron armor with only their eyes visible, passed by. His company had become great. Woe to you! None can withstand him. It was all due to his prophetic office. [...] Abu Sufyan ran in haste. When he reached Mecca, he shouted in the sanctuary, 'People of [the] Quraysh, behold, Muhammad has come upon us with forces we cannot resist.' Hind said, 'Kill this fat greasy bladder of lard! What a rotten protector of the people.' Sufyan replied, 'Woe to you! Don't let this deceive you, for we cannot resist Islam.' [...] 'By Allah, the black mass has spread,' Abu Bakr said, 'There is not much honesty among people nowadays.'"

THE MARCH TO MECCA

Tabari VIII:168: "He departed the tenth day of Ramadan. They broke their fast and encamped at Marr Zahran with 10,000 Muslims. No news reached the Quraysh about the Messenger, and they did not know what he would do."

Tabari VIII:170: "When the Messenger set out for Mecca he appointed no one to military commands and displayed no banners. [...] He sent to the Arab tribes, but they hung back from him. [...] When Muhammad reached Qudayd, the Sulaym met him with horses and full armament. Uraynah joined the Messenger at Arj. Aqra joined in at Suqya."

Tabari VIII:171: "When Muhammad encamped at Marr Zuhran, Abbas said, 'Woe to the Quraysh! If Allah's Apostle surprises them in their territory and enters Mecca by force, it means the destruction of the Quraysh' Abu Sufyan said, 'I have never seen fires like those I see today! These are the fires of men gathering for war. Here is Muhammad, come against us with a force we cannot resist—10,000 Muslims. If he gets hold of me, he will cut off my head.'"

Tabari VIII:173: "[Muhammad said, after Abu Sufyan was captured,]

'Alas, Sufyan isn't it time for you to admit that I am the Messenger of Allah?' Sufyan replied, 'As to that I have some doubt.' [...] Abbas said, 'Woe to you! Submit and recite the testimony that there is no god but Allah and that Muhammad is the Apostle of Allah before your head is cut off!' [...] Muhammad told Abbas to detain Sufyan. [...]"

THE BATTLE OF MECCA

Tabari VIII:175: "[...] The Quraysh aided the [Banu] Bakr with weapons. That is why Muhammad attacked the people of Mecca. [...] Heading for Mecca, the Prophet sent Zubayr after the Quraysh. He [Muhammad] gave him [Zubayr] his banner and appointed him [Zubayr] commander over the cavalry of the Emigrants. He [Muhammad] ordered: 'Zubayr, plant my banner in the upper part of Mecca. Remain there until I come to you.'"

Ishaq:550: "[...] The Muslims met them with their swords. They cut through many arms and skulls. Only confused cries and groans could be heard over our battle roars and snarling. [...]"

Tabari VIII:176: "The Prophet sent out his army in divisions. Zubayr was in charge of the left wing. He was ordered to make an entry with his forces from Kuda. Sa'd was commanded [by Muhammad] to enter with forces by way of Kada. Allah's Apostle said, 'Today is a day for battle and war. Sanctuary is no more. Today the sacred territory is deemed profane.' When one of the Muhajirs [Emigrants] heard him say this, he warned the Apostle, 'It is to be feared that you would resort to violence.' The Prophet ordered Ali to go after him, to take the flag from him, and fight with it himself. [...] [Muhammad said,] 'Fight only those who fight you.' When Khalid came upon them in the lower part of Mecca, he fought them, and Allah put them to the fight. Zubayr encountered a squadron of Quraysh on the slopes of Kada and killed them. [...] When the Prophet arrived, the people stood before him to swear allegiance to him, and so the Meccans became Muslims."

EXECUTIONS AT MECCA

Tabari VIII:178: "Muhammad ordered that certain men be assassinated even if they were found behind the curtains of the Ka'aba. Among them

Abdullah Bin Sa'd. The reason that Allah's Messenger ordered that he should be slain was because he had become a Muslim and used to write down the Qur'an revelation. Then he apostatized, reverted to being a polytheist, and returned to Mecca."

Muslim:B19C18N4360: "[Regarding the seventy prisoners, Umar said to Muhammad,] 'I am of the opinion that you should hand them over to us so that we may cut off their heads, Hand over Aqil [Ali's brother] to Ali that he may cut off his head, and hand over such and such relative to me that I may cut off his head.'"

Muslim:B19C30N4395: "The Messenger of Allah said to the Ansar, 'You see the ruffians and lowly followers of the Quraysh?' And he indicated by striking one of his hands over the other that they should be killed and said, 'Meet me at as-Safa.' So we went [following his orders] and if any one of us wanted that a certain person should be killed, he was killed, and none could offer any resistance. Then came Abu Sufyan and he said, 'Messenger of Allah, the blood of the Quraysh has become very cheap.' Muhammad said, 'There will be no Quraysh from this day on.'"

Bukhari:V3B29N72: "Allah's Apostle entered Mecca in the year of its conquest wearing an Arabian helmet on his head, and when he took it off, a person came and said, 'Ibn Khatal is holding [clinging] to the coverings [curtains] of the Ka'aba.' The Prophet said, 'Kill him.'"

Tabari VIII:179: "Abdullah bin Sa'd fled to Uthman, his brother, who after hiding him, finally surrendered him to the Prophet. Uthman asked for clemency. Muhammad did not respond, remaining silent for a long time. Muhammad explained, 'By Allah, I kept silent so that one of you might go up to him and cut off his head!' One of the Ansar said, 'Why didn't you give me a sign?' Allah's Apostle replied, 'A prophet does not kill by pointing.' [...] Among those who Muhammad ordered killed was Abdallah bin Khatal. The Prophet ordered him to be slain because while he was a Muslim, Muhammad sent him to collect the Zakat tax with an Ansar and a slave of his [Abdallah bin Khatal, the Muslim tax collector, killed the slave for being disobedient. Abdallah did not report his wrongdoing. He then rejected Islam and used the tax money he collected on a few girls.]. [...] The girls used to sing a satire about Muhammad so the Prophet ordered that they should be killed along with Abdallah. Abdallah was killed by Sa'd and Abu Barzah. The two shared in his blood. One of the singing girls was killed quickly, but the other fled. So Umar caused his horse to trample the one who fled at Atbah, killing her."

Tabari VIII:180-181: "Also among those eliminated were Ikrimah bin Abu Jahl and Sarah, a slave girl of one of Abd Muttalib's sons. She taunted Muhammad while he was in Mecca. [...] The Messenger ordered that six men and four women should be assassinated. One of these women was Hind, who swore allegiance and became a Muslim. [...] Having halted by the door of the Ka'aba, the Messenger stood up and said, 'There is no god but Allah alone; He has no partner.' [Then Muhammad said,] 'People of the Quraysh, Allah has taken from you the haughtiness of the Time of Ignorance [Jahiliyyah] and its veneration of ancestors. [...] For now I have humbled you, made you Muslims, submissive unto me. [...] People of the Quraysh and people of Mecca, what do you think I intend to do with you?'"

Ishaq:551: "Another victim was Huwayrith. He used to insult Muhammad in Mecca. Huwayrith was put to death by Ali. [...] The Prophet ordered [the] assassination [of Miqyas] only because he had killed an Ansar who had killed his brother by mistake and then became a renegade by rejecting Islam. [...] Miqyas was slain by Numaylah."

THE MECCANS SUBMIT

Ishaq:552: "When the populace had settled down, Muhammad went to the Ka'aba and compassed [circled] it seven times on his camel, touching the Black Stone with a stick. Then he went inside the Temple. There he found a dove made of wood. He broke it in his hands and threw it away. [...] The Ka'aba contained 360 idols which Lucifer had strengthened with lead. The Apostle was standing by them with a stick in his hand, saying, 'The truth has come and falsehood has passed away.' Then he pointed at them with his stick and they collapsed on their backs one after the other. [...] The Quraysh had put pictures in the Ka'aba including two of Jesus and one of Mary. Muhammad ordered that the pictures should be erased except those of Jesus and Mary. [Their faces were removed]"

Ishaq:554: "Muhammad sat in the Mosque and Ali came to him with the key to the Ka'aba asking him to grant his family the rights associated with custodianship."

Ishaq:555: "[The key was awarded to Uthman instead. The Prophet then proclaimed,] 'Mecca is the Holy of Holies.' [...] [Muhammad said,] 'It is not lawful for anyone to shed blood [to kill anyone] in Mecca. It was not lawful to [kill] anyone [in Mecca] before me and it will not be lawful [to kill anyone in Mecca] after me. If anyone should say, "The Apostle killed men in Mecca,' say, 'Allah permitted his Apostle to do so but He does not permit you.'""

Ishaq:557: "[A Muslim recited:] 'Allah gave you a seal imprinted. Allah's proof is great. I testify that your religion is true and that you are great among men. Allah testifies that Ahmad [Muhammad] is the chosen. You are a noble one, the cynosure [one who attracts admiration] of the righteous, a prince.'"

Ishaq:558: "[Another Muslim recited:] 'Gabriel, Allah's Messenger is with us, and the Holy Spirit [Gabriel] has no equal. [...] Allah said, 'I have sent an army. Every day they curse, battle, and lampoon. [...] He is the pure, blessed Hanif. He is Allah's trusted one whose nature is loyalty.'"

Ishaq:560: "[Another Muslim recited:] 'We expelled the people and smote them with our swords the day the good Prophet entered Mecca. We pierced their bodies with cuts and thrusts. And we shot them with our feathered shafts. Our ranks went in with lances leveled. We came to plunder as we said we would. We pledged our faith to the Apostle on this day of fear.'"

Tabari VIII:182-183: "The people assembled in Mecca to swear allegiance to the Messenger in submission [Islam]. They gathered to do homage to the Apostle in Islam [Submission]. Allah had enabled Muhammad to take the persons of the Quraysh by force, giving him power over them so they were his booty. Their lives were now his spoil, but he emancipated them." [...] Umar remained below the Prophet, lower than the place where he sat, imposing conditions on the people as they paid homage to Muhammad, promising to submit and obey. Umar administered the oath, receiving from the Meccans their pledge of allegiance to Muhammad. They promised to heed and obey Allah and his Messenger. [...] That was the oath administered to those who swore allegiance to the Prophet in submission [Islam]. [...] When the Messenger was finished with the men's swearing of allegiance, the women swore allegiance. [Muhammad said to the women,] 'You are swearing allegiance to me on condition that you will associate nothing with Allah.' 'By Allah, you are imposing something on us that you did not impose on the men,' one of the women said. [...] Muhammad said, 'Do not kill your children.' The woman said, 'We raised them and you killed them. You know better about killing them than we do.' Umar laughed immoderately at her words. [...] He [Muhammad] said, 'Do not invent slanderous tales henceforth [from this point forward].' Hind said, 'Bringing slander is ugly. Sometimes it is better to just ignore it.' He said, 'You will not disobey me in carrying out my orders.' The Messenger told Umar, 'Receive their oath of allegiance and their homage.'" "Now go, for I have accepted your allegiance and praise."

THE MURDERING MISSIONARY

Ishaq:561: "The Apostle sent out troops to the territories surrounding Mecca inviting men to Allah. Among those he sent was Khalid. He was ordered to go as a missionary. Khalid subdued the Jadimah and killed some of them. [...] [Khalid, the missionary, said,] Alas for you, Banu Jadimah! It is Khalid [the sword of Allah and His Prophet.] By Allah, after you lay down your weapons, it will be nothing but leather manacles, and after the manacles nothing but the cutting off of heads.' After they had laid down their arms, Khalid ordered that their hands should be tied behind their backs. Then he put them to the sword, smiting their necks, killing them. When the word got to Muhammad as to what Khalid had done, he said, 'I declare that I am innocent of Khalid's deeds.'"

Ishaq:564: "One of the Banu Jadimah said, 'God take reprisals on the Muslims for the evil they did to us. They stole our goods and divided them. Their spears came to us not once but twice. Their squadrons came upon us like a swarm of locusts. Were it not for the religion of Muhammad, their cavalry would never have attacked.'"

Ishaq:565: "The Prophet sent Khalid to destroy the idol Al-Uzza in the lowland of Nakhlah. The Quraysh used to venerate her temple. When Sulami heard of Khalid's approach, he hung his sword on Al-Uzza, climbed a Mountain, and shouted: 'O Uzza, make an annihilating attack on Khalid. Throw aside your veil, and gird up your train [skirt of your robe]. O Uzza, if you do not kill Khalid, then bear a swift punishment or become a Christian.' [...] When Khalid arrived he destroyed her and returned to the Apostle."

Tabari VIII:187: "The Messenger of Allah married Mulaykah. She was young and beautiful. One of the Prophet's wives came to her and said, 'Are you not ashamed to marry a man who killed your father during the day he conquered Mecca?' She therefore took refuge from him. [...] [After sending Khalid to destroy the idol of Al-Uzza, Khalid came back and said,] 'I have destroyed it.' 'Did you see anything,' Muhammad asked. Khalid said, 'No.' Muhammad said, 'Then go back and kill her [Al-Uzza].' So Khalid returned to the idol. He destroyed her temple and broke her graven image. [...] Whereupon a naked, wailing Ethiopian woman came out before him. Khalid killed her and took the jewels that were on her. Then he went back to Allah's Messenger and gave him a report. [Khalid said,] 'That was Al-Uzza.' [Muhammad said,] 'Al-Uzza will never be worshipped again.'"

A NEVER-ENDING CONQUEST

Tabari IX:1: "The Prophet had been given possession of Mecca following his conquest, but he only stayed [for] a fortnight. He received news that the sheep-herding clans of Hawazin and Thaqif were encamped at Hunayn intending to fight him. [...] These tribes assembled after hearing about how the Messenger had conquered Mecca, thinking that Muslims were intending to invade them next. When the Prophet heard that they had decided to defend themselves he went out to meet them at Hunayn, and Allah, the Great and Mighty, inflicted defeat on them. Allah has mentioned this battle in the Qur'an."

*Muslim:B19N1731: "You will surely pass by a group of people who shaved their hair in the center and left the surrounding hair long braids. Go ahead and kill these people as they are fighters and warriors who carry their swords against you. Go ahead with the name of Allah."

Muslim:B19C9N4321: "The Prophet of Allah, when asked about the women and children of the polytheists being killed during the night raid, said, 'They are from them.'"

Muslim:B19C30N4396: "Muhammad said, 'When you meet them tomorrow, wipe them out.'"

Tabari IX:3: "Since the Hawazin and Thaqif had marched with their women, children, and flocks, Allah granted them as booty to His Messenger, who divided the spoils among those Quraysh who recently embraced Islam."

Tabari IX:6: "The chief sheep tender [Malik] sent out spies to obtain Intelligence But they came back with their joints dislocated. When he asked what had happened, they said, 'We saw white men on black horses. Before we could resist, we were struck as you see us now.' [...] [Muhammad also sent out spies] who mingled among the crowds gathering information."

Ishaq:566: "When Malik [the Chief of the Hawazin] decided to fight the Apostle, he had his women, children, and cattle accompany the men. He explained that by bringing them, the men would have to fight to defend them."

Ishaq:567: "When the spies learned Malik's plans, they returned and informed the Prophet. Muhammad in turn informed Umar [the second caliph], who called the Prophet a liar. [...] [The spy said,] 'Umar, you may accuse me of lying, but you have denied the truth for a long time.' [...] [Muhammad said to some pagans,] 'Lend us your weapons so that we may fight our enemy.'"

Ishaq:568-569: "[...] The Hawazin is diseased so I think that Allah's Apostle will attack them in the morning. [...] We descended through a sloping valley at the twilight of daybreak. [...] But the enemy had gotten there before us and we were waylaid by them in a narrow pass. [...] By Allah, we were terrified! As we descended, their squadrons made their first assaults on us as if they were one man. Our people were routed and fled, no one turning to look back. Allah's Apostle withdrew and cried, 'Where are you going? Come to me. I am Allah's Apostle! I am Muhammad, son of Abdallah!' It was of no avail. The camels just bumped into one another as the Muslims ran away."

Tabari IX:7-8: "Today we will not be overpowered on account of small numbers. [...] The Messenger marched with 2,000 Meccans and 10,000 of his Companions who had come with him to facilitate the conquest of Mecca. Thus, there were 12,000 in all. Muhammad left Abd Shams in charge of Mecca. [...] When the polytheists overwhelmed the Muslims, the Prophet got off his mount and started reciting verses in the rajaz meter: 'I am the Prophet, it is no lie, and I am the son of Abd Muttalib!'"

Tabari IX:10: "When the Muslims fled, the uncouth and rude fellows from Mecca who were with us saw that we were in total disarray. Some of them spoke in a manner that disclosed the hatred they harbored against us. Abu Sufyan, had divining arrows with him but another Muslim said, 'Sorcery is useless today.' Sufyan replied, 'Shut up! May Allah smash your mouth!'"

Tabari IX:11: "When Muhammad saw his men confused and in disarray, he repeated, 'Where are you going, men?' But not even one of them paid heed to his cries, so he went to the biggest man with the strongest voice and had him shout out to rally the troops."

Tabari IX:12: "Ali came upon them from behind, hamstrung their camels and they fell on their rumps. He struck the enemy with such blows he cut off feet and shanks. The men fought, and by Allah, when those who ran away [Muslims who, earlier on, had fled from battle] returned, they found only prisoners already handcuffed with the Apostle."

Tabari IX:13: "Muhammad turned to see Umm, a pregnant woman, who said, 'O Messenger! Kill those who flee from you [Muslims who run away] as you kill those who fight you, for they deserve death. Here is my dagger. If any come near me I will rip them up and slit open their belly with it. [...] Abu Talhah alone took the spoils of twenty men whom he had killed."

Tabari IX:14: "While the men were still fighting, I saw a black-striped garment descending from the sky until it dropped between us and the enemy. I gazed, and lo, it was a mass of black ants strewn everywhere, which filled the valley. I had no doubt that they were angels and that the enemy would be routed."

Ishaq:570: "The Messenger turned to Abu Sufyan, who stood fast fighting that day. He had become an excellent Muslim after embracing Islam."

KILLING TO MAKE A PROFIT

Ishaq:571: "I went up to a man and struck off his hand, and he throttled me with the other. He would have killed me if the loss of blood had not weakened him. He fell, and I killed him while he was down. But I was too occupied with fighting to pay any more attention to him. So one of the Meccan Muslims passed by and stripped him. When the fighting was over and we finished with the enemy, the Apostle said anyone who had killed a foe could have his spoil. I told the Apostle that I had killed a man who was worth stripping but had been too busy killing others at the time to notice who had spoiled him. [Abu Bakr determined who that man was and said to him,] 'To Allah's lions who fight for His religion go the spoils that come from their prey. Return the booty to the man who killed him.' The Apostle confirmed Abu Bakr's words. So I was given the property of the man whom I had killed. I sold it and bought a small palm grove with the money. It was the first property I ever owned."

Ishaq:572: "When the Apostle learned that one of the Meccans died in the battle, he said, 'Allah curses him!' He used to hate the Quraysh. Muhammad is the man, the Apostle of my Lord who errs not [does not commit error] neither does he sin. Any who would rival him in goodness must fail. Evil was the state of our enemy so they lost the day. Fortunes change and we came upon them like lions from the thickets. The armies of Allah came openly, flying at them in rage, so they could not get away. We destroyed them and forced them to surrender. In the former days there was no battle like this; their blood flowed freely. We slew them and left them in the dust. Those who escaped were choked with *terror* [emphasis added]. A multitude of them were slain. This is Allah's war in which those who do not accept Islam will have no helper. War destroyed the tribe and fate the clan. [...]"

Ishaq:574: "Finally a hundred were gathered around the Prophet. They confronted the enemy, and fought. [...] The first cry was, 'Help the Ansar!' And then, 'For the Khazraj!' Looking down at the melee as they were fighting, the Prophet said, 'Now the oven is hot.' [A Muslim recited:] In faith I do not fear the army of fate. He gave us the blood of their best men to drink when we led our army against them. We were a great army with a pungent smell. And we attack continuously, wherever our enemy is found."

Ishaq:576: "One of our Companions told us that the Apostle walked past a woman whom Khalid had killed. He sent word to Khalid and forbade him to kill more children, women, and slaves. [...] Allah's Apostle said, 'If you get hold of Bijad, don't let him escape for he has done something evil.' [...] [A Muslim stated,] 'Allah and his servant overwhelmed every coward. Allah honored us and made our religion victorious. We were glorified in the worship of the Compassionate God [Allah] who destroyed them all. He humiliated them in the worship of Satan. By what our Apostle recites from the Book and by our swift horses, I liked the punishment the infidels received. Killing them was sweeter than drink. We galloped among them panting for the spoil. With our loud-voiced army, the Apostle's squadron advanced into the fray.'"

Ishaq:578: "[Another Muslim sang:] 'Crushing the heads of the infidels and splitting their skulls with sharp swords, we continually thrust and cut at the enemy. Blood gushed from their deep wounds as the battle wore them down. We conquered bearing the Prophet's fluttering standard. Our cavalry was submerged in rising dust, and our spears quivered, but by us the Prophet gained victory.'"

Ishaq:580: "[Muslims said,] 'Allah's religion is the religion of Muhammad. We are satisfied with it. It contains guidance and laws. By it he set our affairs right. Our strong warriors obey his orders to the letter. By us, Allah's religion is undeniably strong. [...] You would think when our horses gallop with bits in their mouths that the sounds of demons are among them. [...] The day we trod down the unbelievers there was no deviation or turning from the Apostle's order. During the battle the people heard our exhortations to fight and the smashing of skulls by swords that sent heads flying. We severed necks with a warriors blow. Often we have left the slain cut to pieces and a widow crying alas over her *mutilated* [emphasis added] husband. It is Allah, not man we seek to please. [...] We helped Allah's Apostle, angry on his account, with a thousand warriors. We carried his flag on the end of our lances. We were his helpers, protecting his banner in deadly combat. We dyed it with blood, for that was its color. We were the Prophet's right arm in Islam. We were his bodyguards before other troops served him. We helped him against his opponents. Allah richly rewards that fine Prophet Muhammad.'"

MURDERING MISSIONARY BECOMES ARMY COMMANDER

Ishaq:583: "Since you have made Khalid chief of the army and promoted him, he has become a chief indeed, leading an army guided by Allah. Firmly clad in mail, warriors with lances leveled, we are a strong force not unlike a rushing torrent. We smite the wicked while we swear an oath to Muhammad, fighting in the quest for booty."

Ishaq:584: "[...] Tell the men with you who have wives: never trust a woman. [...]"

Ishaq:586: "[...] Red blood flowed because of our rage. [...]"

Ishaq:587: "Ka'b ibn Malik reacted to the Apostle's decision. He said, 'We put an end to doubt at Khaybar. But we gave our swords a rest. If our swords could have spoken, their blades would have said, "Give us Daus or Thaqif. We will tear off the roofs in Wajj. We will make homes desolate. Our cavalry will come upon you leaving behind a tangled mass. When we assault a town they sound a cry of alarm but our sharp cutting swords flash like lightning. By them we bring death to those who struggle against us. Flowing blood was mingled with saffron the morning the forces met. They were taken by surprise and we surrounded their walls with our troops. Our leader, the Prophet, was firm, pure of heart, steadfast, continent, straightforward, full of wisdom, knowledge, and clemency. He was not frivolous nor light-minded. We obey our Prophet and we obey a Lord who is the Compassionate. We make you partners in peace and war. If you refuse we will fight you doggedly. Our onslaught will not be a weak faltering affair. We shall fight as long as we live. We will fight until you turn to Islam, humbly seeking refuge. We will fight, not caring whom we meet. We will fight whether we destroy ancient holdings or newly gotten gains. We have cut off every opponent's nose and ears with our fine swords. We have driven them violently before us at the command of Allah and Islam. We will fight until our religion is established. We will plunder them, for they must suffer disgrace.""

Tabari IX:15: "[...] One of the Ansari who was plundering the slain came upon a Thaqif boy. He discovered that he was an uncircumcised Christian.

He uncovered others and then yelled out at the top of his voice, 'Allah knows that the Thaqif are uncircumcised.'"

Tabari IX:18: "[...] While fighting the Banu Sa'd, Muslim horsemen seized Bijad. They herded his family around him like cattle, and they treated them roughly. [...]"

THE FATE OF CAPTIVE WOMEN

Tabari IX:20: "The captives of Hunayn, along with their possessions, were brought to the Messenger. He ordered that their captives, animals, and their possessions be taken to Ji'ranah and held there in custody. [...] The Messenger and companions went directly to Ta'if. [...] Muhammad encamped there for a fortnight, waging war. The townsfolk fought the Muslims from behind the fort. None came out in the open. All of the surrounding people surrendered and sent their delegations to the Prophet. After besieging Ta'if for twenty days, Muhammad left and halted at Ji'ranah where the captives of Hunayn were held with their woman and children. It is alleged that those captives taken numbered 6000 women and children."

Dawud:B2N2150: "They defeated them and took them captive [Battle of Hunayn]. Some of the companions (of Muhammad) were reluctant to have relations with the female captives in the presence of their husbands who were unbelievers. Therefore Allah sent down the Qur'anic verse "married women are forbidden except those who are captives.""

Bukhari:V7B62N136: "We used to practice coitus interrupt us while the Quran was being revealed. Jabir added: 'We used to practice coitus interrupt us during the lifetime of Allah's Apostle while the Quran was being revealed.'"

Tabari IX:21: "Delegations of Hawazin came to the Prophet and embraced Islam. Therefore, he set their women and children free and decided to make the lesser pilgrimage [directly] from Ji'ranah."

THE SEIGE OF TA'IF

Ishaq:588: "Shaddad said this about the Apostle's raid on Ta'if, 'Don't help Al-lat for Allah is about to destroy her. How can one who cannot help herself be helped? She was burned in black smoke and caught fire. Those who fought before her stone are outcasts. When the Apostle descends on your land none of your people will be left when he leaves.'"

Ishaq:589-590: "The Muslims were unable to get through the city wall, for the inhabitants had shut the gate. [...] Muhammad told Bakr, 'I saw in a dream that I was given a large bowl filled with butter. A cock pecked at it and split it.' Abu Bakr said, 'O Messenger of Allah, I don't think that you will attain what you desire today.'"

Tabari IX:22: "Muhammad ordered that Ta'if's walled gardens should be torn down and destroyed. [...] The Prophet continued to besiege the town, fighting them bitterly. Both sides shot arrows at each other until one day the wall of Ta'if was stormed. A number of Muhammad's companions went under a testudo [a Roman-like siege engine] and tried to breach it but they were showered with scraps of iron. They came out from under their testudo and the Thaqif shot them. [...] Muhammad then ordered that their vineyards should be cut down."

REWARDING THE FAITHFUL

Ishaq:592: "The Apostle held a large number of captives. There were 6,000 women and children prisoners. He captured so many sheep and camels they could not be counted."

Ishaq:593: "From the captives of Hunayn, Allah's Messenger gave Ali [his son-in-law] a slave girl called Baytab and he gave Uthman [a future Caliph] a slave girl called Zaynab and Umar [a future Caliph] another [slave girl]. [...] [Abdallah, son of Umar, said,] 'I will take [have sex with] her [his father's slave girl] when I return. [But Muhammad said,] 'Let her go, for her mouth is cold, her breasts are flat. You did not take her as a virgin in her prime nor even full-figured in her middle age!'"

Ishaq:594: "[...] The Apostle gave gifts to those whose hearts were to be won over, notably the chiefs of the army, to win them and through them the people. [...]"

Tabari IX:25: "[A Muslim said,] 'By Allah, I did not come to fight for nothing. I wanted a victory over Ta'if so that I might obtain a slave girl and make her pregnant.'"

Tabari IX:28: "The Banu Tamim were concerned. They did not want to give up their share. So Muhammad said, 'He who holds a share of these captives will get six camels for every slave from the next booty we take' [...]"

GREED

Tabari IX:31: "[Muslims yelled to Muhammad, saying,] 'Muhammad, divide the spoil and booty of camels and cattle among us.' They forced the Prophet up against a tree, and his robe was torn from him. Muhammad cried, 'Give me back my robe. If there had been more sheep I would have given you some. You have found me to be niggardly, cowardly or false.' [...] Then he walked over to his camel and took a hair from its hump. Holding it aloft in his fingers he said, 'Men, I did not have anything of your booty, not even as much as this hair. Just filth. And that filth is what is being given to you. [...] So bring back my cloak, for dishonesty will be a shame, a flame, and a doom to you.' [...]"

Tabari IX:36: "[The Ansar said,] 'Prophet, this group of Ansar have a grudge against you for what you did with the booty and how you divided it among your own people.' After due praise and exultation of Allah, he addressed them, 'Ansar, what is this talk I hear from you? What is the grudge you harbor in your hearts against me? Do you think ill of me? Did I not come to you when you were erring and needy, and then made rich by Allah.'"

Tabari IX:37: "[The Ansar replied,] 'You came to us discredited, when your message was rejected by the Quraysh, and we believed you. You were forsaken and deserted and we assisted you. You were a fugitive and we took you in, sheltering you. You were poor and in need, and we comforted you.' [...] [Muhammad said,] 'Do you hold a grudge against me and you are mentally disturbed because of the worldly things by which I conciliate a people and win them over so that they will embrace Islam and become Muslims?' [...] Allah's Apostle left town to make a lesser pilgrimage and ordered that the rest of the booty be held back, although some of the spoil followed him."

Ishaq:595: "Khuwaysirah [...] said, 'Muhammad, I have seen what you have done today.' 'Well, what did you see?' he [Muhammad] said. 'I don't think you have been fair,' Khuwaysirah answered. Allah's Messenger became angry. [Muhammad said,] 'Woe to you! If justice is not to be found with me, then with whom is it to be found?' Umar said, 'Muhammad, allow me to kill him.' The Apostle said, 'Get him away from me and cut off his tongue.'"

THE REWARDS OF ISLAM AND JIHAD

Bukhari:V4B52N46: "I heard Allah's Apostle saying, 'The example of a Mujahid in Allah's Cause — and Allah knows better who really strives in His Cause — is like a person who fasts and prays continuously. Allah guarantees that He will admit the Mujahid in His Cause into Paradise if he is killed, otherwise He will return him to his home safely with rewards and war booty.'"

Bukhari:V4B52N53: "The Prophet said, 'Nobody who dies and finds good from Allah in the hereafter [Paradise] would wish to come back to this even if he were given the whole world and whatever is in it, except the martyr who, on seeing the superiority of martyrdom, would like to come back to the world and get killed again in Allah's Cause.' [...]"

Bukhari:V4B52N63: "A man whose face was covered with an iron mask came to the Prophet and said, 'O Allah's Apostle! Shall I fight or embrace Islam first?' The Prophet said, 'Embrace Islam first and then fight.' So he embrace Islam [became a Muslim] and was martyred. Allah's Apostle said, 'A little work, but a great reward.'"

Bukhari:V4B52N184, V4B52N182: "Allah's Prophet invoked evil upon the pagans [infidels] on the day of the battle of Al-Ahzab saying, 'O Allah, defeat them and shake them. [...] Allah's Apostle said, 'O Allah! Fill their houses and graves with fire [...].'"

Bukhari:V4B52N256: "The Prophet [...] was asked whether it was permissible to attack pagan warriors [infidels] at night with the probability of exposing their women and children to danger. The Prophet replied, 'They [the women and children] are from them.'"

Bukhari:V4B52N260: "[...] the Prophet said, 'If a Muslim discards [changes or leaves] his religion [Islam], kill him.'"

Bukhari:V4B52N269: "The Prophet said, 'War is deceit.'"

Bukhari:V4B53N374-V4B53N375: "The Prophet said, 'I give to Quraysh people in order to let them adhere to Islam, for they are near to their life of Ignorance (i.e., they have newly embraced Islam and it is still not strong in their hearts.' [...] 'When Allah favored His Apostle with the properties of Hawazin tribe as booty, he started giving to some Quarries [Quraysh] men even up to one-hundred camels each, whereupon some Ansari men said about Allah's Apostle, "May Allah forgive His Apostle! He is giving to (men of) Quraysh and leaves us, in spite of the fact that our swords are still dropping blood (of the infidels)."' [...] Allah's Apostle replied, 'I give to such people as are still close to the period of Infidelity (i.e. they have recently embraced Islam and Faith is still weak in their hearts).' [...] The Ansar replied, 'Yes, O Allah's Apostle, we are satisfied.' Then the Prophet said to them, 'You will find after me, others being preferred to you [If justice is not to be found with me then where will you find it?]. Then be patient till you meet Allah and meet His Apostle at Al-Kauthar (i.e., a fount in Paradise).' [Anas added:] 'But we did not remain patient.'"

KILLING THE OBSTANATE

Ishaq:597: "The people made the pilgrimage that year in the way the pagan Arabs used to do it. [...] When the Apostle returned to Medina after his raid on Ta'if, word spread that he killed some of the men who satirized and insulted him. The poets who were left spread in all directions. [...] The people of Ta'if continued in their polytheism and obstinacy in their city from the time the Apostle left in Dhu al-Qa'da of the year 8 [April 630 AD] until Ramadan of the following year [January 631 AD]."[16]

Ishaq:601: "The best men launch spears as if they were swords. They peer forward unwearied with eyes [as] red as burning coals. They devote their lives to their Prophet. On the day of hand-to-hand fighting and cavalry attacks they purify themselves with the blood of Infidels. They consider that an act of piety. Their habit is to act like lions. They are accustomed to hunting men."

SUMMATION:

IL: Though treaties were made, Allah had the authority through the Prophet to abrogate treaties with infidels. When Allah perceived the good faith of Muslims was violated, they no longer had to abide by the treaty. Therefore, Allah gave instructions against those who worship anyone other than Allah. Idolaters are to be ambushed in order to slay them or make them slaves. Coming to Islam absolves Idolaters unless they make a false oath. In this case they should be fought. Muslims are encouraged to use their wealth to fight in Jihad. If they do, victory is assured. Muslims should never think their family or associations come above their allegiance to Islam. Muslims were told this so they would not hesitate to fight the Quraysh at the mother-town, Mecca. Since the Quraysh refused to believe in Allah's religion, they had to be fought. Muslims should not think this surah only applied to the Quraysh. Verse 29 states this also applies to the People of the Book. Since their beliefs go counter to what Allah commands, they are also enemies of Islam.[17] Jews and Christians refuse to listen to the truth so they are cursed. The People of the Book are labeled as idolaters; therefore, the entirety of surah 9 applies to them. Jews wrongly believe because they hoard wealth for themselves and not for Islam. Muslims commit *haram* when they seek to avoid Jihad. Allah demands that infidels and Muslim hypocrites be dealt with harshly. Muslims who fall in battle are assured paradise because they have given their wealth and lives to Allah. Muslims should slay infidels the same way infidels try to slay them. During Muhammad's time, hypocrites were identified as Medinan Muslims and desert Arabs. Muslims must strive not to be like them. Muslims were commanded to fight the near enemy: idolater, hypocrite, and infidel, before attacking the far enemy. Islam must secure its lands before moving into the lands of the infidels. According to Al-Misri:

> "Jihad means to wage war against non-Muslims and is etymologically derived from the word *mujahada*, signifying warfare to establish the religion."

> —Al-Misri, *Reliance of the Traveller*, o9.0

WA: What we find in this surah is that Allah and his followers are free to break agreements. However; if unbelievers, who have been conquered by Islam, object to dhimmitude they should be slain. Verse 29 placed Judaism and Christianity at odds with Islam. Islamic Literalists know that Allah commanded that Jews and Christians be subjugated under Islam. It is understandable how Muhammad could be wrong about specific details. He could not read and only knew what he was being told. How can one excuse Allah, Lord of the Worlds, from being wrong? Can a god who is wrong be God? Jews never called Ezra, a son of Allah. This is an inaccurate statement that was penned into the Qur'an. Muslims should ask individual Jews if this Qur'anic assertion was ever true. Religious Jews, for certain, will know if this statement is or is not true. When the Islamic texts say things about other religions that are not accurate, non-Muslims have an obligation to point his out. This should be a signal to Muslims to investigate their own texts more closely. Blind faith based solely on the words of others is an ingredient of extremism. Faith based on reason and critical analysis can lead one towards being a more balanced and loving person. One who seeks the truth must consider the possibility that the entity claiming to be God and the Prophet may not be who they claim to be. One needs to be sure about this, especially those who strive for accuracy and really want to know the truth. Finally, in verse 123, one must wonder how Muslims can be taught that their religion is a religion of peace when their god stated, "let them [infidels] find harshness in you."

Consider the tolerance of Tabari VIII:173. There is a demand for one to become a Muslim, and if the person did not convert, then they were to be decapitated. During the battle, the Muslims were merciless towards the resisting Quraysh. After destroying their defenses, Muhammad descended into the heart of Mecca. In the aftermath, Muhammad's Jihadis admitted they came to Mecca in order to plunder. Then there was the account of Abdullah Bin Sa'd. He was killed because he helped write the Qur'an and did not believe it was true. Muhammad did not want him around telling others why Islam was false. As for the attack against Mecca, it occurred because the Meccans gave weapons to the Banu Bakr who attacked a tribe aligned with the Muslims. The Meccan executions were, for the most part, against people who rejected or ridiculed Muhammad. Muhammad even had four women killed because they spoke out against him many years earlier. In the Ka'aba, Muhammad removed the idols and erased the faces of Jesus and Mary. Muhammad then proclaimed Mecca to be the Holy of

Holies. You may recall earlier where the Islamic text stated Lucifer placed the 360 idols in the Ka'aba. Muhammad then proclaimed that no one could be killed in Mecca except if he had them killed—Allah permitted the Prophet to slay in Mecca.

As for the Meccan surrender, to keep their lives, men and women had to swear allegiance to Muhammad. Swearing allegiance to Muhammad meant they agreed to be subjugated. Allah and Muhammad had to be obeyed. Concerning the Prophet's wives, they knew how their husband behaved. He was not satisfied with the wives he had. He liked to marry women after he had their family members killed. His wives saw this and could not remain silent. This discontent also spread to some of his trusted subjects. Khalid was not known as a lover of women, rather a slayer of them as in the case of the Banu Jadimah. The people surrendered and yet he still slaughtered most of them. Survivors blamed the religion of Islam which was perpetually on the attack. Khalid continued his murdering of innocence at the Uzza shrine.

After the conquest at Mecca, Muhammad attacked the Arabs of Hawazin, Thaqif, and Ta'if. Initially, the battle went south as the Muslims were routed. Muhammad's pleas fell on deaf ears. Although tested, the Muslims and 2000 Meccans still won the month-long conflict. Muhammad was gracious towards those who accepted him and his religion by granting them emancipation. However, these new members of the Ummah still had to perform their Islamic duty which would, in time, require them to support the Jihad. Abu Sufyan was reverted to Islam. After his reversion, he was considered a good Muslim because he fought well. In Ishaq:572, we learn Muhammad cursed a Meccan who died fighting for the Muslims. Muhammad evidently remembered something that he did not like about that person. Since Muhammad could not err or commit sin, his perception must have been correct. Those who oppose Islam are evil; therefore, Allah's armies have justifiable rage as they terrorize and destroy. The following is a telling comment, because it came from a Muslim soldier who was only involved in holy war to have sex with a captured girl. One can only imagine what was meant by this quote, "We were glorified in the worship of the Compassionate God who destroyed them all."

When comparing this surah to the corresponding Sirah, it becomes clear that Islamic literalism glorifies itself in the bloodshed of non-Muslims.

How can we reconcile Ishaq:576 with Ishaq:583? Khalid kills women and children, yet he is promoted to the chief of the army by Muhammad?[18] Here is the truth. Muslim Jihadis became more ruthless after Khalid took command. As for Muhammad, he was having his own problems. The Jihadis seemed to only be interested in Islam for the booty. They were not religious people as Westerners understand it. When those who knew Muhammad did not receive the booty they thought they deserved, they were ready to string up their Prophet. Muhammad responded and promised to give them more stolen property from the next raid. In Tabari IX:37, Muhammad admitted he bribed people with the possessions of others so they would become Muslims. This infers that Muhammad was not that successful in convincing people of his truth. However, he was successful in getting them to fight for booty and wedded polygamy in Paradise. The remainder of the Sirah through Ishaq:601 should imprint a sobering realization for every person living in the West. This behavior was considered acceptable, and even holy, in Islam. This surah was the last to be revealed (concerning Jihad) in the Qur'an. This means that this surah is the final word concerning Qur'anic truth and that any verses that are at variance with the words contained in this surah are abrogated. There can be no contradiction in the Qur'an. Therefore, the People of the Book (Jews and Christians) who refuse to convert and refuse dhimmitude can become targets of aggression. This surah makes aggression against non-Muslims obligatory for Muslim believers. According to the Encyclopedia of Islam, Vol. 7, p. 1010, this surah cancelled 124 verses that called for tolerance, compassion, and peace.

"The Prohibition"

(630 AD)

SCRIPTURE:

Qur'an 66:1, 6, 9

Muslim:B9C5N3507-B9C5N3508; Tabari IX:38-39, 42

PREFACE:

This surah was revealed because of jealousy between Muhammad's wives. It got so out of control that Muhammad vowed to stay away from all of them. Allah corrected Muhammad by telling him not to stay away from them. Muhammad was also told that he could have relations with whomever he desired. A judgment was levied against the wives that initiated this incident. They were also told that Muhammad could divorce all of them. (19)

SURAH:

Qur'an 66:1: "O Prophet, why dost thou forbid [deny] thyself that which Allah has made lawful for thee? Seekest thou to please your wives?"

Qur'an 66:6: "O you who believe, save yourselves and your families from a Fire whose fuel is men and stones; over it are angels stern and strong. They do not disobey Allah, but do as they are commanded."

Qur'an 66:9: "O Prophet, strive against the disbelievers and the hypocrites, and remain firm [harsh] against them, and their abode is hell; and evil is the resort."

DOMESTIC UNREST

Tabari IX:38-39: "In this year, the Messenger sent Amr to collect the zakat tax from Ja'far and Amr, the clans of Julanda and Azd [...] He collected the jizyah from the Zoroastrians. [...] In the same year the Prophet married Kilabiyyah. When she was given the choice between this world and the hereafter, she preferred this world. [...] Mariyah [Muhammad's Coptic concubine] gave birth to Ibrahim. The Messenger entrusted the infant boy to Umm. Mariyah told Salma, a bond-maid of the Messenger the good news. She told a Muslim who shared it with Muhammad who in turn gave him a slave as a gift. When Mariyah gave birth to her son, the Prophet's wives became jealous."

Muslim:B9C5N3507: "When Allah's Apostle kept himself away from his wives, I ['Umar b. al-Khattab] entered the mosque, and found people striking the ground with pebbles and saying: 'Allah's Messenger has divorced his wives [...].' [...] So I went to 'Aisha and said to her: 'Daughter of Abu Bakr, have you gone to the extent of giving trouble to Allah's Messenger?' Thereupon she said: 'Son of Khattab, you have nothing to do with me, and I have nothing to do with you. You should look to your own receptacle. He ['Umar] said: 'I visited Hafsa, daughter of 'Umar, and said to her: 'Hafsa, the (news) has reached me that you cause Allah's Messenger trouble. You know that Allah's Messenger does not love you, and had I not been (your father) he would have divorced you. (On hearing this) she wept bitterly. [...] By Allah, if Allah's Messenger would command me to strike her neck, I would certainly strike her neck. [...] I ['Umar], therefore, said: 'Messenger of Allah, what trouble do you feel from your wives [...] Maybe his Lord, if he divorce you, will give him in your place wives better than you...' [...] And it was 'Aisha, daughter of Abu Bakr, and Hafsa who had prevailed upon all the wives of Allah's Prophet for pressing them for more money. [...] I said: 'Messenger of Allah, have you divorced them?' He said: 'No.' [...]"

Muslim:B9C5N3508: "I ['Umar] said: 'Let the nose of Hafsa and 'Aisha be besmeared with dust.

VICTORY IS ASSURED

Tabari IX:42: "Amr said, 'We have been dealt a situation from which there is no escape. You have seen what Muhammad has done. Arabs have submitted to him and we do not have the strength to fight. You know that no herd is safe from him. And no one even dares go outside for fear of being *terrorized* [emphasis added].'"

SUMMATION:

IL: The Prophet was trying to do what was right concerning his wives, but they were not happy. Muhammad received Mariyah as a gift from Egypt. He spent thirty days with her. Eventually, she became pregnant and gave birth. The events concerning this discontent so stirred Allah that he sent down a revelation to deal with Muhammad's rebellious wives. What Allah made lawful, the ungrateful wives did not accept and created a dispute. Believers are not to question Allah's wisdom. As Allah's slaves, they are expected to do what is commanded lest they become as the infidels and the hypocrites.

WA: These events as described were to be expected. A person cannot have relations with this many women and think these women would not be jealous or start a commotion. As these events unfolded, Muhammad was busy collecting Zakat from believing tribes and Jizya from the infidels. In this instance it was the Zoroastrians. Despite his administrative position, Muhammad still found time to marry more women. Muhammad spent so much time with Mariyah, a concubine, the other wives became jealous. When someone did a perceived kindness to Muhammad he repaid them with a slave. Also, the Dhimmis, who were required to pay the Jizya, were forced to comply because they were threatened with terrorism. Jesus, who Muslims consider to be a Rasul who preceded Muhammad by 570 years, never set an example of making, keeping, selling, or gifting slaves. Today, this is called human trafficking."

QUR'AN 5

"The Food"

631 AD

SCRIPTURE:

Qur'an 5:3, 5, 12-15, 17-21, 33, 38, 41, 47, 51, 59-60, 63-64, 70, 72-73, 78, 80, 82, 100-102, 116-117

Ishaq:602-603, 607, 615-616: Tabari IX:46, 48-51, 55, 57-58, 60, 64, 69, 74-76, 78-80

PREFACE:

This surah asserts that Jews and Christians have broken the covenant. Jewish disobedience and Christian transgressions are described. The Jews disobeyed Allah and the Christians broke the covenant by claiming that Jesus is the Son of God. Muslims are warned of Jewish and Christian hostile intentions against Islam. Apostates are also included for reprisal. Since Christians deviated from the truth and show enmity towards Islam, the Qur'an acts justly against them. Christians are placed with those who show aggression against Islam. Christian polytheism has led Christians the farthest from the truth. Christian materialism is subjecting them to harsh punishment. The covenant is with the Muslims because they are behaving justly. Muhammad always rejected the divinity of Jesus. Only the perfection of Islam can cure this error. This surah is mostly aimed at the Christians. Christian error, their rejection of the Islamic Prophet, and their hostility towards Islam, all justify the use of dissimulation and terror by Muslims against them. Christians are guilty of the worst crime against Allah, *Shirk*, and because of this crime, they are doomed in the next life.[20]

Qur'an 5:3: "Forbidden to you is that which [anything] that dies by itself, and blood, and flesh of swine, and that on which any other than that of Allah has been invoked, and the strangled animal, and that beaten to death, and that killed by a fall, and that killed by goring with the horn, and that which wild beasts have eaten — except what you slaughter; and that which is sacrificed on stones and set up for idols, and that you seek to divide by arrows [divination], that is a transgression. This day have those who disbelieve despaired of your religion, so fear them not, and fear Me. This day have I perfected for you your religion and completed my favour to you and chosen for you Islam as a religion. [...]"

Qur'an 5:5: "This day all good things are made lawful for you. [...] And so are the chaste among the believing women [Muslim women] and the chaste from among those who have been given the Book before you [the People of the Book], when you give them their dowries, taking them in marriage, not fornicating, nor taking them for paramours in secret [as secret lovers]. [...]"

Qur'an 5:12-14: "And certainly Allah made a covenant of with the Children of Israel [...]. But account of their breaking their covenant We [have] cursed them and hardened their hearts. They alter the words from their places and neglect a portion of that whereof they were reminded. And thou wilt always discover treachery in them excepting a few of them — so pardon them [who turn to Islam] and forgive [only those who turn to Islam]. [...] And with those who say: We are Christians, We made a covenant [with them], but they neglected a portion of that whereof they were reminded [forgot it] so We stirred up enmity and hatred among them to the day of Resurrection. And Allah will soon inform them of what they did [of their wrong doing]."

Qur'an 5:15: "O People of the Book [Jews and Christians], indeed Our Messenger [Muhammad] has come to you, making clear [explaining] to you much of that which you concealed [used to hide] of the Book [from the Scripture] and passing over much [i.e., leaving out without explaining]. Indeed, there has come to you from Allah, a Light [Prophet Muhammad] and a clear [plain] Book [the Qur'an]."

Qur'an 5:17: "They indeed disbelieve who say: Surely, Allah — He is the Messiah, Son of Mary. Say [Muhammad]: Who then could control anything as against Allah when He wished to destroy the Messiah, son of Mary, and his mother and all those on the earth? [...]"

Qur'an 5:18: "And the Jews and the Christians say: We are the sons of Allah and His beloved ones. Say [Muhammad]: Why then does he chastise you for your sins? [...] He forgives whom He pleases and chastises whom He pleases. [...]"

Qur'an 5:19: "O People of the Book, indeed Our Messenger has come to you explaining to you after a cessation of the messengers, so you won't say: There came not to us a bearer of good news nor a warner. So indeed a bearer of good news and a warner has come to you. And Allah is the Possessor of power over all things."

Qur'an 5:20-21: "And when Moses said to his people: O my people, remember the favour of Allah to you when he raised prophets [sent prophets] among you and made you kings and gave you what he gave not to any other of the nations. O my people, enter the Holy Land which Allah has ordained for you and turn not your backs, for then you will [only] turn back [as] losers."

Qur'an 5:33: "The only punishment of those who wage war against Allah and His Messenger [...] is that they [will be] should be murdered, or crucified, or their hands and their feet should be cut [chopped] off on opposite [alternate] sides, or they should be expelled from the land. This will be a disgrace for them in this world, and in the Hereafter they will have an awful doom."

Qur'an 5:38: "And as for the man and the woman addicted to theft [they are thieves], cut off their hands as a punishment for what they have earned, an exemplary punishment from Allah. And Allah is Mighty, Wise."

Qur'an 5:41: "[...] We believe, and their hearts believe not, and from among those who are Jews — they are listeners for the sake of a lie [they follow a lie], listeners for anther people who have not come to thee. They alter words after they are put into their proper places [the rabbis changed some Bible verses]. [...] Those are they whose hearts Allah intends not to purify. For them is disgrace in this world, and for them a grievous chastisement in the Hereafter." ["Whomever Allah wants to deceive you cannot help. Allah does not want them to know the truth because he intends to disgrace them and then torture them."]

Qur'an 5:47: "And let the People of the Gospel [Christians] judge by that which Allah has revealed in it. And whoever judges not by what Allah has revealed, those are the transgressors."

Qur'an 5:51: "O you who believe [Muslims], take not the Jews and the Christians for friends. They are friends of each other. And whoever amongst you takes them for friends he is indeed one of them. Surely Allah guides not the unjust people [wrongdoers]."

Qur'an 5:59-60: "Say: O People of the Book [Jews and Christians], do you find fault with us for aught except that we believe in Allah and in that which has been revealed to us and that which was revealed before [in the past],while [because] most of you are transgressors [evildoers]? Say [Muhammad]: Shall I inform you of those worse than this in retribution from Allah? They are those whom Allah has cursed and upon whom He brought His wrath and of whom Allah made [turned] into apes [Jews] and swine [Christians, "pork-eaters"], and who serve the devil [idols]. These are in a worse plight and [are led] further astray from the straight path."

Qur'an 5:63: "Why do not the rabbis and the doctors of law prohibit them from their sinful utterances [words] and their devouring unlawful gain? Certainly evil are the works [that] they do."

Qur'an 5:64: "And the Jews say: The hand of Allah is tied up. Their own hands are shackled and they are cursed for what they say. Nay, both His hands are spread out. His disburses as He pleases. And that which has been revealed to thee from thy Lord will certainly make many of them increase in inordinacy [chaos] and disbelief. And We have cast among them [Jews and Christians] enmity and hatred till the day of Resurrection. Whenever they kindle a fire for war Allah puts it out, and they strive to make mischief in the land. And Allah loves not the mischief-makers."

Qur'an 5:70: "Certainly We made a covenant with the Children of Israel and We sent to them messengers. Whenever a messenger came to them with that which their souls desired not [which they did not want to hear], some of them they called liars and some they even sought to kill."

Qur'an 5:72: "Certainly [it is those who] disbelieve who say: Allah, He is the Messiah, son of Mary. And the Messiah said: O Children of Israel, serve Allah, my Lord and your Lord. Surely whoever associates others [partners] with Allah, Allah has forbidden to him the Garden and his abode is the Fire. And for the wrongdoers there will be no helpers."

Qur'an 5:73: "Certainly [it is those who] disbelieve who say: Allah is the third of the three [Trinity]. And there is no God but One God [Allah]. And if they desist not from what they say, a painful chastisement will surely befall such of them as disbelieve."

Qur'an 5:78: "Those who disbelieved from among the Children of Israel were cursed by the tongue of David and Jesus, son of Mary. This was because they disobeyed and exceeded the limits."

Qur'an 5:80: "Thou [will] seest many of them befriending those who disbelieve. Certainly evil is that which their souls send before for them, so that Allah is [became] displeased with them, and in chastisement will they abide [Muslims who befriend unbelievers will abide in hell]."

Qur'an 5:82: "Thou wilt certainly find the most violent of people in enmity against the believers [Muslims] to be the Jews and the idolaters [Christians]. [...]"

Qur'an 5:101-102: "O you who believe, ask not [questions] about things which if made known [plain] to you would [may] cause you trouble; and if you ask about them when the Qur'an is being revealed, they will be made known [plain] to you. Allah pardons this [will forgive]; and Allah is Forgiving, Forbearing. A people before you indeed did ask such questions, then became disbelievers therein [then they lost their faith because of the answers they received]."

Qur'an 5:116: "And when Allah will say: O Jesus, son of Mary, didst thou say to men, 'Take me and my mother for two gods besides Allah?' He [Jesus] will say: Glory be to Thee! It was not for e to say what I had no right to say. If I had said it, Thou wouldst indeed have known it. Thou knowest what is in my mind, and I know not what is in thy mind. Surely Thou art the great Knower of the unseen."

Qur'an 5:117: "[…], and I [Jesus] was a witness of them [among them] so long as I was among them, but when Thou didst cause me to die Thou was the watcher over them. And Thou art Witness over all things."

SUNNAH:

THE TABUK EXPEDITION

Tabari IX:46: "In this year, the Messenger carried out a military expedition to Tabuk. […]"

Tabari IX:48: "Muhammad wanted the people to be prepared so he informed them that his objective was the Byzantines. The Muslims disliked the idea because of their respect for their fighting ability. […]"

Ishaq:602: "The Apostle ordered Muslims to prepare for a military expedition so that he could raid the Byzantines. [With an army of 30,000 at Tabuk, Muhammad declared,] 'The treasures of Caesar have been given to me by conquest. […] The Apostle always referred allusively to the destination which he intended to raid. This was the sole exception, for he said plainly that he was making for the Byzantines because the journey was long, the weather was hot, and the enemy was strong. […] Jadd told Muhammad, 'Will you allow me to stay behind and not tempt me? Everyone knows I am strongly addicted to women. I'm afraid that I will see Byzantine women and will not be able to control myself.' […] The Apostle gave him permission to remain behind. […] It was not that he feared the temptation from the Byzantine women. The temptation he had fallen into was greater in that he had hung back from the Apostle and sought to please himself rather than Muhammad. Verily, hell awaits him."

Tabari IX:49: "One of the hypocrites, feeling an aversion to battle, being skeptical of the truth, and spreading false rumors about Muhammad, said that they should not go out in the heat. With regard to him, Allah revealed: 'They said, "Do not march out in the heat." Say [instead], "The heat of hell is far more intense."' …Muhammad urged the Muslims by way of a meeting to help cover the expenses of Allah's Cause [Jihad]. The men provided mounts in anticipation of Allah's reward."

Ishaq:603: "[...] Some Bedouins came to apologize for not going into battle, but Allah would not accept their excuses. [...] The Apostle went forth energetically with his preparations and ordered the men to get ready with all speed. He urged Muslims to help provide the money, mounts, and means to do Allah's work. Those who contributed earned rewards with Allah. [...]"

Tabari IX:50: "When the Prophet was prepared to set off, a number of Muslims whose intentions had prevented them from following the Messenger, lagged behind without any misgivings."

Tabari IX:51: "Ali seized his weapons and set off until he caught up with Muhammad. 'The hypocrites allege that you left me behind because you found me burdensome and wanted to get rid of me.' He replied, 'They lied [other Muslims]. I left you behind because of what I have left behind [booty]. So go back and represent me in my family.'"

Tabari IX:55: "The Messenger continued his march but his men began to fall behind. The Prophet said, 'Leave them, for if there is any good in them, Allah will unite them; if not, Allah has relieved you of them.'"

Tabari IX:57: "A band of hypocrites [...] going along with the prophet as he was marching toward Tabuk said, 'Do you think fighting these people will be like the others we have fought? It looks to me as if we will be tied with ropes tomorrow.' They said this is in order to intimidate and frighten the faithful. But then they said, 'Every one of us would rather by flogged a hundred lashes to escape Allah revealing a verse about us and what we have said.'"

Tabari IX:58: "When the Messenger reached Tabuk the governor of Aylah came to him, made a treaty, and agreed to pay the jizyah tax. The people of Jarba and Adhruh also offered to pay him the tax. [...]"

Ishaq:607: "[Some village leaders] encountered the Messenger's cavalry which was led by Khalid. Ukaydir was seized and his brother Hassan was killed. Hassan was wearing a silk brocade gown woven with gold in the form of palm leaves. Khalid stripped him of it and sent it to Muhammad. When it arrived, the Muslims felt it with their hands, admiring it. [...] The Prophet said, 'Are you amazed at it? The kerchiefs [neck cloths] in Paradise are better than this.' [...] Khalid brought Ukaydir to Muhammad. He spared his life and made peace with him on the condition that he pays the zakat tax. [...] they left Tabuk and returned to Medina."

CAPTIVES AND KILLERS

Tabari IX:60: "On the way [back to Medina], Muhammad ordered that whoever got to the first well before him should not drink until he arrived. Some of the hypocrites arrived and drew water. The Prophet cursed them and invoked Allah's curse on them."

Tabari IX:64: "Hatim said, 'Adi, whatever you were going to do before Muhammad's cavalry descended upon us, do it now, for I have seen the banners of his army.' When the Islamic cavalry left the settlement they took Hatim's daughter along with other captives. She was brought to the Prophet with slaves from Tayyi. He put her in an enclosure by the door of his mosque where the captives were detained."

Tabari IX:69: "Arabs are the most noble people in lineage, the most prominent, and the best in deeds. We were the first to respond to the Prophet's call. We are Allah's helpers and the viziers [high officer or counselor] of His Messenger. We fight people until they believe in Allah. He who believes in Allah and His Messenger has protected his life and possessions from us. As for those who disbelieve, we will fight them forever in the Cause of Allah [Jihad] and killing him is a small matter to us."

MUSLIMS AND NON-MUSLIMS MUST PAY

Tabari IX:74: "Indeed, Allah has guided you with His guidance. If you wish to do well, obey Allah and his Messenger. You must perform the prayers, pay the zakat tax, and give a fifth of Allah's booty to His Messenger. [...] If anyone pays more, it is to his credit. He who professes this, bears witness to his Islam and helps the faithful [fight and strive] against the polytheists, he has the protection of Allah and His Messenger."

Tabari IX:75: "He who holds fast to his religion, Judaism or Christianity, is not to be tempted from it. It is incumbent on them to pay the jizyah protection tax. For every adult, male or female, free or slave, one full denarius or its value in al-ma'afir [fine cloth]. He who pays that to the Messenger has the protection of Allah and His Messenger, and he who holds back from it is the enemy of Allah and His Messenger."

Tabari IX:76: "The Messenger has sent Zur'ah and his Companions to you. 'I commend them to your care. Collect the zakat [tax] and jizyah [tax] from your districts and hand the money over to my messengers.' The Prophet is the master of your rich and your poor. [...] [Muhammad said,] 'Malik has reported to me that you were the first from Himyar to embrace Islam and that you have killed infidels, so rejoice at your good fortune.'"

Tabari IX:78: "No polytheist shall come near the Holy Mosque, and no one shall circumambulate Allah's house naked."

Tabari IX:79: "In this year the zakat was made obligatory, and the Messenger dispatched his agents to collect it. The verse was revealed: 'Take the zakat from their wealth to purify them.'"

Tabari IX:80: "The obligatory acts of Islam one by one: The zakat tax, fasting, pilgrimage, and all the Sunnah [traditions and sayings] and Shari'a [Islamic law] of the Prophet."

AL-LAT IS DESTROYED

Ishaq:615-616: "They [Thaqafis, who just converted to Islam because they no longer wanted to be attacked] asked the Prophet if they could retain the idol Al-Lat [...] The Prophet refused [...] he sent Abu Sufyan and al-Mughira to destroy her [...] Abu Sufyan and al-Mughira smote her [Al-lat] with the ax [...] When al-Mughira had destroyed her and taken her jewels he sent for Abu Sufyan when her gold and beads had been collected."

SUMMATION:

IL: Allah stated that His religion is Islam; therefore, all other religions are false and misrepresent the truth. In order to bring them to faith in Allah, Muslim men can marry Christian women. Jews broke their covenant with

Allah long ago and He has cursed them. As a group they are treacherous. Since the Christian belief is also in error, Allah will keep conflict between the Christians and the Jews until their day of doom. This is true because Allah sent his mercy, Prophet Muhammad, to the Jews and the Christians. The Qur'an corrects the error of their book, but they refuse to accept it. For instance, Jesus could not be the equal of Allah when Allah could destroy him and his mother if he pleased. Jews and Christians claim the truth, but little do they know, that Allah will punish whom he wants to punish. In terms of punishment, the hands of thieves are to be severed. Allah may also choose to deceive his enemies. They will not know the truth when Allah decides they should be tortured. This especially applies to the Jews who forged the Bible. For this sin, they are damned by Allah. As for the Christians, they are idolatrous unbelievers. It is for these reasons that Muslims can never be friends with Jews and Christians. They are accursed evil doers. Jews are nothing more than apes and Christians are pork-eating swine. Allah fights for Islam against them.

Christians are infidels. They falsely claim the Messiah is God and that God is a Trinity. This is another sin against Allah that earns them damnation. Muslims should know if they befriend these Jewish and Christian infidels, they will also be damned to hell. Why? Jews and Christian idolaters are Muslims greatest enemies. Muslims are not to question Allah or the Prophet about this command. Muslims are to submit and obey.

WA: The Jews were all but destroyed, so Muhammad set his sights on the Byzantines. On the way to battle, Muhammad continued to have problems with Muslims who really did not want to fight. In one instance, a man did not want to fight because he felt the Byzantine women would tempt him. He placed the blame on the Byzantine women and Muhammad damned him to hell. Clearly, Muslims who will not fight or give their wealth in Jihad are of no worth to Allah. When some Muslims drank from a well before Muhammad had a chance to drink from it, Muhammad cursed them. On the march back from Tabuk, the Muslims continued the same behavior. They kept making up excuses so they would not have to fight. The price for temporary peace with Islamic Literalists is tribute that must be paid. Slaves were also in the equation like the ones presented to Muhammad. For Westerners, Tabari IX:69 is the most revealing. It states that Arabs are the best in deeds when they fight people and force them to become Muslims. According to Islam, the best results can be expected when the lives and possessions of non-believers are threatened. Islamic Literalists will never have a problem killing the infidels who refuse to bow to Allah and submit to Muhammad. However, Jews and Christians are not to be tempted from their religion as long as they finance the Islamic Jihad against other non-believers. If Jews and Christians do not pay, then they will be attacked. Jews and Christians are only worth one-third the value of a Muslim male.[21] Good fortune, as defined by Islam, equates to a person reverting to Islam who then is willing to kill infidels. Lastly, Muslims are purified when they pay the zakat tax to the Islamic authority.

QUR'AN 98

"The Clear Evidence"

631 AD

SCRIPTURE:

Qur'an 98:6

Ishaq:617-619, 628, 651-652, 659-660, 675-676; Tabari IX:82-83, 85-86, 88, 108, 111, 112-113, 115, 121-123

PREFACE:

This surah is considered the mightiest of all revelations, and a pure and essential teaching. It confirms all of the revelation revealed by the previous scriptures. In this surah, Jews and Christians are considered the worst of created beings and, thus, are deserving of death and hell.[22]

SURAH:

Qur'an 98:6: "Those who disbelieve from among the People of the Book [Jews and Christians] and the [all] idolaters [those who disbelieve Allah's revelation] will be in Fire of hell, abiding therein [forever]. They are the worst of creatures [created beings]."

SUNNAH:

AGREEMENTS CAN BE BROKEN

Ishaq:617-619: "A revelation came down permitting the breaking of agreements between the Prophet and the polytheists [...] meanwhile there were particular agreements between the Prophet and Arab tribes [...] then there came down (a revelation) concerning the hypocrites who held back on the raid at Tabuk [...] know that you cannot escape Allah and Allah will put the unbelievers to shame [...] Allah and His Prophet are free from obligation to the polytheists [...] if you repent it will be better for you [...] inform those who do not believe about the painful punishment except those polytheists who have agreed to the treaty [...] if one of those whom I ordered you to kill asks for your protection (dhimmitude) give it to him so that he may hear the word of Allah [...]

EMBRACING ISLAM TO BE SAFE

Tabari IX:82: "The Prophet sent Khalid with an army of 400 to the Harith and ordered him to invite them to Islam for three days before he fought them. If they were to respond and submit, he was to teach them the Book of Allah, the Sunnah of His Prophet, and the requirements of Islam. If they should decline, then he was to fight them. [...]"

Tabari IX:83: "The Messenger commanded me, and I sent riders announcing, 'Arabs embrace Islam and you will be safe. They surrendered and did not fight. I stayed, ordering them to fulfill the requirements of Islam.'"

Ishaq:628: "[...] The Quraysh were the [...] people of the sacred shrine, and the pure stock of Ishmael son of Abraham [...] the leading Arabs did not contest this [...] when the Quraysh became subject to him (Muhammad) and he subdued them to Islam, and the Arabs knew they could not fight the Prophet or display enmity towards him, they entered Allah's religion in batches [...] coming from all directions."

Tabari IX:85: "[Muhammad proclaimed,] 'None but the purified shall touch the Qur'an.'"

Tabari IX:86: "Give the people the good news of Paradise and the way to attain it. Warn them of the Hell-Fire and the way to earn it. Teach them the rites of the pilgrimage, its practices, its obligations and what Allah has commanded about the hajj and umrah. [...] He orders you to offer prayer at the appropriate times and proper bowing and humility. [...] He orders you to give one fifth of Allah's booty and pay the zakat tax. It is enjoined on the faithful from their land and property. [...] And don't seduce the Jews or Christians for incumbent on them is to pay the jizyah protection tax. [...] Allah's Apostle dispersed his representatives to every land where Islam had entered to collect the zakat. [...]"

WOMEN'S RIGHTS IN ISLAM

Ishaq:651: "You have rights over your wives and they have rights over you. You have the right that they should not defile your bed and that they should not behave with open unseemliness. If they do, God allows you to put them in separate rooms and to beat them, but not with severity. If they refrain from these things, they have the right to their food and clothing with kindness. Lay injunctions on women kindly, for they are prisoners with you having no control of their persons."

Tabari IX:108: "When Allah's Messenger returned to Medina after performing the hajj of Perfection in Religion, he began to have a complaint of illness [...] News of the Prophet's illness spread, so Musaylima [a Yemini messenger] leapt at the opportunity to claim the prophethood for himself."

Tabari IX:111: "[...] Ali returned from Yemen with an army dressed in white linen to meet Muhammad. [...]"

Tabari IX:112-113: "[The Prophet said,] 'Beware of Satan in your religion. [...] You have a right over your wives and they have a right over you. You have a right that they should not cause any one of whom you dislike to tread your beds; and that they should not commit any open indecency. If they do, then Allah permits you to shut them in separate rooms and to beat them, but not severely. If they abstain, they have the right to food and clothing. Treat women well for they are like domestic animals with you and they do not possess anything themselves. Allah has made the enjoyment of their bodies lawful in his Qur'an."

THE HAJJ IS COMPLETED

Tabari IX:115: "The Messenger completed the pilgrimage, showed the people its rites, and taught them what was required of them including the stations, the throwing of pebbles, the running around the Ka'aba, and what Allah had permitted them to do, and what he had forbidden. [...]"

Ishaq:652: "The Prophet completed the Hajj and showed men [...] what Allah prescribed to their Hajj [...] and what was permitted and forbidden. It was the pilgrimage of farewell because the Prophet did not go on pilgrimage after that."

MORE CONQUESTS

Tabari IX:88: "Abdallah Azdi came to the Prophet, embraced Islam, and became a good Muslim. Allah's Prophet invested Azdi with the authority over those who had surrendered and ordered him to fight the infidels from the tribes of Yemen. Azdi left with an army by the Messenger's command. The Muslims besieged them for a month. Then they withdrew, setting a trap. When the Yemenites went in pursuit, Azdi was able to inflict a heavy loss on them. [...]"

MUHAMMAD'S ILLNESS

Tabari IX:121: "[After assassinating Yusayr, a Jew from Khaybar, by severing his leg] The Messenger said, 'I suspect that Khalid Sufyan is going to attack me. So go to him and kill him.' 'O Prophet, describe him to me so that I might know him.' He [Muhammad] said, 'When you see him he will remind you of Satan.' When it was feasible for me, I struck him with my sword and killed him. Then I departed, leaving his women to throw themselves at him. [Khalid Sufyan was murdered in front of his wife and daughter] When I returned to the Prophet, he asked, 'Is your mission accomplished?' 'Yes. I have killed him.' [...] The Prophet's illness intensified, the pain became fierce, so he said, after entering my apartment, 'Pour seven skins of water over me from different wells, and from skins whose mouths have not been untied, so that I may give advice to the people.' [...]"

Tabari IX:122: "Muhammad sent Uyaynah to raid the Banu Anbar. They killed some people and took others captive. Asma was one of the women taken prisoner."

Tabari IX:123: "Muhammad sent an expedition to Ghalib and to the land of the Banu Murrah. The expedition of Amr and Abi was sent to the valley of Idam. Another by Aslami was sent to Ghabah. And Abd al-Rahman was ordered by the Messenger to lead an army to the seashore."

Ishaq:659-660: "The Prophet took part in 27 raids [...] Waddan [...] the raid of al-Abwa, Buwat[...] Radwa, Ushayrah [...] valley of Yanbu, Badr [...] Kurz b. Jabir, The great Battle of Badr, Banu Sulaym [...] Al-Kudr, Al-Sawiq [...] Abu Sufyan, Ghatafan [...] raid of Dhu Amarr, Bahran [...] Hejaz, Uhud, Hamra ul-Asad, Banu Nadir, Dhatu 'l-Riqa of Nakhal, Last battle of Badr, Dumatu'l Jandal, Al-Khandaq, Banu Qurayza, Banu Lihyan [...] Hudhayl, Dhu Qarad, Banu Mustaliq [...] Khua'a, Khaybar, Mecca, Hunayn, Al-Ta'if, and Tabuk."

KILLING THE POETS

Ishaq:675-676: "Abu 'Afak [an old Jewish poet] was one of the [...] B. Ubayda clan. He showed his disaffection when the Apostle killed Al-Harith b. Suwayd b. Samit and [Abu 'Afak] said, 'Long have I lived [120 years old] but never have I seen an assembly or collection of people more faithful to their undertaking and their allies when called upon than the sons of Qayla when they assembled, men who overthrew mountains and never submitted, a rider who came to them split them in two (saying) "Permitted", "Forbidden", of all sorts of things. Had you believed in glory or kingship you would have followed Tubba.' The Apostle said, 'Who will deal with this rascal for me?' Whereupon Salim b. Umayr, brother of B. Amr b. Auf, one of the "weepers", went forth and killed him [Abu 'Afak, the old Jewish poet]. [...] [Asma bint Marwan, a poetess], was of B. Umayya b. Zayd. When Abu 'Afak had been killed she displayed disaffection. [...] Blaming Islam and its followers she said, 'I despise B. Malik and al-Nabit and Auf and B. al-Khazraj. You obey a stranger who is none of yours, one not of Murad or Maddhij. Do you expect good from him after the killing of your chiefs like a hungry man waiting for a cook's broth? Is there no man of pride who would attack by surprise and cutoff the hopes of those who expect aught [anything] from him?' When the Apostle [Muhammad] heard what she had said, he [Muhammad] said, 'Who will rid me of Marwan's daughter?' Umayr b. Adiy al-Khatml, who was with him [Muhammad], heard him [Muhammad], and that very night he went to her house and killed her. In the morning he [Umar b. Adiy al-Khatml] came to the Apostle and told him what he had done and he [Muhammad] said [reassuring him], 'You have helped God [Allah] and His Apostle, O Umayr!' When asked if he would have to bear any consequences, the Apostle said, 'Two goats won't butt their heads about her.' [...] The day after Amsa bint Marwan was killed, the men of the B. Khatma became Muslims because they *saw the power of Islam* [emphasis added]."

SUMMATION:

IL: Allah is God and cannot be wrong. Muslims must know the most detestable of all people are Jews and Christians. Thus, the Prophet Muhammad and his true followers were justified by any actions they deemed appropriate towards those who rejected the Prophet's revelation of the true religion. This also signifies the point where the Prophet made a complete break in terms of any agreements with the pagans. From this period forward, the pagan Arabs could be killed when they encountered the Muslims.[23]

WA: Entering agreements or treaties with Islamic entities can be problematic. In this instance, Allah and Muhammad are free from obligations with polytheists. Does this apply to Christian idolaters? This would explain why those entering the Dhimmi treaty are offered Islamic protection. Usually, Islamic protection was not offered to those who were not included as People of the Book. Curiously, during Muhammad's last sermon he did not extend physical protection to Muslim wives. After being reminded of all the raids he set in motion by his own command, Muhammad ordered the assassinations of two more men and a pregnant woman who criticized him. The assassins who killed the men had no conscience, but the young assassin of the bint Marwan was troubled by what he did. Enter Muhammad who told the young assassin that this murder of bint Marwan, which included her unborn innocent child, "helped Allah and His Prophet." Are we to believe that Allah *needed* this woman and her unborn child murdered? Sequentially, Muhammad said, "Two goats won't butt their heads about her." Egyptian Islamic Scholar Muhammad Husain Haykal then recorded in his book, *The Life of Muhammad*, p. 242, that her tribe, the Banu Khutmah, became Muslims because they felt the power of Islam. Radicals believe this behavior reaps converts. If it worked then, it should work now.

In the events recorded concerning the Harith, Islam was supposed to be offered to them first before an attack could ensue. If this offer was not accepted, Khalid and his 400 were to attack and defeat them. What seemed gracious towards Jews and Christians was not gracious at all. By keeping Jews and Christians outside of Islam, Muslims collected a much bigger tax to fund their Jihad. If People of the Book resisted Muslim occupiers, then they could be killed and the Muslims would confiscate all of their property. This is a win-win scenario for the Muslim Literalists.

Before the attack against Yemen, Muhammad identified another 'good' Muslim who was willing to wage Jihad. As Yemen was assailed by Islamic invaders, Muhammad completed his religious rites at Mecca and returned to Medina in an ill and weakened state. By displaying his mortality, it did not take long for another to claim Muhammad's place among Allah's chosen.

In Muhammad's last sermon he warned about Satan in Islam. What could he have meant? What immediately followed was his diatribe against women. Muhammad stated that women could be beaten and starved if perceived that they were not acting properly. Women were equated with domestic animals and were said to have been created so that men could enjoy their bodies. One must wonder what Muslim women think of this. Do they question it? After Muhammad had another Jew murdered, his illness got even worse. Why wasn't he blessed for killing Allah's enemy? Muhammad, getting closer to death, suspected—he had no proof—that Sufyan wanted to attack him. So Muhammad ordered the murder of Sufyan. He was murdered in front of his family. A good Muslim, no doubt, hacked Sufyan to death. Even with his health failing, Muhammad was still ordering raids and killing non-Muslim Arabs.

The example of how Muslims are encouraged to behave when they are in the ascent (in power or acquiring power) can be found in the hadith Muslim:B19C2N4294. It is known as the *Medinan-Quraysh Model*. It states Muslims should invite enemies to Islam.[24] If they refuse, demand they pay the penalty tax. If they once again refuse remember; "War is Deception." After striking the enemy of Allah, treat an enemy countermeasure as an unprovoked attack. Respond by fighting anyone who persecutes Muslims. Vanquish those who reject Islam, and ultimately conquer the world in Islam's name.[25] The infidels have three choices: *Conversion, Dhimmitude* ("Subjugation"), or *Death*.[26]

QUR'AN 114

"The Men"

632 AD

SCRIPTURE:

Qur'an 114:1-6

Bukhari:V1B8N428, V2B23N414, V5B59N713, V5B5N727, Ishaq:678, 682-683, 688; Muwatta:B45S5N17; Tabari IX:156, 166-169, 174-175, 178, 181, 183; Tafsir Ibn Kathir

PREFACE:

Protection must be sought from evil men and from the evil that resides in the heart of men. The Qur'an was revealed for the perfection of mankind.[27]

SURAH:

Qur'an 114:1-6: "Say: I seek refuge in the Lord of men, the king of men, the God of men, from the evil of the whisperings of the slinking devil, who whispers into the hearts of men, from among the Jinn and the men."

SUNNAH:

THE OBLITERATOR CURSES JEWS AND CHRISTIANS

Tabari IX:156: "The Messenger of Allah named himself to us in various ways. He said, 'I am Muhammad, the one who is praised, Ahmad, the most praiseworthy, al-Aqib, the last in succession, and Al-Mahdi, the obliterator.'"

Ishaq:678: "The Prophet began to suffer from the illness by which Allah took him…It began when he […] went in the middle of the night to pray for the dead. When he returned to his family in the morning his sufferings began […]

Bukhari:V5B59N713: "The Prophet in his ailment used to say to Aisha, 'I feel the pain caused by the food I ate at Khaybar.' My aorta is being cut by that poison."

Tabari IX:166: "The Prophet ordered the expedition of Usama, but it did not go well because of his illness and because two other Arabs had proclaimed themselves prophets and renounced his authority. The Prophet's head was wrapped around because of the pain. [Muhammad said in pain,] 'May Allah curse those who make the tombs of their Prophets places of worship.'"

Bukhari:V1B8N428: "May Allah curse Jews and Christians for they built their places of worship at the graves of the Prophets."

Muwatta:B45S5N17: "No two religions are to exist in the Arab peninsula."

Tabari IX:167: "Muhammad waged war against the false prophets by sending messengers with instructions to get rid of them by artful contrivance. […]"

Tabari IX:168: "He turned to me saying, 'Abu Muwayhibah, I have been given the keys of the treasures of the world.' […]"

NOT WILLING TO DIE ALONE

Tabari IX:169: "Aisha said, 'When the Messenger returned from the Baqi cemetery he found me. He was suffering from a headache and crying. 'Alas, O my head!' he moaned, 'Nay, by Allah, O Aisha, rather alas, O my head!' […] Then he said, 'Would it distress you if you were to die before me so that I could take care of your body, wrap you in a shroud, pray over you, and bury you?' […] Aisha replied, 'It seems to me that if you were to do that you would return to my apartment and would party with another one of your wives.'"

Tafsir Ibn Kathir: *Muhammad told Aisha that he would be married to Mary the mother of Jesus, Miriam the sister of Moses, and to Assiya wife of Pharaoh Ramses II when he entered paradise.*

Tabari IX:174: "The Messenger's pain became so severe he said, 'Give me pen and paper so I may write a document for you so you will never go astray after me.' […] His companions wrangled over it. But it did not befit them to carry on a dispute before a profit. Some people said, 'What's the matter with him? Is he talking nonsense? He is delusional.' Others said, 'We must ask him for an explanation.' So they went back to him and repeated what had been said. The Prophet replied, 'Leave me alone.'"

Tabari IX:175: "[Muhammad said,] 'Bring me a tablet, or a plank of the shoulder blade and an inkpot, so that I can write for you a document, after which you will not go astray.' Some said, 'The Messenger of Allah is out of his mind.'"

Tabari IX:178: "Some Muslims said that they were afraid he might have pleurisy [fluid around the lungs]. He [Muhammad] said, 'Pleurisy is from Satan and Allah would not inflict it on me.'"

EXONERATION AND AGONY

Bukhari:V5B59N727: "The Prophet said, '[…] whomever I have flogged on the back with a whip, here is my back—let him avenge. Whomever I have reviled, here is my honor—let him retort […] that he should absolve me from it so that I shall meet the Lord while I am exonerated.'"

Tabari IX:181: "Before Muhammad died, he cried, 'O my Lord, help me overcome the severity of the agony of death.'"

THE DEATH OF MUHAMMAD

Tabari IX:183: "Aisha said, 'Muhammad rubbed his teeth with it ["Siwak," a twig] more energetically than I had ever seen him do before. Then he put it down, and I found him getting heavy in my lap...and he died."'

Ishaq:682-683: "The Prophet came back to me from the mosque that day and lay on my lap [...] I found him heavy on my breast [...] his eyes were fixed and he said, "No the most exalted companion is of Paradise [...] When the Prophet was dead Umar got up and said, [...] 'By Allah the Prophet will return as Moses returned (from Sinai) and will cut off the hands and feet of men who allege that the Prophet is dead [...]' Umar said, 'If anyone worships Muhammad he is dead; If anyone worships Allah he is alive, He is immortal [...].' Umar said [...], 'When I heard Abu Bakr recite these words, I was dumbfounded [...] I fell to the ground realizing that the Prophet was indeed dead.'"

Ishaq:688: "Abu Bakr said, 'I heard the Prophet say, "No prophet dies but he is buried where he died." So the bed on which he died was taken up and they made a grave beneath it [...]. The Prophet was buried in the middle of the night on a Wednesday."

Bukhari:V2B23N414: "Aisha said, 'The Prophet in his fatal illness said, "Allah cursed the Jews and the Christians because they took the graves of their Prophets as places for praying."' Aisha added, 'Had it not been for that, the grave of the Prophet would have been made prominent but I am afraid it might be taken as a place for praying.'"

SUMMATION:

IL: The Prophet reaffirmed his commitment to Allah as the 'Lord of men' as his mission on earth was about to conclude. The Qur'an was revealed in its entirety and Allah's will was transmitted to humanity so the world would heed the divine command to submit. In time the world will submit to Allah's religion.

WA: The Prophet of Islam, who brought the Qur'anic revelation, was a self-described obliterator. How are non-Muslims supposed to think and speak of this? It does not give one the feeling that Islam was established to be a good neighbor with those who reject the Qur'anic revelation. Muhammad's demise was now apparent to some. By the year 632AD two other Arabs claimed to be a prophet while Muhammad suffered with his illness. In the hadith of Sahih Bukhari, Muhammad appeared to be unsure of his eternal destination. Why did he ask that he receive the same punishment as he punished others? As Muhammad strived to get rid of his prophetic competition, he selfishly asked Aisha, who was forty-four years younger, to die before him. No one appeared to know Muhammad better than Aisha. She came across as being pretty sharp and told Muhammad that if she died, he would just take up with other women. Muhammad appeared to be losing touch with reality. At the end, he had a difficult time accepting that his god, who so favored him, would allow "His Prophet" to die delusional and in excruciating pain. Unfortunately, before he perished, Muhammad claimed the poison that he spit out two years prior, was the reason for his eventual demise. A Jewess tried to kill him because Muslims, obeying Muhammad's order, killed her family. In pain knowing that death was near, Muhammad cursed the Jews and Christians and forbade them from ever practicing their religion in Arabia.

Why would Muhammad state he would be married to Jesus' mother, Moses' sister, and the Pharaohs' wife after he died? In saying these things, Muhammad predicted the mother of the Christians, the sister of the Jews, and the queen of the polytheists would submit to him and Islam throughout eternity.

"The Help"

632 AD

SCRIPTURE:

Qur'an 110:1-3

Bukhari:V5B59N546, V5B59N727, V9B84N59; Tabari IX:187-188, 196, 204

PREFACE:

A few weeks before Muhammad died he prophesied that people would come to Islam in great numbers. Soon thereafter, all of Arabia was claimed and conquered by Islam.[28]

SURAH:

Qur'an 110:1-3: "When Allah's help and victory comes, and thou seest men [people] entering the religion of Allah in companies [massive numbers], celebrate the praise of thy Lord and ask His protection. Surely He is ever Returning to mercy."

SUNNAH:

MUHAMMAD'S SUCCESSOR

Bukhari:V5B59N727: "Aisha added, 'I had argued with Allah's Prophet repeatedly about his order that Abu Bakr should lead the people in his place. What made me argue so much was that it never occurred to my mind that after the Prophet, the people would ever love a man who had taken his place. I felt that anyone standing in his place would be a bad omen to the people, so I wanted him to give up the idea of choosing dad.'"

Tabari IX:187: "When the Prophet died, Umar stood up threatening the people, saying, 'Some of the hypocrites allege that the Messenger of Allah is dead. I swear by Allah that he is alive, not dead. By Allah, the Prophet will return and he will go after those who are spreading lies about him. He will cut off the hands and the feet of those who claim that he is dead. He will crucify them.' [...] Bakr saw that Umar would not listen. He went forward, saying, 'I swear by the Lord of the Ka'aba that Muhammad is gone. Those people who formerly worshipped Muhammad must know that the deity you worshipped is dead. Those who formerly worshipped Allah must know that Allah is still alive and immortal.'"

Tabari IX:188: "Zubayr drew his sword saying, 'I will not put it back until the oath of allegiance is rendered to Ali.' When this news reached Abu Bakr and Umar, the latter said, 'Hit him with a stone and seize the sword.'"

Tabari IX:196: "Fatimah and Ali came to Bakr demanding their share of inheritance of the Messenger. They demanded Muhammad's land in Fadak and his share of Khaybar's tribute. [...] [Bakr refused, so] Fatimah shunned him and did not speak to Bakr until she died. Ali buried her at night and did not permit Abu Bakr to attend her burial."

Bukhari:V5B59N546: "[...] When Fatima was alive the people used to respect Ali, but after her death, Ali noticed a change in the people's attitude towards him. So he sought reconciliation with Bakr [...] he [Ali] disliked Umar [...] Ali said [to Bakr], '[...] I know your superiority and am not jealous, but you did not consult me in the question of who rules and I thought that I had a right to rule because of my near relationship to Allah's Prophet. [...] As for the trouble that arose between me and you about his property, I will spend it according to what is good, and will not leave any rule or regulation which I saw Allah's Prophet following in disposing of it.' [...]"

Bukhari:V9B84N59: "When the Prophet died and Abu Bakr became his successor and some of the Arabs reverted to disbelief, Umar said, 'O Abu

Bakr! How can you fight these people [...] "Abu Bakr said, 'By Allah! I will fight whoever differentiates between prayers and zakat, as zakat is the right to be taken from property according to Allah's orders. By Allah! If they refuse to pay me even so little as a kid used to pay to Allah's Apostle, I would fight with them for withholding it.' Umar said, 'By Allah…I noticed that Allah opened Abu Bakr's chest towards the decision to fight [Abu Bakr decided to continue the Jihad and credited Allah with his decision], therefore I realized his decision was right.'"

SUMMATION:

IL: Muslims were promised that they would celebrate because Allah predicted that masses of people would come to Islam. At that time in history, there were 200,000 Muslims.[29] The legacy that Prophet Muhammad left in revealing the Qur'an and what it teaches exploded onto the world scene, proving that Islam is the truth.

WA: Islam claimed to be a monotheistic religion. If so, how could some of the earliest Muslims worship Muhammad? After Muhammad's death, Abu Bakr became the first Caliph. Before that happened, Umar, who would later become the second Caliph, threatened numerous acts of violence against the peaceful Muslim hypocrites. Abu Bakr found it necessary to direct all of the Muslims towards Allah since Muhammad was dead. If any of this was true, it suggested that Muhammad set himself up to be obeyed similar to how one would obey a god. After Muhammad died, Abu Bakr wanted to affirm that only Allah should be worshipped. Therefore, we can conclude that some Muslims worshipped Muhammad during his lifetime.

Zubayr's accusations and Umar's response planted the seeds of Muslim rebellion and established the foundation of civil war. The next rift occurred because Abu Bakr would not allow Fatima, Muhammad's daughter, to collect what her father was collecting from the Jews. Fatima had nothing more to do with Abu Bakr. She died years later. As for Ali, he did not like Abu Bakr, but he liked Umar even less, so he appealed respectfully to Abu Bakr. As Arab clans began to abandon Islam, because Muhammad was dead, Abu Bakr and Umar decided to make war on these Muslim apostates. They wanted to ensure the zakat tax would continue to be paid. [30] Muslim spirituality had nothing to do with this situation. They simply did not want to lose their revenue so they went to war.

CHAPTER 7 NOTES

1. Ali, p. 697; Pickthall, p. 253
2. Al-Misri, *Reliance of the Traveller*, pp. 550-553
3. Kathir, *Tafsir Ibn Kathir*, Vol. 7, p. 67
4. Khadduri, *War and Peace*, p. 17
5. Ali, p. 994; Pickthall, p. 364
6. Spencer, *The Truth About Muhammad*, p. 20
7. Ali, p. 1081; Pickthall, p. 395
8. Ali, p. 1004; Pickthall, p. 367
9. Ali, p. 1234; Pickthall, p. 447
10. Swarup, *Understanding the Hadith*, p. 76
11. Ali, p. 499; Pickthall, p. 182
12. Ali, p. 1043; Pickthall, p. 381
13. Ali, p. 1159; Pickthall, p. 423
14. Ali, p. 986; Pickthall, p. 361
15. Ali, p. 395; Pickthall, p. 144
16. Peters, *Muhammad and the Origins of Islam*, p. 239
17. Kathir, *Tafsir Ibn Kathir*, Vol. 1, p. 87
18. Peters, *Jihad in Classical and Modern Islam*, p. 34
19. Ali, p. 1105; Pickthall, p. 404
20. Ali, p. 244; Pickthall, p. 095
21. Al-Misri, *Reliance of the Traveller*, p. xx
22. Ali, p. 1232; Pickthall, p. 446
23. Rubin, *Bara'a: A Study of Some Qur'anic Passages*, pp.17-20
24. Qutb, *In the Shade of the Qur'an*, p. 62
25. Langley, *World Religions*, p. 85
26. Al-Misri, *Reliance of the Traveller*, p. 602
27. Ali, p. 1260; Pickthall, p. 455
28. Ali, p. 1254; Pickthall, p. 453
29. Haeri, *Elements of Islam*, pp. 12 & 15
30. Kathir, *Tafsir Ibn Kathir*, Vol. 4, p. 377

*This quote is related to Muslim:B19N1731. This quote was found in *Misconceptions on Human Rights in Islam* by Abdul-Rahman al-sheha on page 23*

CONCLUSION

Before we conclude let us first do a recap of Muhammad's life. He personally participated in twenty-seven military expeditions (Tabari IX:115). Some sources claim that Muhammad participated in thirty-eight raids.[1] Between 622 AD and 632 AD Muhammad sent Islamic forces on forty-seven battles.[2] According to Sahih Muslim, the total number he ordered and participated in was eighty-two military expeditions. [3] He ordered the assassinations of thirty-six men and women (Tabari IX:118). Muhammad had fifty-nine slaves and thirty-eight male and female servants.[4]

The Prophet of Allah married fifteen women (Tabari IX:126). According to Shi'a Islam, Muhammad married twenty-two times including two captured women.[5] Here are some of the details. The Prophet wanted to marry the infant Ummu'l, but he died before he was able (Ishaq:311). Muhammad, who was fifty at the time, married Aisha who was six years old. When Aisha was nine years old her mother took her from a swing. A nurse cleaned her and she was brought to her house. The Prophet was sitting on a bed. Her mother placed Aisha on Muhammad's lap. The men and women in the house got up and left. Muhammad then had sex with her (Tabari IX:128-131). Muhammad chose Juwayriyah after the Muraysi raid from among the captives. Later, he married Umm after she became a Christian (Tabari IX:133). Muhammad married his daughter-in-law after his adopted son divorced her. Allah did not find any fault in the relationship and ordered the marriage (Tabari IX:134). After the defeat of the Jews at Khaybar, Muhammad chose Safiyah after he had her husband executed (Tabari IX:135). Muhammad chose Rayhana, who was a Qurayza

483

Jewess after she witnessed the decapitation of her father, brother, and saw her mother and sisters taken as concubines. Then Mariyah, a Coptic Christian, was given to Muhammad by the ruler of Alexandria (Tabari IX:137). The Prophet married Aliyah, but he left her and divorced her. He also married Qutaylah, but he died before he could have sex with her (Tabari IX:138). Layla approached the Prophet. When he asked who it was, she said that she came to offer herself to him. Muhammad accepted. After learning what had happened, her parents spoke to her.

> "'What a bad thing you have done! You are a self respecting girl, but the Prophet is a womanizer'"

> —Tabari IX:139

A eunuch named Mubur was given to Muhammad along with two slave girls. He kept one as a concubine and gave the other to Hassan (Tabari IX:147). As for his appearance, Muhammad was a man of average height with a large head, big black eyes, and long chest hair. He was white in complexion and his face had a reddish tinge. He also had a protruding lump of flesh on his back (Tabari IX:157-159).

The Muhammad of history was portrayed in this book according to the authoritative sources of Islam. For Muslims who search after truth they must ask themselves an honest question: Was Muhammad the most wonderful person who ever walked the earth? If your answer is *yes*, then you must agree with his acts of violence, speeches of contempt, and behavior concerning women. If your answer is *no*, then you must also realize that the Qur'an cannot be the sole document among men that reveals the will of the Creator of the universe. This does not mean that God does not exist; rather, it means he must be found elsewhere. Read the New Testament. Assess it on its merits then ask yourself; is the Jesus of the New Testament worthy of Lordship in your life? Pray to the God who Jesus called Abba, Father. Ask this God for the truth. This God of Holiness will answer and bring you inner peace if you can accept His answer.

For those in the West who have been exposed to this material for the first time, try to understand that Muslims have been exposed to this material since the time of Muhammad. In my next book you will learn the impact this ideology has had on the affairs of men over the past fourteen centuries. Be careful to distinguish individual Muslims from Islamic Ideology. Don't assume that all Muslims are aware of this material, or subscribe to it. By coming to understand the concepts discussed in this book, you will now be equipped to ask the proper questions. This is important to determine if individual Muslims are Medinan (Jihadists), Meccan (Muslim Brotherhood sympathizers), or strictly cultural Muslims who reject Political Islam and any application of Islam apart from a personal application.

The threat posed by Islamic Literalists, in their application of Political Islam, will be with us for the remainder of our lives. By understanding the Literalist point of view, we will be in a better position to meaningfully engage Muslims, protect ourselves from Islamic Ideology, and convey these truths to the world to help prevent others from being unaware and unprepared.

CONCLUSION NOTES

1. Ye'or, *Islam and Dhimmitude*, pp. 36-37
2. Richardson, *Secrets of the Koran*, p. 10
3. Swarup, *Understanding the Hadith*, p. 114
4. Ibid., p. 84
5. Ibid., p. 77

BIBLIOGRAPHY

Abdal-Haqq, Irshad. <u>Islamic Law: An Overview of its Origins and Elements,</u> <u>in Understanding Islamic Law; From Classical to Contemporary,</u> Hisham M. Ramadan, 2006.

Ahmad, Barakat. <u>Muhammad and the Jews</u>. New Delhi: Vikas Publishing House, 1979.

Akram, AI. <u>The Sword of Allah</u>. Lahore: Feroze Sons Publishers, 1969.

Akram, Mohamed. <u>The General Strategic Goal for the Group in North America</u>, Shura Council, Muslim Brotherhood, 1991.

Ali, Abdullah Yusuf. <u>The Meaning of the Holy Qur'an</u>, Beltsville, Md.: Amana Publications, 1999.

Ali, Maulana Muhammad. <u>The Holy Qur'an with English Translation and Commentary</u>. Dublin, Ohio: Ahmadiya Anjuman Isha'at Islam Lahore Inc., USA, 2002.

Ankerberg, John; Caner, Emir. <u>Islam & Jihad</u>. Eugene, Oregon: Harvest House, 2009.

Asad, Muhammad. <u>The Message of the Qur'an</u>. Watsonville, Ca, The Book Foundation, 2003.

Al-Azraki, Abu al-Walid Muhammad. <u>Ahkbar Makka</u>. Leipzig, Germany: Wustenfeld, 1858

Bostum, Andrew. <u>The Legacy of Islamic Anti-Semitism</u>. Amherst, N.Y: Prometheus Publishing, 2008.

Caner, Ergun and Emir. <u>Unveiling Islam</u>. Grand Rapids, Mi: Kregel Publications, 2002.

Cook, Michael. <u>Muhammad</u>. Oxford, England: Oxford University Press, 1983.

Crone, Patricia. <u>Slaves on Horses: The Evolution of the Islamic Polity</u>. Cambridge, England: Cambridge University Press, 1980.

Davis, Paul K. <u>100 Decisive Battles</u>; New York, New York: Oxford University Press, 2001.

Demy, Timothy & Stewart Gary. <u>In the Name of God</u>; Eugene, Oregon: Harvest House, 2002.

<u>Encyclopedia of Islam</u>, I: 302, Leiden: E.J. Brill, 1913, Houtsma.

"Encyclopedia of the Middle East," <http://www.mideastweb.org/Middle-East-Encyclopedia/abu-bakr.htm>

<u>Encyclopedia of Religion</u>, I:117, Washington DC, Corpus Pub., 1979.

<u>Encyclopedia of World Mythology and Legend</u>, Anthony Mercatante, New York, The Facts on File, 1983).

Esposito, John. <u>The Straight Path</u>. New York, Oxford University Press, 1991.

Esposito, John. <u>Women in Muslim Family Law</u>; 2nd ed., 2001.

Farah, Caesar. <u>Islam: Beliefs and Observations</u>, New York, Barrons, 1987.

Geisler, Norman; Saleeb, Abdul. <u>Answering Islam</u>. Grand Rapids: Baker Books, 2002.

Al-Ghazali. <u>Counsel for Kings</u>, London: University of Durham Publications, 1971.

Al-Ghazali, Muhammad. <u>Journey through the Qur'an</u>. London: Dar Al-Taqwa, Ltd, 1998.

Grant, George. <u>Blood of the Moon</u>; Nashville, Tennessee: Thomas Nelson Publishers, 2001.

Guillaume, Alfred. <u>Islam</u>; New York: Penguin Books, 1954.

Guillaume, Alfred. <u>The Life of Muhammad</u>; Translated from the Sirat Rasul Allah, known as the Sirah or Biography, written by Ibn Ishaq; edited and abridged by Ibn Hisham. Oxford, England: Oxford Press, 1955.

Hallaq, Waed B. <u>A History of Islamic Legal Theories</u>; New York: Cambridge University Press, 1997.

Hamid, Tawfik. <u>Inside Jihad: Understanding and Confronting Radical Islam</u>, 2007.

Hitti, Phillip. <u>History of the Arabs</u>, 10th ed., 2002.

<u>International Standard Bible Encyclopedia</u>, rev. ed., vol. 5: Chicago, 1929.

Haeri, Shaykh Fadhlalla. <u>Elements of Islam</u>. Great Britain: Zahra Publications, 1993.

Henninger, J. <u>Pre-Islamic Bedouin Religion</u>. Rome: Oxford University Press, 1959.

Al- Kalbi, Ibn. <u>Book of Idols</u>. Princeton, N.J: Princeton University Press, 1952.

Khadduri, Majid. <u>War and Peace: Law in the Middle East</u>. Liebesny eds., 1955.

Kathir, Ibn. <u>Tafsir Ibn Kathir</u>, Houston: Darussalam, 2000.

Khan, Dr. Muhammad Muhsin. <u>Sahih Al-Bukhari-The True Traditions</u>. Al-Madinah: Maktaba Dar-us-Islam, 1959.

Khan, Dr. Muqtedar. <u>The Legacy of the Prophet Muhammad</u>, Issues of Pedophilia and Polygamy, Ijtihad, 2003.

Langley, Myrtle. <u>World Religions</u>; Oxford, England: Lion Publishing, 1993.

Lewis, Bernard. <u>The Crisis of Islam</u>; New York: Random House, 2004.

Lewis, Bernard. <u>The Political Language of Islam</u>; New York: Random House, 1991.

Lewis, Jon E., <u>How it Happened: Great Historical Moments</u>; London, England: Constable Publishers, 2001.

Mawil, Izzi Dien. <u>Islamic Law: Historical Foundations to Contemporary Practice</u>, 2004.

Misri, Ahmad Ibn Naqib. <u>Reliance of the Traveller: A Classic Manual of Islamic Sacred Law</u>; Amana Publications, rev. ed., 2008.

Muir, Sir William. <u>The Life of Mahomet</u>; London, England: 1877.

Nasr, Seyyed Hossein. <u>A Young Muslims Guide to the Modern World</u>; Chicago, Kazi Publications, 1994.

Peters, F.E. <u>Muhammad and the Origins of Islam</u>: Albany: State University of New York Press, 1994.

Peters, Rudolph. <u>Crime and Punishment in Islamic Law</u>; Princeton, NJ: Markus Weiner Publishers, 2005.

Peters, Rudolph. Jihad in Classical and Modern Islam; Princeton, NJ: Markus Weiner Publishers, 1996.

Pickthall, Mohammad Marmaduke. The Meaning of the Glorious Koran. New York: Mentor Book Published by the Penguin Group, 1935.

Qutb, Sayyid. In the Shade of the Qur'an, Translation, Markfield, and Leichestershire: The Islamic Foundation, 1999.

Al-Rawandi, Ibn. Origins of Islam. Amherst: Prometheus Books, 2000.

Richardson, Don. Secrets of the Koran. Ventura, California: Regal Books, 2003.

Rizvi, Syed Saeed Akhtar. The Life of Muhammad the Prophet, 1999.

Rubin, Uri. Bara'a: A Study of Some Qur'anic Passages, Jerusalem Studies in Arabic and Islam, 1984.

Ryckmans, G. Pre-Islamic Arab Religions. Louvain, France, 1951.

Sabini, John, Islam: A Primer. Washington D.C: Middle East Editorial Associates, 1983.

Sa'd, Ibn, Kitab Al-Tabaqat Al-Kabir. Ghazanfar: Kitab Bhavan.

Sekulow, Jay Alan. Shari'a Law: Radical Islam's Threat to the U.S. Constitution. Washington D.C: American Center for Law & Justice, 2011.

Shahrazuri, Ibn Al-Salah. An Introduction to the Science of Hadith. 1st ed., Garnet Publishing, 2005.

Siddiqui, Abdul Hamid. Translation of Sahih Muslim. Los Angeles: Center for Muslim Jewish Engagement, University of Southern California, 2009.

Spencer, Robert. The Politically Incorrect Guide to Islam. Washington D.C: Regnery Publishing, 2005.

Spencer, Robert. The Truth About Muhammad. Washington D.C: Regnery Publishing, 2006.

"Submission.Org," <www.submission.org/suras/sura75.html>

Swarup, Ram. Understanding the Hadith. Amherst, New York: Prometheus Books, 2002.

Tabbarah, Afif A. The Spirit of Islam, 1988.

Al-Tabari, Abu Muhammad bin. Tarikh: the History of al-Tabari. New York: State University of New York Press, 1987-1997.

Tate, Georges. The Crusades and the Holy Land. London: Thames & Hudson Ltd, 1996.

The International Standard Bible Encyclopedia, rev. ed., vol. 5 (Chicago, 1929), pp. 2950-2957.

Warraq, Ibn. Why I am not a Muslim. Amherst, Ma: Prometheus Books, 1995.

Watt, William Montgomery; Cachia, Pierre. History of Islamic Spain. Edinburgh: Edinburgh University Press, 1965.

Watt, William Montgomery. Muhammad: Prophet and Statesman. Oxford: Oxford University Press, 1974.

"Witness Pioneer, The Death of Abu Bakr," <http://www.witnesspioneer. org/vil/Articles/companion/18_abu_bakr.htm>

Ye'or, Bat. Islam and Dhimmitude: Where civilizations Collide; Crandury NJ: Associated University Presses, 2002.

Zakaria, Rafiq. Muhammad and the Qur'an; Middlesex, England: Penguin Books, 1991.

ABOUT THE AUTHOR

Mr. Joseph Butta is an Independent Analyst who provides threat analysis and threat presentations upon request. Mr. Butta specializes in threat, as portrayed by major powers in Asia. He also provides analysis and insight into the ideological threat posed by extremist groups. Mr. Butta is an Operations Security practitioner and focuses on International and Ideological threats that exploit vulnerabilities to gain access to sensitive information.

Joe's first book "The Jewish People and Jesus: Is it time for Reconciliation?" was published in 2010. To learn more about the author's views or purchase additional books kindly visit http://joebutta.wordpress.com